# GENIUS ENVY

# GENIUS Envy

Women Shaping
French Poetic History,
1801–1900

Adrianna M. Paliyenko

THE PENNSYLVANIA STATE UNIVERSITY PRESS

UNIVERSITY PARK, PENNSYLVANIA

Some material in this volume appeared, in an earlier form, in the following publications. "Rereading *la femme poète*: Rimbaud and Louisa Siefert," *Nineteenth-Century French Studies* 26, nos. 1–2 (Fall–Winter 1997–98): 146–60. Reproduced with permission from the University of Nebraska Press. Copyright *Nineteenth-Century French Studies* 1997.
"Illuminating the Poetic Turn to Science: Louise Ackermann, or the Aesthetic Stuff of Cultural Studies," in "The Cultural Currency of Nineteenth-Century French Poetry," special issue, *Romance Studies* 26, no. 4 (2008): 308–22.
"In the Shadow of Eve: Marie Krysinska and the Force of Poetic Desire," in *Women Seeking Expression: France, 1789–1914*, edited by Rosemary Lloyd and Brian Nelson, 159–79. Monash Romance Studies 6. Melbourne: Monash Romance Studies, 2000.

Library of Congress Cataloging-in-Publication Data

Names: Paliyenko, Adrianna M., 1956– , author.
Title: Genius envy : women shaping French poetic history, 1801–1900 / Adrianna M. Paliyenko.
Description: University Park, Pennsylvania : The Pennsylvania State University Press, [2016] | Includes bibliographical references and index.
Summary: "Analyzes the reception of nineteenth-century French women poets, including Marceline Desbordes-Valmore, Amable Tastu, Élisa Mercœur, Mélanie Waldor, Louise Colet, Anaïs Ségalas, Malvina Blanchecotte, Louise Ackermann, and Marie Krysinska, to recover the diversity of women's voices. Places their contributions within the medical and literary debate about the sex of genius"—Provided by publisher.
Identifiers: LCCN 2016027630 | ISBN 9780271077086 (cloth : alk. paper)
Subjects: LCSH: French poetry—Women authors—History and criticism. | French poetry—19th century—History and criticism. | Women poets, French—History—19th century. | Genius.
Classification: LCC PQ149 .P35 2016 | DDC 840.9/9287—dc23
LC record available at https://lccn.loc.gov/2016027630

In memory of my father,

Paul Paliyenko

# CONTENTS

# ILLUSTRATIONS

# ACKNOWLEDGMENTS

In researching and writing this book over a number of years, I have accumulated more debts than I can possibly acknowledge here. My greatest debt is to the nineteenth-century French poets themselves, spirited women who redefined the work of creative genius. Pioneering scholarship by Aimée Boutin, the late Wendy Greenberg, Rosemary Lloyd, Christine Planté, Gretchen Schultz, and Seth Whidden generated a rich framework for my closer look at the way women as poets intervened in the shaping of their legacy. These scholars have also been my critical readers and, in many cases, the source of vital references, encouragement, and friendship.

I express my appreciation for colleagues in nineteenth-century French studies, too numerous to name here, who asked such probing questions about the poets I presented at colloquia in the United States and elsewhere since the late 1990s. Among these colleagues, Joseph Acquisto, Doris Kadish, Edward Kaplan, Stamos Metzidakis, Vicki Mistacco, Allan Pasco, Laurence Porter, Norman Shapiro, Charley Stivale, and Catherine Witt stimulated exchanges and collaborations on edited volumes that inform many of the pages of *Genius Envy*. Still others played a significant role in helping me with archival research, especially Sharon Johnson and Elizabeth Emery. To Elizabeth, in particular, who read the entire manuscript not once, but twice, I am ever grateful. The remarkable team of research librarians at Colby College, particularly Karen Gillum, together with my research assistants greatly advanced my work in the literary archives. The staff at the Bibliothèque Marguerite Durand in Paris also provided support at a crucial stage of my research. Margaret Libby, the visual resources curator at Colby College, offered expert advice and help with all the illustrations.

Other resources that allowed me to bring this project to fruition include my research funds as the Charles A. Dana Professor of French at Colby College and faculty development funds granted by the provost, Lori Kletzer. *Genius Envy* would not have seen the light of day without the gracious invitation and steady backing

I received from Kendra Boileau, the editor in chief at the Pennsylvania State University Press. I extend most sincere thanks to her editorial assistant, Alex Vose, who expertly guided the preparation of the manuscript, and to two readers for the press, whose incisive comments greatly enriched the final version. I would also like to acknowledge Laura Reed-Morrisson, the managing editor of the press, as well as Patricia Mitchell, the production coordinator, for handling the production of my book with consummate professionalism, and my copyeditor, Merryl Sloane, whose careful work polished my prose.

The long journey of *Genius Envy* placed a special burden on my family, especially my spouse, Volodymyr Kurylo, and my children, Ludmila, Yuriy, and Natalia. In living with this book for more years than expected, each of them has been extraordinarily patient, compassionate, and loving. So, too, my first cousin Peter Palijenko and his wife, Andrea Mozarowski, have been a source of strength, joy, and inspiring exchanges about the life of the mind. Had my father lived to hold a copy of this book, I trust he would have recognized how his example of courage and grit spurred me on to recover the history of other unsung heroes.

# Introduction

"Sire, le premier poète de votre règne est une femme: Madame Valmore."[1] This statement recalls a woman who rose from the ranks of the working class to become a leading poet in the 1820s, preserving a foundational chapter in the other history of nineteenth-century French poetry. But why have literary historians passed over all other women in establishing the official literary canon? Only Desbordes-Valmore's verse and prose have gained a prominent place on library shelves as well as in critics' discussion of the Romantic era. Are we to imagine that, apart from her, no other woman contributed to arguably the most fertile century of poetic production in France? What does Desbordes-Valmore's privileged position as a sentimental genius tell us about her legacy, which buries other poetic women? Traditional accounts of literary history offer vastly different answers to these questions than does the reception of individual women's poetry, which underscores the aesthetic force of their rich body of work across the century. Such disparate views of the French poetic past generate the core query pursued in this book. How did women's diverse poetic achievements survive a history that excluded them?

Central to understanding how the narrative of reception obscured yet recorded the women who shaped the history of poetry in nineteenth-century France is the debate about the sexing of genius, which crystallized among Enlightenment thinkers. This debate highlighted the drive to locate the source of genius. Jean-Jacques Rousseau, who derived the force of the mind from the muscles, claimed that a work of genius was beyond women's reach: "Les femmes, en général, n'aiment aucun art, ne se connaissent à aucun et n'ont aucun génie" (*Lettre à d'Alembert*, 138).[2] In *De l'esprit* (1758), his contemporary Claude Adrien Helvétius in turn deliberated whether the superior mind was a gift of nature or bequeathed by nurture, concluding that "l'homme de génie n'est donc que le produit des circonstances dans lesquelles cet homme s'est trouvé" (180). For this thinker, who considered the mind equal in all individuals from birth, intellectual inequality resulted from education and application. Later, by way of response to Rousseau's *Émile; ou, De l'éducation*

(1762), in the posthumous work *De l'homme: De ses facultés intellectuelles et de son éducation* (1772), Helvétius considered the relation of gender and brain power: "L'organisation des deux sexes est, sans doute, très différente à certains égards: mais cette différence doit-elle être regardée comme la cause de l'infériorité de l'esprit des femmes?" (1:153). He responded that a lack of access to education, not innate inferiority, explained the absence of women from the historical record of superior achievements across the disciplines. In *Lettres d'un bourgeois de New Haven à un citoyen de Virginie* (1787), the marquis de Condorcet (known as Nicolas de Caritat) shared Helvétius's ultimate position on why the past had yielded so few women of literary or scientific genius: "De plus, l'espèce de contrainte où les opinions relatives aux mœurs tiennent l'âme et l'esprit des femmes presque dès l'enfance, et surtout depuis le moment où le génie commence à se développer, doit nuire à ses progrès dans presque tous les genres. . . . D'ailleurs, est-il bien sûr qu'aucune femme n'a montré du génie?" (19).[3] The question Condorcet put to history frames the polemic that would surround genius throughout the nineteenth century and imbue the critical reception with ambiguities. If now defined by leading thinkers of the day as an aptitude and linked with superior creativity as well as intellectual power, was genius innate, acquired, or both?[4]

Through the struggle over the meaning of "génie," nineteenth-century writers revealed the stakes of the quest by science to discover the origins of genius and thus determine who could access its property. Representative of those who ignored the impetus to reexamine genius in relation to sex is Arthur Schopenhauer in "Of Women" (1851). Schopenhauer invoked Rousseau to reiterate, "Neither for music, nor for poetry, nor for fine art, have [women] really and truly any sense or susceptibility; it is a mere mockery if they make a pretense of it in order to assist their endeavor to please" (*Works*, 451–52). Biology, asserted Schopenhauer, reinforced the view that women had never produced "a single achievement in the fine arts that is really great, genuine and original; or given to the world any work of permanent value in any sphere" (452). He argued that being male was the fundamental condition of genius, even though medical science offered no such proof. Schopenhauer's deeper narrative of exceptional creativity prefigured a Freudian analysis of female psychology. Because the work of genius was said to preclude femininity, conservative readers equated women's creative ambitions with so-called phallic envy. As expressed in Edmond de Goncourt and Jules de Goncourt's *Les hommes de lettres* (1860), "Le génie est mâle. . . . Une femme de génie est un homme" (176). From the perspective of the dominant genius discourse in nineteenth-century France, women could not create the "great works" later selected for the French literary canon.

And yet, the history of the word "genius" does not privilege a sex. Originally, the word referred to the spirit associated with a person at birth, which the Greeks called a *daimōn* and the Romans a "genius." In the classical sense derived from the ancient view, genius signified a divinely inspired gift that moved the seer, or the *vates*, synonymous with poet, to reveal the unknown. Enlightenment thought maintained a mimetic tradition, but sharpened the notion of genius in relation to the superior application of aesthetic rules.[5] The term "originalité," which the Romantics would use to recognize artistic invention or scientific discovery, simultaneously emerged as a separate category. As Roland Mortier observes about this development in France during the latter decades of the eighteenth century, the adjective "original," synonymous with unique, did not carry over to the noun "un original," a person considered "bizarre," "excentrique," or "ridicule" (*L'originalité*, 32). The link made in French between *génie* (from the Latin *genius*) and creation stemmed from another etymology that allowed generative power to become part of the equation.

In *De l'esprit* (1758), Helvétius argued that the metaphors used to signify genius, "un feu, une inspiration, un enthousiasme divin," failed to distinguish invention, which derives from the root *gignere*, "to beget or produce," as its principal quality (475). Defined as "making" or "discovering," invention accounted for poetic and scientific genius, respectively. Rejecting the belief that genius was "un don de Nature," bestowed upon a select few, he claimed that genius was common. The circumstances needed to produce genius, however, were rare. Its manifestation required learning and work, as he elaborated in *De l'homme*: "Le génie, selon nous, ne peut être que le produit d'une attention forte et concentrée dans un art ou une science" (1:31). Helvétius understood genius as the result of a process, intuiting a synergy between genes and the environment suggestive of modern-day epigenetics. In redefining genius, rather than describing its effect or attempting to situate it, he uncovered physiology as a factor without, however, making one sex the sole originator.

Throughout the nineteenth century, metaphysical accounts of exceptional creativity competed with pseudoscientific explanations. Claims about the source of genius thus shifted between the mind and the body, unwittingly revealing why the attempts to locate the origins of a process inextricably linked to its product, to the creative work itself, would inevitably fail. Early French Romantics gendered the classical view of divine inspiration, locating its effect in men's heads versus women's hearts. With a turn to the Latin *ingenium* (innate ability) and a procreative twist on *gignere*, medical philosophers pulled genius further down into the body, making the male seed, thought to govern human reproduction, its source. This physiology remained undisturbed well beyond the century. Even though embryology's progress accounted for equal female contributions to reproduction, the analogy of male procreativity and cultural production undergirded the collective reception of women as *poètes manqués*.

Women writers' surge overlapped with that of Romanticism in the 1820s, garnering mixed reviews. Although the individual poets among them captivated amateur and elite readers alike, their strength in numbers raised concern, with the sentimental novel also stiffening competition in the market. By then, the notion of "original genius" had taken hold. Imaginative power, associated with spontaneity and authenticity, supplanted the classical tradition of mimesis, or imitation, of the ancients.[6] The meaning of genius developed separately from talent, not in the dictionary, but as a category for distinguishing men's creations from women's.[7] Yet, as late as 1869, in attempting to prove that genius was a male inheritance, Francis Galton exposed the lack of consensus about "the definition of the word" as a serious difficulty "in the way of discovering whether genius is, or is not, correlated with infertility" (*Hereditary Genius*, 330).

In defining "genius" for his dictionary, Émile Littré retained its dual etymology (*genius* and *gignere*) along with the dispute over its origins and makeup. In describing *génie* as inherent, Littré called it a "talent naturel extraordinaire" (1151, 1152). By "talent" he meant a special aptitude, but added that it was either a gift or acquired by work: "aptitude distinguée, capacité . . . donnée par la nature ou acquise par le travail" (2134–35). Herein lies the conceptual way that nineteenth-century women gradually disentangled from sex: by reformulating poetic originality as the work of genius, the process made manifest by the creation that always takes us by surprise. In thinking through their poetry and its reception, women conveyed the depth of ideas with which they engaged to shape for posterity their rightful place in French poetic history.

### Rediscovering Women's Poetic Legacies

In the absence of modern editions of complete poetic works by most women writers of the nineteenth century, except for Desbordes-Valmore, anthologies such as those by Alphonse Séché (1908–9), Jeanine Moulin (1966, 1975), Christine Planté (1998), and Norman Shapiro (2008) have filled many gaps in the record.[8] Though these collections differ in critical apparatus and selection, they suggest how widely French women's writing ranges aesthetically, thematically, and ideologically across the centuries. The nineteenth century exemplifies such diversity, which complicates the traditional ascription of gender to poetry in Wendy Greenberg's 1999 *Uncanonical Women: Feminine Voice in French Poetry*. From a feminist vantage, in *The Gendered Lyric: Subjectivity and Difference in Nineteenth-Century French Poetry* (1999), Gretchen Schultz juxtaposes men's and women's poetry to show the aesthetic axis along which this division was historically constructed. As Alison Finch observes in a critical survey of nineteenth-century women authors, many of these writers argued against gender stereotyping. *Genius Envy* delves into poetic women's contestatory work, in particular, to shed light on the original ways that women inscribed themselves in literary history, not as "women poets" or "poetesses," but as poets.

To expose the problem of gender as a category of literary analysis, this book shows how poetic women experimented with form and content while gravitating toward a multiplicity of voices. Probing and innovative, women's production unfolds as a critical dialogue, not only as a conversation between poets and their readers but also as a revisionist discourse on genius. Within the context of the "discursive combat," or symbolic resistance, in nineteenth-century France, theorized by Richard Terdiman, women seeking expression as poets engaged as much with the gendered discourses that constituted the canons of criticism as with the history of ideas in making their work the counterdiscourse (*Discourse/Counter-Discourse*, 43). The richness of women's achievements as poets emerges from this exchange, their work resisting and thus texturing its reception.

*Genius Envy* begins by reconstructing the history of reception that obscured the scope of women's poetic projects in an era celebrated for aesthetic innovation. In part 1, the chronological organization foregrounds how three principal discourses overlapped in rival assessments of women as poets that linked genius, envy, and femininity. This critical nexus draws sex into the appraisal of women's poetry. When fused with the female body, verse flows directly from the heart. Judged as natural but artless, such effusion precludes the brainy stuff of genius. Relegated to a separate category, "women poets" cannot compete with men. Yet, those women recognized as creators destabilize this narrative of the past. Part 2 presents five distinct trajectories forged by women of different generations: Anaïs Ségalas, Malvina Blanchecotte, Louisa Siefert, Louise Ackermann, and Marie Krysinska. Modern readers encounter the unfolding of each poet's work in its original context and thus can follow the stages of its reception.

Primary and secondary sources—including anthologies, pedagogical manuals, magazines, newspapers, correspondence, and medical treatises—constitute this book's twofold corpus: the critical literature and the creative body. Women galvanized the genius debate in the nineteenth century, testing the history of an idea.[9] In chapter 1, I consider to what extent women who aspired to be remembered as poets disputed the physiology of exceptional creativity, joining those who proclaimed that genius has no sex. Critics consistently attest to the upsurge of women writers in the opening decades of the nineteenth century, but not to the record number of poets among them.[10] What is especially striking about the upsurge of women writers in the nineteenth century is that they represented all classes.[11] French names reveal class; for example, the "de" in Madame de Staël indicates noble rank. Virtually none of the women acclaimed as poets published under male pseudonyms. Though Blanchecotte and Ackermann first used initials, they subsequently signed their full names. Given that they hailed from the working class and the bourgeoisie, respectively, this gesture had more to do with gender than with class and the increasingly hostile environment literary women faced, especially those wanting to preempt being associated with the narrow category of "la poésie féminine."

The mapping of the narrative of literary reception in chapter 2 highlights two major backlashes, in the 1840s and 1870s, which elucidated the critical trend to read women as *poètes manqués*. Yet the semantic drift of the categories used to widen the gap between femininity and creativity reveals the struggle to control the inheritance of genius by passing on a separate "woman's tradition." This paradigm, drawn from a conservative reading of Desbordes-Valmore as the quintessential "woman poet," the *mater dolorosa*, does not account for the various ways that women entered the field across the century. In chapter 3, I examine the different strategies women used to develop poetic agency, beginning with those who came on the scene with Desbordes-Valmore. The sororal network she created with Amable Tastu and Mélanie Waldor did not extend to Élisa Mercœur, Ségalas, and Louise Colet. But, like Desbordes-Valmore, each of these poets formed a distinct creative identity, reconciling femininity with creativity to varying degrees. Women's diverse projects along with their reflections on aesthetics show that even those poets who wrestled explicitly with being placed in Valmore's shadow in the latter part of the century struggled more with the gendering of originality.

Marked differences in form, voice, and vision demonstrate the diversity and multiplicity of women poets throughout the century. In chapter 4, I treat Ségalas's response to France's colonial enterprise during the nineteenth century in order to restore part of her intellectual legacy. From 1831 to 1885, the Parisian writer with Creole roots engaged the century's debate on abolition along with the emergence of scientific racism. The self-styled worker and poet Blanchecotte launched her career in 1855, probing the notion of genius in relation to class and gender. Her project, addressed in chapter 5, exploits the in-between to associate creative production with work. Louisa Siefert, from the literary elite in Lyon, blurred aesthetic categories in works from 1868 to 1881 by expressing pain, yet viewing it with philosophical objectivity. Examined in chapter 6, Siefert's treatment of the mind-body split elicits the dialogic nature of poetic voice, revealing the creative power of the other in the "I." The erudite Ackermann, the subject of chapter 7, considered poetry a science or a way of knowing. In fusing passion with reason, she positioned her voice between poetic writing and thinking. The Polish-born Krysinska, presented in chapter 8, took an interdisciplinary approach to the work of originality in fin-de-siècle Paris. In reconsidering the origins of poetry to write the history of her own *vers libre*, Krysinska revised the biblical creation story and disputed evolutionary science to theorize genius in the work itself.

Nineteenth-century poets who happened to be born women progressively laid claim to the property of genius on their own terms as they untangled their voices from the sentimental writing that, for conservative critics, embodied the "woman's tradition." From the start of the century, women embedded reflections on genius in their verse. They intervened as critical readers of their writing and its reception with increasing confidence, amplifying their poetic output with prefaces. Other paratexts, including correspondence with fellow poets, mentors, and critics, as well as essays and prose collections, illuminate how deeply women examined the centrality of gender in creativity.[12]

The poets featured in *Genius Envy* represent salient ways in which women have broken the so-called feminine mold, imaginatively and conceptually. Their hybrid production, spanning the century, forms a discursive site that resists inherited meanings of genius. Women's thinking through poetry and beyond, as shown in the chapters that follow, provides new canons of criticism for recovering the meaning of their work and the history of ideas about genius it illumines.

# PART ONE

## Reception Matters

# 1   Un/sexing Genius

How could a woman demonstrate genius if the prevailing belief was that women could not be feminine and intellectual at the same time? In a series of forty lithographs published in 1844, Honoré Daumier parodied women who pursued a literary career in nineteenth-century France as *bas-bleus*, or bluestockings (fig. 1).[1] The caricature included here projects the view that a woman who forsakes her femininity for the life of the mind invites sterility. Having shed her outer garments, apart from the semblance of a laurel wreath on her head, the female figure considers her reflection in the mirror: "C'est singulier comme ce miroir m'applatit la taille et me maigrit la poitrine! que m'importe? . . . M^me de Staël et M^r de Buffon l'ont proclamé . . . le génie n'a point de sexe." Removed from its original context, the latter part of this caption does not work as opposition to the established discourse. Rather, as reflected by the figure's masculine traits, it drifts ideologically to uphold the medical opinion that mental labor desexualizes women. Such semantic deviation complicates the historical record, demonstrating more broadly, as Richard Terdiman has observed, "how deeply the struggle for the control of meaning inscribes itself in the language of culture" (*Discourse/Counter-Discourse*, 25). Women's uneven reception as thinkers and artists galvanized their contestatory work in nineteenth-century France. The poets, in particular, engaged in the modern struggle over the meaning of genius.

In defining genius as an aptitude without reference to sex, Buffon (1707–1788) highlighted the endurance, even the pain, that producing great work involves: "Le génie n'est qu'une plus grande aptitude à la patience."[2] Cultural memory also preserves a private exchange as the source of the view expressed by Mme de Staël (1766–1817). Upon surprising Napoleon Bonaparte at his residence in Paris in 1798, Staël learned from his butler that the future emperor, who was "naked in the bathtub," refused her audience. Undaunted, she replied, "Peu importe! Le génie n'a pas de sexe!"[3] With this, Staël championed intellectual equality between the sexes. Her

FIG 1
Plate 10 of Daumier's
series *Les bas-bleus.*
*Le Charivari,* 30
January 1844. Photo
courtesy Yale University
Art Gallery.

pithy rejoinder also prefigured how the unprecedented rise of women as poets early in the nineteenth century would challenge centuries of tradition by testing the scientific explanation of genius.

In this chapter I reconstruct the debate over the nature of genius; it was governed by the claims of physiology at the beginning of the nineteenth century and those of evolutionary science brought it to a close. Divided into two parts, corresponding roughly to the first and second half of the century, the chronological framework shows how the idea of genius evolved. Each part consists of three principal sections. Collectively, they represent the dialogue among medical thinkers, writers, and poets, which alternately sexed and unsexed genius. I begin with the physiological explanation for genius to frame key responses to this discourse from literary men and women of the period. This dialogic structure situates individual poets' approach to the question of genius as part of a forgotten counterdiscourse of protest. By probing the maleness of genius, at once a medical theory and a literary construct, women shaped the conceptual work of their poetry, an intellectual legacy that has been obscured by the canons of criticism.

What was the effect of physiology on the mind, specifically on the work of genius? Women's engagement in the nineteenth-century quarrel about genius reinvigorated this question, which had preoccupied philosophers and medical authorities during the latter part of the eighteenth century. Pierre Roussel had correlated the moistness and softness of a female's organs, including her brain tissue, with mental inferiority. In his view, women were highly sensitive, predisposed to quick feeling rather than to lengthy reasoning (*Système physique et moral de la femme*, 30). The French physician relied on humoral medicine, recalling from Hippocrates that phlegm dominates the female nervous system.[4] For Roussel, this caused a convulsive state in women, a form of hysteria easily confused with the type of "fureur poétique" historically associated with oracles inspired by "le souffle divin" (47). Thus, women's makeup, as Roussel conceived of it, prevented them from being genuine poets. Moreover, in describing females with intellectual and creative ambitions as "misplaced," no longer women but almost men, Roussel anticipated the psychopathology of exceptional women developed during the nineteenth century (105). His contemporary Pierre-Jean-Georges Cabanis agreed that mental exertion unsexes women, asking, "quelle sera la place de ces êtres incertains, qui ne sont, à proprement parler, d'aucun sexe?" (*Rapports du physique et du moral de l'homme*, 363).[5]

The naturalist Julien-Joseph Virey argued that femininity and creativity were mutually exclusive, even as women writers, many of them poets, inaugurated the Romantic era alongside their male counterparts. In *De la femme sous ses rapports physiologique, moral et littéraire*, first published in 1823, Virey equated the word "femme" with reproduction, finding the roots of biological determinism in etymology: "Ce mot FEMME vient de *fœmina*, qui dérive de *fœtare*, *fœtus*, parce que sa destination naturelle est d'engendrer" (211). To buttress this point, he stressed that women had made no contribution "à ces hautes conceptions du génie dans les sciences et la littérature, qui semblent être la plus sublime conquête de l'esprit humain" (5). Like Roussel and Cabanis, Virey described the female body as a cold, moist environment. Drier and hotter, the male body provided all the energy for (pro)creation. Muscular weakness extended from the body to the mind, Virey contended, representing the way "la nature a voulu rendre la femme inférieure à l'homme" (215).

Virey's linkage of genius with sperm, from the roots *genialis* (relative to genius) and *genitalis* (relative to generation), prepared the ground for making poetry a male creation: "S'il existe dans l'univers un principe physique capable d'imprimer à notre intelligence toute l'audace et l'étendue dont elle est susceptible, c'est le sperme sans contredit; [l]e sperme est donc un nouvel . . . *impetum faciens*, une source de vigueur vitale. Par lui, le génie s'échauffe, la poésie s'enrichit de nobles sentiments, se colore de brillantes images; la musique, tous les beaux-arts s'allument à ce flambeau de vie" (*De la femme*, 401, 402).[6] According to Virey, a male boosted his creative output by abstaining from sex: "En s'abstenant de la génération corporelle, on devient plus capable de la génération intellectuelle, on a plus de génie intérieur (*ingenium*), et par la même raison les hommes de génie sont moins capables d'engendrer physiquement" (411). By "génie intérieur," Virey meant an innate, yet embodied, masculine trait. Ironically, Virey's physiology of genius nearly coincided with Karl Ernst von Baer's 1827 discovery of the ovum. The latter laid the foundation for a key finding, in 1843, by the British embryologist Martin Barry: the male and the female each provide half the material necessary for human reproduction.[7] This made the female an equally active player in procreation, which, following the analogy of body and mind applied to men, could be related to women's creative power as well. But even after Barry's finding had been confirmed and circulated,[8] the spermatic imagination prevailed, suffusing the backlash against women writers during the 1840s.

From the perspective of the new medical evidence about how conception occurred, it is instructive to consider Virey's *De la physiologie dans ses rapports avec la philosophie* (1844). Virey likens the phallus to the tongue, making semen the source of fertile thought: "La verge a pour analogue la langue: par l'une est expulsé au-dehors le sperme; par celle-ci est éjaculée la parole, sorte de semence de l'intellect ou de la pensée" (99). Not all sperm that penetrate "l'utérus cérébral," however, carry the seeds of genius because of the mental toll exacted by daily cares (317). The historian Jules Michelet similarly mixes sexual metaphors in defining genius: "Le génie, la puissance inventive et génératrice, suppose . . . qu'un même homme est doué des deux puissances, qu'il réunit en lui ce qu'on peut appeler les deux sexes de l'esprit" (*Le peuple*, 190). However, neither of them meant that a great mind is androgynous, as Samuel Coleridge had stated a decade earlier.[9] An emphasis on male physiology undergirded the Romantic concept of genius as creative individuality, a concept brought to bear on gifted women in France and elsewhere in Europe well past mid-century.

Medicine's influence spread to other disciplines, as shown by Schopenhauer's notion of genius in the second edition of *The World as Will and Representation* (1844): "The fundamental condition [of genius] is an abnormal predominance of sensibility over irritability and reproductive power; and what makes the matter more difficult, this must take place in a male body. (Women may have great talent, but no genius, for they always remain subjective)" (Schopenhauer, *Works*, 311).[10] Only in males could the intellect predominate over instinct, the power of perception superseding reaction to an external stimulus. As encapsulated in Schopenhauer's essay "Of Women" (1851), historically bookending Romanticism, females were thought to "form the *sexus sequior*—the second sex, inferior in every respect to the first" (*Works*, 453). Categorized as females, women had no genius; identified as creative geniuses, women had no gender. In the context of this dominant narrative, which truncated the debate about genius inherited from the Enlightenment, how did women forge a path as writers and thinkers?

## Madame de Staël and the Woman of Genius

Key among the literary women who disputed the masculinist narrative in science from the turn of the century to its midpoint was Germaine de Staël, whose theoretical and imaginative writings began to disentangle genius from sex. Staël made her literary debut with *Lettres sur les écrits et le caractère de J.-J. Rousseau* (1788). Her quarrel with Rousseau stemmed from his assertion, mentioned above, that women have no genius. She challenges the medical view he endorsed, which correlated the female organism with mental inferiority: "[Q]u'il leur refuse cette puissante force de tête, cette profonde faculté d'attention dont les grands génies sont doués: *leurs faibles organes s'y opposent, et leur cœur, trop souvent occupé par leurs sentiments et par leur malheur, s'empare sans cesse de leur pensée, et ne la laisse pas se fixer sur des méditations étrangères à leur idée dominante*; mais qu'il ne les accuse pas de ne pouvoir écrire que froidement, de ne savoir pas même peindre l'amour" (Staël, *Œuvres*, 1:9; emphasis added).[11] Here, Staël pinpoints Rousseau's contradictions. If Rousseau considered women's brains to be weaker because they were excessively sentimental, how could he also claim that their writing was devoid of feeling? By insisting on what women lacked, was the pre-Romantic author more concerned with his own originality? In determining the genius of a given work on the basis of innovation, "masculinist literary criticism . . . has itself at stake," Françoise Meltzer notes in a related context (*Hot Property*, 2). Staël developed her counterdiscourse to such criticism in prefacing the second edition of her volume on Rousseau.

Staël's 1814 preface to *Lettres sur les écrits et le caractère de J.-J. Rousseau* establishes a broader context for considering how her stance on genius separates women's destiny from their anatomy: "On n'a presque jamais nié que les goûts et les études littéraires ne fussent un grand avantage pour les hommes, mais on n'est pas d'accord sur l'influence que ces mêmes études peuvent avoir sur la destinée des femmes" (*Œuvres*, 1:2). French custom did not prohibit women from educating themselves. But women were actively discouraged from becoming writers lest they become professional authors at the expense of their marital and familial obligations, let alone rivals to their male counterparts. Staël thus anticipated how women's massive entry into literary production during the early decades of the nineteenth century would concretely threaten the contested terrain.[12] Was it the expected modesty of women or a tactic to avoid censorship that accompanied Staël's belief that women should not foster ideas for literary glory but purely for intellectual pleasure?[13] She nonetheless raised the profile of women as intellectuals and creators in her genius-conscious age. Staël attempted to disengage genius from sex, using the phrasing "une femme d'un génie élevé" (a woman of lofty genius), rather than the gender-specific term "une femme génie" (a female genius) (1:3).[14]

Staël's cultural moment was the transition from Enlightenment sense to Romantic sensibility, from valuing reason to recognizing the cognitive worth of feeling and intuition. This suggests a propitious time for women, for whom sentiment was said to be a primary source of creative inspiration, to emerge as writers.[15] However, the mobility women gained in the sociopolitical arena during the revolutionary period (1789–99) did not include access to the domains of science, industry, or invention. Separate spheres for men and women, public versus private, were reinforced following the Revolution. The Napoleonic Code, enacted in 1804, reduced women's civil status to that of minors, subjecting females to the authority of their fathers and then to their spouses. This regime also regulated literary property.[16] Yet women like Staël promulgated dissent literally as well as figuratively by exposing the problem of genius.

An exchange from the 1803 memoirs of Napoleon's brother Lucien reveals one source of Bonaparte's animosity toward Staël, whose superior mind inspired admiration:

> LE CONSUL.—Moi, au bout du compte, je suis bon homme; mais voyez-vous, c'est plus fort que moi, j'ai toujours détesté les femmes prétendus beaux esprits, ses pareilles.
> LUCIEN. —Permettez-moi de dire que madame de Staël, en fait d'esprit, n'a point de pareille dans son sexe, et à peine dans le nôtre.
> LE CONSUL. —J'ai cru jusqu'à présent qu'il n'y avait que les sots, ou les hommes d'esprit médiocre qui se prosternaient ainsi devant le génie féminin.
> (Iung, *Lucien Bonaparte et ses mémoires*, 3:238–39)

Staël's international worldview defied the nationalist impetus of Napoleon's empire, and her widely recognized intellect contradicted his view of reproductive fertility as the measure of a woman's greatness. The tension between them led to her exile from France in 1803.[17] One may be tempted to see the woman of genius in *Corinne; ou, l'Italie* (1807) as Staël's literary double, the eponymous heroine mirroring the exile experienced by the author at personal and political levels. However, as Christopher Herold notes, "[Staël's] object was not merely to exhibit or justify herself; rather, it was to criticize a society that stifled generous impulses and that discouraged half of mankind (the feminine half) from developing its gifts" (*Mistress to an Age*, 199). Central to the novel, which Laurence Porter has treated more recently as "a key transitional work," was whether society would allow the woman to thrive separately from the genius (see *Women's Vision*, 69–72).

Staël's fictional woman of genius makes her entrance upon an international stage from the perspective of the male protagonist, English nobleman Oswald Nelvil: "*Vive Corinne! vive le génie! vive la beauté!*" (Staël, *Œuvres*, 2:444; emphasis in original). Oswald finds Corinne doubly striking, her appearance as beautiful as the genius demonstrated by the elegiac poetry she performs. It is the first time "qu'il était témoin des honneurs rendus à une femme, à une femme illustrée seulement par les dons du génie . . . les plus beaux dons de la nature, l'imagination, le sentiment, et la pensée" (2:444). Staël represents Corinne from the viewpoint of the male character smitten with her and, at the same time, portrays her heroine as an inspired priestess with a poetic gift. This figuration invokes the categories of "woman" and "genius," thus integrating femininity and creativity.

Whereas men such as Roussel and Cabanis used scientific works to promulgate the theory that women could not sublimate their sexuality into creative output, Staël exploited her writerly gifts to suggest that women possess the transcendent power of thought over passion. Staël's heroine links genius with originality in a pre-Romantic fashion, connecting the capacity with the individual possessing it: "Le génie est essentiellement créateur; il porte le caractère de l'individu qui le possède" (Staël, *Œuvres*, 2:540). A classical sense of divine inspiration lingers, however, reflective of Staël's role as a transitional figure. As a "poëte" inspired by "un enthousiasme surnaturel," Corinne traces her genius to an external source, separating the creative voice from the conscious self (2:469).

Oswald contradicts an earlier opinion that women were to be seen rather than heard in thinking about Corinne's giftedness: "[P]ouvait-on espérer de [*sic*] captiver jamais un génie doué de si brillantes ailes? Il était impossible de le décider; mais au moins on sentait que ce n'était pas la société, que c'était plutôt le ciel même qui avait formé cet être extraordinaire, et que son esprit était aussi incapable d'imiter, que son caractère de feindre" (Staël, *Œuvres*, 2:463). He calls her a "génie," using the indefinite masculine article "un," as is customary in French when referring to the person rather than the gift, which requires the definite article "le." Though he wonders whether a superior woman born with such a gift could still be loved, this is not necessarily "the main question of *Corinne*," as Alison Finch proposes (*Women's Writing*, 28).

Staël uses another male character's comments about her gifted heroine to examine the relationship between genius and gender. The comte d'Erfeuil says to Oswald: "[M]ais c'est une personne d'un esprit si supérieur, d'une instruction profonde, d'un tact si fin, que les règles ordinaires pour juger les femmes ne peuvent s'appliquer à elle" (Staël, *Œuvres*, 2:470). Corinne also voices the idea of unbinding creativity from sex: "Chaque femme, comme chaque homme, ne doit-elle pas se frayer une route d'après son caractère et ses talents? et faut-il imiter l'instinct des abeilles, dont les essaims se succèdent sans progrès et sans diversité?" (2:685). In a society dominated by the gender binary, whereby one could be *either* a genius *or* a woman, this was indeed a remarkable insight.

The struggle for such a woman, however, was also internal. Corinne later admits to Oswald that "[l]e talent a besoin d'une indépendance intérieure que l'amour véritable ne permet jamais" (Staël, *Œuvres*, 2:734). In response, Oswald issues an ultimatum. Corinne finds little room to maneuver in seeking expression as an artist who wishes to retain a place as a woman: "Ah! s'il en est ainsi . . . que ton génie se taise, et que ton cœur soit tout à moi!" (2:734). Societal expectations prevail along with the latent desire for an ideal female companion in Oswald's decision to wed the Englishwoman, Lucile Edgermond, rather than Corinne, who dies of grief.

Corinne's downward spiral left Staël open to criticism. For Christine Battersby, Staël "rehearses the grand gestures of genius, but then remembers that she needs to adjust the posture of the truly womanly woman" (*Gender and Genius*, 99). These tensions are not productive, Battersby concludes, because at the end of the novel Corinne "is a woman, her life and her genius destroyed by passion" (99–100). Another interpretation of the heroine's fall is possible from the perspective of the male observer's initial recognition of Corinne's genius and her self-portrait, both dissociating genius from sex. In this way, Staël exposes the sharp conflict between the selflessness that society expected of a woman and the individuality that genius required, precisely what women would have to negotiate in order to pursue creative work that would outlast them.

### Sand in/on the Gendering of Genius

The literary woman George Sand (1804–1876), née Aurore Dupin, whose career began in the early 1830s and spanned more than forty-five years, did not deny women genius, as has been erroneously recorded.[18] Sand echoed Staël as a point of departure for disputing the idea that "anatomy is destiny."[19] But Sand vacillated in considering her era's debate, initially unsexing genius to seek equal opportunity for women and, at times, asserting intellectual inequality between the sexes.[20]

"La fille d'Albano" (1831), one of George Sand's first short stories, likely written with Jules Sandeau,[21] engages with the view of genius evolving in the medical realm at the time. Sand represents the quandary facing her female character Laurence, a young Italian artist betrothed to a bourgeois Frenchman, with an international cast of characters like those in Staël's *Corinne*. Sand, like Staël, borrows a male character's voice to reproduce her society's mores. However, a twist in Sand's plot reminds modern readers not to expect a monolithic narrative of the past, that is, not to reduce all men's voices (whether real or imagined) to misogyny, or women's to feminism. On the eve of Laurence's wedding, a male stranger arrives to save her from sacrificing her artistic gift on the altar of marriage. "Le génie n'a pas de sexe," he asserts (287). That a woman could possess genius was not the issue. Absent from the male character's assertion is the irony observed in Daumier's portrayal of the counterstance, first attributed to Staël (and Buffon). For Sand, too, genius transcends sex, but not work. The latter introduces a class distinction in the way that women thought about genius, the more elite among them not needing to write for a living. Nevertheless, all gifted women had to reckon with the institution of marriage, usually tied to motherhood, which placed constraints on creative pursuits. In "La fille d'Albano" and elsewhere, Sand diametrically opposes marriage, which she considered a form of slavery,[22] to the independence of mind and lifestyle that genius requires: "Autre chose est la femme née pour perpétuer l'espèce, et l'artiste qui vit de la vie de tout un monde. L'artiste ne s'appartient pas, les détails de la vie commune ne vont pas à sa taille" ("La fille d'Albano," 287). Sand returned to the genius debate throughout her career, swerving at times toward the dominant discourse she contested.[23]

Was Sand being provocative or ironic in knotting genius with sex in a review of *Souvenirs de Madame Merlin* in 1836?[24] Explanations of women's negligible achievements in the arts and sciences, she argues, fall more within the realm of phrenology than philosophy. Because of the shape of women's heads, generally larger in the back with lower foreheads, it was determined that the organs needed for success in the arts and sciences were underdeveloped in females.[25] Sand then addresses the other side of the argument, whether creativity is inborn or acquired, by attributing women's absence from cultural history to a lack of education. In the context of these remarks, Sand makes no reference to women's contributions as prose writers and poets in her day.[26] Yet this was a salient moment in French history, as Charles Augustin Sainte-Beuve had emphasized three years prior in an essay that Sand had surely read. In the first line of his 1833 review of *Lélia*, the lyrical and philosophical novel published by Sand that year, the critic highlighted her position in the upsurge of literary women he observed, the "singulier mouvement moral et littéraire qui se déclare en France chez les femmes, d'une manière croissante, depuis les dernières années" (Sainte-Beuve, "George Sand," 495).[27]

One can only speculate why Sand weighed the evidence of women's literary work at the time differently in her review of Merlin, stating, "nous nous prononcerions pour la supériorité intellectuelle de l'homme" (84). In drawing out the psychophysiology of superior women as "des hommes de seconde classe," Sand ranks genius according to sex: "C'est pourquoi nous ne pensons pas qu'un génie mâle puisse être envieux et inquiet des triomphes d'un génie femelle: il faut qu'un homme soit bien médiocre pour en être blessé, et pour vouloir en souiller l'éclat offensif" (85). Though medical science offered no proof, Sand invokes the analogy of muscular and cognitive inferiority in describing Merlin's volume of childhood reminiscences as poetic and sentimental. For Sand, its flaws showed that women had yet to excel as writers despite their striving. Did Sand take this universalizing stance as a critical reader, as an astute writer, or as both, wishing to separate her own literary voice from gender? Nearly concurrently, she resumed her contestatory position in a cluster of texts that disputed the power structures along with the creative hierarchy.

The narrator of "Lettres à Marcie" (1837), a series of philosophical fragments addressed to the fictional Marcie, contemplates her sex-conscious age: "Beaucoup d'hommes aujourd'hui font profession d'affirmer physiologiquement et philosophiquement que la créature mâle est d'une essence supérieure à celle de la créature femelle" (228). However, history did not support this difference. If one were to reexamine the past, one would discover the range of women's achievements, Sand's narrator continues, on the basis of their writings during the Middle Ages and the Renaissance, in particular as poets (whom she does not name) (231). The eponymous heroine of *Gabriel* (1839) counters her preceptor's sexing of the mind along similar lines: "La femme! la femme! je ne sais à quel propos vous me

MIROIR DROLATIQUE.

Si de Georges Sand ce portrait
Laisse l'esprit un peu perplexe,
C'est que le génie est abstrait
Et comme on sait n'a pas de sexe

FIG 2

Caricature of George
Sand by Alcide
Lorentz. *Le Charivari,*
5 August 1842.

parlez toujours de la femme. Quant à moi, je ne sens pas que mon âme ait un sexe, comme vous tâchez souvent de me le démontrer" (18).[28] To this point, in the revised version of Sand's novel *Lélia* (1839), the title character, whose "vaste front révèle en effet le génie," has the physiognomy of genius (69).[29] Contrary to the mediocre grade that Sand had given women as writers and thinkers in 1836, in an 1841 letter to the great intellectual the abbé de Lamennais, she stated, "je ne suis pas convaincue de l'infériorité des femmes" (Sand, *Correspondance: 1812–1876*, 168). Indeed, as illustrated by a mocking depiction of Sand as a presiding genius the following year, "[c]ounter-discourses inhabit and struggle with the dominant which inhabits them" (Terdiman, *Discourse/Counter-Discourse*, 18).

The caricature "Miroir drolatique" appeared in 1842 in the illustrated newpaper *Le Charivari*, which also published Daumier's *bas-bleu* series (fig. 2). Alcide Lorentz's caption of the cross-dressed Sand suggests that a woman of genius—said to have no sex—cuts a droll, if not perplexing, figure: "Si de Georges [*sic*] Sand ce portrait / Laisse l'esprit un peu perplexe, / C'est que le génie est abstrait, / Et comme on sait n'a pas de sexe." Sand's feminine features are covered by a dark, masculine costume, but not entirely concealed. Enveloped by the "feu sacré" of the cigarette she holds in her left hand, Sand strikes a curious pose in an ethereal realm. Represented as weightless sheets of paper, her cloudy ideas are as tenuous as her claim to genius.

Though "le génie est abstrait" suggests a concept blind to sex, Lorentz's play on "le génie n'a pas de sexe" in relation to Sand constructs the categories of "genius" and "woman" as irreconcilable. Elizabeth Barrett Browning drew out this agonistic relationship in her 1844 tribute, "To George Sand: A Recognition," with the opening line, "True genius, but true woman!" (*Poems*, 148). Browning expresses the tension between creativity and femininity in imagining how Sand's genius would live on, decorporealized and thus without sex:

> We see thy woman-heart beat evermore
> Through the large flame. Beat purer, heart, and higher,
> Till God unsex thee on the heavenly shore,
> Where unincarnate spirits purely aspire!
>
> (148)[30]

Whereas some French women with poetic ambitions revisited Staël's narrative of the exceptional woman, virtually none of them turned explicitly to Sand.[31] In tracing women's diverse paths during the first half of the century, following the order in which their first poetic volume appeared, I show that Corinne's shadow faded as Romantic era poets explored whether genius was inspired or innate.

### The Limits of Genius

In "Corine [*sic*] à Oswald" (1813), an epistle in verse by Adélaïde Dufrénoy (1765–1825), the heroine seeks to reconcile her place as a womanly woman with her poetic work. Has not the literary glory she achieved made her all the more beautiful in her suitor's eyes? Or does she have to renounce her gift in order to assuage her lover's anxiety about her creative power? Dufrénoy leaves the imaginary woman of poetic genius (and her readership) wondering, "Faut-il haïr les arts pour te garder sa foi[?]" (*Œuvres poétiques*, 146).

In shifting from the character Corinne to her gifted creator, the elegist Victoire Babois (1760–1839) cleverly authorizes the political section of her *Élégies nationales* (1815). Babois measures the distance between her voice and Staël's genius, but gains critical agency via her self-effacing stance: "Il est probable que beaucoup de personnes trouveront que ces trois morceaux . . . sortent des limites qu'on prescrit tacitement aux femmes, en France peut-être plus qu'ailleurs. Pour oser les franchir, il fallait être madame de Staël; elle l'a fait avec la conscience d'elle-même et toute l'assurance de son génie. Je la regarde de si loin qu'il ne m'appartient pas de l'imiter" (*Élégies et poésies diverses*, 111). In light of the ethical standards set by the bourgeoisie during the Restoration (1814–30), which restricted women's work to home life, a literary woman had to protect her social reputation. Babois's prefatory comments offer a pre-Romantic example of the narrative of reception from the side of women. Romantic era women intervened in this narrative, beginning with Marceline Desbordes-Valmore (1786–1859), who did not invoke Staël's heroine as a poetic foremother.[32] The itinerant actress-turned-poet considered the cultural interdiction against women's professional aspirations as she entered the literary arena from the ranks of the working class.

Desbordes-Valmore's inaugural volume, *Élégies, Marie, et romances* (1819), marked the leading edge of French Romanticism.[33] From the outset, as expressed in the elegy "L'inquiétude," her lyrical expression blended deep thought with feeling.[34] Anxiety stirs pensive sadness in the poem "Prière aux muses." A first-person feminine subject forecasts her fall into oblivion—"l'obscurité que le sort me destine"—while affirming her heart as the wellspring of her verse (Desbordes-Valmore, *Œuvres poétiques*, 1:49). This was the source belatedly claimed by her male counterpart Alphonse de Lamartine, whose *Méditations poétiques* (1820) would displace Desbordes-Valmore's volume in traditional literary histories to signal the birth of modern French Romantic poetry. The nascent aesthetic valorized emotion together with imagination. And why did this not apply equally to women? Desbordes-Valmore's poem "Un beau jour" (1820) reflects the power of public opinion over women's private lives as the female poetic subject bids farewell to her muse at the thought of her impending marriage: "Adieu, Muse! on me marie. / . . . Adieu, vague rêverie, / Songe de la volupté! / Mon âme plus attendrie / S'ouvre à la réalité" (*Œuvres poétiques*, 1:123). Nevertheless, the voices of a doleful "poetess" and a reflective poet emerge from the same corpus published during Desbordes-Valmore's lifetime.

Desbordes-Valmore also crafted a feminine persona, as illustrated in "À M. Alphonse de Lamartine," initially published in *Mémorial de la Scarpe* (1832), then in *Les pleurs* (1833).[35] In this poem, responding to Lamartine's public admiration of her "génie poétique," she invokes the sexual binary. Physiology regulates intellectual property in Desbordes-Valmore's self-portrayal. Weakness paired with a lack of culture characterizes her lyre, used metaphorically to evoke her work or skill as a poet. Her expression pales in comparison with his inspiring poetry:

> Car je suis une faible femme;
> Je n'ai su qu'aimer et souffrir
> Ma pauvre lyre, c'est mon âme,
> Et toi seul découvres la flamme
> D'une lampe qui va mourir.
>
> Devant tes hymnes de poète,
> D'ange, hélas! et d'homme à la fois,
> Cette lyre inculte, incomplète,

> Longtemps détendue et muette,
> Ose à peine prendre une voix.
> (Desbordes-Valmore, *Œuvres poétiques*, 1:225)[36]

Did Desbordes-Valmore pen these lines with exaggerated humility because "[s]he knew the kind of woman her public could allow to become a poet," as Barbara Johnson argues ("Gender and Poetry," 167)? Or, at once sentimental and reflective, did Desbordes-Valmore weave the "frêle voix de femme" into her writing alongside thoughts about other women's imaginative ability or her own?[37]

Representative of the dual identity Desbordes-Valmore formed is her poem "Louise Labé," also in *Les pleurs*. The renaissance of lyric poetry during the early nineteenth century stemmed in part from poets' reading of their sixteenth-century predecessors, such as Pierre de Ronsard (1524–1585) and Louise Labé (1524–1566). Indeed, the epigraph, which cites Labé, suggests that Desbordes-Valmore had consulted Breghot du Lut's 1824 edition of Labé's complete works. This evidence belies Desbordes-Valmore's depiction of her voice as uneducated and unrefined ("Cette lyre inculte, incomplète") in "À M. Alphonse de Lamartine" and elsewhere, which she often tied to being a working-class woman with no time to read.[38] That Desbordes-Valmore showcased Labé's fourteenth sonnet and the first seven lines of Labé's third elegy reveals, moreover, a sophisticated blurring of the boundary between poetic forms gendered as masculine and feminine, respectively. Though Desbordes-Valmore eschewed the sonnet, this gesture is not necessarily "anti-masculine," as Schultz proposes (*Gendered Lyric*, 77–80). Rather, Desbordes-Valmore's choice of form, which can be interpreted as anticlassical, aligns her more closely with the Romantic project in Labé's œuvre. In paying homage to Labé's resonant verse, Desbordes-Valmore defines poetic writing as a personal expression that also reflects the world in all its diversity: "l'âme poétique est une chambre obscure / Où s'enferme le monde et ses aspects divers!" (*Œuvres poétiques*, 1:230).

Social issues and political themes, such as the movement for emancipation linking women, workers, and black people, open Desbordes-Valmore's poetic thought to the world. The overarching sense of divine inspiration that she retained without reference to sex also places her so-called natural genius beyond gender.[39] Yet conservative readers would establish Desbordes-Valmore's legacy as the quintessential "woman poet" who embodied femininity by associating her voice with frailty and her verse with an outpouring of tears. The titles of her principal volumes, *Les pleurs* (1833), *Pauvres fleurs* (1839), *Bouquets et prières* (1843), and *Les anges de la famille* (1849), played into societal expectations.[40] The theme of motherhood further domesticated her work by making it fit the category of "poésie féminine." This token status evolved from the discursive categories of literary reception I treat in chapter 2. Valmore's sentimental legacy worked, moreover, to conceal her fuller output as well as other women's contributions to poetic production during the Romantic era and beyond, a point that is taken up in chapter 3.

## The Social Problem of Genius

Among Desbordes-Valmore's more visible contemporaries was Delphine Gay (1804–1855), partly thanks to her mother, the novelist and dramatist Sophie Gay (1776–1852), whose salon drew an elite audience. Named after one of Staël's gifted heroines, the young Delphine brought forth her first volume of poetry in 1824 to acclaim.[41] After her marriage to the journalist Émile de Girardin in 1831, she turned from poetry to prose, as if following the market. This change in genre also relates to the matter of genius treated in her narrative poem "Napoline" (1833): "Napoline mourante est le Génie—éteint, / Énervé par le monde, en ses élans contraint" (Girardin, *Poésies complètes*, 140). Staël's Corinne lingers as a shadow figure, representing "the failed social integration and suicide of a young woman of genius," Cheryl Morgan notes ("Delphine Gay de Girardin," 229).[42] The allegory of Napoline foretold the bleak view espoused by Delphine de Girardin who, by 1836, identified herself as a novelist: women of poetic genius had no future, either as women or as geniuses. No single stance, however, subsumes how women negotiated their relationship to poetic originality. Discourses of religion and science mingle in women's thinking through the problem of genius, with the Romantic period setting the stage for their hybrid production and the multiplicity of their voices throughout the rest of the nineteenth century.

The Académie française recognized Amable Tastu for her inaugural volume, *La chevalerie française* (1821), a collection of prose and poetry related to the work's historical theme. Her 1825 poem about Charles X's coronation as the king of France that year, "Les oiseaux du sacre," brought more praise. A young female's poetic gift is the subject of "L'ange gardien," first published in *Poésies* (1826) and then reprinted in *Poésies complètes* (1858). Tastu's text, consisting of thirteen stanzas, presents a palimpsest of interiority. An inner dialogue in which notions of genius and gender overlap externalizes a poetic mind divided against itself, staging a woman's life from birth to death. The speaker, first identified as a child, invokes the immortal spirit to reflect upon personal ambition versus moral duty, thus raising the question of destiny:

> Oh! Qu'il est beau, cet esprit immortel,
> Gardien sacré de notre destinée!
>
> .  .  .  .  .  .  .  .  .  .  .  .
>
> Dès le berceau sa voix mystérieuse,
> Des voeux confus d'une âme ambitieuse,
> Sait réprimer l'impétueuse ardeur,
> Et d'âge en âge il nous guide au bonheur.
>
> (Tastu, *Poésies complètes*, 54)

Ancient and classical meanings of genius mingle, respectively, with the guardian angel or tutelary spirit guiding the young female subject and the sacred flame inspiring her poetic voice. This semantic tension juxtaposes a call to womanhood with the life of the mind:

> Dans cette vie obscure, à mes regards voilée,
> Quel destin m'est promis? à quoi suis-je appelée?
>
> . . . . . . . . . . . . .
>
> Quel immense horizon devant moi se révèle!
> À mes regards ravis que la nature est belle!
> Tout ce que sent mon âme ou qu'embrassent mes yeux
> S'exhale de ma bouche en sons mélodieux!
> Où courent ces rivaux armés du luth sonore?
> Dans cette arène, il est quelques places encore:
> Ne puis-je, à leurs côtés me frayant un chemin,
> M'élancer seule, libre, et ma lyre à la main?
>
> (54–55)

Here, as in other women's writing examined in this book, the myth of Eve's transgressive desire competes with that of Mary's motherly sacrifice.

The institution of religion underlies the angel's response in Tastu's "L'ange gardien." To seek coronation not with poetic laurels but with Marian humility is the only destiny that does not lead Eve's daughters astray: "Seule couronne à ton front destinée . . . / D'un saint devoir doucement enchaînée, / Que ferais-tu d'un espoir mensonger?" (*Poésies complètes*, 55). In order to preserve her virtue, a woman must avoid the treacherous path of literary glory and thus allow inspiration to consume itself in her soul:

> Ce feu sacré, renfermé dans ton âme,
> S'y consumait loin des profanes yeux;
>
> . . . . . . . . . . . . .
>
> D'un art heureux tu connus la douceur,
> Sans t'égarer sur les pas de la gloire.
>
> (57)

Overt conformity, however, does not erase the sense of "lost opportunity" nor the embedded testament to a woman's poetic gift (Schultz, *Gendered Lyric*, 40).

"La gloire" (1826) closes Tastu's first poetic volume on a similar note. The poet begins by depicting her voice as weak and thus not destined for literary glory, preempting in this way any charge of envy:

> Qui! moi, moi l'envier, la chercher ou l'attendre?
> Moi, d'un immense écho flatter ma faible voix?
> Non, je n'y prétends point, mais je crois la comprendre;
>     Et je m'applaudis de mon choix!
>
> (Tastu, *Poésies complètes*, 158)

Here, as in "L'ange gardien," modesty overlaps with poetic power. Erudition and a mastery of classical prosody belie the leitmotifs of reception in "La gloire." In describing her poetry as artless in form and as feminine and maternal in content, Tastu conforms to the canons of male criticism. Elsewhere, she forges a path of resistance.

Tastu, like Desbordes-Valmore, crafted a feminine identity in her verse. And, like Desbordes-Valmore, Tastu interjected the voice of a critical reader, making her corpus a discursive site as well as a reflection on the literary culture of the time:

> Qu'importe si nul bruit ne survit à ma tombe,
> Si dans le cercle étroit, par mes accords rempli,
> Sitôt que de mes mains le luth s'échappe et tombe,
> Règnent le silence et l'oubli!
>
> (Tastu, *Poésies complètes*, 160)

In "Chant de Sapho," recalling Desbordes-Valmore, Tastu laments the fate that befell a woman with poetic aspirations: "Celle pour qui la honte à la gloire est unie, / Qui de tout son bonheur a payé son génie, / Et n'en a point joui" (113). But Tastu also celebrates the Greek poet Sappho's genius, demonstrating how cleverly women have inscribed their creative authority and contribution to poetic history in relation to each other even as they have denied their own gifts. Others, such as Élisa Mercœur, directly challenged convention by authorizing the view that genius is blind to sex.

### The "Virility" of Genius

Unlike Desbordes-Valmore and Tastu, Mercœur portrayed herself as a genius in the context of her poetry. She wearily contemplated the future, even more so while ailing from tuberculosis.[43] "L'avenir" (1826) conveys the aesthetics of mental and physical suffering adopted by Romantics of both sexes, making intense pain a font of genius.[44] Despite the symbolic resonance of the name Mercœur, it is overstating the case to say that she portrays "the life of the genius as misery, a debilitated psychological condition" (Greenberg, "Élisa Mercœur," 87).[45] Rather, in the twenty-first and final stanza, this ode evokes the idea of long suffering in Buffon's linkage of genius with patience. After death, the young poet's lyre is transformed into an eagle that soars into the future, with the stanza concluding thus: "Qu'importe un jour de pleurs! L'avenir du génie / Est l'immortalité!" (Mercœur, *Œuvres poétiques*, 52). This open ending preserves Mercœur's desire to transcend history by living on in readers' minds, as other literary geniuses have.

Mercœur's Pindaric ode "Le sublime" (1827) recalls literary glory from ages past in an arc from Homer to Tasso to Milton. Two epigraphs set a dialogue in motion, placing Mercœur in a broader conversation about the nature of poetic creativity, which boldly projects the posterity of her sublime expression. The opening epigraph, which cites the first half of the poem's tenth stanza, represents the poet's voice as majestic and timeless: "Il chante, et ne craint pas le rire d'un Zoïle. / L'aigle échappe au venin que jette le reptile: / Rien n'empoisonne l'air que l'on respire aux cieux" (Mercœur, *Œuvres poétiques*, 133).[46] The eagle, symbolizing the poet of genius who fears no reproach ("le rire d'un Zoïle," referring to Zoilus, a grammarian and literary critic from ancient Greece), reaches lofty heights. The first line of the second epigraph, taken from Charles Nodier, traces the origins of genius to Greek mythology: "Le berceau du génie est le berceau d'Alcide" (133). The reference to Alcide, the French name for Hercules, equates genius with superhuman strength, but also with combat. This male-defined model of exceptional power is precisely what Mercœur appropriates, but she unsexes it to represent the force inhabiting the creative mind that surpasses all obstacles, including time and space.

In stanza 4 of "Le sublime," the speaking subject solicits her imagination to capture with consummate lyricism the trace of inner vision, showing the extraordinary way that a poet sees the ordinary:

> Invente! immortalise un moment d'existence;
> Effeuille les pavots que jette l'ignorance;
> Des regards de ton âme embrasse l'univers.
> Vole au sommet sacré t'abreuver d'harmonie:
> Chacun de ces instants ravis à ton génie
>> Est tout un âge que tu perds.
>>> (Mercœur, *Œuvres poétiques*, 134)

The capacity of genius, possessed by the divinely inspired poet, has no association with gender. In stanza 7, "éclair" represents the effects of genius, a rush of energy along with insight. For Mercœur, the sublime (from the Latin *sublimis*, to elevate), meaning "exquisite form or thought," is a product of genius:

> D'un seul mot, t'ai-je dit, la rapide puissance
> Charme, captive, entraîne, et quelquefois dispense
> Aux amants de la gloire une immortalité.
> C'est l'éclair s'échappant du caillou qui s'enflamme;
> Enfin, c'est le sublime, ou c'est un son de l'âme
>> Que le génie a répété.
>>> (135)

Why would a young woman, determined that readers remember her as a poet of genius, allude to a masculine concept of the sublime? In a reputedly "unfeminine" quest for fame and immortality, did Mercœur mistakenly adopt the Romantic personality type of the (male) genius, as Wendy Greenberg has argued ("Élisa Mercœur")?

In the subsequent stanza of "Le sublime," the adjective "mâles" (male in the sense of energetic or vigorous) refers to the ideals or aesthetics of beauty:

> En cédant à l'effort d'un magique délire,
> Le sublime jamais ne peignit un sourire:
> Il faut à ses crayons de plus mâles beautés.
> Au bruit inspirateur de la voix des orages,
> Pour le poète ému par ces accords sauvages,
> L'effroi même a des voluptés.
>
> (Mercœur, *Œuvres poétiques*, 135)

Is one to conclude from this nominal evidence that, "for Mercœur women were subjects of sublime creations, but they could not create themselves" (Greenberg, "Élisa Mercœur," 94)? Does Mercœur's genius discourse unwittingly recall the link between virility and genius à la Virey? Or might one interpret this discourse in the combative way Mercœur thought about originality, calling, in stanza 17, the poet's lyre a "glaive"? From such a perspective, "Le sublime" counters the failure to recognize women as innovators, which renders their struggle against oblivion all the more acute, echoing poems such as "La pensée," "La gloire et l'indigence," "La gloire," and "La France littéraire."

Introductory comments to *Mélanges*, a collection of Mercœur's writings posthumously published in 1843 and reprinted in her *Œuvres poétiques*, mention an article that denied women a soul while claiming that poetry belonged exclusively to men. In response, Mercœur had argued against the sexed mind: "Quoi! vous qui avez presque idéalisé les femmes, vous leur refusez la pensée, vous leur refusez une âme! Comment nommez-vous donc le feu qui les anime? . . . Ah! qu'il soit à jamais annulé l'arrêt injuste qui ne fait de la femme qu'une statue mouvante. Le vaste domaine de la pensée est-il une carrière où l'homme seul a droit de courir? Non, l'étincelle sacrée du génie ne s'étouffe pas dans notre cœur; elle nous dévore comme vous" (Mercœur, *Œuvres poétiques*, 2:392–93). Her rebuttal develops the paradigm shift, lost since Helvétius, from metaphors capturing the effect of genius to an interactive model locating the advent of genius between nature *and* nuture: "Comme vous, ne pouvons-nous donc mériter, conquérir la gloire? . . . vous réservez à vous seuls la poésie, cette musique intérieure dont chaque note est un sentiment, une émotion. . . . Peut-être existe-t-il quelque Sapho dans les préjugés où l'ignorance enchaîne l'imagination; peut-être n'a-t-elle besoin que d'être devinée ou de se deviner elle-même. Il faut briser une pierre pour trouver un diamant. Eh bien! l'éducation, les circonstances, un moment quelquefois peuvent briser la pierre, et le génie du poète peut s'en échapper" (393, 394). To make their mark as thinkers and poets, women have to wrestle with the idea of their ostensible lack of aptitude for reflection and creativity. In thinking beyond gender, Mercœur depicts genius as a force cultivated by knowledge or propelled by circumstances, which breaks through barriers to reveal the creative mind.

The question of genius weighed heavily, yet differently, on women whose poetic forays intersected with the rise and fall of Romanticism during the 1830s and '40s. Anaïs Ségalas, who emerged on the literary scene in 1831, and Mélanie Waldor, who first published poetry in 1835, were less explicit than Mercœur in seeking literary glory. Their trajectories, along with Louise Colet's, whose inaugural volume of verse dates to 1836, complicate how women understood their contribution to poetic history, the issue being whether they disputed, or reinforced, the sexing of genius.

### Negotiating Genius Otherwise

The rival ideas of genius in the hybrid production of the poet, novelist, and dramatist Mélanie Waldor have been overshadowed by her role as Alexandre Dumas père's muse. Waldor's self-fashioning as a "poetess," inspired by feeling instead of thought, differs from the critical authority she established. Although Waldor promoted her female contemporaries as original poets alongside their male counterparts, she approached critics to gain favorable press for her self-styled "feminine" writing. For example, writing to a critic for the newspaper *Le Moniteur* in 1834, she asked that he redress a blurb announcing her poetic volume: "Voici les quelques lignes, monsieur, pour lesquelles j'ai sollicité votre aimable obligeance pour moi. Veuillez les revêtir d'une robe plus gracieuse, afin que le public fasse un bon accueil à mes poésies, là est tout mon avenir" (Waldor, *Lettres inédites*, 11). What future did Waldor have as a poet if, in deploying the sartorial metaphor of dress and fashion, she made her work fit the category of "poésie féminine"?

The first three lines of "À mes amis," the opening poem of *Poésies du cœur* (1835), explain the volume's title. Calling her verses "chants" that flow directly from the heart, the poet uses an avian allegory to represent her relationship to creativity: "Ne me demandez pas de donner à mes chants / Un vol plus élevé: ce qu'ils ont d'harmonie / Je le dois à mon cœur, et non pas au génie" (3). The speaking subject compares herself to a bird lacking the wings of inspiration. Were she to attempt, as Mercœur had, to follow the majestic eagle that could reach lofty heights, she would surely fail. Unable to elevate thought, her verse holds no promise, apart from being recalled by her friends: "Que puis-je désirer de plus dans l'avenir, / Moi qui n'attends de lui ni couronne ni gloire!" (4). Waldor retreats further from the quest for glory that energizes Mercœur's project. Read closely, Waldor adds, a woman's verses reveal their sentimental charm or genius: "Car il est son génie, et rien ne le remplace. / Ce qu'elle gagne en force, elle le perd en grâce" (5). Here, in "À mes amis," Waldor uses "génie" to mean an identifying character or spirit. Grace, not creative force, represents the poetic embodiment of femininity. Elsewhere, however, Waldor does not distinguish between the sexes of poetic genius. In *Poésies du cœur*, she records her contemporaries' poetic achievements via epigraphs and poems dedicated to a wide circle of women and men. For example, in "À Madame

Victoire Babois," Waldor recognizes Babois's "éclair du génie" alongside the success of "ce livre où la douleur / En vers harmonieux, échos de votre cœur, / S'exhale tour à tour sublime et déchirante" (Waldor, *Poésies du cœur*, 306).[47]

Similarly, in "À Madame Marceline Desbordes-Valmore," Waldor lauds her contemporary's poetic originality. The epigraph selected by Waldor ("Ma pauvre lyre c'est mon âme!") comes from Desbordes-Valmore's poem "À M. Alphonse de Lamartine." This textual echo structures Waldor's poetic tribute. Desbordes-Valmore, using "âme" as a synonym for her heart, had portrayed her voice as wretched and plaintive, lacking the divine inspiration she attributed to Lamartine. Waldor uncouples the Romantic notion of genius from gender, altering the gist of Desbordes-Valmore's self-portrayal, on the one hand, and her own authority as both a writer and a reader, on the other. "Âme," from the Latin *anima*, connotes breath (in French, "souffle") or life. Waldor's depiction pivots on the term "souffle," reading Desbordes-Valmore's inner force from her physiognomy: "Le souffle du génie / A caressé ton front sans s'arrêter au mien . . . / Mais je suis ton amie, et non pas ta rivale, / Qu'importe entre nos chants s'il est un intervalle?" (Waldor, *Poésies du cœur*, 37; ellipses in original). In mapping Desbordes-Valmore's genius on her forehead and likening her verse to a "chant divin," Waldor elevates her contemporary's inspired flame above her own writing from feeling (36). In thinking about genius, however, Waldor inscribed her work in the Romantic chapter of French poetic history.

In the autobiographical essay "Ma mère," published in *Pages de la vie intime* (1836), Waldor recalls the year 1826, approximately six years into the Romantic movement inaugurated by Lamartine, Desbordes-Valmore, and Tastu, which she describes as the turning point in her desire to become a writer. Though her mother had warned against such a vocation, Waldor immersed herself in reading, ever fascinated by the concept of genius, "le sublime, l'idéal, l'infini, mystérieuse trinité dont se compose le génie" (Waldor, *Pages de la vie intime*, 2:242–43). Like other Romantic era women, Waldor worked within the framework of divine inspiration in making the transition from a classical view of genius, focused on a universal ideal, to a Romantic notion of originality. In the essay "Les femmes auteurs," Waldor has innovation in mind as she distinguishes women's poetic work since the outset of the century from the commodification of literature during the Romantic heyday. "Le génie de la gloire," the phrasing she uses to evoke the pervasive commercialism and attendant cult of personality of the 1830s, has threatened the survival of true genius and the value of poetry (253). As authors, women also have to grapple with virtue, an issue Waldor traces to the biblical account of the transgression associated with women's pursuit of knowledge: "Et quelle est la femme, la mère surtout qui, tout au délire du moment, ne se repentirait d'avoir crié à son génie: 'Élance-toi à travers cette génération avide de ce qui frappe et remue: oublie le ciel, l'avenir!'" (254–55). Waldor addresses societal pressures, rather than any organic physiological problem between the energy a woman expends as a mother and as an author.

For Waldor, the question was not whether women could possess genius, but how they could maintain the integrity of their intellectual property in an age of mechanical reproduction. When writing about her own work, whether in the context of her poetry, prose, or letters, Waldor nonetheless portrayed herself as a feminine woman with talent but no claim to genius. As she expressed in a letter of 1839 to a critic reviewing her novel *Alphonse et Juliette*, which had appeared that year, "Écrire est quelquefois un besoin de mon cœur, jamais de mon esprit" (Waldor, *Lettres inédites*, 18). Waldor deftly negotiated her identity as a writer, interlocking her poetry and prose with the gendering of literary engagement that she contested as a critical reader. Her contemporary Louise Colet was more explicit in stating that the life of the mind transcends a woman's lived experience. The story of the men in Colet's life, as in Waldor's, however, later usurped her poetic history.

A cluster of poems in *Fleurs du Midi* (1836), Colet's first published volume, interweaves the poet's reflections about her craft with autobiographical notes. In the opening poem, "Tourments du poète," the speaking subject contemplates genius in relation to inspiration, feeling, pain, thought, and work. While emotional and mental anguish inform the creative process, the rhetoric of combat associates the poet and "l'homme de génie" beyond gender, recalling Mercœur's paradigm. The poetic inheritance claimed by Colet in "Enthousiasme" emerges along a similar axis: "Dieu me fit poète!" (Colet, *Poésies complètes*, 16). The aspiring poet fuses sensibility ("Le trop plein de mon cœur") and sense ("mes rapides pensées"), adopting the aesthetics of Romanticism while domesticating her verse: "Là j'ai laissé ma vie empreinte dans mes vers! . . ." (16; ellipses in original). "L'inspiration," another early poem by Colet, composed from 1833 to 1834, develops a biography of the creative mind; the fledgling poet described therein as a "jeune aiglon" (a young eagle) echoes Mercœur's metaphor for transcendent genius and Waldor's rejection of it (17).

In "Les doutes de l'esprit," Colet represents herself as a born poet, "celui qu'en naissant la poésie embrase" (*Poésies complètes*, 20). Her self-portrait foregrounds the notion of poetic genius as an inherent capacity, which evolved from an ancient view: "cet instinct inné qui nous suit au berceau, / Qui guide à notre insu nos sentiments intimes, / Et nous révèle Dieu par ses œuvres sublimes" (20). Consistent with this stance, Colet imagines a different ending to *Corinne*, thirty years after Staël's fictive woman of genius first appeared. In "Corinne à Oswald," published in Colet's second poetic volume, *Penserosa* (1840), the title of which means "contemplative woman," the heroine transcends the gender binary that restricted genius to males. Her suitor embraces both the womanly woman and her creative mind: "Ton amour me révèle une sphère infinie; / Je crois à ma beauté, je crois à mon génie, / Puisque tu sais m'aimer" (*Poésies complètes*, 182).[48]

But the public had yet to learn from her example and that of other creative women to separate the woman from the poet, as expressed by the speaker contemplating her reception in Colet's poem "À ma mère," also in *Penserosa*: "Oh! que tu savais bien que, dans ce monde infâme, / Le céleste rayon qui ceint un front de femme, / Hélas n'attire pas le respect et l'honneur" (*Poésies complètes*, 224). The laurel wreath crowning a woman's superior mind, metonymically represented by the "front" in Colet's text, is entwined with sarcasm:

> En posant le laurier sur le front d'une femme,
> Froidement à l'éloge on mêle l'épigramme;
> On brille en déchirant, et l'esprit satisfait,
> Frondeur insoucieux, rit du mal qu'il a fait!

> (226)

The poem closes with the female subject dwelling on the possibility that someone would dissociate the woman from the poet: "vivant noblement du fruit de la pensée" (227). In "Un mystère" (1842), Colet explicitly links her legacy to genius, asking:

> Qui m'écoute et me suit ainsi de rêve en rêve?
> Qui recueille les bruits laissés sur mon chemin?
> À mes œuvres d'un jour quelle prodigue main
> Élève un monument qu'on ne doit qu'au génie.

> (298)

Colet garnered a number of prizes for her works, becoming one of France's most visible poets in the 1840s. As a strong woman, the writer was "a paradigm of that bluestocking French men so feared and derided" (Gray, *Rage and Fire*, 97). What would Colet think of the legacy she has retained, not as the poet Flaubert recognized her to be but, rather, as his muse?[49]

By the early 1840s, Delphine de Girardin had all but buried the shadow of Staël's woman of genius in whose image she had cast her figure of Napoline in 1833, "tombée avant la gloire et morte avant l'amour" (*Poésies complètes*, 140).[50] In 1843 she brought forth under the title *Lettres parisiennes* the contemporary sketches she had penned under the pseudonym Charles de Launay and published in *La Presse* from 1836 to 1839. In a later sketch reflecting on the absence of women in the Académie française, she filters females' access to literary authority through the metaphor of inheritance: "Pourquoi voulez-vous leur octroyer la plume, quand vous leur avez refusé le sceptre? Pourquoi, lorsqu'elles ne sont rien par leur naissance, seraient-elles quelque chose par leur génie?" (*Lettres parisiennes*, 3:2). She wonders if men have refused women the right to inherit property, including that of genius, because they somehow envy them.

Nevertheless, in modeling genius on psychic androgyny, where masculine force balances feminine sensibility, Girardin asserts a cerebral inequality between the sexes: "Le génie de la femme (une brillante exception ne prouve rien) ne possède pas ce double avantage; il n'a jamais ni les qualités ni les défauts masculins, alors même qu'il s'exerce le plus à les acquérir" (*Lettres parisiennes*, 3:5). "Factice et fébrile," as Girardin describes, the energy a woman spends on creative endeavors is always fruitless, in a word, "stérile" (3:5). Though she uses the latter word in a figurative sense, her argument anticipates the theory of infertility in fin-de-siècle physiology: a woman who feeds her brain starves her reproductive body (3:5). Her analysis of "ces attaques d'épilepsie intellectuelle" as bordering on hysteria conveys a pathological bent related to the nervous system.[51] In sum, Girardin reproduces the physiological binary à la Virey, concluding that excessive brainwork depletes a woman's "force naturelle" (3:5).

As of the late 1840s, the Parisian bourgeoise Anaïs Ségalas had also shifted from progressive to conservative views on women and their intellectual activity. Ségalas had launched her career in 1831 with a poetic volume on France's invasion of Algeria the previous year, in which her speaking subject, bearing literary arms, joins ranks with the women who entered into that combat. In prefacing *La femme: Poésies* (1847), however, Ségalas no longer aligns her voice with the women demanding emancipation on the eve of the 1848 revolution: "Dieu me préserve de ces idées révolutionnaires; je ne suis pas de celles qui font de leur écharpe un drapeau" (9). She positions herself as a womanly woman writer, parting ways with the militant feminists of the time: "Sans demander pour la femme plus de place au soleil, j'ai cherché tout simplement le bien qu'elle peut faire dans la société actuelle. . . . Tout le bien-être matériel, toutes les grandes découvertes de la science et de l'industrie viennent de l'homme; mais les chastes et douces vertus, l'amour pur et l'influence poétique et religieuse viennent presque toujours de la femme" (10, 11–12). As a man's muse, a woman inspires his creative work and ethical behavior. Was it for her intended female readership or her own reputation that Ségalas upheld bourgeois values? Her poem "Les trois amours" attributes imaginative ability to males and love of virtue to females: "Un feu sacré, pareil à celui du poëte: / L'homme en fait le génie, et la femme l'amour" (150). Ségalas also intertwined the question of genius with race in considering the effects of colonial slavery, its abolition, and women's civilizing role, a forgotten aspect of her œuvre treated in chapter 4.

As illustrated by women's engagement in the debate about genius during the first half of the nineteenth century, the biological explanation of creativity did not supplant the belief in divine inspiration. The latter belief, though traditionally patriarchal, involved a counterparadigm. Romantic era women invoked inspiration beyond gender as a discarnate force. Women's questioning of religious versus scientific accounts of the capacity to innovate, especially as poets who pondered the human condition to reassess their relationship to the work of originality, the modern attribute of genius, was more pronounced from the 1850s onward. During the second half of the century, biology dominated efforts to define genius in relation to its source, internal versus external. Scientific attempts to measure intelligence, however, shifted from the muscles to the brain. Whereas social scientists considered nature versus nurture in human development, evolutionary science focused the debate on sexual selection. The vocabulary and tenets of physiology pervaded the genius debate in the letters and sciences to the century's end. The final section of this chapter turns to poetic women from the second half of the century, who marshaled the history of ideas about genius within the context of richly imaginative projects.

### Brighter by Nature or Nurture?

During the second half of the century, conservative thinkers popularized advances in anatomy, biology, embryology, psychophysiology, and pathology.[52] This synergy among the sciences, encouraged by concerns with depopulation, galvanized the backlash against creative and intellectual women, whose numbers were steadily rising. In 1857, the naturalist writers Jules de Goncourt and Edmond de Goncourt speculated that autopsies of Staël and Sand would reveal both male and female genitals, reflecting the tone of the backlash as well as its interdisciplinary texture: "Le génie est mâle. L'autopsie de Mme de Staël et de Mme Sand auraient été curieuses: elles doivent avoir une construction un peu hermaphrodite" (Goncourt and Goncourt, *Journal*, 1:396). Genius, they suggested, generated an intersex condition in women whose superior intellect made them virile. The Goncourts' fanciful anatomy captures the nature of the threat that such women were thought to pose to society: a nonreproductive sex.

At nearly the same moment, in *De la justice dans la révolution et dans l'église* (1858), the French politician and socialist Pierre-Joseph Proudhon recycled the physiology of genius that Virey had mapped from an incomplete understanding of reproduction thirty years prior. Women, Proudhon confirmed, lacked the seeds of genius in a literal sense but also figuratively: "des germes, c'est-à-dire des idées" (3:354). With a loose recourse to etymology ("ce que les Latins appelaient *genius*, le génie, comme qui dirait la faculté génératrice de l'esprit"), Proudhon fused the maleness of mind and body: "Le génie est donc la virilité de l'esprit, sa puissance d'abstraction, de généralisation, d'invention, de conception, dont l'enfant, l'eunuque et la femme sont également dépourvus" (3:356). Genius requires male procreative force, he argued, comparing the effects of sexual abstinence on the athlete and the thinker, "comme si la résorption de la semence n'était pas moins nécessaire au cerveau de l'un qu'aux muscles de l'autre" (3:356). This proponent of the spermatic imagination did not go unchallenged.

That same year, the feminist writer Juliette Adam brought forth *Idées anti-proudhoniennes sur l'amour, la femme et le mariage* (1858) under the pseudonym Mme Juliette La Messine. Having consulted with a distinguished physiologist (whom she does not identify), she dismisses all of Proudhon's claims, especially his "théorie de la résorption des germes" (72).[53] By attributing creative power to semen, Proudhon could maintain that "le cerveau n'est pas fécondé chez la femme" (73). Adam argues against the transposition of sexual differences into cerebral attributes, noting that creative men express so-called feminine sensibilities and gifted women display "masculine" thought. For her, there is no organic difference between the sexes' mental capacity. Women's work, in and outside the home, she concludes, is as vital as men's work to France's future.

The physician/midwife Jenny d'Héricourt wrote with similar conviction about the need for women to cultivate their intellect, which would better all of humanity. In *La femme affranchie: Réponse à MM. Michelet, Proudhon, É. de Girardin, A. Comte* (1860), d'Héricourt disputes, as Adam had, the role ascribed exclusively to the male in both reproduction and cultural production. The opposition to creative and intellectual women recalled a comparable attack during the Romantic period, which the protofeminist Charles Fourier had aptly described as an outburst of "la jalousie masculine" (quoted in d'Héricourt, *La femme affranchie*, 1:49). D'Héricourt counters her contemporary Proudhon's view of females' passive, procreative role: "Vous dites: l'homme seul produit les germes physiques, l'anatomie répond: *C'est la femme qui produit le germe*; l'organe qui, chez elle, comme chez les autres femelles, remplit cette fonction, est l'ovaire" (*La femme affranchie*, 1:176; emphasis in original). Does not this scientific truth dislodge the traditional paradigm of procreativity and, with this, the sexing of genius?

There is no evidence to support the view, inherited from Aristotle, that women are mutilated or incomplete men and thus are governed by any form of "male" envy, continues d'Héricourt: "Vous dites: la femme est un diminutif de l'homme; c'est un mâle imparfait, l'anatomie dit: *l'homme et la femme sont deux êtres distincts, chacun complet, mais chacun d'un appareil spécial, aussi nécessaire l'un que l'autre*" (*La femme affranchie*, 1:176; emphasis in original). Moreover, on what basis could Proudhon deny genius in women? Each previous century had produced several famous women, d'Héricourt stresses, citing among others the achievements of Sand and the artist Rosa Bonheur in her century (1:182–83). How could one restrict women to mindless, domestic tasks, when their work across the disciplines also contributes to cultural production?

Ten years after Proudhon's death, his unfinished response to Adam and d'Héricourt appeared under the title *La pornocratie; ou, Les femmes dans les temps modernes* (1875). For Proudhon, the liberated woman (also called the New Woman) embodied depravity. He correlated the influence of emancipated women with a pornocracy (loosely translated as the reign of prostitutes). Gifted women, writers in particular, displayed symptoms of an idiosyncratic hermaphrodism, which he attributed to the envy of male genius. In this context, it is important to recall the opinion that intellectual labor reduced both sexes' fertility. As the Harvard physician Edward Clarke wrote regarding females, by the 1870s it was "a doctrine of physiology" that excessive cerebration redirected blood from the uterus to the brain, at the same time shrinking a woman's ovaries and rendering her sterile (*Sex in Education*, 137).[54] Against the backdrop of depopulation and the "woman question,"[55] Proudhon emphasized the toxic effect of brain labor on female reproduction: "Faut croire que les fatigues cérébrales agissent sur la matrice à la façon de l'*agnus-castus* ou des cantharides. . . . Une femme ne peut plus faire d'enfants quand

33

son esprit, son imagination et son cœur se préoccupent des choses de la politique, de la société et de la littérature" (*La pornocratie*, 170). Proudhon refused to recognize female geniuses, even though women's originality in various realms as well as interventions on their behalf proved the contrary. As Empress Eugénie of France proudly observed upon awarding the Légion d'honneur to Bonheur in 1865, "le génie n'a pas de sexe."[56] This counterdiscourse, repeating Staël and Sand, further increased women's visibility as creators. Its resonance at that time sheds light on how Lamartine revisited Staël's legacy in making the history of poetry a product of male genius.

### Making Poetry Male

Among the articles Lamartine published in the periodical *Cours Familier de Littérature* was an essay about his mother written in 1857. She had fostered his poetic genius by reading Anne Le Fèvre Dacier's translation of Homer's *Odyssey* to him during his childhood.[57] Sensitive, but not erudite, "elle n'avait de transcendant que la sensibilité; toute sa poésie était dans son cœur: c'est là en effet que doit être toute celle des femmes," Lamartine observes (*Souvenirs et portraits*, 51). He further defines what a woman's poetry is and is not: "L'art est une déchéance pour la femme: elle est bien plus que poëte, elle est la poésie. La sensibilité est une révélation, l'art est un métier; elles doivent le laisser aux hommes, ces ouvriers de la vie; leur art, à elles, est de sentir, et leur poésie est d'aimer" (51). Imbued with post-Romantic notions of psychophysiology and *dégénérescence* (degeneration), Lamartine's view of divine inspiration includes sexual difference. Poetic genius acquires two natures and poetry has a dual effect, the creative spark enlivening a man's thought while touching only a woman's heart: "C'est que le génie a deux natures: flamme dans la tête de l'homme, chaleur dans le cœur de la femme. . . . Malheur aux femmes qui excellent dans les lettres ou dans les arts! Elles se sont trompées de génie. Si elles se ravalent à imaginer, soyez sûrs que c'est qu'il leur a manqué quelque chose à aimer" (51). The deeper question was far from resolved, however. If genius had a sex, how could one account for Staël and other women of superior intellect and creativity?

Lamartine reflects on Staël's legacy in 1868, a half-century after her death: "On agite sans cesse, sans la résoudre jamais, cette question en effet insoluble: *Convient-il aux femmes d'écrire et d'aspirer à la gloire des lettres? S'il s'agissait de résoudre cette question d'une manière absolue, nous aimerions presque autant dire: Convient-il à la nature de donner du génie aux femmes?*" (*Souvenirs et portraits*, 203; emphasis in original).[58] Whereas being male or female is a biological fact, nature (in the sense of makeup), society, and family determine gender roles. Even though Staël had crossed these lines, Lamartine admits that her century deserves praise for having produced such a mind. However, her gift was not a poetic one, an opinion he bases on her early attempts at writing verse. Literary history, even the recent past, corroborates this limit to Staël's talent. Except for "la virile Sapho," declares Lamartine, no woman has displayed the type of energy associated with a great poet (218). He thus ignores all of women's poetic production through the late 1860s, including the Romantic era poets he had previously recognized: Desbordes-Valmore, Tastu, and Mercœur, among others.

In pondering the dearth of female poets, Lamartine reviews the art of poetry, which involves four faculties: imagination, sensibility, love, and enthusiasm. For him, women naturally possess these gifts, but they lack the cognitive strength that allows men to transcend their biology in order to produce works of genius.[59] Lamartine further muses, "le vers est un instrument exclusivement viril qui veut . . . une main d'homme pour le faire vibrer complètement à l'oreille, au cœur, à la raison, à la passion de l'humanité" (*Souvenirs et portraits*, 219). He associates original poetry with male fecundity, wryly adding, "Peut-être la tension prodigieuse d'esprit nécessaire au grand poëte pour cette éjaculation à la fois passionnée et raisonnée des vers, est-elle disproportionnée à la force et à la délicatesse des organes de la pensée dans la femme?" (220). Physiology would remain central in the way that women's creative pursuits were pathologized. This trend intensified after the fall of the Second Empire in 1870, especially with the push for higher instruction for girls, which had a direct impact on the literary canon taught in schools, as I discuss in chapter 2.

Reminiscent of the backlash against women after the French Revolution, antipathy toward gifted women intensified after the 1871 Paris Commune. The women Communards, mocked in contemporary caricatures as Pétroleuses, built street barricades and fought the national government troops alongside the men. Both moments represented, in the French psyche, the danger that freethinking women of any sort posed to society. France's declining birth rate, which doctors blamed on feminism, also factored in the hostile environment for literary women from the 1870s to the century's end.[60] Ideological warfare between detractors and supporters focused on the brain and the hereditary nature of genius (promulgated by Galton in 1869), mirroring the ascendancy of experimental physiology, psychology, and neuroscience alongside the specter of degeneration.[61] An exchange between the feminist writer Olympe Audouard and the critic and writer Jules Barbey d'Aurevilly exemplifies the core debate during that period.

In 1870, Audouard published a talk she had given that year, *M. Barbey d'Aurevilly: Réponse à ses réquisitoires contre les bas-bleus*. In preparing her rebuttal, Audouard had paraphrased a passage from Barbey d'Aurevilly's novel *Un prêtre marié* (1865): "La femme bas-bleu est une virago de l'intelligence, chez laquelle l'hypertrophie cérébrale déforme le sexe et produit la monstruosité" (13).[62] According to Barbey d'Aurevilly, writing caused cerebral inflammation that deformed a woman's sexual organs, making her manly (the Latin *virago*, from *vir* "man"). Audouard dryly notes, "À qui la faute, si les hommes ont la prétention de se réserver exclusivement toutes les choses de l'esprit?" (*M. Barbey d'Aurevilly*, 21). Claims about the size, shape, and volume of the brain, which were correlated with higher degrees of intelligence in the male, are baseless: "Avoir du génie, ce n'est pas donc avoir un cerveau d'homme; le génie peut se placer aussi dans un cerveau de femme" (22). She argues that the brain is adaptable and that genius is gender-blind, a mental quality not inborn but nurtured: "On ne naît pas homme [ou femme] de génie . . . on naît seulement apte à le devenir; l'intelligence humaine a besoin de culture" (22). Audouard, predating Simone de Beauvoir, articulated how gender roles are socially constructed, even as the spread of evolutionary theory ascribed genius solely to males.

### The Deeper Question of Genius

In *The Descent of Man* (1871), developed from *On the Origin of Species*, Charles Darwin claimed that man had evolved to be more powerful than woman in body and mind.[63] Men possessed greater courage, energy, intellect, and inventive genius, inevitably excelling in art, science, and philosophy. Darwinism influenced the view of degeneration in psychology and sociology, a view that sidelined the modern understanding of natural reproduction (confirmed in 1876), which discredited the inherited physiology of genius.[64]

Genius in women continued to be seen as an aberrant sexual selection, as in Cesare Lombroso's *The Man of Genius*, published in 1891 and translated into French (*L'homme de génie*) that same year.[65] Lombroso linked genius with epilepsy and added (from the neurologist Jean-Martin Charcot's work on anatomical pathology) the element of hysteria to explain why women failed to produce works of originality: "L'excitation épileptoïde de l'écorce cérébrale, que nous considérons comme la condition essentielle du travail du génie, ne se transforme pas chez la femme en grandes excitations physiques, mais seulement en phénomènes moteurs et en convulsions hystéro-épileptiques" (Lombroso, *L'homme de génie*, 223).[66] The Italian criminologist argued that women of genius presented organic anomalies (226).[67] By this he meant masculine characteristics that robbed women of their femininity. In a journal entry of 1893, Edmond de Goncourt similarly imagined the effect of sublimated male sexual energy well before Freud: "[J]e dirais crûment être persuadé que, si on avait fait l'autopsie des femmes ayant un talent original, comme Mme Sand, Mme Viardot, etc. on trouverait chez elles des parties génitales se rapprochant de l'homme, des clitoris un peu parents de nos verges" (Goncourt and Goncourt, *Journal*, 4:485). The gap between creativity and femininity was widened because of the perspective of degeneration adopted by the social sciences in the late nineteenth century.

In arguing the contrary in *La femme devant la science contemporaine* (1896), the sociologist Jacques Lourbet asserts that there is no scientific evidence to support the analogy between brain and brawn: "Et non seulement on ne connaît pas le rapport entre la cellule nerveuse et l'intelligence, mais nul n'a prouvé que l'énergie nerveuse soit proportionnelle à la force musculaire: à plus forte raison ignore-t-on si la puissance mentale est proportionnelle à celle des muscles" (24). He reverses, moreover, the history of thought about biological determinism: "Supposons qu'on eût trouvé le contraire dans les phénomèmes de la fécondation, c'est-à-dire que le spermatozoïde eût les qualités visibles de l'ovule et inversement. On aurait dit: le germe femelle, plus petit, plus agité, plus instable, est déjà l'image de ce que sera la femme, être faible, nerveux, mal équilibré, incapable d'un effort soutenu et, par suite, de grandes choses, de grandes créations qui exigent une longue patience" (114–15).[68] In essence, Lourbet prepares the way for rethinking the categories of "genius" and "woman" in relation to procreativity, adding, "D'ailleurs la femme est le produit *artificiel* d'un milieu qui doit changer" (119; emphasis in original).

In probing the inheritance of genius during the latter half of the nineteenth century, women poets revealed complicity with, as well as resistance to, the sexing of the mind. Sand's writings from the mid-1850s through the late 1870s provide a framework for this discursive complexity. In her autobiography *Histoire de ma vie* (1855), Sand distinguishes between the sexes, denying women a role in cultural production: "Que la femme soit différente de l'homme, que le cœur et l'esprit aient un sexe, je n'en doute pas . . . la femme sera toujours plus artiste et plus poëte dans sa vie, l'homme le sera toujours dans son œuvre" (*Œuvres autobiographiques*, 2:127).[69] These lines blur in her novel *Le marquis de Villemer* (1861), where a male character portrays a woman with a gift for abstract thought but not all of the creative attributes associated with genius (140). However, in her essay *Pourquoi les femmes à l'Académie?* (1863), Sand recalls the stance from "La fille d'Albano" by disengaging genius from sex: "Les dons de l'intelligence sont le produit plus ou moins spontané d'une culture *sui generis* que personne ne peut réglementer, et les traditions se brisent comme le verre là où le génie commence" (14). Her later essay "L'homme et la femme" (1873) addresses the construct of gender, anticipating the modern view that knowledge is the product of discourses.

During the second half of the century, women experimented with objective lyricism, thinking between identities as they developed multiple voices in relation to and beyond gender. The work of the self-described "ouvrière et poète" Malvina Blanchecotte, recognized by the Académie française for her first volume of poetry, *Rêves et réalités* (1855), illustrates such experimentation. Treated in chapter 5, her poetic output tests the notion of genius (inborn, made, the work of originality, and/or an exceptional individual) both with and without reference to gender and class. In considering the relationship between work and cultural capital, Blanchecotte thought deeply about being a worker and a poet or *voyant*, an intellectual legacy revealing that Arthur Rimbaud may in fact have been in her debt. Ultimately, as affirmed in her prose volume *Impressions d'une femme: Pensées, sentiments, et portraits* (1868), Blanchecotte disputes the "othering" of women along with their exclusion as originators:

> Ou trop haut ou trop bas, sur le piédestal ou dans la boue, le diadème au front
> ou l'éventail à la main, on vous a placées et déplacées, on a dénaturé votre rôle,

on a troublé votre vue, on vous a faites *autres*, et vous vous y êtes trompées vous-mêmes. Facilement crédules, peu sérieuses, miroirs qui reflétez autrui, vous avez accepté ces appréciations de fantaisie. Et, en effet, vous êtes devenues . . . esprits de convention . . . et c'est avec vous-mêmes que je veux essayer de vous reconstruire, de vous restituer à votre vraie nature. (157–58; ellipses in original)

The worker born a poet develops her creative voice beyond the clichés of feminine subjectivity, elaborating "le génie du *vrai voir*" while cultivating "[le] travail de la pensée" (Blanchecotte, *Impressions d'une femme*, 141; *Le long de la vie*, 216).

Blanchecotte's contemporary Louisa Siefert, whose first volume of poetry, *Rayons perdus* (1868), sold out within a month, produced a body of lyrical and philosophical work in which creative reverie mingles with stoic detachment. As shown in chapter 6, Siefert forged a hybrid expression on the boundary between Romantic and Parnassian aesthetics. She refuted critics who placed her in Valmore's shadow and also rejected Staël's woman of genius: "Ta Corinne autrefois tant aimée, / Elle doit être maintenant assez déplumée" (Siefert, *Comédies romanesques*, 87). Rather, she identified her drive with the inner force that harked much further back, to the first woman who sought the unknown on her own terms: "Où donc avais-je la tête, moi qui croyais pouvoir me passer d'esprit. Hélas! c'est la pomme de l'arbre de science, et je viens d'y mordre à en avoir faim toute ma vie" (Siefert, *Méline*, 10). Eve's desire for knowledge represents "cette marque originelle du génie de la femme, cette puissance dans le désir, ce déploiement de toutes ses facultés sur un point unique, cet élan irrésistible" (216). Siefert grasped how poetry embodies sensation and thought, formulating in this way its dialogic nature: "Sentir, expérimenter, deviner, savoir, c'est une soif qui la dévore, c'est une impulsion qui l'emporte malgré tout, parfois malgré elle" (258). Her project, which positions the subject or the "I" between the unconscious and conscious realms, illumines poetry as a way to transcend the dualism of mind and body.

Louise Ackermann, who began writing poetry in the late 1820s, spent a lifetime contemplating the reach of science against the claims of religion. Discussed in chapter 7, her major work *Poésies philosophiques* (1871) reveals her pessimism about the problem of absolute truth. To counter the suggestion that her bleak view of the human condition stemmed from personal loss, Ackermann intervenes with an autobiographical account and other critical writings to shape her intellectual legacy. She distances herself as much from Romantic poets as from women writers, even women of genius about whom she writes, eschewing any facile identification between her creative voice and her gender: "J'éprouve parfois une vraie colère en voyant qu'une grande intelligence ne met pas les femmes à l'abri de toutes sortes d'erreurs et de faiblesses. Au contraire, on dirait que c'est la monnaie dont elles paient leur supériorité. Pauvres femmes de génie, c'est à vous que le cœur et surtout les sens gardent leur plus mauvais tours!" (*Pensées d'une solitaire* [1903], 59). She also makes a contrary statement about the antagonism between the female brain and the maternal body: "On ne peut concevoir ni mettre au monde de deux côtés à la fois" (quoted in Haussonville, "M^me Ackermann," 350). Ackermann's way of complicating women's relationship to cultural production illustrates the dialectical thought in her body of work, which places the source of knowledge between rational power and poetic sensitivity.

Marie Krysinska, considered in chapter 8, disputed the narratives of religion and science to reposition originality in the work, inextricably linking the process and the product. She had in mind her innovative *vers libre* and its place in the history of French poetry. Her treatment of the biblical creation story restored the positive view of the first woman's original fall into knowledge. In turning from metaphysics to the physical realm, she contended that evolutionary science could neither predict nor explain what drove genius: "Le propre du Génie c'est d'être révélateur par sa manifestation soudaine, et c'est avec les exemples qu'il laisse sur son passage que sont faites la tradition, la science et la règle" (*Intermèdes*, v). Krysinska understood that genius reveals itself in the work of originality without, however, disclosing its origins.

In a probing study of the origins of genius closer to the contemporary moment, the modern psychologist Dean Simonton shows that biology alone cannot account for the forms that genius takes nor when, how, or where it appears. Having discerned from Darwin's laws of sexual selection that male and female species must co-evolve, which allows for aesthetic discernment on the part of both sexes, Simonton posits that "the low representation of women in the annals of creative genius is the consequence of cultural rather than biological forces" (*Origins of Genius*, 219).[70] From his broader perspective, "[c]ulture rather than the genes may determine whether a genius will be black or white, male or female" (222). In the nineteenth-century debate on genius, a fluid concept involving the mind, the body, and work of originality, it is clear that men and women from a broad range of disciplines questioned its relationship to sex, as did women who shaped nineteenth-century French poetic production. That one finds these original poets in the same history in which all women have been lost as poetesses is the paradox of reception history, to which I turn in the next chapter.

# 2  Literary Reception and Its Discontents

Women surged as professional writers during the Romantic era. Their rise as poets, in particular, alarmed the conservative men who would uphold the French literary tradition by adopting the biology of the creative mind. The caricature reproduced here from Daumier's 1844 *bas-bleu* series suggests the laden narrative of literary women's reception (fig. 3). Mesmerized yet uneasy, the exclusively male audience beholds the towering woman, who identifies herself in the caption accompanying the image: "L'auteur! . . . l'auteur! . . . l'auteur! . . . —Messieurs, votre impatience va être satisfaite. . . . vous désirez connaître l'auteur de l'ouvrage remarquable qui vient d'obtenir un si grand, et je dois le dire, si légitime succès . . . cet auteur . . . c'est môa!" Positioned to disturb the gender hierarchy, the author's masculine head replicates the hard, vertical line of the adjacent column, belying her soft, feminine curves. Masculinity does not overwhelm, but rather cohabits with femininity in the same body. Daumier's portrayal of the woman author unwittingly shows how creativity exceeds the normalizing force of conceptual categories marked off by sex.

The various terms used by critics throughout the nineteenth century to identify women as poets capture the struggle over the source and meaning of the verse they produced.[1] Those critics who used the word "poète"—also spelled "poëte," which draws from etymology the sense of "maker" or "creator"—recognized the originator apart from the woman, thus unsexing creative voice. Interestingly, both supporters and detractors used the wording "femmes poètes." This label, often written with a hyphen (a sign that both divides and connects), suggests the ambivalence that thickened poetic women's reception: femininity was not entirely reconciled, or was rendered incompatible, with creativity. Similarly, the wording "poètes femmes," like "poètes femelles," evokes the gender binary; the space between the terms represents an ideological gulf between creators and females.

FIG 3

Plate 17 of Daumier's series Les *bas-bleus*. *Le Charivari*, 17 March 1844. Photo courtesy Yale University Art Gallery

"Poétesse," derived from "poète," though initially not pejorative in designating a poetic woman acquired the sense of a second-rate muse lacking in originality.[2] Antagonistic critics added envy on the part of women to the physiology of male genius, anticipating the Freudian analysis of femininity in relation to a masculinity complex.[3] In the latter half of the nineteenth century, the protopsychoanalytic bent of literary criticism fused with the discourse of degeneracy. The chiasmic linkage of mental fertility and reproductive infertility associated with poetic women resurged as the history of reception repeated itself in the early decades of the twentieth century.

Archival evidence shows women's contributions to poetic production together with their male counterparts' in both mainstream and nonmainstream venues throughout the nineteenth century. How, then, can one account for women's virtual erasure from the nineteenth-century poetic canon? In this chapter I map the discursive categories used by literary critics in response to the rise of poets from the ranks of women writers, highlighting two major backlashes. The first of

41

these, in the 1840s, reduced Romantic era women to one and the same "poetess," wholly effusive and artless. The second reactionary period coincided with the battle over female education that gathered force from the 1860s onward. Conventional readings of Marceline Desbordes-Valmore from the same period engendered her token status as the century's only woman poet. Other women's aesthetic and intellectual achievements thus faded from the French poetic canon established at the century's close.

## (Mis)placing Women in Poetic History

During the first half of the century, individual poems by women appeared alongside men's in newspapers, magazines, and keepsakes (a type of literary album popular at the time), such as *L'Almanach des Dames* (1802–40), *Almanach Dédié aux Dames* (1807–30), and *Hommage aux Dames* (1813–35).[4] Collections devoted to women's poetry also proliferated: *Guirlande des dames* (1815–29), *Les femmes poètes* (1829), and *Le génie des femmes* (1844–46), among others. Women also succeeded in publishing individual volumes and collected poetic works. The rise of the sentimental novel, however, began to stiffen the competition in the book market.[5] This shift in literary tastes occurred under the July Monarchy (1830–48) as the upper bourgeoisie gained a strong political foothold along with moral clout. By the 1840s, literary physiologies, a genre made popular by Balzac, flourished, and the satirical figure of the *bas-bleu* eclipsed the favorable reception poetic women had enjoyed.[6]

Why adopt the term *bas-bleu* to designate the woman of ideas in nineteenth-century France? Thus the popular novelist and journalist Frédéric Soulié opens his *Physiologie du bas-bleu* (1841), a source for Daumier's caricatures, and follows with this answer: "[J]'aime ce nom, qui ne signifie absolument rien, par cela seul qu'il dénonce cette espèce féminine par un mot du genre masculin" (5–6). As a category for thinking of women as authors, *bas-bleu* conveys a biologistic ideology via a grammatical error between feminine and masculine pronouns, linking intellectual women's misplaced ambitions with depravity and disease: "[D]u moment qu'une femme est *Bas-Bleu*, il faut absolument dire d'elle: il est malpropre, il est prétentieux, il est malfaisant, il est une peste" (Soulié, *Physiologie du bas-bleu*, 6; emphasis in original). It remains to be seen "si les Bas-bleus sont des femmes," adds Soulié, fusing the methods of naturalists and physiologists who study the functions and vital processes of living organisms in order to categorize various "species" of literary women, not only according to class but also in relation to their milieu, appearance, manners, and marital status (19).

In the history Soulié traces of the *bas-bleu* from Staël to the mid-1840s, the "bas-bleu poète" enjoyed popularity during the Bourbon Restoration. This period followed Napoleon, whose military campaigns had depleted, if not wounded, France: "À ce moment, la lyre a pris un développement effroyable, et, Corinne vivante, en chair et en os, s'est promenée dans les rues de Paris. . . . Toute cette nation, fatiguée du fracas des armes et du canon, frémissait d'une douce émotion à sa moindre parole" (*Physiologie du bas-bleu*, 35).[7] Alarming yet appealing, the surge of poetic women lulled the beleaguered nation into Romanticism. For Soulié, all of these poets were one and the same. Anonymity cuts short the history of Romantic era poets in Soulié's physiology, as does his conclusion: "Le Bas-Bleu est toujours le même" (109).

The critic Paul de Molènes matched Soulié's totalizing approach to women's poetic aspirations. Addressing the readers of the *Revue des Deux Mondes* in 1842, Molènes asks: "Comment, en effet, concilier l'idée que nous avons de l'existence du poète avec celle qu'on doit se faire de la vie des femmes, d'après les données de la nature et les notions du sens commun?" ("Simples essais d'histoire littéraire," 49).[8] For him, however innate women's poetic sensibility might be, the domestic realm in which women are expected to dwell—together with their maternal instincts—contradicts the freedom to nurture their creativity. Even male geniuses, he observes, often do not produce "une longue suite d'enfans" (50).[9] Though Molènes's analogy generalizes the struggle over re/productive energy between the brain and body, he tips the balance against intellectual and creative women: "Comment appeler une créature dont le sein, destiné à allaiter des enfans et à renfermer les joies maternelles, demeure stérile et ne bat que pour des sentiments d'orgueil?" (53). Medical preoccupations with the effect of mental work on reproductivity inflect the terms "femme poète" and "poète femelle," used interchangeably by a critic who entangles all "Sapphos" in a woman's body, which lacks the seeds of genius.[10]

Yet Molènes unwittingly helps modern readers to recover poetic women's texts by citing some of them at length. His close readings aim to dissociate women from the art of poetry, but instead he has preserved their names and selected works while demonstrating the differences among them. For example, he describes Tastu as displaying prosodic control and distinguishes her from the passionate Desbordes-Valmore, whose elegies he likens to love letters with no universal appeal.[11] Whereas Delphine de Girardin and Colet created bold personae, further observes this critic, Ségalas treated contemporary topics, such as France's conquest of Algiers in 1830. However, as Molènes concludes, all women lack the divine inheritance of genius: "nées pour mettre au monde autre chose que des volumes de vers" (75).

With similar assumptions, in 1843 the critic Charles Labitte called women "poetæ minores" whose uninspired verse could not compete with the lyrical genius of Lamartine and Hugo (132). Like Molènes, Labitte invokes the analogy of mental exertion and disease in females to pathologize poetic women: "[L]a poésie devient, chez eux qui ne sont pas ses vrais élus, une carrière maladive et dangereuse" (138). Metaphors of disorder alternated with those of pathology from mid-century onward. Critics of both sexes filtered women's poetic creativity through religion's faltering authority and/or science's ascendancy. Those advancing maternalist arguments imbued with bourgeois ideology had girls' higher education in mind.[12]

Representative of the orthodox stance promoted by some women is *Les femmes illustres de la France* (1850), a primer for young French women by the prolific Catholic writer Madame la comtesse Drohojowska (née Symon de Latreiche). Drohojowska considers the genius debate from a religious perspective, evoking the original division of labor: "Aux hommes, Dieu a donné l'amour du bruit et de la gloire. À eux les vertus éclatantes, les mâles conceptions du génie . . . et aux femmes, dans le calme et le saint recueillement du foyer domestique, que de vertus aussi sont destinées! vertus cachées et modestes" (*Les femmes illustres*, 1). Because the first woman initiated the trespass against God, stresses Drohojowska, she received the harsher punishment and was cast out of Eden as "l'esclave de l'homme plutôt que sa compagne" (2). Once named by Adam, Eve forsook her own desires to become the mother of humanity, fulfilling divine design.

Drohojowska continues by stating that, though the rare genius among them protests, females are born to be mothers. For her, even a writer remains, above all, a woman "[qui] n'outrepasse ni ses droits ni ses privilèges, puisque c'est la loi naturelle, émanant directement de Dieu, qui l'a faite la première ou plutôt la seule véritable institutrice de l'humanité" (*Les femmes illustres*, 15). In celebrating the women of France who extol such moral virtue,[13] Drohojowska endorses the idea of the "womanly woman writer," disseminating the bourgeois values of motherhood and self-sacrifice. This ideal worked to limit women's creativity to the embodiment of femininity, a woman's poetic "tradition" passed on from readings of Desbordes-Valmore as its archetype.

### Is a Woman Poet Born or Made?

In 1861, two years after Desbordes-Valmore's death, Charles Baudelaire, the most celebrated French poet of the mid-nineteenth century, gauged her achievement against the tenets of Romantic lyricism. If cries and sighs, spontaneity, and instinct, "tout ce qui est gratuit et vient de Dieu, suffisent à faire le grand poète," argues Baudelaire, then "Marceline Valmore est et sera toujours un grand poète" (*Œuvres*, 146). If one reads closely, however, her greatness diminishes because she lacks artistry, or in Baudelaire's words, "ce qui peut s'acquérir par le travail" (146). As Baudelaire's appraisal shifts from Desbordes-Valmore's originality to her femininity, his gender bias surfaces along the lines proposed by Barbara Johnson: "When they are not excluding women poets altogether, the guardians of poetic taste often enforce their views by singling out one woman writer, praising her extravagantly, and using her as a pretext to denigrate the work of *other* women" ("Gender and Poetry," 164; emphasis in original).

By virtue of the womanly persona Desbordes-Valmore constructed, however strategically not laying claim to genius, she avoided what was considered "monstrosity" or "masculinity." This made her the exception to all other poetic women, who are grouped by Baudelaire as "ces sacrilèges pastiches de l'esprit mâle" (*Œuvres*,

146). In Baudelaire's tribute to Desbordes-Valmore, however, the concept of femininity absorbs her creativity: "Mme Desbordes-Valmore fut femme, fut toujours femme et ne fut absolument que femme; mais elle fut à un degré extraordinaire l'expression poétique de toutes les beautés naturelles de la femme" (146–47). His portrayal of Desbordes-Valmore, yet to include any of her texts, evokes the ideal woman embodying gentleness and compassion, on the one hand, and a blend of female passion with motherly devotion, on the other: "la souplesse et la violence de la femelle, chatte ou lionne, amoureuse de ses petits" (147). This maternal yet animalistic image associates woman as poet with reproduction, eliding sensuality and sexuality to privilege Desbordes-Valmore's transcription of "*l'éternel féminin*" (147; emphasis in original).

The "woman poet" endorsed by Baudelaire is heartfelt, the carrier of sentimental rather than aesthetic beauty: "[Desbordes-Valmore] a les grandes et vigoureuses qualités qui s'imposent à la mémoire, les trouées profondes faites à l'improviste dans le cœur, les explosions magiques de la passion. Aucun auteur ne cueille plus facilement la formule unique du sentiment, le sublime qui s'ignore" (*Œuvres*, 147). For Baudelaire, Desbordes-Valmore's vigor meshes with her passion and feeling. Sublime but artless, her poetry emanates spontaneously from the heart. After impressing upon readers the span of Desbordes-Valmore's poetic collections, from 1818 to 1860, he cites only four lines of verse from her posthumous *Poésies inédites* (1860; reprinted in *Œuvres poétiques* [1973]), two from the same poem, "À celles qui pleurent."[14] Though a keen reader of Desbordes-Valmore, Baudelaire eclipses the socially engaged and reflective poet.[15] His uneven rendering makes Desbordes-Valmore's work fit a script of femininity.[16] As Gretchen Schultz observes, "[Desbordes-Valmore] is all that the *homme de génie* is not" (*Gendered Lyric*, 49).

In 1862, Jules Barbey d'Aurevilly evaluated Desbordes-Valmore's posthumous collection in his first series on poets, widening the gap between the woman, "qui n'a jamais joué au génie androgine [*sic*]," and the poet of genius (*Les poètes*, 146).[17] Barbey d'Aurevilly separates the agony of Staël's *Corinne* from the figuration of her genius and uses this paradigm to reduce Desbordes-Valmore's writing to pathos. While Baudelaire used the term "cri," like "soupir," metonymically to assess Desbordes-Valmore's Romantic sensibility, Barbey d'Aurevilly amplifies the trope to separate her "poésie du Cri" from works of poetic originality (148). To emit a cry, uttering inarticulate sounds, as the expression of grief or suffering, usually accompanied by tears, relates to sentience rather than to thought. Barbey d'Aurevilly's binary thinking, which equates a woman's body with her poetic "cry," conveys the sense of being overcome by emotion and thus unable to speak with clarity or eloquence.

To capture the instinctive nature and energy of Desbordes-Valmore's "cris pathétiques," Barbey d'Aurevilly recalls the abandon and spontaneity with which the actress Marie Dorval performed on the Paris stage. Such effusion was the hallmark of Romanticism and had no aesthetic value from the perspective of the

Parnassian school emerging at that time, which emphasized form. The veiled question about Desbordes-Valmore concerns genius, whether "cette femme, d'une passion si grande et si naturelle, a réellement assez de langage pour faire *fond de poète* aux sublimités de l'émotion," as Barbey d'Aurevilly states (*Les poètes*, 150; emphasis in original). Does her example disprove history? The critic approaches this from Corneille's alleged statement describing women as failed poets: "Je ne sais pas ce qui manque aux femmes . . . mais pour faire des vers, il leur manque quelque chose" (151).[18] This notion of lack, later related by Barbey d'Aurevilly to intellectual women's envy of the male genius, inflects how he reads Desbordes-Valmore's *Poésies inédites* back into her poetic history.

Barbey d'Aurevilly stresses how the Romantic turn of Lamartine's classical expression in 1820 overshadowed Desbordes-Valmore's elegiac writing, which he criticizes as formally loose "vers *libres*" (*Les poètes*, 153; emphasis in original). At the time, the poet Paul Verlaine had not yet attributed to Desbordes-Valmore the innovative hendecasyllabic verse that would be practiced by Symbolist poets in the 1880s and '90s: "Marceline Desbordes-Valmore a, le premier d'entre les poètes de ce temps, employé avec le plus grand bonheur des rythmes inusités, celui de onze pieds entre autres, très artiste sans *trop* le savoir" (Verlaine, *Les poètes maudits*, 59; emphasis in original). For Barbey d'Aurevilly, attuned instead to how Desbordes-Valmore's early work embodies femininity at the level of form and content, her *Poésies inédites* demonstrates more prosodic control and includes topics beyond the domestic sphere. But, in the latter, Desbordes-Valmore does not display the work of true genius because "la femme, dont la gloire est de refléter ceux qu'elle aime, ne peut jamais avoir de profonde ou de saisissante originalité" (*Les poètes*, 154).

Focused on the thematic division of *Poésies inédites* ("Amour," "Famille," "Foi," "Enfants et jeunes filles," "Poésies diverses"), Barbey d'Aurevilly ascribes the volume to personal biography. The critic names fourteen poems from the collection, which show formal and thematic range. He quotes at length from "La fileuse et l'enfant" ("que les âmes tendres et chrétiennes diront divine") to represent the arc of Desbordes-Valmore's legacy: "Tout n'y est-il pas des meilleures qualités de cette femme, adorable par moments, qui n'est pas un poète, mais une femme qui, pour le coup, a passé bien près de la poésie, en nous passant si près du cœur" (*Les poètes*, 158). By representing Desbordes-Valmore as a sentimental woman, but not as a poet in the robust sense of the word, Barbey d'Aurevilly confirms his view of women as *poètes manqués*. He describes her contemporary Delphine Gay de Girardin and her trajectory in analogous terms, illustrating how deeply gender mattered in the canons of literary criticism.

## From *Poëte* to *Bas-Bleu*: Girardin

Barbey d'Aurevilly's chapter on Girardin's complete works (published in 1860–61) recalls her poetic debut with a dual image: "le génie de Corinne et la beauté de

Lucile Edgermond" (*Les poètes*, 294). To encapsulate how the young Delphine reconciles her gift with conventional feminine qualities by balancing pride with modesty, he cites her verse, albeit out of context: "Mon front était si fier de sa couronne blonde! / Anneaux d'or et d'argent, tant de fois caressés! / Et j'avais tant d'espoir quand j'entrai dans le monde, / Orgueilleuse et les yeux baissés!" (294). This stanza, restored to its original context, outlines instead the quandary elaborated in Girardin's poem "Désenchantement" (1834): "Oh! les brillants succès de poète et de femme, / Succès permis et défendu" (*Poésies complètes*, 338). The speaking subject mulls over the uneven reception of women as poets, presaging the retreat from poetry inscribed in the last lines: "Jamais on ne rendra le sublime prestige / Au poète désenchanté" (340). Here Girardin is self-conscious as a writer, and she reiterates the difficulty of being a "femme de génie, et femme comme il faut," as expressed in her poem "Napoline" (96). For readers today, Delphine Gay's reflective texts disclose how she, like other poetic women, embedded in her creative writing a counterdiscourse of dissent.

Barbey d'Aurevilly's account pulls the trajectory of Girardin the poet-turned-prose-writer through categories rather than through close analysis, demonstrating how conservative critics often read women's works at a distance from the texts themselves. The young Delphine had waxed poetically and thus fit the category of a "bas *lilas*, c'est-à-dire qu'il y a en elle de la femme encore, de la grâce de femme!" (*Les poètes*, 295; emphasis in original). She had not yet entered the literary profession, which made her an "auteur dans le sens laborieux et disgracieux du mot, et le *bas-bleu*, cette affreuse chose, apparaît dans son *foncé* terrible" (295; emphasis in original). However, Barbey d'Aurevilly considers her forays beyond topics related to a woman's lived experience as failed, a point he underscores by applying sexual differences to poetry: "C'est que pour l'homme et pour la femme, en raison d'organisations combinées pour des fonctions diverses, la poésie n'est pas aux mêmes sources" (299). Motherhood being a principal subject for women, he adds, the childless Girardin could not become "une Valmore" (300). Barbey d'Aurevilly reads the influence of the reproductive organs on the mind *à la lettre* to suggest that poets inhabit their texts the way they inhabit their body.

Marriage, which involves sexual union, is fatal for poetry, even for men, Barbey d'Aurevilly further asserts, "car la poésie veut presque des prêtres" (*Les poètes*, 300). For women, marriage is all the more lethal because it replaces the work of poetry: "Evidemment pour moi, Mlle Delphine Gay aurait eu du génie,—le génie, par exemple que ses amis . . . lui ont attribué si longtemps,—que ce génie serait mort de son mariage. Seulement avait-elle du génie?" (300–301).[19] For Barbey d'Aurevilly, Girardin falls short of genius for reasons other than the alleged incompatibility between females' procreative and intellectual energies. In his view, her attempt to treat contemporary topics in *Improvisations* (*Œuvres complètes*, vol. 1) proves "l'impuissance radicale de toute femme poète, quand il s'agit de chanter quoi que ce puisse être, en dehors de la maternité et de l'amour" (301). But Girardin is more than an elegist, he admits. To support this point, Barbey d'Aurevilly notes that Girardin's narrative poem "Magdelaine," consisting of nine cantos, has "une vigueur d'invention encore plus étonnante pour un cerveau de femme, dont le destin est d'imiter" (303).

For Barbey d'Aurevilly, the allegory "Napoline," a narrative poem divided into four chapters, is Girardin's best work, with the womanly woman outshining the woman of genius. Had Girardin not become a professional writer, a *bas-bleu*, he concludes, she could have made her mark as "UNE poète, cette chose si rare que, pour la dire au féminin, il faut faire une faute de français" (*Les poètes*, 304).[20] Barbey d'Aurevilly's study exemplifies the irony of literary criticism that aimed to show why women had no poetic history and yet preserved their work for posterity. At whatever moment and from whatever distance nineteenth-century critics read women (as) poets, whether staying close to the text or close to their own context, they recorded women's names and their works (via the titles, excerpts, or full citations). The same holds true for their successors in the early twentieth century, discussed later in this chapter.

### Recovering Women's Poetic Work

Archival evidence forms a retrospective framework for unearthing the body of poetry produced by women in all its diversity and for evaluating the discourses that determined its reception. Some nineteenth-century anthologies fill in gaps created by critical studies of the time by adding names to the record. For example, the fourth volume of Eugène Crépet's anthology, *Les poëtes français* (1863), includes, along with Desbordes-Valmore and Girardin, Tastu and Ackermann. Though this selection greatly underrepresents women's contributions, ample introductions treat the four women's trajectories in the context of their works.[21] Other poetic collections, such as *Le Parnasse contemporain* (1866–76) and the multivolume *Anthologie des poètes français du XIXᵉ siècle* (1887–88), both edited by Alphonse Lemerre, feature a greater number of women alongside men. In the second volume of *Le Parnasse contemporain* (1869–71), for example, one finds Colet, Blanchecotte, and Siefert, as well as Nina de Villard de Callias and Madame Auguste Penquer.[22] The third volume, published in 1876, includes Ackermann, Blanchecotte, Colet, and Siefert, as well as Mélanie Bourotte and Isabelle Guyon. Lemerre's *Anthologie* adds to this roster, among others, Ségalas, Daniel Stern, and Madame Alphonse Daudet.[23] These and other compilations that document women's success as poets provide a fresh gloss on the second of Arthur Rimbaud's 1871 *lettres du voyant* in which he appraised women as future poets. This letter, unpublished until 1912, illuminates how literary archives at once provide and obscure evidence. Women's absence, like their presence, shapes understanding of the French poetic past.

On 15 May 1871, the young Rimbaud, only seventeen at the time, redressed nineteenth-century French poetry to position his own visionary poetics. He wrote to his friend Paul Demeny: "Quand sera brisé l'infini servage de la femme, quand elle vivra pour elle et par elle, l'homme,—jusqu'ici abominable—lui ayant donné son renvoi, elle sera poète, elle aussi! La femme trouvera de l'inconnu! Ses mondes d'idées différeront-ils des nôtres?—Elle trouvera des choses étranges, insondables, repoussantes, délicieuses; nous les prendrons, nous les comprendrons" (*Œuvres complètes*, 252). Reminiscent of the nineteenth-century illuminists who carried forward Saint-Simonian ideals, the aspiring poet imagines himself a seer and links women's social and poetic liberation.[24] His use of the future tense implies that French women have not yet emerged as poets. Yet Rimbaud was aware of Desbordes-Valmore, whom he encouraged Verlaine to read.[25] As I discuss in chapter 6, Rimbaud's correspondence is the source of an excerpt from a poem by Siefert, whom he strongly recommended to his mentor Georges Izambard. Given that Rimbaud was familiar with Lemerre's editorial projects promoting poets,[26] he could also have mentioned other female contemporaries to Demeny. Why did Rimbaud dwell on women's creative potential rather than on their actual writing? Could one attribute this oversight to an unwitting association of women's rise as poets and the advent of Romanticism, a movement indebted to classical form yet imbued with an exaggerated pathos scorned by Rimbaud?

That passage from the *lettre du voyant*, often cited by modern feminists,[27] does not explicitly engage with the way women had already marked French poetic history. However, near the beginning of the same missive, Rimbaud declares, "Je est un autre," encapsulating his theory of the self or the "I" in poetry (*Œuvres complètes*, 250). His dictum, which gestures toward the unconscious origins of the creative impulse, can be read as a figure for the heterogeneous voice of the poetic text.[28] This experimental paradigm also relates to the dialogism that Siefert explores (see chapter 6), which opens up multiple subject positions and identifications, regardless of a writer's sex. Despite this perspective and Rimbaud's gender-neutral language, it is nonetheless clear that, in affirming that women would become poets—"elle sera poète, elle aussi!"—he did not envisage the separate canon of "feminine poetry" that would obscure the scope of individual women's creativity.

My examination of reception has thus far shown that primary and secondary sources form a repository of cultural memory that tells a different story about the literary past than does traditional history. Text and context remain intertwined. Their interaction shows how women continued to raise the stakes of the dominant narrative of reception by thinking creatively and critically. The issue of educational equality, related to "brain sex," stirred the backlash against poetic women that would intensify during the 1870s on both sides of the Atlantic. By the early 1860s in France, Paul Broca, a comparative anatomist, neurologist, and anthropologist, had established the view that the smaller female brain correlated with intellectual inferiority.[29] Hostile readers drew this discourse into literary criticism, alleging that women lacked higher cerebral function (notably reason and creativity) and thus could not produce works of originality.

In 1874, the British psychiatrist Henry Maudsley summarized the chief stance (not only in Europe but also in America) that contemporary movements for improving the higher education of women and raising their social status ignored the effect of superior mental training on females. "There is sex in mind as distinctly as there is sex in body," Maudsley asserted, and because of this, educational reformers needed to heed the difference between the male and female brains ("Sex and Mind in Education," 468). Given their physiology, women were equally sensitive to mental labor and "morbid irritation of the reproductive organs" (469). Maudsley emphasized the "excessive educational strain" on American girls in reports by American doctors, like Harvard's Clarke (discussed in chapter 1), in making his ultimate point: "[I]t cannot certainly be a true education which operates in any degree to unsex her; for sex is fundamental, lies deeper than culture, cannot be ignored or defied with impunity" (477).

Biology's grip on the qualities of the mind had nonetheless loosened as science made strides toward understanding human reproduction. By 1876, embryology had confirmed the sexes' mutual, generative role, thus refuting the long-standing theory that male seed governed physical and mental conception. Traditionalists, however, held fast to the primacy of sperm in reproduction and artistic creation. Under the French Third Republic, intellectual fertility remained tied to procreative infertility in literary analysis that measured women's deficient as well as excessive creativity against normative femininity.[30]

### "Women who write are no longer women"

From the 1870s onward, France witnessed an even greater movement of women writers than the one Sainte-Beuve had observed in the 1830s. As literacy rates rose, the popular novel thrived, and self-described "ouvrières des lettres" responded en masse to public demand.[31] Opponents of this movement purported that there were brain differences between the sexes to analyze all women who took up writing.[32] Barbey d'Aurevilly's *Les bas-bleus* (1878), a study of twenty-six literary women, including Staël, Sophie Gay, Girardin, Sand, and Colet, develops the protopsychoanalytic bent of *bas-bleu* criticism.[33] His introduction, which restates Baudelaire's portrayal of the *bas-bleu* as "un homme manqué,"[34] reflects the contemporary synergy between physiology and psychology: "[L]es femmes qui écrivent ne sont plus des femmes. Ce sont des hommes,—du moins de prétention,—et manqués! Ce sont des Bas-bleus. *Bas-bleu* est masculin. Les Bas-bleus ont plus ou moins donné la démission de leur sexe" (*Les bas-bleus*, xi; emphasis in original). No longer a woman but not yet a man, continues Barbey d'Aurevilly, "[c]'est la femme qui fait métier et marchandise de littérature. C'est la femme qui se croit cerveau d'homme et demande sa part dans la publicité et dans la gloire" (xii).

In Barbey d'Aurevilly's analysis, the act of picking up a pen, an *acte manqué* (a socially maladjusted behavior that manifests an unconscious wish), projects phallic desire.[35] Women's writerly ambition, born of penis envy *avant la lettre*, robs them of femininity: "La première punition de ces jalouses du génie des hommes a été de perdre le leur,—le génie de la mise, cette poésie d'elles-mêmes" (*Les bas-bleus*, xi). Their attempt to lay claim to genius, "cette immense virilité," not only strains the brain but also stimulates in women the bodily habits of men (xvii). Further still, the surfeit of *bas-bleus* in France could lead to social hermaphrodism, "où l'homme s'effémine et la femme s'hommasse, et quand ces fusions contre nature se produisent, c'est toujours, pour que l'ordre soit troublé davantage, la femelle qui absorbe le mâle jusqu'à ce qu'il n'y ait plus là ni mâle ni femelle, mais on ne sait plus quelle substance neutre," Barbey d'Aurevilly argues (xix). Faced with female overeducation, Maudsley had also wondered whether it might be "in the plan of evolution to produce at some future period a race of sexless beings, who undistracted and unharassed by the ignoble troubles of reproduction, shall carry on the intellectual work of the world" ("Sex and Mind in Education," 477).

Barbey d'Aurevilly stays close to a biologistic line of thought, which assumes primary Darwinism, in pursuing the question of a woman's capacity for creative work: "Et comme il ne s'agit ici que de littérature et d'art, est-elle d'organes, de cerveau, et même de main, lorsqu'il s'agit d'art, capable des mêmes œuvres que l'homme, quand l'homme est supérieur?" (*Les bas-bleus*, xxi). For him, femininity edges out creativity in all women's writing: "Les femmes peuvent être et ont été des poëtes, des écrivains et des artistes, dans toutes les civilisations, mais elles ont été des poëtes femmes, des écrivains femmes, des artistes femmes" (xxii). Here, in *Les bas-bleus*, the term "poëte femme" reverses the syntax of "femme poëte," used by Barbey d'Aurevilly in *Les poètes* (1862) in reference to Desbordes-Valmore and the young Delphine Gay. The orthographic variation "poëte" recalls the Greek *poiēsis*, "a making," which underscores the link between poetry and creation, synonymous with originality. The cerebral difference assumed by Barbey d'Aurevilly fills the blank space that separates the categories of "poëte" and "femme," from the Latin *femina* (belonging to the female sex).

Women's texts, continues Barbey d'Aurevilly, offer proof as evident as natural history that "elles n'ont ni l'invention qui crée ou découvre, ni la généralisation qui synthétise. . . . Elles restent donc incommutablement femmes, quand elles se montrent le plus artistes" (*Les bas-bleus*, xxii). In his view, it remains to be seen whether any of the writers he proposes to engage will escape the law of inferiority also inherited from Christianity (xxiii). For him, the discourses of science and religion present a united front against granting women equal authority in cultural production.

Advocates for female intellectual development built on the momentum created by Victor Duruy, the national minister of education, who founded secondary courses for women in 1867, gaining more ground in 1880. That year, the Camille Sée law provided *lycées* for girls. The following year, Jules Ferry, the minister of education and president of the Council of Ministers, established free education and, in 1882, mandated secular and compulsory education for children aged six to thirteen. However, this legislation did not represent a commitment to intellectual equality, but rather the republican agenda: national unity and competent citizenry.[36]

51

## Sex in Mind and Education

Curricular reform of classical education under the Third Republic, which relegated Latin and Greek to a minor role in comparison with the French literary tradition, was geared toward maintaining traditional gender roles. Though French literature was considered appropriate for girls, texts were carefully selected to provide moral training for future homemakers and mothers.[37] The call for pedagogical manuals still expressed the danger of "allowing girls to cultivate their mental space" (Gale, "Education, Literature and the Battle over Female Identity," 111). Some women's poetry survived in the more inclusive manuals of the time, such as *Les femmes de France: Poètes et prosateurs* (1886), edited by Paul Jacquinet, the inspector general for state education. Though many works had yet to be exhumed from library shelves, for Jacquinet, the corpus he had uncovered substantiated the authority women had acquired by the 1880s. The renaissance of poetry in the nineteenth century, he believed, owed much to women displaying creativity and artistry far superior to that of previous centuries: "Les femmes ont deployé dans ces concerts assez d'imagination, de sentiment et d'art pour qu'une part distincte et bien à elles leur soit acquise dans l'histoire de la renaissance poétique de notre temps" (xvii–xviii). Jacquinet named Tastu, Desbordes-Valmore, Girardin, Ackermann, and Blanchecotte in observing how powerfully nineteenth-century women had shaped the century's poetic output. However, he emphasized that their legacies alone did not encompass women's poetic production in all its forms. Interestingly, in Jacquinet's manual, which was focused exclusively on women's contributions to France's intellectual history and intended for girls in the *écoles normales supérieures* (originally established to train teachers), poets outnumber prose writers in the section devoted to the nineteenth century.

Another collection from the same period reveals the state's strong hand in forming a national curriculum. Gustave Merlet, a professor and member of the High Council on Public Instruction, published the *Anthologie classique des poètes du XIXème siècle: Cours élémentaires et moyens* (1890) in response to the council's December 1889 mandate that "une Anthologie serait désormais obligatoire dans toutes les classes, en particulier pour les cours élémentaires et moyens" (i). The adjective "classique" in the anthology's title relates not to classical Latin or Greek, but to the making of a modern canon consisting of contemporary "classics" or "great works." In structuring his anthology thematically, per the letter of the mandate, Merlet selected nineteenth-century poets of both sexes, who "célébrant la famille et la patrie, idéalisent la vie domestique, populaire, et nationale, de manière à toucher les cœurs et à frapper vivement l'imagination" (i–ii).[38] Unique for the time, this pedagogical tool reflected a newly created coeducational system that matched, at least in principle, the century's poetic evolution.

The education of girls and the teaching of a national tradition worked both for and against women's writing at a key moment of canon formation. Although ped-

agogical manuals and anthologies of the time expanded the place of women's production, including that of poets, literary histories greatly reduced the range of women's work, often erasing their poetry altogether. In 1889, the critic Ferdinand Brunetière limited French women's influence to the epistolary genre, and in a later book (1913) he excluded their work from the evolution of nineteenth-century poetry. Likewise, Gustave Lanson's *Histoire de la littérature française* (1895) silenced nineteenth-century women as poets.

However patchy the official historical record, the cultural memory of poetry produced by women is thick, as suggested by critical studies such as Henri Marion's *Psychologie de la femme* (1900). Marion, a professor of education at the Sorbonne and a self-professed naturalist, knotted with biology the narrative that excluded women from the body of "great works" that formed the pedagogical canon at the twentieth century's turn. Marion invokes Maudsley's claim that "le sexe est plus au fond que toute culture," arguing that education would not fundamentally alter female nature (4). Marion's wide-ranging volume recaps the cross-fertilization of modern scientific ideologies and literary criticism, as elucidated by the interaction already discussed between the discourses of medicine and reception. Marion suggests the intellectual equality of the sexes in countering the categorical sexing of the mind: "La raison proprement dite, au sens étroit et philosophique du mot, n'a pas de sexe: c'est la faculté des principes" (197–98). Yet he maintains a cognitive difference by depicting women's imagination as too lively and thus lacking "puissance" and "fécondité" (205). Marion draws the discourse of physiology into the reception of women as creators, meeting some resistance, however, in the realm of poetry: "M^{me} Ackermann compte comme poète aux yeux de tous les connaisseurs. . . . M^{me} Desbordes-Valmore a eu de grandes parties du génie poétique" (206). However, Marion concludes that work of such originality is not the goal of female education: "de nous aider à elever des hommes et des citoyens" (306). Nationalist ideologies, which reinforced educational and curricular reforms that were based on sexual difference, carried through to canon formation well past the turn of the century. That women's contributions to poetic production during the nineteenth century in France survived the construction of a "woman's tradition" from rival masculinist and feminist perspectives is another irony of their reception history.

## Between Literary Criticism and History

The Parnassian poet Catulle Mendès's 1902 report on poetic production during the nineteenth century for the minister of education and fine arts represents the paradoxical way that hostile critics have marginalized women, yet recorded their contributions in detail. The first part of Mendès's volume is an essay of two hundred pages, which reviews the history of French poetry to contextualize the century's chief movements: Romanticism, Parnassianism, and Symbolism. The second part, covering more than three hundred pages, offers a dictionary of principal poets. Replete with bibliographies, critical references, and a chronology spanning the century, this part of Mendès's report provides the histories of some forty women. However, Mendès does not treat the few women in his body of analysis as central to the century's poetic evolution.[39]

Desbordes-Valmore elicits one of Mendès's longer commentaries. In the second part of his volume, Mendès restates Baudelaire's 1861 essay as well as conservative reviews by Sainte-Beuve, Hugo, and Alfred de Vigny: "[I]l y eut Mme Desbordes-Valmore, la chère et douleureuse Marceline, la seule femme qui soit poète sans cesser d'être femme, qui n'ait pas été un 'travesti' de la littérature, celle par qui ont été exprimées, en leur naturel de sexe, les piétés, les douleurs, les forces, les faiblesses de l'âme féminine,—la seule Femelle de la poésie française" (*Le mouvement poétique français*, 77–78). Mendès lingers at greater length on his contemporary Krysinska, conceding that her early poems (1881–82) may have resembled what the Symbolists later theorized as *vers libre*. Nonetheless, in placing her in the category of the "poétesse," associated with artlessness, Mendès emphasizes that her work falls short of a true poet's: "En vérité, je pense que, satisfaite d'être célèbre pour l'aimable spontanéité de ses vers (puisqu'on dit que ce sont des vers), Marie Crysinska [*sic*] fera bien de ne point prétendre à la gloire d'avoir été une novatrice" (152). Women's poetry should be considered like their physical beauty, concludes Mendès, "un charme de plus dans la maison" (201).

Domesticated by analogy, female creativity merged with womanliness and did not threaten either the literary tradition or the social order. The poetic embodiment of unbridled feminine sensibility, however, aroused hostility. This antipathy comes into greater relief in various studies at the turn of the twentieth century, including the retrospective account of women's Romantic inheritance by the poet and critic Charles Maurras, also the principal spokesman of the reactionary Action française.[40] In "Le romantisme féminin: Allégorie du sentiment désordonné," first published in *Minerva* (1 May 1903), Maurras scorns turn-of-the-century poets Renée Vivien (1877–1909), Gérard d'Houville (1875–1963),[41] Lucie Delarue-Mardrus (1874–1945), and Anna de Noailles (1876–1933). He alludes to their nineteenth-century predecessors, naming only Desbordes-Valmore, then reads each poet closely. Maurras's appraisal targets their collective expression as "le romantisme féminin," but associates each writer's foreign origin or sexual orientation with perversion and anarchy.[42] Along the latter axis unfolds the Romantic revolt against classicism, on the one hand, and the censuring of Romanticism as a form of excessive, unnatural femininity, on the other. In his view, "sous le nom d'originalité, pour principe d'art," creative individuality had supplanted classical mimesis ("Le romantisme féminin," 215). By "le romantisme féminin," Maurras does not mean the poetry Romantic era women produced, which he obscures, but the womanish sensibility that usurped traditional French genius: "Au lieu de dire que le romantisme a fait dégénérer les âmes ou les esprits français, ne serait-il pas meilleur de se rendre compte qu'il les effémina?" (218).[43]

For Maurras, while Hugo's genius exemplifies "un mode de sensibilité aussi féminine que celle . . . d'un lamartinien," Lamartine's demonstrates "cette vérité que le Romantisme entraîna chez les mieux organisés un changement de sexe" ("Le romantisme féminin," 218). In repudiating the male Romantic legacy by correlating it with excess femininity,[44] Maurras also mocks turn-of-the-century women's poetry: "Leurs modèles les avaient, plus ou moins, volées de sexe. Ils s'étaient mis à écrire et à penser comme il est naturel que pense et écrive une femme. Depuis qu'il retombe en quenouille, le romantisme est rendu à ses ayants droit" (219). Maurras imputes to modern feminism a neo-Romantic movement of poetry saturated with sentiment and tinged with sensuality. In formulating a separate category of female genius, he extends his subtitle, "allégorie du sentiment désordonné," to equate "le génie féminin" with anarchic immorality. Maurras's contemporary Alphonse Séché uses the same formulation, albeit to *promote* women's poetic writing.[45] The ambiguity of constructs such as "le génie féminin" and "la poésie féminine" discloses the semantic shifts underlying literary criticism and the recording of history. This reflects how the power of any discourse depends on context, demonstrating another dimension of the paradox of reception.

## Anthologies and the Poetic Canon

In prefacing his two-volume anthology, *Les muses françaises* (1908–9), Séché argues that, to date, anthologies of French poetry that aimed to show that art makes no distinction between the sexes had placed men and women together but in so doing had grossly underrepresented the latter. To address this lacuna, he collected women's poetry from 1200 to 1891. His anthology provides detailed biographies and selective bibliographies for each poet and an appendix of critical views of so-called *poésie féminine.* If ambiguously framed by such paratextual material, however, anthologies devoted to women risk upholding the separate "female tradition" that women, as poets, questioned or explicitly contested, especially during the nineteenth century. From this perspective, Séché's indiscriminate terminology contradicts his aim to celebrate the scope of women's poetic work. The word "muses" in his title suggests the passive role traditionally assigned to women as the source of a male artist's inspiration. Séché's alternate use of "femme-poète" and "poète" in referring to the poets he uncovers further muddies his perspective by tangling and untangling women's relationship to creativity on the basis of sex.

Séché believed that women were poised to garner a prominent place in French poetic history. Given the substantial body of poetry women had produced and the greater freedom they now sought, their expression would shift even more from personal subjectivity to lyricism tempered with artful reflection, acquiring, in Séché's view, "cette impartialité qui a été l'honneur et le génie des grands poètes et des grands romanciers" (*Les muses françaises*, 12). No moment was more propitious for women writers, he notes, and thus *Les muses françaises* was timely and needed: "une éclatante affirmation du génie féminin" (13). Here, in Séché's preface, the adjective "féminin" does not mark off the "inferior sex" from genius, as in Maurras, but designates the poetic creativity or "génie" displayed by women across the centuries.

Nevertheless, the significant body of work anthologized by Séché competes with the authority of the paratexts surrounding it, both his prefatory assessment and that of critics he solicited to offer their opinion on "la poésie féminine." Their views, appended to Séché's anthology, carry forward the nineteenth-century nature-versus-nurture debate over genius, together with the reading of nineteenth-century women as poetesses versus poets. Although a couple of critics cited by Séché affirm that poets of genius would emerge or perhaps had already emerged from the ranks of women, most of them pass on variations of the theme that women have no poetic history and thus no future as poets. For example, Marcel Ballot maintains two separate canons of poetry, but blurs the line between them by adding that women could become "great" poets: "Qui sait même si elles ne nous l'ont pas donné?" (quoted in Séché, *Les muses françaises*, 2:355). Jules Bertaut's sweep across centuries of poetry confirms, to the contrary, "l'absence parmi elles, de tout génie" (2:356). His commentary reproduces the contemporary debate: The source of this inferiority was not females' lack of education, their lower social standing, or even the hostility greeting their literary aspirations, but a cognitive deficit. In Bertaut's view, the mind of the poet of genius and that of a woman are diametrically opposed, "car le génie est nécessairement objectif, au lieu que la femme est, par nature, entièrement, irréductiblement subjective" (2:357). It would require more than education for women to develop the capacity for genius. The latter, stresses Bertaut, would demand a complete transformation of their nature, which he does not consider possible or even desirable.

With a comparable tone, Ernest Charles insists that there is nothing original about "la poésie féminine contemporaine" and places Noailles and her cohort in Valmore's sentimental shadow: "Les femmes-poètes de notre temps ont exprimé avec une abondance effrayante des sentiments que Marceline Desbordes-Valmore et que la plupart des poètes contemporains ont exprimés avant elles" (quoted in Séché, *Les muses françaises*, 2:358). Unlike Charles, who alleges that no woman has exerted any influence as a poet, his contemporary Émile Faguet, a member of the Académie française, observes that Sappho, Corinne, Marie de France, Labé, and Desbordes-Valmore had produced poetic masterpieces. By focusing on the sentimental genius displayed by women, however, Faguet overlooks the intellectual legacy represented by Ackermann, for example, an achievement on par with the work of Lamartine and Vigny.

The literary journalist and poet Fernand Gregh contests the master narrative of reception more productively than does Faguet by rejecting gendered categories of poetry informed by the sexing of the creative mind. In recalling the aura surrounding genius, Gregh underscores that one can neither explain nor predict when great poets emerge: "Il n'y a pas de poésie féminine. Il y a la poésie. Certains et certaines y excellent, d'autres non. On ne peut donc parler d'un avenir spécial de telle poésie, masculine ou féminine. La poésie a toujours tout l'avenir. Il naîtra toujours de grands poètes, hommes ou femmes, des Hugo, des Musset, des Louise Labbé [*sic*] ou des Marceline Desbordes-Valmore. Où? Quand? *Cela gît sur les genoux des dieux*, et nul ne peut prophétiser là-dessus" (quoted in Séché, *Les muses françaises*, 2:360–61; emphasis in original). Unlike Gregh, Edmond Pilon narrows the category of "feminine poetry" to the dolorous and maternal strand of Desbordes-Valmore's production, which he gleaned from Baudelaire's reading. From this perspective, he places in Valmore's shadow the turn-of-the-century poets Noailles, Hélène Picard, Cécile Perin, and Nicolette Hennique, insisting that they produced nothing original. For Paul Reboux, apart from Sappho, whose poetry is masculine, women could not become great poets. Similarly, for Édouard Trogan, women would remain muses or the embodiment of poetry itself. The only such collection until the early 1960s, *Les muses françaises* sheds considerable light on how unevenly twentieth-century critics evaluated women as poets, expanding, contracting, or altogether erasing their achievements in the nineteenth century. Discerning readers of Séché's anthology, such as Irène Chichmanoff, however, weigh the original poetic corpus it restored against the inconclusive critical literature.

## Reading Women Back into Poetic History

Chichmanoff acknowledges Séché as a principal source of her doctoral thesis, "Étude critique sur les femmes poètes en France au XIX$^e$ siècle" (1910). Unfortunately, her thesis had very limited circulation and thus minimal impact at the time. Considered retrospectively, however, it places French women's poetic works during the nineteenth century in their original context. Chichmanoff's revisionist study highlights women's diverse achievements, drawing parallels with, or departures from, their male counterparts': "Elles ont triomphé avec eux et les noms . . . de Girardin, de Mme Desbordes-Valmore, Colet, Mercœur, Siefert, et surtout de Mme Ackermann ne périront pas" (22). Women advanced as poets during the early decades of the century, observes Chichmanoff, using the label "femmes poètes" to designate the leading group: "Ne peut-on pas dire que ces femmes poètes ont fait ce que les hommes n'osaient pas faire, à une époque où la littérature allait changer d'inspiration et de direction?" (29).

Chichmanoff argues that poetic women succeeded from 1800 to 1830 because they excelled in cultivating emotion, a principal feature of the Romantic aesthetic Baudelaire emphasized: "Dans ce domaine-là, elles peuvent atteindre au génie, elles peuvent être inimitables, témoin cette Desbordes-Valmore qui avait instinctivement trouvé les plus beaux accents d'amour qui soit dans la poésie lyrique" (quoted in "Étude critique," 69). Desbordes-Valmore was not the only poetic innovator to emerge from the ranks of Romantic era women, however. This period, which valorized sentimental genius, as Chichmanoff describes, was "favorable à la poésie féminine" and saw "l'éclosion d'œuvres de femmes que l'on pouvait considérer comme absolument originales et novatrices" (69). By the term "poésie féminine," Chichmanoff does not mean a separate category of poetic expression. Rather, by this, she designates women as poets and shows that they treat not only matters of the heart, such as love, marriage, and maternity, but also philosophical topics with universal appeal. Individual women's histories developed alongside close readings of poems and brief bibliographies enrich, yet also disprove, some of Chichmanoff's broader claims.

The subsequent period of Romanticism (1830–50), which Chichmanoff characterizes as "à la fois pittoresque et déclamatoire," anticipated the Parnassian turn from sentiment to sensation ("Étude critique," 69). She considers this era, in which the focus shifted from personal lyricism to objective description of the external world, to be less favorable to women who tended to copy their male counterparts' labored style.[46] The women selected by Chichmanoff to represent these two decades, among them Ségalas, the later Desbordes-Valmore, Girardin, Colet, Blanchecotte, Ackermann, and Siefert, were nonetheless innovative.[47] Though Chichmanoff registers individuality among poetic women of different generations, she comments that "[une femme] met toujours de ses sentiments dans son art," adding that most women could not achieve the objectivity championed by the male Parnassian poets (101). These claims limit her discussion of women's poetic expression during the second half of the century. From 1850 to 1900, she identifies "deux grands poètes féminins," Ackermann and Siefert, ignoring, for example, the unique way Blanchecotte bridges subjective and objective lyricism and how Krysinska theorizes her own foundational *vers libre*.

As Chichmanoff underscores, Ackermann explored the reaches of philosophy with unique force: "Aucune femme, dans aucun temps, n'a poussé si loin l'esprit philosophique, la profondeur de l'idée, la hardiesse de l'inspiration. On peut même dire que la littérature française n'a pas de poète philosophique plus complet, plus original que Mme Ackermann" ("Étude critique," 103). For Chichmanoff, Alfred de Vigny and Sully Prudhomme also rank as great philosophical poets, but do not surpass Ackermann, whose *Poésies philosophiques* represents "un coup de génie" (104). Siefert also has a distinctive trajectory in Chichmanoff's revisionist history; her poetry deepens Romantic lyricism: "cette poésie du cœur déçu et douloureux dont Mmes Desbordes-Valmore et Blanchecotte avaient déjà su exprimer de si profonds accents" (117).

By virtue of Siefert's formal mastery and greater reflection, Chichmanoff continues, "l'expression de cette poésie a acquis dans ses mains une précision, une netteté, un réalisme auquel le mouvement naturaliste a beaucoup contribué" ("Étude critique," 117). Here, Chichmanoff implies a continuum linking poetic women, but it is not an overarching assumption of her study. Though Chichmanoff, like other critics, invokes Desbordes-Valmore to position some of her female successors in French poetic history, she also situates women's accomplishments in relation to men's and even more broadly. In Siefert's lyrical rendering of stoicism,

Chichmanoff recognizes "une véritable conception de la vie, une philosophie, un pessimisme d'une portée universelle" (118). This intellectual element in women's poetic work, highlighted by Chichmanoff and others, disputes the centrality of sentiment traditionally used to categorize "la poésie féminine." So, too, the multiplicity of voices Chichmanoff recalls from the century's end helps to recover other trajectories that have informed the broader history of French poetry, a history that includes women's shaping of their poetic work on their own terms.

The legacies sketched by Chichmanoff include those of the philosophical Daniel Lesueur, nom de plume of Jeanne Lapauze, née Loiseau (1860–1920); Jean Bertheroy, pseudonym of Berthe-Corinne Le Barillier (1868–1927), whose inspiration was historical and picturesque; Rosemonde Gérard (1872–1953), described as having poetic verve;[48] Lydie de Ricard (1850–1878), characterized as the most Parnassian of all nineteenth-century women ("Étude critique," 126); Thérèse Maquet (1858–1891), whose work Chichmanoff considers deliciously sentimental and musical (127); and Lucie Delarue-Mardrus, who embodies "la poésie féminine contemporaine et la femme contemporaine, dont le caractère est la franchise dans le désir and la passion" (130). Whereas a number of Chichmanoff's contemporaries used the latter assessment to criticize such poetry, as seen in Maurras and others, she extols in Delarue-Mardrus "un vocabulaire tout nouveau, absolument original" (130).

Chichmanoff cites space limitations and the year 1900 as her study's end point and simply lists another seventeen poets. In contradistinction to Séché, she places Krysinska in this secondary group of women, whose work she considers less original but deserving of mention.[49] In sum, however, for Chichmanoff, the body of poetry produced by nineteenth-century women is superior in quantity and quality to the poetry of previous centuries. According to her, the number of women who emerged as poets in France from 1890 to 1910 was twice that of the Romantic generation.[50] She stresses the hostile social and ideological environment these women encountered, citing Mendès's 1902 report. Though Chichmanoff does not endorse two canons of poetry, she notes that many nineteenth-century women tended to be conservative "pour la pensée et pour la forme," except perhaps Krysinska, whose boldness she attributes to "son sang polonais" ("Étude critique," 153).

In closing, Chichmanoff returns to the question unresolved by the critics that Séché surveyed. If women do not inherently possess genius, can they acquire it? For her, nineteenth-century French women's poetry offers compelling evidence of creativity. It also raises the deeper issue at stake in forming the canons of criticism, notably the construct of "genius," both its meaning and attribution. As she puts it, "Avant de se désespérer du génie de la femme, il faudrait que tous les âges s'entendissent sur ce mot et sur ceux à qui on l'attribue" ("Étude critique," 153). To underscore this final point, Chichmanoff quotes Fernand Gregh: One cannot predict the birth of great poets, whether from the ranks of men or women.

However, few critics of the time disputed the claim that women demonstrated no capacity for poetic genius, even in the recent past. A cluster of studies of contemporary women's poetry, intersecting with Chichmanoff's, silenced the multiple voices recovered in her project until the latter part of the twentieth century. Subsequent studies in the late 1920s buried the expansive production uncovered by Chichmanoff, whether diagnosing women's surge during the Romantic period, categorizing all women's poetry in the nineteenth century as sentimental, or reproving their verse in the early twentieth century as perversely sensual. Nevertheless, in reiterating that women had left no mark, critics and historians alike unwittingly provided modern readers glimpses of those women remembered as gifted poets.

### "So accurately does history repeat itself"

However narrow or broad a sampling one considers, the critical literature shows how the dominant narrative of reception history repeats itself, thus conflating women's poetic past, present, and future.[51] In 1909, the critic Paul Flat broached the genius question by prefacing his study of contemporary women writers (the poets Noailles, Delarue-Mardrus, d'Houville, and Vivien and the novelist Marcelle Tinayre) with Schopenhauer's claim some sixty years prior: "Que peut-on attendre de la part des femmes, si l'on réfléchit que, dans le monde entier, ce sexe n'a pu produire un seul esprit véritablement grand, ni une œuvre complète et originale dans les Beaux-Arts, ni, en quoi que ce soit, un seul ouvrage de valeur durable" (*Nos femmes de lettres*, i).[52] The only exception for Flat was the philosophical Ackermann (v). In Flat's view, Schopenhauer's "diagnosis" was still accurate regarding contemporary women as not having evolved poetically. Flat thus deems the sensual expression of carnal desire as monstrous and characteristic of all women writers: "La Femme littéraire est un *monstre* au sens latin du mot. Elle est un monstre, parce qu'elle est anti-naturelle. Elle est anti-naturelle parce qu'elle est anti-sociale . . . c'est qu'elle reproduit . . . la plupart des ferments de dégénérescence qui travaillent notre monde moderne" (218; emphasis in original). This discourse of degeneracy echoes the *bas-bleu* criticism that emerged in the 1840s and 1870s. Flat reflects his own context and Schopenhauer's influence in judging the upsurge of women writers at the turn of the twentieth century from the perspective of the German philosopher's notion of the will in the world. The pursuit of literary culture threatens women's maternal instincts and thus modern society.

In prefacing *La littérature féminine d'aujourd'hui* (1909), the literary historian Jules Bertaut exposes the male angst generated by modern women writers: "[L]e succès de la littérature féminine actuelle a été foudroyant, il nous a tous surpris, il nous a tous mortifiés, il nous a tous un peu humiliés" (1). One can see here recognition mixed with the scorn of the previous century. However extraordinary women's success as poets and novelists at that time, it was temporary, as Bertaut describes, "une mode, un snobisme qui passera comme tous les snobismes et qui ne comptera pas plus dans le développement de notre art national que la vogue de la crinoline ou celle du corset droit" (2). In his view, women writers' popularity in 1909 owed much to the fact that their readers were primarily women who lacked discernment.[53]

Bertaut places all women's writing in a single category, fusing the criticism of their prose and poetry with their sex: "Qu'elles fassent des romans de mœurs, des romans psychologiques, des romans historiques, de la poésie romantique, de la poésie parnassienne ou de la poésie décadente, la femme de lettres est avant tout la Femme, c'est-à-dire un être d'une certaine sensibilité, d'une certaine intelligence, d'un certain goût et d'un certain tempérament, caractères qui varient fort peu selon les individus et qu'on est toujours assuré de retrouver en chacun d'eux" (*La littérature féminine*, 16). For Bertaut, love remains the essence of women's poetry, varying little from the sentimental Desbordes-Valmore to the sensual neo-Romantics d'Houville, Delarue-Mardrus, Noailles, and Vivien, among others. Passionate excess, symptomatic of psychological imbalance, however, characterizes the style and content of the latter contemporary verse (303). Only those women authors who preserve the cult of the family avoid such excess, Bertaut concludes, and with this he prescribes the "cure" for women's future poetry.

Bertaut's contemporary the vicomte Hervé de Broc questioned the critical trend in 1911: "Si l'on prétend frapper les femmes d'incapacité littéraire, de nombreux exemples protestent en leur faveur" (*Les femmes auteurs*, 1). In redressing women's absence from the French poetic past, Broc names from the nineteenth century Dufrénoy, Desbordes-Valmore, Tastu, Mercœur, Élise Moreau, and Ségalas. Brief commentaries on highlights from their work nuance his preface, which assumes all women's poetic legacy to be sentimental. This enables modern readers not to lose sight of the fact that the Romantic generation as well as later poets explored a broader range of themes; some of these poets also experimented with various forms. Other twentieth-century critics related women's poetic writing to their physiology. Their accounts place "la poésie féminine" in the shadow of their male counterparts' genius, past and present, further reducing the footprint of women who emerged as poets in the nineteenth century.

### What "Women Poets" Want

In introducing *Muses d'aujourd'hui: Essais de physiologie poétique* (1910), Jean de Gourmont,[54] the literary editor for *Mercure de France*, adapts the lexicon of evolutionary science to aesthetic developments: "La sensibilité n'évolue pas, mais seulement les formes qu'elle suscite" (14). Gourmont adds physiology to the synergy between poetry and music, which he traces to Verlaine and also associates with Wagner: "Nous restituer la sensation même, la vibration nerveuse, c'est ce que doit faire la poésie" (18). From his paradigm of males' poetry as the transposition of sexual desire, Gourmont forms the corollary for females: "la nécessité d'une vibration eurythmique qui régularise son équilibre nerveux" (24). Women's verse releases strong emotions and thus restores balance (from the Latin *eurythmia*) to their nervous system. Gourmont claims to have read nearly all the "poétesses" writing in his day, which would have been quite a feat, according to one author's statistics.[55] He observes that most contemporary women's poetry remains too close to the feeling or physical sensation it describes to be considered art (28).[56] The sensual, rather than strictly sentimental, accents of women's current poetic expression, however, await "un grand poète pour être fixés en art" (30). For Gourmont, the exception to this rule is Desbordes-Valmore, whose prosodic experiments inspired Verlaine: "Il faut comprendre que Verlaine, par exemple, loin d'être un novateur, fut au contraire l'aboutissement de toute une poésie féminine. Mme Desbordes-Valmore est une sorte de précurseur de Verlaine" (30). Generally, however, Gourmont does not consider women innovative. He describes their poetry as devoid of "toute culture intellectuelle," applying Buffon's definition of genius as "une longue patience" only to males (238). By stating that "le génie de la femme poète est une spontanéité," natural and artless, Gourmont, too, perpetuates the critical topos of the Romantic "poetess" (238).

At nearly the same moment, Jean Dornis, pseudonym of Mme Guillaume Beer (née Elena Goldschmidt-Franchetti), published a less truncated account of the recent poetic past in *La sensibilité dans la poésie contemporaine* (1912). Dornis's psychological analysis of French poetry since the mid-1880s compares the sensibility of contemporary male and female poets. In her view, many of the latter write through the desiring body, in contrast to Desbordes-Valmore's allegedly chaste embodiment of femininity as presented by Baudelaire and others, whose views Dornis recaps from Mendès's 1902 tome. Dornis considers Desbordes-Valmore's legacy among the Symbolists, evoking Verlaine's tribute to her as well as Krysinska's role in *vers libre*'s history.

Against this background, Dornis observes that contemporary women poets' work carries virtually no historical residue, no trace of the lyrical accents vacillating between tenderness and boldness "échappés à une Siefert, à une Ackermann, à une Desbordes-Valmore" (*La sensibilité*, 179). More liberated in body than in mind, however, modern women still grapple with the self-questioning that haunts much of women's poetry from previous centuries. On this, Dornis cites two lines from Desbordes-Valmore's posthumously published poem "Une lettre de femme": "Les femmes, je le sais, ne doivent pas écrire; / J'écris pourtant" (180). In evoking the hostile environment for gifted women in her day, Dornis suggests that the deep-rooted prejudice against them masks male detractors' sense of "impuissance" and "envie" (190). Greater artistry, she believes, will allow women's future creations to survive the test of time.[57] Dornis argues against the discourse of male genius that has governed the reading of and writing about women's place in poetic history. However, her study eclipses their contributions by not referencing more women from the nineteenth century (whether of the Romantic or post-Romantic eras). The concurrent forming of the modern French canon also precipitated poetic women's fall into oblivion, as did studies that evoked their rise as a monolithic and unduly sentimental group in the 1820s, instead of examining the diversity within individual women's œuvres and between their bodies of work.

## Against the Canon

The retrospective study of women's place in French poetic history in the 1920s and '30s takes on a fuller meaning against the backdrop of the canon of "great works" emerging during those years. Éditions Conard, established in 1902 to publish the collected works of nineteenth-century authors, was adding to its list modern editions of the works of Baudelaire, Dumas, Maupassant, Flaubert, and Balzac. With a similar aim, in the 1930s the independent editor Jacques Schiffrin launched the Bibliothèque de la Pléiade, a series of complete works by "classic" French authors (still published by Gallimard). During this key period of canon formation, Marcel Bouteron published *Les muses romantiques* (1926). A literary historian and member of the Institut de France (which includes the Académie française), Bouteron was also a specialist on Balzac, whose works he was editing for Conard at the time.

Bouteron invokes Balzac's *Illusions perdues* to position his own account of women's place in the Romantic heyday.[58] Metaphors of disorder and disease tinge Bouteron's portrayal of women glutting the literary scene: "[T]outes les variétés de muses ont, au temps du Romantisme, envahi le Bois Sacré, *à la manière d'une épidémie*" (*Les muses romantiques*, 14; emphasis added). In his view, women as writers had not succeeded in gaining a place in the French literary tradition because their excessive emotion and melancholy delimited their collective production. Bouteron retains only Desbordes-Valmore among the poets. His role as an elite reader of literary history overlaps with the dominant discourses constituting her sentimental legacy: "Dites-moi si vous connaissez ailleurs que dans un cercle de raffinés, de lettrés, beaucoup de lecteurs de la tendre Marceline? Et pourtant cette femme n'est-elle pas la poésie même? N'a-t-elle pas, dès 1819, publié des *Élégies* qui, au moins autant que les *Méditations* de Lamartine, marquent le début du romantisme sentimental?" (105). Her work anchors the Romantic movement in French poetic history as much as Lamartine's. Despite this fact, had male readers such as Baudelaire, Verlaine, Montesquiou, and especially Lucien Descaves not promoted her canonization after her death, argues Bouteron, referring to the public celebration in her honor in 1894, "peut-être le public ne s'aviserait-il pas d'y reconnaître des chefs-d'œuvre?" (105). That Desbordes-Valmore's collected poetic works were not published in a modern edition until 1973 exposes her dual status as the one and only "woman poet" of the nineteenth century and yet a minor Romantic.[59]

Already forgotten were Valmore's contemporaries Waldor, Mercœur, and Ségalas. As Bouteron states, these were "des noms vieillots sur les titres de livres qu'on n'a jamais fait qu'entr'ouvrir ou même que l'on n'a pas du tout lus" (*Les muses romantiques*, 105). In the next line, however, he recalls some of their works, as if from memory: "*Enfantines* de Ségalas, *Poésies du cœur* de Waldor, *Poésies* de Mercœur,

63

etc." (105). Bouteron's *Muses romantiques*, like other studies consulted for this book, exemplifies the paradox of literary criticism that relegates poetic women to the margins of the canon it helps to form but, in so doing, helps posterity to discover and study them anew.

Alexandrina Baale-Uittenbosch's *Les poétesses dolentes du romantisme* (1928), which purports to contest Romantic era women poets' absence from literary history, further illustrates this double edge in women's reception as *poètes manqués*. Baale-Uittenbosch proposes to explain why, apart from Desbordes-Valmore, most of the women forming the spectacular poetic movement of the first half of the nineteenth century virtually vanished from the official record. She reiterates the critical view that their success partly stemmed from the exuberant spirit of the age: "L'époque romantique 'n'ayant guère le sentiment de la mesure, ni le goût de la sobriété,' les femmes sont parvenues à exciter un véritable enthousiasme pour leurs écrits" (21). Almanacs, keepsakes, and albums also contributed to poetic women's visibility at that time. However, "dans un temps de névrose romantique où il fallait être pâle, fatal, poitrinaire et lys penché," the surfeit of "muses" who cultivated a melancholic persona devalued in turn all women's poetry (30). Baale-Uittenbosch counters such imposture by concentrating on the thematic diversity of women's poetic writing across the century. A veritable gold mine of primary texts, amply documented and contextualized with secondary references, Baale-Uittenbosch's volume is an invaluable resource for scholars today. However, her account of women's poetic originality, or rather lack thereof, has a blind spot: the constructed maleness of genius.

In turning from women's rise as poets during the Romantic era to their descent into oblivion by the turn of the twentieth century, Baale-Uittenbosch invokes the sentimental source assumed to limit women's innovative capacity. She cites the writer Antoine Rivarol, whose stance calls to mind the two sexes of genius later elaborated by Lamartine: "Le ciel refusa le génie aux femmes pour que toute la flamme pût se porter au cœur" (*Les poétesses*, 163). Because women ostensibly write according to impulse, argues Baale-Uittenbosch, they neglect the *art* of poetry at which their male counterparts excel. Her final analysis, punctuated with pejorative labels, echoes masculine opinion on the inferior poetic sex: "Tout en ayant eu la même conception des thèmes lyriques, nos *authoresses* n'ont pu égaler les grands poètes. *Auteures* de second ordre, elles forment un cortège de *poetae minores* qui ont balbutié ce que les Maîtres ont chanté d'une manière autrement profonde et artistique, les laissant dans l'ombre de leur gloire rayonnante" (265–66; emphasis in original). The production she recovered notwithstanding, Baale-Uittenbosch fails to introduce a new narrative of women's poetic past. Such a narrative was Jean Larnac's stated purpose in *Histoire de la littérature féminine en France* (1929).[60]

In publishing a comprehensive account of "la littérature féminine" through the ages, Larnac aimed to settle, once and for all, whether women could produce works of genius: "Est-il vrai que les différences physiologiques qui opposent la femme à l'homme conditionnent des différences intellectuelles que le temps et la volonté n'effaceront jamais?" (*Histoire*, 5). In Larnac, one finds condensed the physiology of genius invoked by literary critics to construct male versus female canons. As Elaine Marks observes, "The masculine is inevitably the sign of intelligence, reason, effort, abstraction, production, muscles, and normality; the feminine is just as inevitably the sign of sensitivity, inspiration, spontaneity, emotion, reproduction, nerves, and abnormality" ("1929: Jean Larnac," 888–89). Larnac's view of the nineteenth century passes on the one-woman poetic tradition I examine in greater detail in chapter 3, reinforcing the myth that, "après [Desbordes-Valmore], la poésie féminine sembla morte" (*Histoire*, 201). For Larnac, from 1850 to 1870, only Blanchecotte, Siefert, and Ackermann warrant any mention. And only Ackermann receives a closer look because of her intellectualism, which he considers "un sentiment, non une construction de l'esprit" (203). In his view, one could only speculate whether access to education would deepen women's future literature.

At this juncture, Larnac reflects on genius that "souffle où il veut. Nulle culture ne peut le provoquer" (*Histoire*, 224). For him, however, the absence of women from literary history disproves the trend to unsex genius, which he traces back to Staël. Because women write from the heart, he argues, their writing lacks the objectivity that true literary art requires: "Les femmes n'ont pleinement réussi que dans la correspondance qui n'est qu'une conversation à distance, la poésie lyrique et le roman confession, qui ne sont qu'un épanchement du cœur. Elles n'ont produit rien qui compte dans tous les domaines qui exigent de l'auteur un complet détachement de soi-même et dans ceux qui ne se fondent pas sur le concret" (257). The want of reflection would always limit "le génie féminin," Larnac concludes, using this category not to celebrate women's achievements, as Séché had, but to mark a sexual difference that creative females could not transcend (279).

Fernand Gregh's *Portrait de la poésie française* (1936) diverges from the traditional lines of criticism in various anthologies and literary histories, exposing how cultural context determines the labels used to record poetic history. In writing the history of modern French Romantic poetry, Gregh asserts that Desbordes-Valmore should precede Lamartine. That he calls her a "poétesse" has no bearing on her work of poetic originality, "un des plus beaux triomphes du don sur la technique, et du génie sur le talent" (66). Gregh's appraisal contests the prevalent sexing of genius but not the singling out of Desbordes-Valmore, which, as already mentioned, obscures the other women whose poetry diversified Romantic production. Along with Desbordes-Valmore's contemporaries Tastu, Delphine Gay, Mercœur, and Ségalas, Gregh puts Ackermann in a minor category of poets, doubly marginalizing her, as both a woman and in Valmore's shadow. Yet, in describing her as "l'éloquente madame Ackermann, volcan rationaliste, dont quelques strophes sont parmi les plus mâles de notre poésie" (142), Gregh expresses how the ideological power of her poetry, like that of other women, engages us not in the criticism of sex, but in the creative work. Indeed, the vagaries of literary reception from the nineteenth century through the twentieth form a thick nexus. The critical force of rival narratives beckons us, time and again, to read women's absence from poetic history against the grain.

## Critical Displacements

In 1949, Simone de Beauvoir argued that women have no poetic legacy because their production reflects no creative agency. Instead, patriarchal thought defines women as the "other" to men: "Les femmes ne se posant pas comme Sujet n'ont pas créé de mythe viril dans lequel se refléteraient leurs projets; elles n'ont ni religion ni poésie qui leur appartiennent en propre; c'est encore à travers les rêves des hommes qu'elles rêvent" (*Le deuxième sexe*, 1:235). Here, the adjective "viril" means "strength" and "energy" and, in the context of Beauvoir's argument, evokes the idea of a strong feminocentric tradition that would pass on myths (in the sense of narratives) of women's own making. Familiar with French literary history, Beauvoir was in a position to reconsider the "woman poet question." However, at the close of each volume of her revisionist cultural history, which disputes the second sex narrative, she cites Rimbaud on women's poetic future, thus reburying their rich past. It remains to be seen, she reiterates, whether women will become poets, for they have just begun to liberate themselves from the idea of being physically and intellectually inferior to men, a deep-rooted sense of lack that has prevented their creative achievement. She, too, denies that there have been women among the poets who shaped the French tradition.

Beauvoir returns to the question of women's relationship to creativity in the 1966 lecture "La femme et la création." For her, the chief impedient to women's self-perception as creators is the idea that "les femmes d'autrefois n'ont rien fait de supérieur" (474). In theory, Beauvoir rejects the inherited canons of criticism with her final statement: "[I]l ne faut pas qu'elles se laissent intimider par le passé, parce que d'une manière générale, dans ce domaine-là, comme dans tous les domaines, jamais le passé ne peut servir de démenti à l'avenir" (474). In practice, however, she questions neither the record nor the categories of analysis used to evaluate women's poetic work, as does Jeanine Moulin who, that same year, published the volume of her anthology devoted to women's poetry from the twelfth century to the nineteenth, *La poésie féminine*.[61]

A question raised by Moulin's title and aspects of her prefatory overview of women's writing in relation to gender prescriptions is whether her anthology leaves in place the principal construct used to isolate women in the "poetess" tradition.[62] In addition, the epigraph to her volume, a passage from Rimbaud's *lettre du voyant*, carries forward from the future tense of his remarks the view that women have yet to become poets in the fullest sense of the term. More directly than Beauvoir, however, Moulin targets gender as the principal difficulty that has plagued the writing and reading of women's poetic history. Though Moulin does not espouse feminism, she questions the literary past, as suggested by the query heading the volume: "Existe-t-il une poésie féminine?" (*La poésie féminine*, 13). She broaches the problem of separating the woman from the poet. For her, women's poetic expression "reflète une pensée, une sensibilité, et une attitude devant la vie, propres aux femmes" (13). To put her remark another way, poetry is a form of discourse or a way of thinking.

In her lengthy preface, Moulin acknowledges the social conditioning that underpins women's verse, which often reflects the female experience. She also pulls in the biological blueprint determining "la poésie féminine," which leaves her open to criticism.[63] However, in commenting on the diversity of women's modern poetic trajectories, which Moulin could also have drawn from their contributions in the past, she questions the construct of "feminine poetry": "Peut-être, un jour, n'existera-t-il plus de poésie féminine?" (*La poésie féminine*, 64). Thus, Moulin envisages reading women's poetry beyond gender. Neverthe-less, Domna Stanton presented her own 1986 anthology of French women's feminist poems from the Middle Ages to the modern era as a corrective to Moulin's anthology, which "iterates the stereotypes of femininity and the clichés of feminine writing that pervade traditional literary histories" (*Defiant Muse*, xvii–xviii). It should be noted that Stanton's single volume, tracing feminist thought in women's poetry across the centuries, cannot match the scope of Séché's and Moulin's collections.

Any compilation risks being reductive, a risk that increases in response to the volume's critical framework. A modern compiler's reading of the historical record to determine women's presence in or absence from the poetic past may distort the reading of contemporary poetic production as well. In *Elles: A Bilingual Anthology of Modern French Poetry by Women* (1995), for example, Martin Sorrell introduces the "substantial body of poetry written or published by French women during the last twenty years," which he hopes "may persuade future historians that this was something of a golden age" (1). For Sorrell, this body of work contrasts with "almost three centuries of apparent infertility," separating the distant voices of Christine de Pisan, Marguerite de Navarre, and Labé from the "richly romantic and Roman-tic Marceline Desbordes-Valmore" and "Louise Ackermann . . . full of pre-modernist *angst*" (1; emphasis in original). Louis Simpson's *Modern French Poets: A Bilingual Anthology* (1997) reduces the record even more. Simpson chooses Desbordes-Valmore as the only excellent and innovative "female poet" of the nineteenth century: "Throughout the span of time I have measured there were very few women in France whose poetry even approaches the excellence of the poetry of Desbordes-Valmore. . . . [T]he poetry women wrote in France in the nineteenth century and early decades of the twentieth is unadventurous in form and style. It is sentimental. In short, there is nothing modern about it" (xx).[64] Yet the basis upon which Simpson selects Desbordes-Valmore contradicts why her reputation as a sentimental genius endured to the exclusion of all other women of her century. If by "sentimental" Simpson means Romantic, what would he call Desbordes-Valmore's effusive lyricism, which Baudelaire considered her greatness? What, moreover, does he consider modern about Desbordes-Valmore, who did not figure for Stanton as a "defiant muse"?

The double meaning of femininity has allowed misogynists to applaud Desbordes-Valmore and feminists not to embrace her completely. Desbordes-Valmore's "very success in constructing an unthreatening poetics of sincerity, which enabled her to maintain a place in the French poetic canon as a 'romantique mineur' . . . has tended to render her unusable and invisible for feminism," Johnson argues ("Gender and Poetry," 170). That Desbordes-Valmore's reputation as the *only* "woman poet" of her century survived well into the twentieth century partly explains the slow recovery of other women's contributions, with the restrictive category of *la poésie féminine* being another principal factor. But, as Jean-Paul Somoff and Aurélien Marfée stated in "Les muses du Parnasse" (1979), "[Desbordes-Valmore] ne fut pas la seule à pouvoir rivaliser avec les plus grands poètes" (6). In 1987, Évelyne Wilwerth reiterated the point with emphasis: "Mais, Marceline Desbordes-Valmore résume-t-elle à elle seule la création poétique [des femmes] du XIXᵉ siècle des femmes? Non!" (*Visages de la littérature féminine*, 181).[65]

During the 1990s, scholars amplified the record of the poetry produced by women across the nineteenth century. For example, *Femmes poètes du XIXᵉ siècle: Une anthologie* (1998), edited by Christine Planté, features 19 of 70 major poets plumbed from the archives.[66] An index lists another 120 women not featured in the anthology.[67] The body of scholarship has also broadened to include poets other than Desbordes-Valmore, though, apart from Krysinska, principally through scholarly articles. In calling for a new history of nineteenth-century French poetry that would include women's contributions in all their diversity, thus encouraging commensurate study, I seek in this book to illuminate the strategies women developed for intervening in the dominant narrative, which not only belittled their aesthetic ambitions but also barred their entry to the canon.[68] Chapter 3 prepares a new critical direction by expanding Desbordes-Valmore's trajectory and reception from the perspective of women who engaged with, or ignored, her poetic work, starting with the Romantic period, which reveals how actively women thought about their relationship to creativity and, in so doing, rethought the notion of genius.

# 3

## The Other History
## of French Poetry, 1801–1900

Rival discourses sexing and unsexing genius, which affected creative women's reception throughout the nineteenth century, called into question the critical literature that excluded them. From this paradox of reception an even fuller narrative of the French poetic past emerges. In an era that defined creativity as a male inheritance, did French women poets in the nineteenth century form a separate canon, mirroring "the formation among French women novelists of a conscious tradition"?[1] Or did they strive to position themselves with their male counterparts as carriers of a national poetic tradition? In what ways did the poetry women produced respond to their reception? Does their body of work resist the so-called maleness of genius, female envy, and the feminine shadow cast by Desbordes-Valmore, the discursive nexus that usurped their texts and muffled their prominence? And, finally, how do women as creative thinkers invite us to read their individual legacies beyond gender?

In this chapter I chart through representative trajectories the poetic authority that women established during the nineteenth century. A chronological framework, roughly following the poets' dates of publication, allows an examination of the ways their projects intersected and diverged. Individually but also together, women expose the problem of "tradition," which entails the pull of influence (from the Latin *influentia*, "a flowing in") as well as the push for originality (from the Latin *originalis*, "beginning, source, birth"). Their output across the century reveals a multiplicity of aesthetic and conceptual projects.

The pre-Romantic poets Adélaïde Dufrénoy and Sophie Gay also became editors and critics who followed women's poetic writing. Their foundational appraisals of Desbordes-Valmore differed from those of Romantic male writers who admitted her originality but related her work to normative womanliness. The latter element dominated Valmore's canonization, which began shortly after her death in 1859, even though she was neither solely "féminine" nor "féministe," as Christine Planté argues ("Marceline Desbordes-Valmore," 80). The same could be said of Tastu who, like Desbordes-Valmore, embedded social critique in her verse. Waldor, another member of their Romantic circle, published essays about women's position in the modern history of French letters. Mercœur, Ségalas, and Colet interacted with female peers, albeit not as so-called sister poets. They each invoked male poets as models or equals in positioning their own work, as did the later poets Blanchecotte and Siefert. Ackermann and Krysinska, like Siefert in particular, were even more explicit in distancing their voices from the poetics of femininity that Desbordes-Valmore had come to represent. Their experiences illustrate how the meaning of genius evolved, and what it meant for a woman to display creative power.

### The Romantic Edge

The mass entrance of women as writers in post-revolutionary France coincided with the rise of industrialization, capitalism, and the publishing revolution.[2] Literacy among women increased from 14 percent to 27 percent in the first two decades of the nineteenth century as the new middle class became consumers of culture (Hoock-Demarle, "Lire et écrire en Allemagne," 149). Nevertheless, the shift in women's literary activity was double-edged. Though authorship widened women's sphere, Patrick Vincent observes, "new literary institutions such as women's magazines and annuals . . . transformed women poets into objects of circulation and exchange and lowered the symbolic value of their poetry" (*Romantic Poetess*, 124).[3] As self-conscious authors, however, Romantic era women turned their conflicted position in the industry to their advantage by making their poetic ambitions a theme of their writing. This work of counterdiscourse progressed even as women insisted that their verse emanated solely from the heart. Interestingly, the inspiration they claimed is precisely the source that Lamartine later identified in asserting his originality as a feeling genius: "Je suis le premier qui ai fait descendre la poésie du Parnasse, et qui ai donné à ce qu'on nommait la muse, au lieu d'une lyre à sept cordes de convention, les fibres mêmes du cœur de l'homme" ("Préface," 10). Various exchanges among poets of both genders, including critical reviews and correspondence, as well as paratexts, such as prefaces and epigraphs, tell anew the forgotten story of Romanticism's shared history.

Victoire Babois and Dufrénoy were among the forerunners to French Romanticism. Their works *Élégies par M^me Babois sur la mort de sa fille âgée de 5 ans* (1805) and *Élégies, suivies de poésies diverses* (1807), respectively, were recognized for infusing the classical elegy (a poem in couplets that expresses sorrow or lamentation, usually for one who has died) with personal lyricism.[4] As the novelist Sophie Ulliac-Trémadeure writes, "[L]e nom de M^me Babois était dans toutes les bouches, ses élégies faisaient partout couler les larmes, les journaux retentissaient de son nom" ("Madame Babois," 128).[5] Waldor notes that Babois's *Élégies maternelles* (1805) had placed her "au premier rang des femmes poètes" (*Poésies du cœur*, 306). Dufrénoy's reputation as a poetic model and professional mentor for female contemporaries stemmed in part from her position as the editor of women's periodicals, such as *La Minerve Littéraire*, *L'Almanach des Dames*, and *Hommage aux Demoiselles*. She collaborated with Tastu on *Le livre des femmes: Choix de morceaux extraits des meilleurs écrivains français, sur le caractère, les mœurs et l'esprit des femmes* (1823). Their discussion of male and female writers considers ideas about women not only to intervene in the social and moral issues raised by expanding their sphere, but also to endorse their writerly aspirations. Women acquired critical authority through such editorial work, demonstrating erudition and literary activism. Their verse, which explores feelings as well as the big questions of life, reveals artistry and thematic diversity. Those women who held to the feminine line during the Romantic era, in particular, did so deftly by admitting societal expectations without, however, entirely conforming to them.

## A Poet Is Born, a "Woman Poet" Made

In 1819, Marceline Desbordes-Valmore published her first collection, *Élégies, Marie, et romances*, which drew little notice. When reissued without the prose piece under the title *Poésies* the following July, however, her volume won acclaim. Éliane Jasenas speculates that readers belatedly recognized in Desbordes-Valmore "une nouvelle forme d'harmonie élégiaque, sincère et essentiellement musicale" by association with Lamartine's *Méditations poétiques*, which had been published five months earlier (*Marceline Desbordes-Valmore*, 18).[6] Barbara Johnson proposes, to the contrary, that "readers in 1820 turned to Lamartine as a way of marginalizing Marceline Desbordes-Valmore" ("1820: The Lady in the Lake," 630). These arguments juxtapose Desbordes-Valmore's rise to prominence alongside Lamartine in the 1820s with her invisibility in the traditional Romantic canon represented by Lamartine, Hugo, Vigny, and Musset at the turn of the twentieth century. The arguments in turn raise the issues of class and gender emphasized by Aimée Boutin to explain the initial silence that greeted Desbordes-Valmore's work.[7] Although some of Desbordes-Valmore's contemporaries subsequently ranked her first among the Romantics, others positioned her in relation only to female predecessors. The impetus of a separate tradition dissipated as women defined paths for their poetic innovation.

In October 1820, Sophie Gay reviewed Desbordes-Valmore's *Poésies* against the backdrop of the tensions between the opposition liberals and the ultras. This took place before the November election, which established the second legislature and restored the conservatives' power. In February, a Bonapartist had assassinated the duc de Berry, the son of the future Charles X, thus precipitating the turmoil. Gay encouraged readers to seek relief from such tumult in Desbordes-Valmore's elegies, which she recommended "comme modèles en ce genre,"[8] quoting the volume's opening poem, "L'arbrisseau":

> La tristesse est rêveuse, et je rêve souvent.
> La nature m'y porte, on la trompe avec peine:
>     Je rêve au bruit de l'eau qui se promène,
> Au murmure du saule agité par le vent.
> J'écoute: un souvenir répond à ma tristesse;
> Un autre souvenir s'éveille dans mon cœur:
> Chaque objet me pénètre, et répand sa couleur
>         Sur le sentiment qui m'oppresse.
>         Ainsi le nuage s'enfuit,
>         Pressé par un autre nuage:
>         Ainsi le flot fuit le rivage,
>         Cédant au flot qui le poursuit.
>             ("Compte rendu de *Poésies*," 157–58)

In "L'arbrisseau," Desbordes-Valmore embeds her aesthetics of poetry. The notion of echo, which she connects to memory, represents both her verse's inner source and its expansive rhythm.

Desbordes-Valmore dedicated "L'arbrisseau" to Jean-Louis Alibert, her doctor, who had suggested that she write to alleviate symptoms related to the loss of her singing voice, which stifled her career as an actress.[9] Desbordes-Valmore mined her inner musicality, as she later described to Sainte-Beuve, disclosing her poetic way of thinking: "À vingt ans, des peines profondes m'obligèrent de renoncer au chant, parce que ma voix me faisait pleurer: mais la musique roulait dans ma tête malade, et une mesure toujours égale arrangeait mes idées, à l'insu de ma réflexion. Je fus forcée de les écrire, pour me délivrer de ce frappement fiévreux, et l'on me dit que c'était une élégie (*Le Pressentiment*). M. Alibert . . . me conseilla d'écrire, comme un moyen de guérison, n'en connaissant pas d'autre" (quoted in Sainte-Beuve, *Portraits contemporains*, 360).[10] Desbordes-Valmore disproves those who classified her writing as pure instinct by linking poeticity with rhythm and reflection. Her pain ceded to creative reverie, she writes ("à l'insu de ma réflexion"), suggesting the fusion of conscious and unconscious thought. Early in her literary career, Desbordes-Valmore also produced socially engaged poems.

In "À Délie," also cited by Gay, Desbordes-Valmore alludes to the disadvantages of having intially made acting, then writing, her life's work. The poem, addressed to an actress friend, begins thus: "Du goût des vers pourquoi me faire un crime? / Leur prestige est si doux pour un cœur attristé!" (*Œuvres poétiques*, 1:57). Biography yields to introspection as the poet registers her culture's ambivalence about women's creative pursuits. Included in the excerpt Gay highlights, these lines near the poem's end capture the poetic woman's quandary:

Oh! des erreurs du monde inexplicable exemple,
Charmante Muse! objet de mépris et d'amour
  Le soir on vous honore au temple,
  Et l'on vous dédaigne au grand jour.
   (quoted in Gay, "Compte rendu de *Poésies*," 159)

Though fraught with contradictions, public opinion counts. The stanza of "À Délie" that follows the excerpt in Gay's review suggests that a woman's literary success meets with social disapproval:

Je n'ai pas pu supporter ce bizarre mélange
  De triomphe et d'obscurité,
Où l'orgueil insultant nous punit et se venge
  D'un éclair de célébrité.
   (Desbordes-Valmore, *Œuvres poétiques*, 1:57)

Self-aware, Desbordes-Valmore inscribes herself *avant la lettre* in the lineage of accursed poets with these closing lines: "Seule, je suis pourtant moins seule avec ma lyre: / Quelqu'un m'entend, me plaint, dans l'univers" (1:58). "À Délie" refutes the idea that a woman's verse conveys no reasoning. With this choice of text, Gay also encouraged sympathy for Desbordes-Valmore and, more broadly, for all women writers and artists.

Desbordes-Valmore had another advocate in Dufrénoy: "[J]e lis l'éloge de Mme Desbordes-Valmore dans les journaux, je souhaite la lire elle-même; ses poésies sont sous mes yeux, je les dévore, et je sens que je ne pourrai m'empêcher d'unir ma voix à celle des estimables écrivains qui lui ont donné leurs suffrages" ("De Mmes Bourdic-Viot, Desroches," 557). Dufrénoy's review illustrates the form-ing of a "sorority" of poets described by Boutin, which "implies that women poets show support for their peers and acknowledge that they form a feminine tradition" ("Marceline Desbordes-Valmore," 165). Indeed, Dufrénoy links Desbordes-Valmore to the seventeenth-century elegist Antoinette Deshoulières: "Notre siècle possède une véritable Deshoulières, plus peut-être qu'une Deshoulières; et je m'efforcerai de lui faire des amis de tous nos lecteurs" ("De Mmes Bourdic-Viot, Desroches," 557–58).[11] In selecting Deshoulières as a model, Dufrénoy intimates that Desbordes-Valmore surpassed *her* precursor and thus relates poetic evolution to originality, the attribute of genius surfacing at the time. Dufrénoy follows this line of thought to compare her peer Babois's elegies with Desbordes-Valmore's. For Dufrénoy, although both women excel in this genre, with "Le ruisseau" Desbordes-Valmore exceeded Babois in the realm of the idyll, a short poem based on pastoral themes. While Dufrénoy, like Gay, focuses on Desbordes-Valmore's craft, Victor Hugo considers her gender.

Hugo, only nineteen at the time, evaluated Desbordes-Valmore's *Poésies* for *Le Conservateur Littéraire* in 1821. He had founded the journal with his brothers in

1819 to promote aspiring writers like himself against the vagaries of censorship. Despite Hugo's liberal politics, he was morally conservative with regard to women writers. He prefaces his review by admitting that he first saw Desbordes-Valmore's name in the *Almanach des Muses* (which had published "Le pressentiment" in 1818).[12] Not only does he consider most elegiac poetry bland, he also objects to seeing "*l'encre salir des doigts de rose*" ("*Poésies* de Mme Desbordes-Valmore," 339; emphasis in original). The image of a woman's ink-smeared fingers evoked by Hugo implies that such work tarnishes her virtue and conveys the physical strain associated with mental labor. Desbordes-Valmore's *Poésies*, however, challenged his belief.

Like Gay, Hugo draws readers' attention to the first stanza of "L'arbrisseau," cited above. This contemplative text ascribes feeling to inanimate nature, an example of the "pathetic fallacy,"[13] which he recognizes as a feature of Desbordes-Valmore's poetic creativity. In this regard, he comments about a long excerpt from her melodious idyll "Les roses": "Il y a dans ces vers plus que de la poésie, il y a une observation du cœur, peut-être profonde" ("*Poésies* de Mme Desbordes-Valmore," 340). Much like reverie, her sentimental expression hints at a depth akin to thinking. Hugo continues in this vein, citing copiously from elegies, including "Prière aux muses," "La nuit d'hiver," "Le concert," "À l'amour," "Le miroir," and "Adieu mes amours" (340–44). Her verse, which he describes as being virtually free of artifice and of a simple beauty, strikes him as almost natural. Hugo acknowledges the impact of her work as "un des recueils poétiques les plus remarquables qu'on ait publié depuis longtemps" without invoking Lamartine, or any other poet for that matter (344). This implies originality, but not yet the work of poetic genius. For Hugo, there are technical imperfections in her verse along with infelicitous repetitions that Desbordes-Valmore could surmount. Her passionate writing touches the heart, though she would achieve even greater glory by infusing her work with "un caractère religieux" that would penetrate the soul, Hugo ends, mirroring his own nascent project (345).

At nearly the same moment, the playwright Jacques Ancelot claims that, with *Poésies*, Desbordes-Valmore has revealed "toute sa force et son éclat" ("Critique littéraire," 202). In tracing an aesthetic lineage from the eclogue (a short pastoral poem, usually in dialogue) to the elegy, practiced by poets of both genders, Ancelot invokes the ancient past: the Greek poet Corinne, whose texts have all vanished, and Sappho, whose work, apart from a single ode, has been recovered in fragments.[14] Against this background, he writes that "nos Corines [*sic*] françaises" have also struggled to survive (201). The more analytical Dufrénoy had acquitted herself well, but Desbordes-Valmore had breathed new life, or emotion, into the elegy.[15] To give readers "une idée du véritable talent qui brille dans ce recueil," Ancelot amply cites from Desbordes-Valmore's texts, balancing praise with a critique targeting instances of weak form and unclear meaning (202). For Ancelot, her work deserves "un grand succès" (211).

Critics of the time overlooked Desbordes-Valmore's *Veillées des Antilles* (1820–21), a prose collection containing verse, which further diversifies her voice.[16]

In the novella *Sarah*, for example, Desbordes-Valmore juxtaposes through the prism of loss her mother's death and the effects of slavery in the French Caribbean in 1802.[17] This engagement with abolitionism adds social critique to her repertoire.[18] Yet, this topic, like other issues and current events that Desbordes-Valmore considered as "une femme à l'écoute de son temps,"[19] did not survive in criticism of the time, which focused almost exclusively on her Romantic expression. She published a third edition of *Poésies* in March 1822, the same year that Hugo's *Odes et poésies diverses* and Alfred de Vigny's *Poèmes* appeared. In 1824, she brought forth *Élégies et poésies nouvelles*. Though Desbordes-Valmore would continue to struggle with her lower-class origins, she joined the ranks of celebrated poets with Tastu, who benefited from a bourgeois standing and education.

### Tastu in/on the Guise of a Poetess

Unlike Desbordes-Valmore, who pursued verse after having to abandon the stage, Amable Tastu (1798–1885) was encouraged from an early age to develop her poetic gift. In 1809, at the age of eleven, she presented a versified play to Empress Josephine. Tastu rose to prominence in 1825 with "Les oiseaux du sacre," which Sainte-Beuve crowned a success, naming her *"la muse de la patrie"* ("Poésie," 664; emphasis in original).[20] Tastu won prizes for her poetry and prose, producing some thirty volumes during her life. Though a prolific writer who moved male peers to acknowledge poetic genius in women, she adopted the image of a mutilated bird, first deployed in "Les oiseaux du sacre," to symbolize the feeling of impotence with which she wrestled throughout her career.[21] Nevertheless, the fact that women articulated the difficulties they encountered as writers "creat[ed] a curious dialectic: they were becoming more confident in turning their unconfidence into the matter of literature," as Finch observes (*Women's Writing*, 94). Tastu, like Desbordes-Valmore, consistently describes her voice and verse as weak in the guise of a poetess who lacks both power and art.[22] Within the same corpus, however, Tastu recognizes other women's contributions to poetic history.

In "À ma muse: Le jour de la fête de Madame Dufrénoy," for example, Tastu honors her mentor, whom she considers divinely inspired, as suggested by the classic poetic symbol of the laurel wreath adorning "le front d'Adélaïde" (Tastu, *Poésies complètes*, 74). However, in the ode "Sur la mort de M^me Dufrénoy" (1825), originally published by Joseph Tastu, whom she married in 1816, Tastu acknowledges Dufrénoy without expressing the sense of belonging to a feminine tradition: "C'est moi qu'elle a nommée; / La crédule amitié l'aveuglait dans son choix; / C'est à mes faibles chants que de sa renommée / Elle a légué le poids" (*Poésies complètes*, 75). Tastu expresses critical acumen as she relates Dufrénoy's legacy to the transition from classicism to Romanticism, displaying an intellect not customarily associated with Romantic era women's verse.[23] In this poem, characteristic of her œuvre, Tastu's access to culture resonates in the image of "l'Hélicon," the mountain celebrated in Greek mythology and a symbol of poetic inspiration (75).[24] Tastu thus attributes to Dufrénoy the modern renaissance of lyric poetry by invoking its ancient origins, but defends herself against any charge of impropriety. Against "le poids" of Dufrénoy's achievement, her "faibles chants" fit the physiology of feminine poetry.

This, however, is not how a critic reviewed Tastu's first collection, *Poésies* (1826). Noting her "esprit supérieur," Victor Chauvet ("*Poésies*, par Mme Amable Tastu," 649) praised the blend of force ("la vigueur de la pensée") and grace ("fidèle aux bienséances") in her volume, directing readers to selected texts (650). On 29 January 1827, the public session of the Académie des sciences, arts et belles-lettres de Besançon ended with "Les deux génies: Hommage poétique à Amable Tastu." The epigraph of this tribute cites her poem "Les deux poètes": "J'aime des luths unis l'harmonieux essor; / J'aime des sons divers le merveilleux accord" (86). The tribute to Tastu, "Les deux génies," elaborates in her work the shift from classicism ("l'ancien Génie") to Romanticism ("le moderne Génie"): "Modèle des vertus dont s'honore une femme, / Sous le ciel de Paris, vers nous s'élève une âme / . . . / S'exhale vers les cieux, plein de suavité. / . . . / Des vers qui semblent nés sans pretendre à la gloire / Et déjà sont inscrits au temple de mémoire" (94–96). Hugo had defined this aesthetic evolution in prefacing his *Odes et ballades* (1826), which was listed among other recent publications during the session but not discussed.

Hugo argues against the hierarchy of genres by comparing "les deux littératures dites *classique* et *romantique*," the former requiring adherence to strictly defined forms, such as the sonnet, and the latter allowing for freedom of expression (*Odes et ballades*, xv; emphasis in original). He advocates for the turn from "imitation" (mimesis) to "originalité," by which he means "génie" (xvi, xvii). His stance conveys the semantic drift that complicates the idea of tradition discussed at the start of this chapter. The second epigraph to his ode "Promenade" cites Tastu's "La lyre égarée" ("Voici les lieux chers à ma rêverie / Voici les prés dont j'ai chanté les fleurs"), suggesting that he considered her work to be part of the current poetic development (135).[25]

A fellow poet, Antoine de Latour, found Tastu equally striking, especially her "netteté de la pensée" ("Les femmes poètes," 272). Her *Poésies* demonstrates a perfect balance between respect for prosodic tradition and innovative thought: "le développement naturel d'un génie sobre et réservé" (273). Latour appreciates Tastu's development in *Poésies nouvelles* (1835), commenting that "une révolution s'était accomplie dans le talent du poète" (276). Her lyricism has deepened and also broadened in response to historical events, tracing a path like Lamartine's.[26] To illustrate her new confidence coupled with imaginative strength, Latour quotes "La mer" in its entirety (281–84). In this exuberant poem, Tastu memorializes the July revolution of 1830 and its aftermath, revealing the world of ideas from which she drew inspiration.

Other appraisals in the 1830s recognized Tastu alongside peers of both genders. In 1835, for example, a reviewer (self-identified only as Y.) for *Le Citateur Féminin* referred to Tastu's genius, placing her in the company of Lamartine, Delphine Gay, Hugo, Desbordes-Valmore, and Sainte-Beuve ("Poésies nouvelles," 45). For this reviewer, despite prose's onslaught, poetry was still very much alive, as demonstrated by the "cri d'admiration" won by Tastu's *Poésies nouvelles* (46). A repository of history, her volume expresses wider cultural and political currents, like "un miroir," observes the critic, "où vient se réfléter la société tout entière, avec ses tergiversations et ses craintes, ses vœux et ses espérances" (46). Sainte-Beuve also praises Tastu as a "vrai poète," noting the artistry and mastery of form in her *Poésies nouvelles* ("Poètes et romanciers," 355). Yet he emphasizes the doubt Tastu expressed about her talent ("qui n'est, dit-elle *qu'une lutte intime d'ardens pensers et de frêles accords*"), embodying the "femme-poète" who places familial duty before literary glory (355, 357; emphasis in original).

Tinged with melancholy and mourning, *Poésies nouvelles* represented her "last song."[27] Tastu's husband was financially ruined after the revolution of 1830 devastated the book industry, and she abandoned poetry for the more profitable educational prose.[28] Against this background, Sainte-Beuve reproduces "Réponse à Madame Tastu," a poem written by Lamartine after he read the copy of *Poésies nouvelles* she had sent to him. Lamartine recognizes Tastu's poetic genius while seeking to console her: "À ces vains jeux de l'harmonie / Disons ensemble un long adieu: / Pour sécher les pleurs du génie, / Que peut la lyre? / . . . / Il faut un Dieu!" (quoted in Sainte-Beuve, "Poètes et romanciers," 360). This exchange, like many others, chronicles the significant readership and favorable reception individual poetic women enjoyed throughout the century.

In 1836, Ségalas confirmed that God had made Tastu a "poète," one who succeeded in reconciling creativity with femininity ("Madame Tastu," 17). By that time, Tastu's *Poésies*, "que nous savons tous par cœur," as Ségalas writes, was in its fifth edition (18). In Tastu's verse, she further observes, "la raison qui pèse et qui calcule marche à côté de l'inspiration" (18). Ségalas balances her reading the way that Tastu measured her writing: against societal expectations. Both women were editors for the *Journal des Femmes*, a newspaper characterized by Évelyne Sullerot as "très bourgeois, raisonnablement catholique et relativement féministe" (*Histoire de la presse féminine*, 164).[29] The term "féministe," not coined until 1872, applies more to Ségalas than Tastu, and loosely at that, a point developed in chapter 4.[30] Ségalas uses sartorial terms to change her peer's aesthetically pleasing work into the portrait of a properly attired bourgeois woman: "Vous ne verrez rien de dérangé dans sa parure, car avant de se mettre en chemin elle arrange avec soin les plis de sa robe et les fleurs de sa guirlande. Elle exhale un charme infini; sa voix a des sons qui viennent de l'âme" ("Madame Tastu," 18). Ségalas brings her own knowledge of classical prosody to bear on Tastu's artful form, which is virtually free from "hémistiches brisés" or "vers enjambés" (19).

Unlike other critics, Ségalas admires Tastu's *Chroniques de France*, a poetic volume inspired by history.[31] Ségalas highlights Tastu's nine-syllable lines from "Chant" and "Peau d'âne" in *Poésies nouvelles* as "un rhythme [*sic*] neuf, tout artistique, que l'on aime par son étrangeté" ("Madame Tastu," 22). For Ségalas, Tastu matches the existential despair expressed by Lamartine and Hugo. Ségalas cites Lamartine's poem (above) as if rereading the final lines to Tastu, entreating her to ignore his advice and return to poetry for the public's sake: "[I]l lui a donné la gloire, 'cette splendide royauté du génie; il a entouré son nom de rayons éclatants, et il l'a mise au nombre des poëtes qu'il distingue entre tous'" (23).[32] As discerning readers, women interacted through such intertextuality with peers of both genders. From this dialogue, which demonstrates how actively poets followed each other's writing, one can better imagine their community, which transcended class and gender.

MARCELINE DESBORDES
*Crayon de Constant Desbordes*
1820

FIG 4

Marceline Desbordes by Constant Desbordes, 1820. From *Lettres de Marceline Desbordes à Prosper Valmore* (1924).

FIG 5
Amable Tastu by Émile Lassalle, 1840. Photo © RMN–Grand Palais/Art Resource, New York.

## Valmore and Tastu: Poetic Sisters

As Desbordes-Valmore (fig. 4) expressed in a letter of 23 December 1837 to Latour, in Tastu (fig. 5) she had a sister: "Douce femme que je voudrais oser nommer *sœur*" (quoted in Pougin, *La jeunesse de Marceline Desbordes-Valmore*, 238–39; emphasis in original). By this, Desbordes-Valmore meant the bond of friendship and mutual admiration they had forged as poets whose paths had intersected in Paris beginning in 1832.[33] Allied not by class, but by literary community, they shared similar financial difficulties. Desbordes-Valmore, like Tastu, had to take up prose after her husband's theater was shuttered in 1831. Writing on 11 May 1833, Desbordes-Valmore shared her sorrows with Tastu: "Hélas! oui, Madame, je fais tant que je peux de la pénible prose pour n'être pas tout à fait inutile ou nuisible à ma chère famille. Mais que cela me donne de mal! et que je regrette mes pauvres petites chansons qui m'aidaient à endormir mon cœur!" (quoted in Pougin, *La jeunesse de Marceline Desbordes-Valmore*, 195–96).[34] Despite her own economic hardships, Tastu relieved Desbordes-Valmore's burden by soliciting her contribution to *Soirées littéraires de Paris* (1832), a collection of verse and prose by male and female writers, and by finding buyers for her stories. Tastu later introduced Desbordes-Valmore to Sainte-Beuve, who played a principal role in what would become Desbordes-Valmore's sentimental legacy, promoting her as a "womanly woman" poet.

In an 1832 letter to her husband, Desbordes-Valmore describes Tastu as equally creative and feminine: "ce talent sans enflure" also "une tendre mère" (*Lettres de Marceline Desbordes à Prosper Valmore*, 1:33). She underscores Tastu's celebrity in an 1837 letter to Latour, suggesting that her own poetic output is inferior: "C'est une âme pure et distinguée qui lutte avec une tristesse paisible contre sa laborieuse destinée. Son talent est, comme sa vertu, sans une tache. Je lui ai fait des vers. Ils sont là depuis deux ans. Je n'ai pas osé les lui envoyer. Je suis toute anéantie devant ces charmantes célébrités, et quand j'entends mon nom sonner après les leurs, Dieu seul sait ce que je deviens dans le tremblement de mon cœur!" (quoted in Pougin, *La jeunesse de Marceline Desbordes-Valmore*, 228).[35] Desbordes-Valmore also refers to the dedicatory poem "À Madame Tastu" (1835), in which she attributes Tastu's gift to divine inspiration without any reference to sex: "Vous! qui tenez du ciel ce don frais et sacré" (*Œuvres poétiques*, 2:419). The epigraphs in Desbordes-Valmore's œuvre reveal that, though not formally educated, she read widely. However, in "À Madame Tastu," she claims a lack of sophistication: "Je n'ai pas eu le temps de consulter un livre, / Pour ciseler les cris dont mon sein se délivre" (420). Desbordes-Valmore thus evokes her class in espousing a hierarchy of poetic labor: "Est-ce au front incliné d'une vulgaire femme / Que vous devez ainsi secouer votre flamme?" (420).

Tastu, however, separates Desbordes-Valmore the poet from the humble woman. She uses Dante's verse to embellish the medallion that Pierre-Jean David d'Angers had carved of Desbordes-Valmore in 1833: "E per che dalla sua labbra si mova / Un spirito soave, pien d'amore, / Che va dicendo all'anima: Sospira" [And from her lips there seems to emanate / A gentle spirit, full of tender love, / Which to the soul enraptured whispers: "Sigh!"].[36] Desbordes-Valmore's aristocracy of heart echoes in the memory of her Tastu would express in a letter of 1869 to Sainte-Beuve: "cette femme distinguée, dont le talent et la personne m'ont toujours inspiré l'admiration la plus sincère et la plus vive sympathie" (quoted in Sainte-Beuve, *Madame Desbordes-Valmore*, 116–17). Desbordes-Valmore and Tastu enjoyed the rise of lyric poetry, but also survived its fall. They were established poets by the time the young Mercœur brought forth her *Poésies* (1827) with glory in mind.

## The Immortality of Genius

Élisa Mercœur (1809–1835; fig. 6), first recognized by academic societies in her native city of Nantes, contemplates her poetic aspirations in "Le sublime," as if wrestling with a premonition: "Le poëte au tombeau retrouve l'existence; / Qui laisse un nom, peut-il mourir?" (*Poésies*, 152). This query at the heart of Mercœur's œuvre resonated among her first readers. Georges-Adrien Crapelet, the editor of the second edition of her *Poésies* (1829), embedded Mercœur's early reception in his preface. The following passage, taken from a letter Mercœur wrote to the Académie provinciale of Lyon in 1826 upon being elected to the society over which Chateaubriand presided, addresses women's relationship to creativity: "Rivaliser de gloire avec ces Muses aimables et célèbres dont la patrie s'enorgueillit, en adoptant tous leurs succès, n'a point été mon espérance; mais j'ai éprouvé un sentiment d'orgueil, en songeant que mon nom pourrait trouver une place auprès de leurs noms chéris. Cette espèce de rapprochement est la première feuille de ma couronne littéraire. Puissent, à l'avenir, des suffrages mérités joindre quelques lauriers à cette feuille précieuse!" (Mercœur, *Poésies*, viii–xi). Here, Mercœur uses the term "muse" to

FIG 6

Élisa Mercœur of Nantes by Achille Deveria, 1835. Photo courtesy Ville de Nantes, Bibliothèque municipale (Frank Pellois).

mean "poet," as suggested by her view that her female contemporaries' contributions enriched a national tradition and by her own ambition to mark French poetic history. Mercœur's mother later wrote that Desbordes-Valmore, Tastu, and Delphine Gay were the "Muses" her daughter had in mind.[37] In her poetic corpus, however, Mercœur invoked genius in developing a much bolder persona.

Mercœur's *Poésies* opens with a dedicatory poem to Chateaubriand. The speaking subject uses the familiar form ("tu") in an interior monologue, linking her poetic trajectory to his by addressing him as an equal:

> Quoi! pas un de mes jours n'a laissé de mémoire?
> Quoi mon nom reste encor dans l'ombre enseveli?
> Ah! pour moi chaque instant qui s'écoule sans gloire
> Est un siècle fané par la main de l'Oubli!
> Mais toi, chantre sublime, à la voix immortelle,
> Demain, si tu l'entends, la mienne qui t'appelle
> Aura des sons plus purs que ses chants d'aujourd'hui.
>
> (4)

In a letter of 18 July 1827, Chateaubriand ensured the glory Mercœur sought: "Si la célébrité, Mademoiselle, est quelque chose de désirable, on peut la promettre, sans crainte de se tromper, à l'auteur de ces vers charmants" (quoted in Mercœur, *Poésies*, x). Had Staël still lived, Hugo, another of Mercœur's advocates, might have encouraged Mercœur to seek endorsement from her.[38] He considered Staël "une femme de génie, qui, la première, a prononcé le mot de *littérature romantique* en France" (Hugo, *Nouvelles odes*, 9; emphasis in original). Mercœur's quest for immortality, which she associated with genius, also won support from Lamartine, who stressed her momentum as further evidence of women's creative power: "J'ai lu avec autant de surprise que d'intérêt les vers de mademoiselle Mercœur, que vous avez pris la peine de me copier. Vous savez que je ne croyais pas à l'existence du talent poétique chez les femmes: j'avoue que le Recueil de madame Tastu m'avait ébranlé; cette fois-ci je me rends; et je prévois, mon cher, que cette *petite fille* nous effacera tous tant que nous sommes" (quoted in Mercœur, *Poésies*, xii–xiii; emphasis in original).[39] Lamartine's backing of Mercœur over Tastu veils a sense of rivalry not with either of them, but with the poet he does not name: Desbordes-Valmore. That Lamartine did not escape being compared with her may partially explain why later, in *Cours Familier de Littérature* (1856–68/69), he retreated from supporting women's poetic ambitions.

Crapelet stressed that reception mattered, yet the patronage Mercœur obtained from the minister of the interior, Jean-Baptiste-Sylvère Gay, the vicomte de Martignac, to whom she had sent a copy of her volume, was just as vital to her future success. With Charles X's fall in 1830, however, Mercœur, who was of humble means, found herself without the promised pension. By 1832, she and her mother, who had resided in Paris since 1828, were in dire straits. Appeals on her behalf by

Hugo, among others, to Adolphe Thiers, the minister of the interior under the new king, Louis-Philippe, were to no avail. Mercœur, like Desbordes-Valmore and Tastu, turned to prose, as did their male peers, in order to survive the depressed market for lyric poetry.[40] There is scant evidence of any actual interaction among the three women, apart from the poor impression that Mercœur made upon Desbordes-Valmore when they met by chance in 1832 at Dr. Alibert's home. In a letter dated 6 December 1832, Desbordes-Valmore wrote to her husband: "J'y ai vu Mlle Mercœur . . . peu élégante, l'air sincere et très bizarre. Elle m'a fait beaucoup d'accueil" (*Lettres de Marceline Desbordes à Prosper Valmore*, 1:37). Whatever the reason for this negative recollection, Desbordes-Valmore immortalizes a much more sympathetic figure in the poem "Élisa Mercœur, à sa mère."[41] This tribute was more in keeping with how deeply the literary world mourned Mercœur's death in 1835, as expressed in line 43: "Un soupir, s'il vous plaît, à la poète fille" (Desbordes-Valmore, *Œuvres poétiques*, 2:402).

In "Élisa Mercœur, à sa mère," Desbordes-Valmore draws Mercœur into her sororal circle, moved as much by the poet's voice as her youth and hardships, much like her own. Class mediates Desbordes-Valmore's portrayal of Mercœur as "une sœur inconnue," whose voice nevertheless has a familiar echo:

> Moi, sans racine aussi, née aux bords des voyages,
> Posant à peine un pied sur de fuyants rivages
>
> . . . . . . . . . . . . . . . . . . .
>
> J'écoutai, quand sa voix à mon cœur parvenue,
> M'apprit le nom charmant d'une sœur inconnue;
> Sa voix, qui n'avait pas encor de souvenir,
> Sa voix fraîche et nouvelle en perçant l'avenir,
> Lançait l'hymne de vie et de gloire trempée,
> Où sa tombe précoce était enveloppée.
>
> (2:402)

In granting Mercœur the glory she sought, Desbordes-Valmore scorns the mercantile environment of the 1830s that devalued poetic work by treating it as just another commodity. This contrast draws out the tension in Mercœur's project: the quest for immortality versus the fall into oblivion.

Social critique folds into the way Desbordes-Valmore memorializes Mercœur. Whereas the elite revere poetry as "le chef-d'œuvre de l'imagination,"[42] unsophisticated readers consider it like any other marketable product:

> On épuisait alors cette vivante lyre;
> Sa souffrance voilée, on la lui faisait lire;
> Car le monde veut tout quand il daigne écouter;
> Et quand il dit: Chante! il faut toujours chanter!
>
> (2:402)

Recall from chapter 1 the immortal heights Mercœur aimed to reach as an eagle, symbolic of genius. Here, Desbordes-Valmore modifies the figure of the mutilated bird, used by Tastu in portraying herself as an impotent poet, to depict Mercœur in the image of a long-suffering Romantic:

> Par d'innocents flatteurs innocemment décue,
> Son âme s'écoulait victime inaperçue,
> Et quand l'oiseau malade à son toit remontait
> Sous son aile traînante et fiévreuse il chantait!
> Il cherchait d'autres sons pour saluer la foule,
> Cette foule qui cause, et qui passe et qui roule;
> En vain, ses chants mêlés de courage et d'effroi,
> Dirent bientôt: "Je souffre et j'attends! . . . sauvez-moi!"
>
> (2:402; ellipses in original)

Desbordes-Valmore's tribute suffuses Mercœur's lyricism with emotional pain, rather than philosophical angst, unwittingly obscuring her more philosophical and objective expression.

In the 1843 edition of Mercœur's complete works, her mother placed Desbordes-Valmore's poem at the start, thus leading with a womanly woman's voice rather than with "À M. de Chateaubriand," as in the first and second editions of Mercœur's *Poésies.* This choice may have anticipated the backlash against women writers at that time. Madame Mercœur nonetheless cited among her daughter's contemporary reviews that of Émile Deschamps, one of the leaders of the Romantic school: "On est frappé d'étonnement quand on songe qu'une poésie si élevée, si vigoureuse, une versification si mélodieuse et si savante, se trouvent sous la plume d'une demoiselle de dix-huit ans, élevée loin de la capitale et hors du cercle et du mouvement littéraire; c'est plus que jamais le cas de s'écrier: *Nascitur poeta!*" (quoted in Mercœur, *Œuvres poétiques,* clxvi–clxvii; emphasis in original). The ambitious Mercœur "au cœur mâle," as Léon Séché later wrote, nonetheless faded from view, systematically associated with "la poésie féminine" and consequently subsumed by Valmore's model of conservative femininity (Séché, "À propos du centenaire de sa naissance," 189). Even though Ségalas, Mercœur's contemporary, began with a male model and then turned to feminine ideals, but continued to engage with current events, in particular France's colonial enterprise, a "woman's tradition" similarly homogenized her voice.

## Shaping Influence

For a young bourgeois woman, Anaïs Ségalas (fig. 7) exhibited an unusual independence of mind. Determined to pursue her passion for poetry, the newlywed

FIG 7

Anaïs Ségalas by Émile
Lassalle, 1840. From
Huart and Philipon,
*Galerie de la presse, de
la littérature et des
beaux-arts* (1841).

demanded that her husband, Victor Ségalas, a lawyer appointed to the royal court
in Paris, not thwart her writerly ambitions.[43] She was also savvy in responding to
the initial decline in the market for sentimental poetry following the 1830 revolu-
tion. In prefacing her first collection of verse, *Les algériennes: Poésies* (1831), Séga-
las acknowledges the influence of Hugo's *Orientales* (1829) in her choice and
treatment of a current event: the 1830 invasion of Algiers by the French. Treated
in detail in chapter 4, Ségalas's inaugural volume anchors the issue of colonization
and the attendant discourse of race that would span her output. This theme in her
writing would be virtually erased, however, later in her career by critics who would
emphasize her works geared toward mothers, children, and families.

Ségalas's subsequent volume, *Les oiseaux de passage* (1836), which saw a second
edition in 1837, drew notice from Théophile Gautier for its mastery of rhyme and
rhythm, absence of love lyrics, and thematic diversity. The table of contents yields
titles such as "Les morts," "Le cavalier noir," "Le voyageur," "La jeune fille," "Le
marin," "Le sauvage," "L'assassin," "Le brigand espagnol," "À une tête de mort," and
"Un nègre à une blanche," some featuring her interest in colonial matters (317, 318).

The fact that her poem "À une tête de mort" was mistakenly attributed to Hugo shows that Ségalas's contemporaries did not readily identify her voice as feminine.[44] Gautier, for example, placed Ségalas in Hugo's lineage and Tastu closer to Lamartine: "Madame Anaïs Ségalas est avec madame Tastu une des femmes qui font le mieux les vers de ce temps-ci" ("*Les oiseaux de passage* par Madame Anaïs Ségalas," n.p.). By relating the females to male precursors—"L'une relève de M. Hugo, l'autre relève de M. de Lamartine"—Gautier positions them in the same poetic tradition, in particular the Romantic school, but implies a hierarchy (n.p.). His comparison, however, does not invoke the centrality later ascribed to Desbordes-Valmore, which would sideline other poetic women across the century.

Even though Ségalas collaborated with other female contemporaries, such as Antoinette Dupin and Waldor, who were also editors for the *Journal des Femmes*, she recorded few of them in her œuvre.[45] Epigraphs in *Les oiseaux de passage* include the following names: Desbordes-Valmore, the duchesse d'Abrantès, Mercœur ("La jeune fille mourante"); Marie Mennessier-Nodier, Salm ("La petite fille"); Dupin ("À une tête de mort"); Tastu ("Éducation de l'enfant de chœur"); and Sand ("Les oiseaux de passage").[46] Of these poems, "La jeune fille mourante" draws Ségalas most closely into the "sorority" of poets. Lines from Desbordes-Valmore's "Élisa Mercœur" and Mercœur's "Le déclin du jour, une élégie" outline an interior monologue in which the first-person speaker, also known as the expiring Mercœur, gives her own eulogy: "Je vais mourir. Déjà! . . . mourir! . . . oh! c'est horrible! / [ . . . ] / On m'admirait pourtant, moi, fantôme, ombre vaine; / La foule m'entourait comme une jeune reine" (Ségalas, *Les oiseaux de passage*, 178, 179; ellipses in original, except those in square brackets). Ségalas archives other women's texts in her own corpus via the homage paid to Mercœur without, however, consciously invoking a female tradition.[47] In fashioning a more maternal persona from the 1840s onward, Ségalas called herself a "poëte" in relation not to other women, but to a new mission: moral influence.

As hostility against literary women increased in the early 1840s, Ségalas turned to personal lyricism, likely having calculated the risk of publishing other than what was considered womanly (topics related to love and motherhood). In 1844, she published *Enfantines: Poésies à ma fille*, dedicated to her only child, Bertile. That a virtual dialogue between mother and daughter structures the volume resonates with the maternal echoes Aimée Boutin has analyzed in Desbordes-Valmore. Yet, there is no indication that Ségalas was looking back to Valmore's model. In identifying her new voice as maternal, Ségalas "domesticates" her poetic identity: "Cette voix de poëte est une voix de mère: / Le chant est faible, mais sacré" (*Enfantines*, 244). In *La femme: Poésies* (1847), Ségalas shifts from moderate feminism to a conservative stance on women's poetic influence. A similar political move complicates how she engages with French colonial history. As shown in chapter 4, the abolitionism in her verse of the 1830s and '40s cedes to racial prejudice in her prose from the 1850s onward.

## Waldor's Other Legacy

The work of Mélanie Waldor (1796–1871; figs. 8 and 9) also diversifies the sphere in which Romantic era women operated. In her poetry and prose, Waldor promoted women as creators alongside their male peers, developing her literary production as a repository for forgotten or ignored history. Waldor's father, Guillaume Villanelle, a lawyer and book collector, hosted events in their home, exposing her to creative writers and artists. Present at one such gathering in 1827, Alexandre Dumas père was smitten by Waldor.[48] In discussing their liaison, critics have narrowed Waldor's legacy, treating her simply as his muse.[49] Theirs was a fiery affair, inspiring Dumas's play *Antony* (1831), which he described in his *Mémoires* as "une scène d'amour, de jalousie, de colère en cinq actes" (quoted in Croze, "Une héroïne romantique," 170).[50] However, the letters they exchanged from 1827 to 1831 reveal literature as the other passion they shared.[51]

Their correspondence expresses mutual support along with a sense of intellectual equality as avid readers and writers in the literary field. By 1830, Waldor's verse had begun appearing in keepsakes and annuals. In a letter that year, Dumas encouraged her poetic creativity: "Fais des vers, mon amour, et envoie-les moi [*sic*]—puis nous publierons ton recueil et nous soignerons ta réputation poétique qui pousse à merveille en terre parisienne" (Dumas, *Lettres*, 90). Waldor in turn followed his career as a playwright, recognizing his contribution to Romantic

FIG 8
Mélanie Waldor, circa 1830, dressed as the female character Gulnara in Byron's play *The Corsair*. Artist unknown. Photo © AKG-Images/ Gilles Mermet.

FIG 9

Mélanie Waldor by
Julien Léopold Boilly,
n.d. Photo © RMN–
Grand Palais/Art
Resource, New York
(Franck Raux, Musée
Magnin).

theater in 1831, even as their relationship succumbed to his infidelity: "Oh! travaille, tu as un immense avenir de gloire devant toi" (quoted in Dumas, *Lettres*, 151). Waldor also focused on establishing herself as a critic and essayist without, however, claiming the poetic authority she attributed to other women.

In the 1833 essay "De l'influence que les femmes pourraient avoir sur la littérature actuelle," Waldor emphasizes women's output, especially their poetic works, during the 1820s and 1830s.[52] Nothing killed literature, writes Waldor, "comme un travail à tant la page" (223). For her, in resisting the mercantile trend with their deeply reflective and heartfelt writing, women would leave a profound legacy. Waldor thus anticipated Sainte-Beuve's 1839 stance against "la littérature industrielle," influenced by his perspective as the literary editor for the *Revue des Deux Mondes* since 1831.[53] Sainte-Beuve opposed the book industry in his reviews of women's poetry, which preserve the aura of femininity associated with private spaces, such as literary salons and the home. By praising "the kind of elegiac, sentimental lyricism that mirrored his own—or rather, his poetic alter ego Joseph Delorme's—poetry," Patrick Vincent argues, Sainte-Beuve effectively "imagined the poetess's role as one of resistance to these institutional changes" (*Romantic*

*Poetess*, 123). Whereas Sainte-Beuve stressed women's modesty more than their craft, Waldor celebrated the power with which women had emerged as writers in post-revolutionary France.[54]

Poetic women's rise to prominence had required tremendous energy since the drive for intellectual equality expressed by Constance de Salm in her "Épître aux femmes" (1797): "Si la nature a fait deux sexes différens, / Elle a changé la forme et non les élémens" (quoted in Waldor, "De l'influence," 223). Never had women's intellect been championed with such force and enthusiasm, and Salm's poem planted "les germes du génie" (224). Women, who also had male supporters, promised to exert a lasting influence on French literature. Waldor names Babois, Dufrénoy, Tastu, Desbordes-Valmore, Ségalas, and Mercœur among the poets who had shaped the recent past and present. Regarding Desbordes-Valmore, who had just published *Les pleurs* (1833), Waldor comments: "Sa vie, toute d'amour et de souffrance, l'a fait poète" (225). Here, a woman's life and creative work are not mutually exclusive. Waldor's wording "l'a fait poète" also leaves gender out of the equation, suggesting instead the element of pain recognized by poets of both genders as crucial to the Romantic aesthetic.

In reviewing *Les pleurs* some two months later, Sainte-Beuve perceived "de grands rapports d'instincts et de génie naturel" between Lamartine and Desbordes-Valmore ("Mᵐᵉ Desbordes-Valmore," 250). Though the male poet displays more power, for Sainte-Beuve, they belong to the same Romantic tradition: "[T]oute proportion gardée de force et de sexe, ils sont l'un et l'autre de la même famille de poètes" (250). A decade later, in endorsing the 1842 edition of Desbordes-Valmore's *Poésies*, Sainte-Beuve removed this hierarchy to identify her as an originator. To the contrary, Waldor never wavered on the question of Desbordes-Valmore's creativity, in particular as their voices intersected. Some contemporaries viewed Desbordes-Valmore and Waldor as equals, yet they retained uneven places not only in each other's archive but also in poetic history.[55]

The sororal network in Paris, which Desbordes-Valmore first discussed in 1833 in letters to her husband, included Tastu, Babois, and Waldor; Mercœur received only a passing mention. It remains unclear why Desbordes-Valmore did not record Waldor in her own corpus via a poem or epigraph. Desbordes-Valmore did support her peer's literary aspirations, but mostly in correspondence. One of Waldor's romances graced the pages of the *Almanach des Grâces* in 1833, thanks to Desbordes-Valmore, who evoked their kinship in writing to her on 2 November 1833: "*Il faut sourire*, ce brave éditeur a été heureux d'avoir nos deux noms qui riment comme nos pauvres cœurs" (Desbordes-Valmore, *Correspondance intime*, 1:47; emphasis in original).[56] In 1834, regarding a preview of Waldor's collected verse, which she called "doux et beaux," Desbordes-Valmore wrote to Waldor, "J'étais persuadée aussi du soin élégant que vous apporteriez au volume de vos poésies" (1:77).

Waldor gave a stronger sense of Desbordes-Valmore's place in the context of her own trajectory. In the dedicatory poem "À Madame Marceline Desbordes-Valmore," previously discussed in relation to how poetic women joined the broader debate on genius, Waldor gauges her talent against her contemporary's gift: "Le souffle du génie / A caressé ton front sans s'arrêter au mien" (*Poésies du cœur*, 37). But Waldor invokes Desbordes-Valmore as a peer, not as a foremother.[57] They are joined as "poètes par le cœur," states Waldor, echoing the volume's epigraph: "Le cœur seul est poète, ô Chénier! tu l'as dit" (37). Waldor recalls how Desbordes-Valmore's verse first resonated in her soul as a "chant divin," linking poetic creativity with transcendence: "Nos noms, nos cœurs, nos lyres / N'ont eu qu'un même accord" (36). As one critic later noted, the poet in Waldor was effusive and philosophical: "derrière cette âme de femme qui jaillit de chacune de ses poésies il y a une intelligence de philosophe" (Grandeffe, *La pie bas-bleu*, 179).

A sense of loss pervades Waldor's *Poésies du cœur* (1835),[58] suggestive of the grief in Musset's "La nuit de mai" (1835): "Rien ne nous rend si grands qu'une grande douleur. / . . . / Les plus désespérés sont les chants les plus beaux, / Et j'en sais d'immortels qui sont de purs sanglots" (*Poésies complètes*, 304).[59] Melancholy and mourning, however, form a capacious framework for Waldor's poetic inspiration. Sentimental poems (such as "Souvenirs," "Rêverie," "Regrets," and "Jalousie") merge with philosophical verse about the search for meaning and truth (such as "L'amour et l'ambition" and "La foi") as well as art ("À David, statuaire"), history ("La France," "Légende polonaise"), and poetry ("À Madame la duchesse d'Abrantès," "À Madame Victoire Babois"). Waldor's volume knits together lived and imagined experiences, reverberating with the multiplicity of voices she engages as a reader and writer.

Waldor's use of paratexts in *Poésies du cœur* demonstrates her sophistication via a broad cultural history that integrates men and women. Goethe, Dumas, Pierre-Simon Ballanche, Pierre Gavarny, Jean-Baptiste de Pongerville, Soulié, Casimir Delavigne, Eugène Sue, and Hugo are among the male peers she invokes. Women named or cited include Ségalas, Hortense de Céré-Barbé, Aimée Harelle, Louise Arbey, Tastu, Salm, Mercœur, Ernestine Panckoucke, and Constance Aubert (née d'Abrantès). A dialogic structure joins celebrated dedicatees with the authors Waldor cites in her poems. These multilateral links texture the fifty-three poems in her volume as a conversation and reflection among artists and writers. Thought tempers spontaneity as work shapes feelings into poetic art that also records history, some now forgotten. In *Poésies du cœur*, like elsewhere,[60] Waldor's œuvre performs vital archival work by identifying other members of the community of poets that passed down Romantic traditions, voices later silenced by editors and critics.

The more visible paratexts, in particular prefaces, shape understanding of the editorial context in which women's poetic legacies evolved across the century. Sainte-Beuve, for example, prefaced the 1842 edition of Desbordes-Valmore's *Poésies*. She could not have imitated Lamartine, insists Sainte-Beuve, harking back to the 1820 edition of *Poésies*: "Il m'est bien clair quand je tiens ce volume-là, de cette date, qu'elle n'avait pu lire encore Lamartine, dont les *Méditations* ne paraissaient qu'au moment même" (Desbordes-Valmore, *Poésies*, v). Sainte-Beuve recognizes her genius without marking it by sex, as he did in reviewing *Les pleurs* (1833): "Eh bien! Voilà un génie charmant, léger, plaintif, rêveur, désolé, le génie de l'élégie et de la romance, qui se fait entendre sur ces tons pour la première fois: il ne doit rien qu'à son propre cœur" (v).[61] The originality Sainte-Beuve attributes to Desbordes-Valmore predates her overshadowing of all other women after her canonization in the 1890s: "Que pourriez-vous lui comparer dans nos poètes, et surtout dans nos poètes-femmes d'auparavant?" (vi).

Despite how strongly Sainte-Beuve endorsed Desbordes-Valmore's 1842 poetic volume, in a letter to Frédéric Lepeytre the same year, she lamented the poor value assigned to women's writing, now a separate category of literature: "Ce que l'on appelle *littérature de femme* ne produit pas plus que le travail d'aiguille" (Desbordes-Valmore, *Lettres inédites*, 142; emphasis in original). Like other women, she found outlets for her prose, primarily focused on mothers and children,[62] yet struggled to survive. In 1843, though her poetic volume *Bouquets et prières* had appeared, Desbordes-Valmore wrote to Waldor: "Moi, chère amie, je porte avec résignation la monotonie d'une destinée grave" (*Correspondance intime*, 2:98). Self-cast as the *mater dolorosa*, Desbordes-Valmore published stories,[63] but no poetry in the 1850s, the final decade of her life. It was at this time that her relationship with Waldor unraveled.

FIG 10
Marceline Desbordes-Valmore by Nadar, 1854. Digital image courtesy Getty Museum's Open Content Program.

Waldor had virtually abandoned poetry since the mid-1830s, establishing herself primarily as a novelist. She was still confused with Desbordes-Valmore (fig. 10), however, because of their rhyming names. This confusion exasperated Desbordes-Valmore not only in the case of a custody suit between Waldor and Valmore's son-in-law in 1853,[64] but also when Valmore was accused of having published verse against Hugo in 1855. In self-defense, Desbordes-Valmore wrote: "Ce qu'il y a de douloureux dans la similitude des noms, c'est que je reçois toutes sortes de lettres à ce sujet, les unes de louanges, les autres de mépris et d'indignation" (quoted in Pougin, *La jeunesse de Marceline Desbordes-Valmore*, 359). Waldor expressed her allegiance to the imperialist government against the exiled Hugo,[65] which alienated her from Desbordes-Valmore, who had always taken the people's side.

Yet another poet, the latecomer Colet, expressed no sense of a sorority of poets in launching her career in the mid-1830s or later, in the mid-1840s, when she crossed paths with Desbordes-Valmore. Posterity would forget the passion that inspired Colet's poetic creativity by focusing on her notoriety as a passionate woman who counted Flaubert among her lovers.

### Colet the Poet: Flaubert's Other Muse

The first poetic collection of Louise Colet (1810–1876; fig. 11), *Fleurs du Midi* (1836), opens with "Tourments du poète." The aspiring poet imagines the posterity she seeks in terms of two Romantic authorities cited in the opening epigraphs. Taken from Chateaubriand, the first epigraph below measures the journey of sacrifice to glory—associated with genius—against the weight of tradition:

> Après tout, qu'importent les revers, si notre nom, prononcé dans la postérité, va faire battre un cœur généreux deux mille ans après notre vie?[66]
>
> Amour, vertu, génie, tout ce qui a honoré l'homme, l'homme l'a persécuté. (Colet, *Poésies complètes*, 5)

The second epigraph above, which comes from Staël's *Delphine* (1802; *Œuvres*, 1:779), expands its own context in Colet's poem: "D'amour, de poésie, [Dieu] a pétri mon âme, / Et j'ai dû lutter seule avec un double feu" (Colet, *Poésies complètes*, 6). Indeed, Colet fought to justify being born female and a poet, one who searched for inspiration and feared its lack, as expressed in the 1833 poem "L'inspiration": "J'implorais, pour donner un corps à ma pensée, / Ton langage éthéré, musique, écho d'Éden!" (17). Colet's poem "Enthousiasme," dated July 1834, evokes the ardor with which she sought to develop her gift, "cet enthousiasme auquel on doit un culte" (15). She qualifies her early verse as being "sans art," but does not align herself with Desbordes-Valmore, Tastu, and Waldor (16). Rather, as

FIG 11
Louise Colet by
Charles-Philippe-
Auguste Carey.
From Mirecourt, *Les
contemporains* (1857).

expressed in the dedicatory poem "Chateaubriand et Lamartine," Colet identifies her gift with the "génie inspiré" of male poets touched by the creative breath of God (37–39).[67]

Undaunted by a culture obsessed with feminine propriety, Colet took her poetic work seriously. Kennedy Fraser imagines Colet in the mid-1830s, "jump[ing] feet first into the city's seething literary scene. She was a lovely woman who wanted to be valued as a first-rate poet. She chased after publishers, critics, and any great men who could help her get prizes, subsidies, or a blurb. . . . She was a genius at keeping herself in the public eye" (*Ornament and Silence*, 107). For the poet Pierre-Ange Vieillard de Boismartin, Colet's *Penserosa: Poésies nouvelles* (1840) reveals scholarly breadth.[68] The biographer Eugène de Mirecourt suggests that the year 1842 marked Colet's peak, her "gloire poétique à son apogée" (*Les contemporains*, 34). However, that same year, Paul de Molènes included Colet in his dismissive account of Romantic era "poetesses," ridiculing her *Fleurs du Midi* while accusing her of servile imitation that bordered on plagiarism: "C'est une effrayante abondance de mots et de tours empruntés au langage des poètes en vogue" ("Simples essais d'histoire littéraire," 72).[69]

In prefacing her *Poésies complètes* (1844), Colet responds to such criticism. She does not consider her development in agonistic terms, as a struggle between poets seeking their own voices. Rather, her creative process represents a broader conversation among different *poems*, all expressing similar, yet individual, moments of inspiration: "Une pensée m'a retenue: avais-je cherché à imiter? Non, sincèrement, non: ces chants furent l'écho, peut-être inhabile, mais fidèle, de ce que j'éprouvais alors. Beaucoup de poètes ont traversé ces phases et les ont décrites; ce n'est pas qu'ils se soient copiés l'un l'autre; c'est qu'avant d'atteindre à l'originalité, ils ont passé . . . par des sensations douloureuses et délicates traduites en plaintes élégiaques qui se ressemblent naturellement entre elles" (ii). Colet positions her voice by invoking the category of originality, now used to identify a poet of genius. While Colet's persona recalls Mercœur's from the perspective of Romantic era women's production discussed to this point, a philosophical quality ties both of them to Tastu and their erudition to Waldor. Colet's feminist principles also recall the young Ségalas. Desbordes-Valmore, however, was peripheral to Colet's poetic trajectory.

In 1841, Colet made a late entry into Desbordes-Valmore's circle via the salon of patron of the arts Juliette Récamier. The biographer Francis Ambrière suggests that scruples and the memory of her own indiscretions might explain why Desbordes-Valmore kept her distance from Colet (*Le siècle des Valmore*, 2:227–46). It was not until 1845 that an exchange about *La Corbeille*, a keepsake to which both women contributed, gave Colet occasion to contact Desbordes-Valmore directly. Subsequently, Colet sought Desbordes-Valmore's support when she was accused by the families of Mme Récamier and Benjamin Constant of having manipulated Récamier. Upon Récamier's death, Colet published correspondence with Constant that Récamier had entrusted to her. The case went to trial, and publication of the letters was halted as a result.

Interspersed with Ambrière's retelling of the affair are Desbordes-Valmore's 1848 letters to Colet. Desbordes-Valmore wrote a poem for Colet, reproduced by Ambrière as proof of Desbordes-Valmore's attachment to Colet at a time when she felt extremely isolated. One finds therein a faithful transposition of Colet's self-portrait ("Dieu me fit poète"): "Car c'est pour nous aussi que Dieu fit votre voix!" (quoted in Ambrière, *Le siècle des Valmore*, 2:231). Colet dedicates her volume *Ce qui est dans le cœur des femmes: Poésies nouvelles* (1852) to Desbordes-Valmore.[70] However, the title of the volume is misleading, for the power Colet reveals in this collection is more intellectual than sentimental. Flaubert had long since recognized and encouraged this aspect of Colet's poetic expression.

The Flaubert-Colet correspondence, spanning the years from 1846 to mid-1848 and 1851 to 1855, shifts from the throes of passion to a mutual love of literature. Like the Dumas-Waldor letters, this corpus is not complete from both sides. Colet's letters to Flaubert were destroyed, allowing her legacy as a writer to be absorbed into her role as Flaubert's muse. The letters Flaubert wrote to Colet reveal not only "the writer's struggle with his own literary efforts" but also the role of anatomy and physiology in his gendering of style (Beizer, *Ventriloquized Bodies*, 77; see the analysis 76–95). His missives during the first phase of their relationship maintain the gap between women and the work of art, as in this letter of 6–7 August 1846: "Les femmes qui ont le cœur trop ardent et l'esprit trop exclusif ne comprennent pas cette religion de la beauté abstraction faite du sentiment" (Flaubert, *Correspondance*, 1:278). In a letter the next day, 8 August 1846, Flaubert stresses to Colet, whom he praises for her beauty as well as her intelligence, that literary creation involves labor: "[T]ravaille, aime l'art" (1:283).[71] The latter is the source of the rift that develops between them, as expressed in his letter to Colet on 2 September 1846: "Oh, va, aime plutôt l'Art que moi" (1:325). What divides Flaubert from Colet is the line between inspiration and genius, that is, subjective lyricism and the objectivity of art, described in his letter of 14 September 1846: "Je veux dire qu'il me semble que tu n'adores pas beaucoup le Génie, que tu ne tressailles pas jusque dans tes entrailles à la contemplation du beau. Ce n'est pas tout d'avoir des ailes. Il faut qu'elles vous portent" (1:342). In the collection of poems Colet dedicates to Desbordes-Valmore, she reinscribes aesthetic ideas from her letters to Flaubert, which counter his critique of her Romantic sensibility.

*Ce qui est dans le cœur des femmes* restores the gist of Colet's side of her conversations with Flaubert about aesthetics.[72] A cluster of poems links the love of art with passion in two different, but closely related, senses of suffering and desire. This rhetoric of contrasts involves the quest for the ideal developed by Colet, who transposes her exchanges with Flaubert in terms of the encounter between Romanticism and realism. "L'art et l'amour" (1846) begins by restating Flaubert's counsel to his new lover, Colet, who was already an established poet and was eleven years his senior. She discloses his principle of aesthetic creation, that is, sublimating passion into art:

> Tu me dis: Aime l'art, il vaut mieux que l'amour;
> Tout sentiment s'altère et doit périr un jour!
> Pour que le cœur devienne une immortelle chose,
> Il faut qu'en poésie il se métamorphose.
>
> . . . . . . . . . . . . . . . .
>
> Sentir, c'est aspirer! . . . c'est encore la souffrance;
> Mais créer, c'est jouir, c'est prouver sa puissance;
> C'est faire triompher de la mort, de l'oubli,
> Toutes les passions dont l'âme a tressailli!
>
> Et moi, je te réponds: La langue du poëte
> Ne rend du sentiment que l'image incomplète;
>
> . . . . . . . . . . . . . . . .
>
> Et ne t'es-tu pas dit, du réel t'enivrant:
> La beauté seule est belle, et l'amour seul est grand!
>
> (Colet, *Ce qui est dans le cœur des femmes*, 5–7)

Interwoven in the virtual conversation between creative peers is another trace of the lost archive, which illumines the Platonic élan in Colet.

One can read between the lines of Colet's poem "Sonnet" (1847), which invokes Flaubert as a creator ("Veillant et travaillant, ô mon noble poëte"), the epistolary echo of Flaubert as an appreciative reader of her verse: "Où tu m'as dit: Je t'aime et je relis tes vers" (*Ce qui est dans le cœur des femmes*, 95, 96).[73] In the sonnet "Orgueil" (1847), the speaker wrestles with the pain of forsaken love, exposing the desire for perfection linked with inspiration: A desire at once corporeal and mental suffuses the creative impulse. Life, like art, falls short of the ideal, as Colet expresses in "Deuil" (1851) and "Le rayon intérieur" (1852). Whereas the Romantic finds reality flat, the realist considers Romanticism hollow. Both, however, fail to grasp Plato's world of perfect ideas evoked in "Veillée" (1852):

> Les autres n'étaient que des fantômes pâles,
> Repoussant mon cœur d'un cœur épouvanté;
> Mais toi, fier amant des choses idéales,
> De ma passion t'émut l'immensité!
>
> Tu la sentis vraie et tu compris en elle,
> Ainsi que dans l'art, ta passion, à toi,
> Était contenue une essence éternelle;
> Ton cœur s'attendrit, et tu revins à moi!
>
> Dans tes visions d'homme et de poëte
> Passa l'idéal, et vers lui tu marchas;
> . . . . . . . . . . . . . .
> Va, je le sais bien que l'idéal échappe;
> . . . . . . . . . . . . . .
> Va, je le sais que jamais n'est saisie
> L'altière beauté qui plane devant nous.
> À notre toucher s'enfuit la poésie,
> Et comme la mort nos bonheurs sont dissous.
>
> Va, je le sais bien que l'impossible attire;
> Que tu cherchais ce qui te manque en moi.
>
> (115, 116, 117)

"Veillée" represents Colet's hybrid production. The thinker complements Colet the poet crowned by the Académie française for *Le musée de Versailles* (1839), *Le monument de Molière* (1843), *La colonie de Mettray* (1852), and *L'acropole d'Athènes* (1855).[74] Regarding the latter text, Mirecourt writes, "La poésie en est grande et simple tout à la fois; elle caractérise merveilleusement, selon nous, le génie de l'auteur, qui appartient au romantisme par le fond et au génie classique par la forme" (*Les contemporains*, 77). Unsympathetic critics, however, attributed Colet's awards to her connections with men in positions of power, especially the philosopher Victor Cousin, who was also her lover. But she did not remain silent: "Nous avons concouru quatre fois pour le prix de poésie, et quatre fois nous l'avons remporté. Comme cela n'était jamais arrivé à aucune femme, le public s'est étonné, et quelques-uns ont crié à la faveur. Nous avons repoussé du sourire, et aujourd'hui nous repoussons de la parole cette opinion. Chaque fois que nous avons eu le prix, la protection a été accordée à l'œuvre, jamais à la personne" (quoted in Mirecourt, *Les contemporains*, 78–79).[75] By writing back to their critics in prefaces, epigraphs, and poems, women like Colet shaped their own poetic identity for posterity. Those women who emerged as poets during the second half of the century responded in various ways to Desbordes-Valmore's self-fashioning of a feminine voice, which the more conservative critics made from the 1860s onward the principal legacy of all "femmes poètes."

## Valmore's Dual Legacy

In the last collection of poetry she published during her lifetime, *Bouquets et prières* (1843), Desbordes-Valmore maintained the persona she had crafted throughout her career. Her preface, titled "Une plume de femme," begins thus: "Courez, ma plume, courez: vous savez bien qui vous l'ordonne" (1). Desbordes-Valmore describes herself as long-suffering and weak as well as untrained ("mes doigts ignorants"), displacing agency from the author to the pen, as Schultz observes (*Gendered Lyric*, 56). "Desbordes-Valmore, knowing what she was up against," adds Schultz, "artfully protected herself with the image of artlessness" (57). Boutin proposes that the "backlash against women poets effectively prevented the second generation of nineteenth-century women poets from espousing Desbordes-Valmore as a model or even seeking a feminine tradition of any kind" ("Marceline Desbordes-Valmore," 172).[76] But, perhaps, later poets championed other models to escape the category of "femme poète," as Planté argues, a category that placed them in Valmore's shadow (*Femmes poètes du XIX^e siècle*, 41–42).

In a quatrain attached to the poem "Renoncement," Desbordes-Valmore expresses this bequest: "Que mon nom ne soit rien qu'une ombre douce et vaine" (*Œuvres poétiques*, 2:547). This, in effect, was the feminine aura as well as the greatness attached to Desbordes-Valmore's name. Homage paid to Desbordes-Valmore at her gravesite on 4 August 1859 included Vigny's calling her "le plus grand esprit féminin de notre temps" (quoted in Sainte-Beuve, *Madame Desbordes-Valmore*, 243). Hugo's tribute identified the woman with the poet: "Vous êtes la femme même, vous êtes la poésie même" (244). The dolorous, Marian figure eulogized by Sainte-Beuve that day would continue to echo. In "Celle qui chantait," for example, Banville makes pain the font of Desbordes-Valmore's poetic genius, her voice embodying an inner cry: "La douleur, qui fut ton génie, / T'arrachait de tremblants aveux" (quoted in Desbordes-Valmore, *Œuvres poétiques*, 2:811).

In reviewing Desbordes-Valmore's *Poésies inédites* (1860), Émile Montégut lamented how the public had always misread her, her reputation constructed *avant la lettre*: "Le nom de M^me Desbordes-Valmore réveillait en lui l'idée d'une femme poète, auteur de vers faciles, mélodieux, élégans: il la considérait comme un écho de la poésie lyrique de ce siècle et la rattachait au groupe de l'école romantique; il n'a jamais su très nettement qu'elle ne devait sa poésie qu'à elle-même, et qu'elle était, dans le genre qui lui était propre, un poète aussi original, sinon aussi puissant, que les grands poètes de l'école romantique" ("Portraits poétiques," 999–1000). The poet Auguste Lacaussade, in a long preface to the 1886 edition of Desbordes-Valmore's complete poetical works, tied her originality to the elegy: "le vrai domaine lyrique de M^me Valmore, le champ d'inspirations où son expansif et doux génie se donnait carrière" (*Œuvres poétiques de Marceline Desbordes-Valmore*, xxiii). That same year, Verlaine argued that critical attention drawn to Desbordes-Valmore's gender by Sainte-Beuve, Baudelaire, and Barbey d'Aurevilly, among others, had obscured her creativity, "la seule femme de génie et de talent de ce siècle et de tous les siècles, en compagnie de Sapho peut-être, et de sainte Thérèse" (*Les poètes maudits*, 62). Her reputation loomed large by the end of the nineteenth century, as captured by this line from Verlaine's 1895 poem evoking the woman and the genius: "O grande Marceline, ô sublime poète" (quoted in Desbordes-Valmore, *Œuvres poétiques*, 2:826).[77] In a sonnet that Verlaine composed to commemorate the bronze statue of Desbordes-Valmore, which Montesquiou had arranged to have erected in her hometown of Douai in 1896, he wrote: "Et ton œuvre de mère à jamais survivra!" (2:826). By this, Verlaine meant that she was a precursor, the first poet of her time to use the eleven-syllable line. But because of the feminine shadow cast on Valmore as emotional, women seeking to position themselves as poets from the 1850s onward either looked past her or openly contested her as a model. They wanted to disengage their poetic works from their gender.

Malvina Blanchecotte, long employed as a seamstress, was one of these poets and shared common ground with Desbordes-Valmore.[78] Both women came from working-class families and struggled financially all their lives. They were also mothers who wrote sentimental verse and reluctantly turned to prose to earn a living. As the poet and songwriter Pierre Jean de Béranger's protégée, Blanchecotte was drawn into Colet's literary salon and could very well have met Desbordes-Valmore there. However, I have found no mention of Desbordes-Valmore in Blanchecotte's writings. Apart from a single epigraph in *Les militantes* (1875), where she quotes Colet, Blanchecotte does not establish links with other women (49). Rather, she aligns herself with Lamartine, but positions her voice between categories.

In a letter Blanchecotte wrote to Lamartine four years before her first volume, *Rêves et réalités* (1855), appeared, she forges her creative identity as a poet *and* a worker:

[V]otre nom est le premier mot que mes doigts ont formé; vos vers sont la première musique dont mon cœur se souvienne; votre influence politique fut la source de mes premières pensées sérieuses de patrie et de révolution. . . .

Je n'ose pas espérer, Monsieur de Lamartine, que vous vous souviendrez d'une ouvrière, très pauvre, un peu souffrante et encore enfant, que vous reçûtes plusieurs fois, qui vous écrivit souvent. (Quoted in Blanchecotte, *Tablettes d'une femme*, vii)

A concern with originality and origins, both from the Latin *origo* ("beginning" or "source"), underlies the word "premier," which Blanchecotte repeats three times in close proximity to claim Lamartine, the poet turned statesman, as the source of her poetic development and class consciousness.[79] Born and raised under the July Monarchy in France (1830–48), she witnessed the bourgeoisie rise and workers fight for civic status. In blending Romantic and Parnassian aesthetics, Blanchecotte would bridge manual and cognitive labor to consider the relationship between work and cultural capital as she questioned the masculine traditions that defined genius.

Louisa Siefert (fig. 12) also invoked a male precursor to dispute having been categorized as a carrier of "la poésie féminine." In prefacing the second edition of Siefert's inaugural volume, *Rayons perdus* (1868), Charles Asselineau casts her voice as Valmore's echo: "Et Elle . . . celle de qui on l'a rapprochée comme une digne élève, la grande femme-poëte du XIXe siècle, Marceline Valmore, de quels sourires

FIG 12
Louisa Siefert, *carte de visite*, n.d. Photo: Bibliothèque nationale de France.

maternels . . . n'eût-elle pas salué cet essor d'un jeune talent où revivent ses ten-
dresses & son génie!" (*Rayons perdus*, viii). In "Sur la première page de *Joseph
Delorme*," a sonnet composed in July 1869 and published in *Les stoïques* (1870),
Siefert reveals Sainte-Beuve and his sonnet practice as her model:

> Chacun a son poëte entre tous préféré,
> Interprète choisi de sa pensée intime,
> Ami sûr qu'on recherche, idéale victime
> Dont on fait son écho, son modèle inspiré

(94)

A roster of favorite poets forms an alternative anatomy of influence in a nonlinear
manner. Siefert thinks aesthetically as she distills, in the stanza closing the octave
and the subsequent stanza opening the sestet, the century's turn from Romanticism
to Parnassianism with hints of Symbolism:

> Les uns ont Lamartine, & les autres André;
> Hugo, le fier génie au vol ample & sublime;
> Gautier, l'inimitable artiste, avec sa lime;
> Musset, avec sa lyre & son verre doré
>
> Sans le savoir ainsi chacun donne sa norme;
> Et souvent, inconstance ou d'humeur ou d'amour,
> Après Valmore en pleurs Baudelaire a son tour.

(94)

Here, Siefert responds to Asselineau not by singling out Valmore as a poetic fore-
mother, as he did, but by reducing her voice to tears. No other woman is named,
which is consistent with the aesthetic choice that Siefert makes to anchor her place
as a poet: "Pour moi, c'est Sainte-Beuve & son Joseph Delorme, / Martyr mystérieux
d'un rêve inaperçu, / Cœur qu'il faut deviner & chant qu'on n'a pas su!" (94). The
hero of Sainte-Beuve's *Vie, poésies et pensées de Joseph Delorme* (1829) recalls Cha-
teaubriand's *René* or Goethe's *Werther*. Yet Sainte-Beuve distinguished himself
from other Romantics through the sonnet he revived from Ronsard, which Siefert
adopted.[80]

Moreover, Siefert's choice of Sainte-Beuve distanced her from Desbordes-
Valmore, who was as explicit as Hugo about rejecting the classical genre: "[C]e
genre régulier n'appartient qu'à l'homme, qui se fait une joie de triompher de sa
pensée même en l'enfermant dans cette entrave brillante" (*Lettres*, 1:151).[81] One
could align Siefert as a practitioner of the sonnet with Baudelaire, who "found in
its very constraints the beauty of the form," as Schultz observes (*Gendered Lyric*,
77).[82] Aesthetics sideline the inscription of gender when one considers that the
Renaissance poet Louise Labé, who mastered the sonnet alongside her male peers,

is the only woman with whom Siefert established a link.[83] Siefert did not align herself with feminine tradition, nor did she express a feminist sensibility, that is, a perception of herself as a woman writer. By invoking Sainte-Beuve, who recovered the sonnet and thus the shared origins of modern French lyricism, Siefert claimed the various subject positions she explored beyond gender to cultivate the dialogism that constitutes poetic voice.

In a similar manner to Siefert, Louise Ackermann did not write in ignorance of women's poetic production, but rather rebuffed being associated with any feminine, feminized, or feminist tradition. Ackermann expressed little sympathy for Romanticism and even less for the elegy cultivated by Desbordes-Valmore: "M^me Valmore est l'élégie même. Sa plainte éternelle a quelque chose de maladif. Pendant quarante ans, elle a chanté la même note. Les gens qui aiment cette note doivent être dans le ravissement. Ceux qui n'ont pas le goût particulier pour cette note unique peuvent la trouver monotone" ("Journal," 538). Possibly written in response to Baudelaire's essay on Desbordes-Valmore, which had appeared in the *Revue Fantaisiste* on 1 July 1861, Ackermann's statement of 22 July 1861 conveys her own break with subjective lyricism in taking a scientific approach to the pain of being human.

Although Romantic idealism informs some of the verse Ackermann wrote in the late 1820s and 1830s, her philosophical poetry in the 1870s exhibits Parnassian objectivity. In retrospective accounts of her poetic development, she insists that her pessimism about the limits of science is intellectual. Ackermann thus deflects being read as a late female Romantic, identifying herself instead as a creative thinker. To this point, André Thérive characterizes Ackermann as the anti-Valmore: "On range ce type féminin à l'opposé de Marceline Desbordes, la froide pessimiste en regard de la douce blessée" ("À propos de Mme Ackermann," 142). Jeanine Moulin further elaborates Ackermann's unique place in French poetic history: "Première femme écrivain à échapper aux écoles littéraires, Louise Ackermann est aussi le premier poète du XIXe siècle à exprimer avec art la philosophie et la science de son temps. Imprégnée de Darwin, de Comte et de Schopenhauer, elle refuse Dieu mais en souffre profondément" (*La poésie féminine*, 286).

Marie Krysinska questioned the established narratives of religion and science as deeply as Ackermann did, claiming no precursor. In separating the woman from the poet more resolutely than any of her predecessors examined to this point, Krysinska makes the evolution of poetic form the subject of her œuvre. The free-verse poetry Krysinska produced from 1879 to 1903 engages the history of ideas on women and their relationship to creativity, which she challenges to rethink the work (in the conjoining senses of effort and output) of originality. Krysinska theorizes "le propre du Génie" with her own *vers libre* in mind, its work made manifest through a break with the past, which forms tradition anew (*Intermèdes*, v).

The diverse trajectories brought to light in this chapter, from the poets who surrounded Desbordes-Valmore to those who pursued a career after her, show that few women discovered their voices through links with female peers. They claimed instead affinities with male precursors or, more boldly, with no forebear, testing categories of analysis and new forms of expression to disengage creativity from gender. In reading each other, women also envisaged their own history, resisting in different ways critics' attempts to homogenize so-called poésie féminine. Yet they all operated with the understanding that "the term 'woman poet' has no meaning, not intellectually, not morally, not historically. A poet is a poet."[84] To recover the ideological work of women's poetic output and relate it to their imaginative and critical prose, I next chart their intellectual legacy across the nineteenth century, using the case of Ségalas to further develop the range of Romantic era women's voices. I examine Ségalas's poetry in its original context to show how the traditional reception of her work has obscured the questions of race and gender she raised by thinking through France's neocolonial enterprise as it gained force across the century.

# PART TWO

## Women Thinking Through Poetry and Beyond

# 4

## Anaïs Ségalas on Race, Gender, and "la mission civilisatrice"

The slave uprising of 1791 in the French colony of Saint-Domingue sparked the war for independence that ended in 1804 with the founding of the first black republic under the island's original name of Haiti.[1] Nearly concurrently, in 1788, one year before the French Revolution, activists of both genders established the Société des amis des noirs in Paris. The antislavery movement in France, which was suppressed in the wake of *les massacres de Saint-Domingue*, reorganized during the 1820s.[2] Political debate that centered on the gradual versus immediate abolition of slavery spread to the literary realm. In Romantic era women's writing, abolitionist and feminist currents overlapped without, however, always merging. Various political stances thus diversify the way women's literary works archive the colonial past, as does the multiplicity of their poetic voices and individual legacies. As illustrated by the writings of Anaïs Ségalas (1811–1893; fig. 13), the ideological drift of individual authors further complicates the intersection between literature and history. The Parisian-born writer's poetry in the 1830s and '40s leaned toward the emancipatory projects that linked feminists and abolitionists. A Eurocentric view of history surfaces in this verse, however, which adumbrates Ségalas's conservative turn at mid-century toward the civilizing mission declared by France under the Third Republic and the racist overtones of her related prose from the 1850s and later decades.[3]

In this chapter I examine the colonial strand of Ségalas's verse and prose, spanning the years from 1831 to 1885, to illumine the impact of gender, memory, reading, and collective attitudes on her engagement with history.[4] The Romantic era, which coincided with renewed abolitionism and the definitive end of slavery in France's colonies in 1848, provides the broader context in which I analyze her poetry. Racial physiology emerged during the same period, however, bracing

FIG 13
Anaïs Ségalas by
Pierre Petit, n.d.
Photo: Archives
Larousse, Paris /
Bridgeman Images.

aggressive empire building from the mid-century forward. Ségalas conveys this radical sociopolitical shift through her appraisal of race before and after the abolition of slavery, which I trace from her early verse to late prose. The depth and permanence of Ségalas's interest in France's colonial empire challenges the accounts of literary history that ignore her unique contribution to understanding the rise of French colonialism in the nineteenth century.

Women disputed the inferiority of blacks and females, beginning with the political activist Olympe de Gouges, the author of "Réflexions sur les hommes nègres" (1788) and "Déclaration des droits de la femme et de la citoyenne" (1791). This intellectual element often mingled with empathy in French women's antislavery prose and poetry. Only the sentimental aspect, however, prevailed for critics who later ascribed the colonial topics addressed by women writers in the 1820s and '30s to the Romantic yearning for the exotic fueled by "le goût des voyages" and "la fièvre de lectures comme les *Natchez* ou *Paul et Virginie*" (Pilon, "Les muses plaintives du romantisme," 207).[5] Ségalas's output, however, extends well past the issue of slavery, which captured the "distanced imagination" of male and female pre-Romantics as well as their successors.[6] Her original path of thought tracks the rise of biological racism and its influence on French colonial expansion, expressing the individuality of creative genius.

## Slavery and the Romantic Imagination

Staël located her novella *Mirza; ou, Lettre d'un voyageur* (1795) within the French Atlantic triangle. Ximéo's relationship with Ourika (a woman of his tribe to whom he was promised in marriage) and Mirza (a woman of an enemy tribe and a poet of "genius" whom he betrays) is the focal point of Staël's commentary on how Africans' lives were rent asunder by slave trading.[7] The Caribbean island of Saint Barthélemy during the British occupation from 1801 to 1802 is the setting for Desbordes-Valmore's *Sarah* (1821). This novella exposes the inhumanity of slavery from a dual perspective: that of Arsène, a former slave who sells himself back into bondage to protect Sarah, the white Creole in his care, and that of his charge, who is tricked into thinking that she is a slave by a white foreman.

Entwined with the debate over slavery, which seized the literary imagination in the early nineteenth century, was the emergent "scientific" notion of race. Whereas proponents of monogenism, like Buffon, claimed that blacks and whites shared the same origins, polygenists followed Cuvier, arguing that blacks descended from a different ancestral type.[8] In *Histoire naturelle du genre humain* (1801), Virey also drew on skull differences "du nègre et du blanc" to dispute the climatic explanation for different skin tones inherited from the eighteenth century. He theorized instead that color represents an organic difference, asserting that "le genre humain, dans sa totalité, doit se diviser en deux espèces distinctes": the white and the black races (1:436). In a dictionary entry on "Nègre," which invoked Pierre Barrère's 1741 anatomy of black skin, Virey confirmed that "le nègre n'est donc pas seulement nègre à l'extérieur, mais encore dans toutes ses parties, et jusque dans celles qui sont les plus intérieures" ("Nègre," 425).[9] He thus refuted "les amis des noirs," specifically Henri Grégoire (known as Abbé Grégoire), who had stated that blacks possessed genius ("Nègre," 429).[10] In the corresponding entry in the *Dictionnaire des sciences médicales*, Virey insisted that blacks' muscles, tissues, organs, and secretions were all dark in color. Regarding "cette teinture noirâtre," concluded Virey, "[i]l faut donc que cette qualité soit innée et radicale" (388). His physiology, which transposes physical traits into signs of mental capacity and moral attributes, carried through the debate over slavery as well as the biological notion of race that bolstered imperialism.

The question raised early in the nineteenth century about the meaning of race—ancestry versus color—hovers in the background of Claire de Duras's *Ourika* (1823). Set in Paris during the French Revolution and the Reign of Terror (1793–94) that coincided with the rebellion in Saint-Domingue, the novella stems from the true story of a Senegalese girl. Ourika is rescued from a slave ship and raised by an aristocratic French family, whose perspective and experience of persecution she internalizes. Her discovery of her blackness produces a sense of shame and alienation from which she never recovers.[11] While Hugo's *Bug-Jargal* (1826) evokes the early months of the Saint-Domingue revolt, Sophie Doin's *La famille noire* (1825), published the year that France recognized Haiti's independence, takes place after the long revolution. Their narratives show the principal black male characters' humanity and intelligence. In so doing, they contest the narrative of "black terror" grafted onto Toussaint Louverture, the former slave who became a leader of the Haitian revolution.[12] Ségalas's treatment of race does not fit squarely within either the feminist-abolitionist binary or the Romantic resistance to the slave trade and slavery by analogy. Rather, in considering the idea of race from multiple perspectives, Ségalas archives her century's push for the abolition of slavery and the paradox of its ultimate regression to scientific racism.

Although Duras and Desbordes-Valmore had firsthand knowledge of the Caribbean islands,[13] Ségalas never traveled there. She learned about the French colonies from her mother. Biographers generally agree that Ségalas's mother, Anne Bonne-Portier, was a white Creole from Saint-Domingue and that her father, Charles Ménard, hailed from the Picardy region of France.[14] No account mentions when Ségalas's mother arrived in France. Like other French Creoles, she likely fled from the island soon after the slave uprising began. In mistakenly recording that both parents were Creoles, Camille Delaville alludes to Ségalas's appearance: "Leur fille, née à Paris, très parisienne d'esprit et de goût, a physiquement l'aspect des femmes de nos colonies" (*Mes contemporaines*, 69).[15] The British author Charles Hervey remembers Ségalas in a similar fashion from a gathering he attended at Vigny's home: "Mme Anaïs Ségalas was announced, and a lady, apparently on the sunny side of forty, whose dark lustrous eyes and singularly clear complexion sufficiently denoted her Creole origin, entered the room" ("A Reception of Alfred de Vigny's," 486).[16] The sense of Creoleness that Ségalas exploits in her creative production is less obvious, however. The figure of "la belle Créole," in particular, comes laden with ambiguity, for a mixed heritage mingles with a distinctly French European descent in Ségalas's poetry and prose. Germane to the various colonial sites evoked in Ségalas's poetry is the issue of racial identity she first raises in engaging with the history of French conquests.

## The Algerian Conquest

Ségalas's interest in the Antilles was likely nurtured by memories of Saint-Domingue that her mother shared with her. Another major chapter in the history of French colonization, closer to home and to Ségalas's moment, however, unfolds in her first poetic collection. Ségalas's *Les algériennes: Poésies* (1831) commemorates France's conquest of Algiers the preceding year.[17] In prefatory comments, Ségalas invokes as her model Hugo's *Orientales* (1829), a volume inspired by the Greek War of Independence, which portrays the eastern Mediterranean's rich landscapes: "Je résolus de me hasarder dans ce monde nouveau dont M. Victor Hugo nous a montré le chemin; mais, trop faible pour marcher sur les traces d'un si vaste génie, je consacrai peu de vers à la peinture des mœurs Africaines. Dans le reste de cet ouvrage, je n'ai parlé que de la valeur de notre armée, espérant que dans un tel sujet l'admiration m'inspirerait et suppléerait au talent" (*Les algériennes*, 2). Though Ségalas's verse charts new terrain, she purports not to possess enough imagination to transport her readers there, as Hugo had. One can interpret the ambivalent way Ségalas authorizes her poetic work as a strategy to disarm her critics. This ambivalence can be also understood to mirror the uneasy encounter with the exotic other, an encounter that displaces the site of memory from personal experience to the collective domain.

Ségalas's notes to *Les algériennes* add her knowledge of history and current events derived from print culture, including newspapers and books, to the ethos of sympathy highlighted in Romantic era women's antislavery writing. She also nuances her opening treatment of slavery by considering the practice apart from race. In the first poem, "L'esclave," the first-person speaker, not yet identified, challenges the reader to imagine what it means to be a slave: "Esclave! esclave! moi! . . . sais-tu bien, homme libre, / Ce que c'est qu'un esclave?" (5; ellipses in original). From chains to torment, shipwreck, torture, and captivity, servitude begets inhumanity. Ségalas's portrayal condenses the nascent humanitarian argument for the immediate emancipation of black slaves: "Son âme plane aux cieux, son corps est dans la fange" (7). But here in "L'esclave," the slave represents a universal, "un homme animal" (7).

As Ségalas's speaking subject further states, regardless of race or context, once a slave, one becomes an object of exchange: "Être exposé, vendu! . . . mais devenir encor / D'intrépide soldat marchandise Africaine / Qu'un maître possède à prix d'or!" (*Les algériennes*, 9–10; ellipses in original). Ségalas charts an unconventional course for indicting the slave trade by attempting to enter the mind of a "guerrier Français" captured in Algiers. The anxiety about being sold into slavery, on the part of a white French soldier, projected what was a historical reality for black Africans. Even though England had banned slave trading in 1807 and France had followed suit in 1815, the practice continued. Firsthand accounts of the "bloody commerce," to use the subtitle of the British abolitionist Thomas Clarkson's tract, which appeared in French translation in 1821 (*Les cris des Africains*), circulated as part of the antislavery platform that had gained strength in France by the 1830s.[18]

In "L'esclave," the protest against slavery as unjust and cruel drifts to the concerns of the ruling class in France:

> Un maître! . . . Ce mot tue, et d'horreur il pénètre
> L'âme du Français révolté,
> Lui qui n'a point d'esclave et qui n'a point de maître,
> Qui sous son drapeau voit paraître
> La victoire et la liberté.
> (*Les algériennes*, 10; ellipses in original)

Nationalism underlies the speaker's cry for freedom from captivity. The banner of liberty shaken for the French male soldier extends the memory of past French victories. Linked with Napoleon's military campaigns in subsequent poems, the thread of conquest develops the Eurocentric perspective twinned with Bonapartism in *Les algériennes*.

The issue of slavery merges with war in "La captive." Unlike the tour of local color admired by Hugo's subject in a poem of the same title in *Les orientales*, Ségalas's speaker, imprisoned by her Algerian captors, remains fixated on thoughts of "divine France" and her "belle patrie" (*Les algériennes*, 17, 21). It is not that she is blind to the exotic paysage of Algiers, which the poet presents in detail.[19] Instead, the landscape beyond the walls of her prison has no appeal because the prisoner cannot separate herself from the memory of the one who loved her "d'un cœur français" (21). The allegiance in "La captive," as in "L'esclave," is the abiding sense of Frenchness, which is conveyed as imperialism in the way Ségalas next imagines the encounter with the Algerian other.

In juxtaposing "L'arrivée des Français" with "Le cri de guerre des Algériens," Ségalas envisions the battle from the perspectives of both the French and the Algerians.[20] The daily press is the source she claims for locales such as the campsite in "Le jeune soldat," a poem revealing what was at stake for the French. Placed at the heart of the battle, the first-person speaker boasts:

> Le plus beau modèle est la France,
> Et sa gloire est de s'égaler!
> Quelle tâche imposante elle donne à mon zèle!
> Quel plus noble héritage, ô guerriers d'Austerlitz,
> Pouviez-vous, en mourant, confier à vos fils!
>
> (*Les algériennes*, 57–58)

To spur the French to victory, the young soldier recalls another of Napoleon's famous battles:

> France, enorgueillis-toi de tes anciens hauts faits,
> Frissonne de plaisir, comme au jour d'un succès!
> Algériens, craignez notre ardeur meurtrière!
> Soldats, de chants joyeux, frappons tous leur écho!
> Et couronnons de fleurs nos armes qu'on révère:
> Voici l'auguste anniversaire
> Du jour sacré de Marengo!
>
> (60)[21]

The colonial dimension of the French invasion fades against the backdrop of the Napoleonic wars. So, too, the ground of combat shifts from race to gender as the poet extends the call to patriotic arms to all women and as she thinks across cultures.

In her notes to "La captive," Ségalas comments, "Les Algériens, qui regardent les femmes comme des esclaves, ont soin d'en appareiller de toutes les nations et de toutes les couleurs" (*Les algériennes*, 131–32).[22] Women's condition was universal; the institution of marriage enslaved women in France, as characterized by Sand in *Indiana* (1832).[23] In "Les Françaises à Alger," Ségalas combats sexism by celebrating two French women who made headlines when they were decorated with the Légion d'honneur for their valor on the battlefield:

> L'une, affrontant la mort, et s'offrant en échange
> D'un malheureux blessé, succombant sous les coups,
> À l'amour du pays joint l'amour d'un époux;
> Et son glaive à la main le remplace et le venge:
> L'autre a vu mutiler son corps noble et guerrier;
> Cette illustre victime est souffrante et meurtrie,
>     Mais pour battre pour la patrie,
>     Son cœur reste encor tout entier.
>
> (66)

In the alternative poetic space explored by Ségalas, nationalism and feminism are not mutually exclusive. To the contrary, women unite with their male counterparts to reclaim France's glory as a European nation:

> Les guerrières d'Alger, fières de leur licence,
> S'unissent aux Français, sous les murs assiégés;
> Leur courage enfermé rompt sa froide contrainte,
>     Et franchit la stupide enceinte
>     De la prison des préjugés.
>
> (*Les algériennes*, 67)

To root out her own country's sexual bias, Ségalas refutes those who doubt that women possess the same courage as men:

> Vous doutez du courage et de l'ardente flamme,
> Qui font voler la femme au milieu des combats!
> A-t-elle moins que vous, intrépides soldats,
> D'amour pour son pays et de force dans l'âme?
> Et de son prompt essor doit-on être étonné?
>
> (67)

The aspiring poet intervenes in the celebration of feminine patriotism to identify with these female warriors.[24]

Inspired by the example of the French heroines of Algiers, Ségalas reveals her desire to be crowned with laurels. In commemorating these soldiers, she invokes another battle, the one waged by poetic women like herself to gain a foothold in another field dominated by men:

> Mais qui peut à present douter de notre audace?
> Héroïnes d'Alger, votre éclatante ardeur
> Doit rejaillir sur nous . . . que le laurier vainqueur,
> Aux roses du plaisir sur nos fronts s'entrelace!
> Que dis-je! où m'égarait l'aveugle vanité?
> O vous, dont la valeur me séduit et m'inspire,
>> Daignez pardonner à ma lyre
>> Son ambitieuse fierté.
>>> (*Les algériennes*, 68; ellipses in original)

The self-reflective writer covers her poetic aspirations with the same flag she raises to honor these women as soldiers of France: "Et nous nous abritons chacune / Sous les coins de votre drapeau" (68).

National pride dominates "Le drapeau tricolore" in which Ségalas evokes the history of the flag adopted in 1794. Hoisted to recall Napoleon's expedition into Egypt (1798–1801), the French flag also anchors the final lines of Ségalas's poem, which gesture toward Eugène Delacroix's painting *La liberté guidant le peuple* (1830):

> Mais lorsqu'on voit soudain, dans ces temps de malheur,
>> Les trois couleurs paraître en France,
> Le peuple peut alors, d'ivresse transporté,
>> Saluer avec confiance
>> L'aurore de la liberté.
>>> (*Les algériennes*, 77)

In portraying the revolution that brought Louis-Philippe to power in 1830, Delacroix elevated the figure of a working-class woman of the time as the ideal of freedom that guided the people's struggle. In Ségalas's "Le drapeau tricolore," Bonapartism and republicanism, though incompatible in political theory, align along the revolutionary axis to symbolize the modern French nation. France is situated alongside its colonial empire, now expanded to Algeria.[25]

Ségalas had revealed her gift in 1829, at the age of eighteen, with verse published in the keepsake *Psyché* and the literary magazine *Le Cabinet de Lecture*. "La plus jeune des femmes poëtes," Paul Jacob ("le Bibliophile") stresses, "Mme Ségalas s'est élevée tout à coup au premier rang" ("Mme Ségalas," 37). For Jacob, *Les algériennes* exhibits the precise meter and careful rhyme she had acquired. In his view, her mind is as expansive as Hugo's: "Mme Ségalas trouva donc dans son imagination les couleurs que demandait ce voyage imaginaire en Afrique, et souvent elle s'éleva jusqu'au ton de l'ode en exprimant avec énergie des pensées toutes masculines, que le patriotisme avait transplantées dans le cœur d'une femme" (41).

In explaining "l'accueil empressé" enjoyed by *Les algériennes*, Francis Roch under- scores the poems' conceptual and creative power. Ségalas's reputation soared, Roch recalls: "À partir de ce moment, revues littéraires et journaux se disputèrent à qui aurait le premier l'honneur d'insérer dans ses colonnes une production nouvelle d'Anaïs Ségalas" ("M^me Anaïs Ségalas," 3). Her next collection, *Les oiseaux de pas- sage* (1836), sold out in a few months, as did the second edition in 1837.[26] Poems in this work weigh the nascent biology of race against abolitionism.[27] The volume was republished under the title *Poésies* (1844), drawing her cluster of texts, which con- figure the colonial world through a series of encounters, historically closer to the final push for slavery abolition.

## The Other French Empire

In "Le voyageur," Ségalas imagines foreign lands where she will never set foot, having renounced all major travel early in her life because of a boating accident.[28] Based on this biographical detail, one is wont to identify her as the speaker in these opening lines:

> Je veux partir, je veux partir,
> Et laisser ma ville en arrière,
> Ses toits, son clocher, sa barrière:
> C'est ma prison, j'en veux sortir.
>
> (*Les oiseaux de passage*, 69)

The speaking subject projects herself across the Atlantic: "ce pont mouvant / Qui va du vieux au nouveau monde" (70). An armchair traveler, the poet aims to dis- cover the diversity of the human race by using the mind's eye to traverse unknown regions:

> Peuples divers, j'irai vous voir;
> Voir l'espèce géante, et noire, et blanche, et naine,
> Et le moule que Dieu fit pour chaque pays;
> Voir comment il tailla tous vos corps infinis,
> Le grand sculpteur en chair humaine!
>
> (71)

The virtual journey leads to the Antilles, where Ségalas's poetic narrator imag- ines volcanoes, palm trees, and scented paths.[29] She expects to see black people, who are pictured initially in terms that associate the color black with evil: "Nègre, ô frère des démons, / Nègre aux deux yeux ardens sur une face noire" (*Les oiseaux de passage*, 72). But does this race—said to be accursed according to the Ham myth—not share other human characteristics?[30] The poet wonders whether "l'âme change ou lance un même éclair, / Quand on la voit briller sous les masques de fer, / Sous ceux d'albâtre et ceux de cuivre" (72). This questioning of the view that skin tone determines moral fiber, reprised in the second edition of Virey's influential *Histoire naturelle du genre humain* (1824),[31] reiterates the stance developed by the abolitionist Grégoire.

In *De la noblesse de la peau* (1826), Grégoire recalls the first era of French colonization during the early seventeenth century, comparing the construct of the gentry or "parchment nobility" with that of the contemporary "aristocracy" of color: "La noblesse des parchemins était dans tout son lustre quand l'avarice coloniale établit la *noblesse de la peau*, car c'est une invention moderne" (39). The stigma of dark skin was added to the crime that whites had committed in tearing Africans from their homeland and enslaving them: "Ce préjugé parut aux blancs une invention merveilleuse pour étayer leur domination" (39).[32] Grégoire pursues the racial implications of the counterdiscourse "l'esprit n'a point de sexe,"[33] challenging the linkage of physical and mental characteristics: "Mais les âmes ont-elles une couleur?" (64).[34] His query aims at the tenets of biological racism. In "Le voyageur," Ségalas likewise assumes sexual equality as she probes racial diversity.

In exercising her imagination to visualize other worlds—"Toi, ma vaste pensée, à mon retour, je veux / Que tu rapportes tout le globe"—Ségalas ponders what separates yet unites the diverse peoples across the globe (*Les oiseaux de passage*, 73). Can the cultured Parisian bridge the distance between herself and her colonial double, who is and is *not* French, by constructing "an imaginative space for mutual alterity and mutual empathy" (Lee, *Slavery and the Romantic Imagination*, 42)?[35] In "Le voyageur," the sketch of the Creole has the contours of orientalism. The speaker transforms the primitive nature of the exotic other into an object of beauty, linking via word association the issue of color and racial identity:

> Créole, odalisque, sauvage,
> Oh! délice de vous aimer!
> Mon cœur sera comme une cage
> Où l'on se plaît à renfermer
> Des oiseaux de chaque plumage.
>
> (*Les oiseaux de passage*, 76)

In the original French usage, the noun "Créole" referred to whites of European descent born in the colonies.[36] In adjectival form, the term denoted all island-born people and creatures as well as a manner, style, and temperament with no reference to color.[37] Ségalas exploits this lexical difference through appositions that link the Creole with both the odalisque (a female slave or concubine in a Turkish harem) and the indigenous woman. The term "sauvage" also has a double meaning: the primitive viewed as either uncultured or barbaric (in the sense of cruel or bestial). In the context of romantic primitivism—which valued the simple and unsophisticated—the word promotes the Eurocentric conception of the "noble savage." This construct works dialogically in Ségalas's poem "Le sauvage," which disputes colonization from the perspective of the native inhabitant untouched by "civilization" and thus still naturally good.

Ségalas's writing at the time of the slavery debate sharpens the dialectic by turning from the sentimentalism associated with the Romantic imagination. "Le sauvage" enacts an interior monologue to weigh the argument for and against France's colonial enterprise. The native denizen frames his encounter with the white man by placing in opposition civilization and nature:

> Il s'en va, l'homme à la peau blanche,
> Qui disait: Viens voir ma cité.
> Fuir mes forêts de liberté,
> Mon enfant, mon hamac qui penche,
> Fuir ma compagne au teint si beau,
> Au pagne fin, au doux visage!
> Qu'il rejoigne seul au rivage
> Sa case qui marche sur l'eau.
>
> (*Les oiseaux de passage*, 127–28)

The periphrasis "Sa case qui marche sur l'eau" recalls the fetishistic "beau brick *L'Espérance*," symbolizing knowledge, which bewilders the mutinous slaves in Prosper Mérimée's *Tamango* (1829). This possible intertext introduces a note of condescension toward the "sauvage" and his lack of culture. However, Ségalas's text resonates with the abolitionist current by defending the native inhabitants' way of life.

Unlike the orientalist impulse to take imaginary possession of the other, the view of colonization in "Le sauvage" maintains the difference between European and indigenous cultures, the latter preserved by virtue of topography, vegetation, species, and customs. Details suggestive of various regions of the Americas, such as "ces savanes" and "ces long déserts" along with "gommiers" and "goyaviers," on the one hand, and "serpens," "tigres rouges," and "jaguars," on the other, depict the environment. Speaking for his people, the native dwells in harmony with the natural world and impugns the superiority attributed to material progress:

> Là-bas, une pendule, où l'aiguille s'avance,
> Marque instant par instant chaque jour qui s'enfuit;
> Ici, nous mesurons largement l'existence
>         Par le matin et par la nuit.
> Tout le luxe mesquin de sa riche demeure,
> Je le méprise, moi. Voici, dans ce ciel bleu,
> Notre pendule à nous, ce beau soleil, où l'heure
>         Se lit sur un cadran de feu!
>
> (*Les oiseaux de passage*, 130)

The speaker rejects not only the white man's technology but also his religion: "Le blanc voulut ici faire un temple de pierre, / Mais nous avons brisé son temple et son autel" (132). In discussing other examples of the value placed on wealth and physical possessions, the "sauvage" displays his ability to reason. He also expresses his humanity and capacity for love along with an aesthetic sense of his culture's difference. In the last stanza, which echoes the first stanza, the person of color to whom Ségalas gives voice celebrates freedom ("À moi mes bois de liberté") and the beauty of his people. This is exemplified by his partner "au teint si beau / Au pagne fin, au doux visage!" (132). Here, the respect for other cultures applies equally to the indigenous woman.

Ségalas's poem "Un nègre à une blanche" expresses a further intervention in the discourse of black people's inferiority. Up until 1818, the 1777 version of the Code Noir prohibited blacks or other people of color from entering France as well as interracial marriage. Love between a black man and a white woman was thus unthinkable. But this is precisely the possibility that Ségalas entertains, mixing empathy with thought. Her black speaker uses an apostrophe to his beloved to draw a parallel between the diversity of the human race and that found in nature:

> O blanche, tes cheveux sont d'un blond de maïs,
> Et ta voix est semblable au chant des bengalis!
> Si tu voulais m'aimer, ce serait douce chose!
> Un peu d'amour au noir, jeune fille au teint frais:
> Le gommier n'a-t-il pas, dans nos vastes forêts,
> Sur son écorce brune une liane rose!
>
> (*Les oiseaux de passage*, 255)

Passionate yet lucid, Ségalas's speaker refers to himself in the third person, outlining the ideological work announced by the poem's title. He counters the pejorative connotation of "nègre," synonymous with "esclave," by using the term "noir," which had been adopted by the first abolitionist circle, the Société des amis des noirs, to refer to blacks.[38] Ségalas's text works for abolition, using semantic and imagistic synergy. The image of the ivy wrapped around the gum tree illustrates an adaptive harmony that allows different beings to coexist without dominating or assimilating each other.

"Un nègre à une blanche" also calls into question the color hierarchy established by Cuvier: "La race blanche, à visage ovale, à cheveux longs, à nez saillant, à laquelle appartiennent les peuples policés de l'Europe, et qui nous paroît la plus belle de toutes, est aussi bien supérieure aux autres par la force du génie, le courage et l'activité" (*Tableau élémentaire*, 71). Virey in turn portrays blacks at the opposite end of the spectrum as "une race, ou plutôt une espèce distincte d'hommes de couleur noire, à cheveux frisés, à nez épaté, à grosses lèvres avec des mâchoires prolongées en museau" ("Nègre" [1818], 422). As if to expose such offensive typecasting, Ségalas's speaker compares racial physiognomies. He reiterates the counterdiscourse in "Le voyageur," that color is not a moral attribute, assessing black as beautiful:

> Un nègre a sa beauté: bien sombre est ma couleur,
> Mais de mes dents de nacre on voit mieux la blancheur;
> Tes yeux rayonnent bien sous tes cils fins, longs voiles,
> Mais regarde, les miens ont un éclat pareil:
> Ton visage est le jour, tes yeux c'est le soleil;
> Mon visage est la nuit, mes yeux sont des étoiles!
> . . . Oh! suis-moi, blanche femme,
> Afin que je te serve et te parle à genoux!
> Qu'importe ma couleur, si je suis bon et doux,
> Et si le noir chez moi ne va pas jusqu'à l'âme!
>
> (*Les oiseaux de passage*, 256)

Could love, which inspires such blind devotion ("Afin que je te serve et te parle à genoux!"), also transcend the racial divide that now dominated science?[39] The final lines disappoint the hope expressed in the first stanza: "Mais quoi! tu fuis le noir, jeune fille au teint frais; / Oh! plus heureux que moi, le gommier des forêts / Sur son écorce brune a sa liane rose!" (*Les oiseaux de passage*, 257–58).[40] Abolitionism was a movement of the elite that polarized the French on the continent and, even more so, their Creole counterparts in the colonies, who turned a blind eye to the system that implicated them. Ségalas's verse on slavery and race straddles the divide between the French in Europe and those in the colonies, presenting the same arc as her feminist bent, which grew increasingly conservative.

### Literary Abolitionism

Ségalas's writing examined to this point conveys the remove from which she considered the racial question along with her evolving position as a moderate feminist. Poems about the institution of slavery and the construct of race as color show her to be more of a thinker stirred by current events than an activist directly championing abolition. In the absence of an explicit statement from Ségalas, one can only speculate how, through her collaboration with the *Journal des Femmes*, she may have reacted to Mme Letelier's "Mœurs coloniales," which the newspaper published in 1833, just months before England abolished slavery. The fact that this sketch of colonial manners was brought forth under a pseudonym, and appears to be the author's only work, may explain why Letelier has not been included in critics' discussion of women's literary activism during the decades that led to slavery's end. Referenced in the push for immediate abolition, however, Letelier's portrayal of colonial Guadeloupe suggests an unacknowledged source of the site to which Ségalas returned again and again in thinking about the effects of abolition.

In 1833, Letelier used the pseudonym Mme Aline de M*** to publish her "feuilleton" (serial story) over six installments, condemning slavery while revealing French Creole women's cruelty toward their black slaves. Letelier was in Paris at the time, on extended leave from Pointe-à-Pitre, Guadeloupe, where she lived with her husband, an administrator of the French navy. Republished in *Revue des Colonies* (1835–36),[41] Letelier's account incited protest in Guadeloupe in the summer of 1835 upon her family's return from Paris. This direct impact is striking and in fact rare for women's antislavery writing.[42] Fanny Richomme, the editor of the *Journal des Femmes*, later described the "émeute d'aristocrates":

> Il se fit un soir un grand tapage devant leur maison. Un "commando" de jeunes gens fortunés, fils de planteurs, que le journal local qualifie d'aristocrates s'était massé là et criait des injures ignobles. Ils forcèrent l'entrée de la maison et n'ayant pas trouvé Mme Letelier se portèrent en hurlant vers la maison d'une de ses amies de couleur, Mlle Reine Ledoux. On injuria celle-ci, brisa sa porte, la somma de livrer Mme Letelier ou de mettre le feu à sa maison. . . . Des scènes semblables se déroulèrent le lendemain à Basse-Terre. (quoted in Sullerot, *Histoire de la presse féminine*, 183)[43]

The plantation owners saw only the price of abolition, not the moral implications of slavery, a system that corrupted both "master" and "slave," as Letelier stressed.

At once a Romantic bildungsroman and a social critique, Letelier's story unfolds over the period of a month. The protagonist, Charles Delacroix, long envisaged Guadeloupe as the ideal place to develop his artistic talent. When the young Parisian arrives in the French colony for the first time, however, he encounters the French Creoles' inhumanity. Shortly after meeting his hostess in Pointe-à-Pitre, Charles is stunned when she refers to her slaves as "ces êtres dégénérés" ("Mœurs coloniales," 92). An omniscient narrator mediates his thought that, to the contrary, *she* embodies the dehumanizing effects of colonization: "Ce qu'on voyait en elle d'absurde et de presque féroce, *était* avant qu'elle ne fût; cette nature ajoutée à la sienne faisait partie de l'air qu'elle avait respiré en naissant, de l'état social qui l'avait formée à son image" (93; emphasis in original). Charles later observes his hostess flogging an enslaved child. Appalled by other forms of cruelty and racism, he minces no words in declaring to Fournier, "Ces créoles! Oh! Je ne crains plus de les trop haïr" (182). A French naval officer stationed in Guadeloupe, Fournier observes that France is to blame for sanctioning the Creoles' attitudes, having created territorial dependencies solely for its own gain: "Il serait injuste de punir les créoles d'un état social qu'ils ont trouvé tout fait. Ce qui est étrange, c'est que cet état, ces mœurs, subsistent dans un pays que la France possède et gouverne; mère indifférente, les enfans qui lui naissent aux colonies ne sont point appelés à partager ses lumières et sa civilisation" (182). Letelier develops this irony through a character named Maurice, Charles's childhood friend, who hails from Pointe-à-Pitre. When reunited with Maurice in Guadeloupe via a chance encounter, Charles recognizes him as having "la plus noble et la plus belle figure" along with "un front empreint de génie" (240).[44] Letelier borrows Maurice's voice to assess the moral consequences of slavery through a comment made to Charles: "Ce dégradant système, on l'a dit avant moi, *corrompt le maître et l'esclave*" (329; emphasis in original).[45] This statement anticipates Lamartine's 1836 call to action: "Une telle propriété [l'esclave], Messieurs, ne corrompt-elle pas la race qui possède autant que la race qui est possédée?"[46] This is also the way Waldor portrays everyday life in the French colonies in the antislavery narrative "Clara," which she published in *Pages de la vie intime* (1836).

Waldor's father, one of the presidents of the Société de la morale chrétienne, established in 1821, likely exposed her to abolitionism. Because of her relationhip with Dumas, whose paternal grandmother was a Haitian slave, and with her god-mother the poet Hortense de Céré-Barbé, originally from Mauritius, Waldor had other sources of information about colonial culture. Recall that Waldor was also part of Richomme's editorial team and, like Ségalas, may have read Letelier's story before it went to press. Like Letelier's hero, Waldor's eponymous French European heroine, Clara, travels for the first time to a French colony, the island of Mauritius in the Indian Ocean, and is shocked by her relatives' attitude toward their slaves. Like Letelier's protagonist, Waldor's decries slavery for debasing all of humanity: "Les mœurs des colonies me révoltaient, l'esclavage, cette plaie honteuse de la civilisation, faisait rougir mon front et remplissait mon cœur d'une noble indig-nation. Je ne savais, ni ne voulais commander à aucun des nègres que mon oncle avait placés près de moi" (*Pages de la vie intime*, 1:12). Whereas Letelier's work is radical in advocating for abolition, Waldor's colonial narrative straddles the line between sentimental prose and social realism in treating abolitionism, in a similar manner to feminism, as a contemporary issue rather than a cause. The same could be said about Ségalas whose writing about these issues represents literary activism rather than political action.

The broader debate about race reproduced in Waldor's "Clara" enriches under-standing of how text and context interlock. Polygenism authorizes the colonists' view expressed by Clara's uncle: "[L]es noirs sont venus au monde pour obéir aux blancs" (*Pages de la vie intime*, 1:13). The opposing idea of monogenism underlies the stance articulated from memory by the female slave whom Clara befriends: "[L]es âmes étant sans forme, n'ont point de couleur" (19). This statement, made in reference to Catholicism, establishes a possible link with a literary source.[47] Duras's *Ourika* is the subject of a subsequent exchange between Clara and her uncle. He mocks her choice of reading material, calling it "un roman de femme" (24). To break the ensuing silence, he asks Clara: "Avez-vous apporté de France beaucoup de livres de ce genre?" (27). The male character takes the book and quickly exits the room, leaving Waldor's heroine and the reader to ponder his reaction. This scene can be read as a comment on "littérature féminine." Waldor contests this category, defined as strictly sentimental, by hinting at the sociopolit-ical dimension of Duras's novella. The corresponding element in the first part of

Waldor's own story broaches miscegenation, the cultural gap between France and its colonies, and the racial prejudice common to both. Upon Clara's return to the continent, however, the theme of unrequited love overtakes the narrative, which isolates the colonial theme in Waldor from the broader corpus devoted to abolitionism.

The influential statesman Victor Schœlcher, however, drew Letelier's narrative into the political arena. After a second trip to the Antilles from 1840 to 1841, Schœlcher rejected the planters' economic concerns and promoted a humanitarian platform calling for the immediate abolition of slavery. In 1842, Schœlcher detailed the conditions in which he had observed the population of black slaves in France's Caribbean colonies, emphasizing the effects of slavery on women: "elles si bonnes, deviennent aux colonies d'une cruauté spéciale" (*Des colonies françaises*, 88). Having witnessed French Creole women beat enslaved children, along with other forms of abuse, Schœlcher declares: "L'esclavage rend les femmes cruelles, vous voyez bien qu'il faut détruire l'esclavage" (89). On this point, he cites Letelier's analysis: "Il y a dans les rapports des créoles avec leurs esclaves une barbarie qui s'ignore elle-même et qui, si l'on peut profaner cette expression, a quelque chose de candide" (89).[48] At considerable remove from the lived experience of slavery exposed by Letelier and Schœlcher, among others, Ségalas considered the idea of its gradual abolition, redressing the image of "la belle Créole" in a colonial space fraught with racial and political conflict.

## Slavery and "la belle Créole"

In the colonial context, the Romantic figure of "la belle Créole" embodies the ideals of civilization, as in Bernardin de Saint-Pierre's *Paul et Virginie* (1787). As a carrier of European Frenchness (a white yet island-born woman), this archetype also mediates between colonization and slavery. For example, in Hugo's *Bug-Jargal* (1826), the character Marie, who exemplifies the virtuous white Creole woman, is contrasted with the violent backdrop of the 1791 slave revolt in Saint-Domingue: "Elle était rayonnante, et il y avait dans sa douce figure quelque chose de plus angélique encore que la joie d'un amour pur: c'était la pensée d'une bonne action" (49). She asks her father, who has promised to grant whatever she desires as a wedding gift, to free the slave who saved her life: Pierrot, also known as Bug-Jargal. However, Sand's *Indiana* (1832) destabilizes the image of "la belle Créole" with a racial ambiguity that conveys a shadow sense of cultural contamination.[49]

A global crossing *à rebours*, from the French colony of Réunion to Europe, enmeshes three characters in a fatal love triangle: the beautiful noblewoman Indiana ("une créole nerveuse et maladive"), her *sœur de lait* Noun ("la jeune créole aux grands yeux noirs qui avait frappé d'admiration toute la province"), and the handsome Raymon de Ramière (Sand, *Indiana*, 73). In a narrative aimed at emancipating women, if only psychologically, Sand also has in mind the black people subordinated to the building of the French empire. As she expresses in prefacing the 1842 edition of her novel, "Le malheur de la femme entraîne celui de l'homme, comme celui de l'esclave entraîne celui du maître, et j'ai cherché à le montrer dans *Indiana*" (Sand, *Préfaces*, 93). By associating women's lack of civil status in a patriarchy with slavery, Sand echoes Olympe de Gouges. To the contrary, Ségalas rejects republican feminism to reinvigorate the French Creole woman's civilizing mission on the eve of slavery abolition, as if sensing the political shift that will follow the short-lived Second Republic proclaimed in 1848.

In prefacing the fourth edition of *Enfantines: Poésies à ma fille* in 1845 (it was first published in 1844 without introductory comments and saw two editions that year), Ségalas depicts the place that society reserved for women at the time: "Aimer, prier, rêver, voilà l'existence de toutes les femmes; au lieu de suivre la colonne de vapeur et de fumée du dix-neuvième siècle, elles suivent la colonne de feu qu'on appelle la foi" (vi).[50] She dedicates the new edition, "qui n'est faite que d'amour et de croyance," to mothers (vi). Religion and education remain central to the way Ségalas approaches the issue of assimilating former black slaves as French citizens in her narrative poem "La Créole (L'esclavage)," published twice in 1847, first in *Le Magasin des Demoiselles*, then in her collection *La femme: Poésies*.[51]

Ségalas opens her preface to *La femme* with two questions, which reveal the hostile reception a woman writer anticipates: "La femme, se dira-t-on (si toutefois on jette un coup d'œil sur cet ouvrage), que nous promet ce titre? L'auteur veut-il nous peindre une esclave révoltée qui jette un cri de Spartacus ou de Saint-Simonienne?" (9). Her vocabulary, linking feminism and abolitionism as threats to the social order, suggests a form of ironic distancing, which allowed her to avoid censorship, real or imagined, at a time of backlash. Ségalas associated with groups, such as Éducation mutuelle des femmes, that sought educational reform in the late 1840s.[52] Yet she was clearly more circumspect as an author who, at the same time, promoted the bourgeois ideals of womanhood. Women's poetic work was part of a broader mission "d'adoucir, de purifier, et, en quelque sorte, de spiritualiser ce monde que l'homme dirige, fait mouvoir, rend plus puissant et plus riche," Ségalas writes (10). Although making women's poetic influence spiritual or moral, she nonetheless celebrates the work of her imagination: "Ses pensées les plus caressées, ce sont de poétiques rêveries ou des élans vers l'infini: c'est une grande voyageuse qui part tous les jours pour le pays des rêves" (11). Ségalas envisions a way for women to promote social reform via poetic production, including slavery among "les grandes plaies de la société" they needed to treat (13).

In "La Créole (L'esclavage)," Ségalas advances the moral platform for gradual abolition without, however, addressing racial inequality. The title associates, yet more clearly separates, the French Creole woman and the institution of slavery. In the first printed French text, the second term is aligned underneath the first. So, too, the parentheses mark off a space. This discursive interstice structures the poem, which privileges the aesthetic figure before addressing its political dimension in situ. In the opening stanza, a first-person plural speaker portrays the

Creole as the "perle des mers." This association between natural beauty and moth-
erliness (via homophony with "mère") alters the French epithet for the former
colony of Saint-Domingue: "la perle des Antilles." In so doing, the speaker reclaims
via the image of "la belle Créole" a positive link between France and its remaining
empire in the Americas:

> Oh! nous t'aimons ici, notre sœur d'Amérique,
> > Blanche aux yeux noirs, perle des mers.
> Nos aïeux sont les tiens, Française du tropique
> > Nous vivons sous des cieux divers:
> À toi les bananiers, les palmistes immenses,
> > À nous le chêne au large front:
> Dans deux mondes, ma sœur, nous habitons deux Frances
> > Qu'un navire unit comme un pont.
>
> > > > (*La femme*, 201–2)

A common heritage of Frenchness bridges the geographical distance between the
speaker and the Creole woman. The gap between them then closes further, the
speaker calling the island-born woman "ma sœur," as if she presents an idealized
reflection of her European self.

Stanzas 2 and 3 move away from the ode-like tone of the poem's start. They
peel back the layers of the aesthetic figure, inviting readers to look past "la sirène"
envisioned from afar as well as "la déesse" behind "la moustiquaire en gaze" (*La
femme*, 202, 203). In the fourth stanza, the speaker draws even closer to the French
Creole woman and the enslaved blacks in her charge:

> Dans l'habitation, maîtresse étincelante,
> > Tout un peuple noir suit tes pas;
> Ton trône est un hamac, ô reine nonchalante,
> > Et ta couronne est un madras.
>
> > > > (203)

This close-up produces a hybrid figure, "creolized" by her environment.[53] The
Creole of arresting beauty and sensual indolence, powerful yet weak, fuses with
her surroundings and thus exudes the apathy induced by the tropical climate.
However, the "sœur d'Amérique" must assume a new role as abolition looms.

A space in the text signals a break in Ségalas's narrative and a shift toward "la
belle Créole" as a political figure. The time has come for "la belle Créole" to shed
her island accoutrements and exhibit her European roots, for she has a duty to
fulfill toward her slaves:

> C'est assez te bercer, et vivre avec paresse
> > Entre ton perroquet, ton singe et ta négresse.

Du hamac, enfermant ton corps souple et douillet,
Sors comme un jeune oiseau s'échappant du filet;
Car ta main doit sécher des pleurs, briser des chaînes.
Prends pitié de tes noirs, marchandises humaines.

(*La femme*, 203)

Ségalas's poetic narrator expresses sympathy. Yet the word "pitié" (from the Latin *pietas*), repeated twice more in subsequent lines, also gains the etymologically related sense of piety or self-righteousness. In addressing the Creole, the narrator implores her to have mercy on "la nourrice . . . / Qui donne à ton enfant, malgré sa couleur noire, / Un amour toujours pur et du lait toujours blanc" as well as "le bon nègre . . . / Qui, la nuit, à son tour, vient veiller à ta porte" (204). The moralistic tone nevertheless conveys a sense of superiority along with anxiety rooted in the deeper memory of the massacres in Saint-Domingue.

The speaker expresses a primal fear of the male slave, whose "coutelas" (large knife) symbolizes the potential vengeance of the oppressed:

Un coutelas reluit dans sa main large et forte,
Mais son arme protège au lieu de massacrer:
Femme, l'esclave armé pourrait te déchirer
Comme un tigre, et pourtant te garde comme un dogue.

(*La femme*, 204)

Here, the ambivalence about the colonial other registers scientific racism à la Virey: "En tout pays le blanc est supérieur au nègre sensuel, le civilisé dompte le barbare" (*De la physiologie dans ses rapports avec la philosophie*, 175). "La Créole (L'esclavage)" reflects simultaneously the campaign among the "French abolitionists from the Amis des Noirs [and] the Morale chrétienne [who] stressed the need for gradually preparing slaves for freedom in order to avoid the disruptions and upheavals that had occurred in the 1790s" (Jennings, *French Anti-Slavery*, 22). In approaching abolition as a moral action that requires the French Creole woman's intervention, Ségalas's poetic narrator transposes the white-black binary into virtue versus vice: "Tu ne peux de ton front lui donner la couleur: / Oh! du moins donne-lui la blancheur de ton âme!" (*La femme*, 205).

Ségalas's narrator maps the rhetoric of colonization onto the native topography to elucidate the path the Creole must clear for the population of uneducated black slaves, soon to be assimilated as citizens of France. She thus expresses "la mission civilisatrice" *avant la lettre*: "Fais marcher aux vertus ce peuple encor farouche; / À ton tour, sers de guide, et, de ta blanche main, / Écarte la broussaille et trace le chemin" (*La femme*, 206). Sympathy mixes with cultural imperialism. Ségalas's European speaker envisages that slaves placed under the tutelage of the Creole—the agent of the motherland—would eventually be liberated from vice as well as from ignorance, given instead "une vertu dans l'âme, un livre dans la main" (208).

123

The Creole, whose moral purity is transposed into a sign of immaculate whiteness ("beau cygne"), is further solicited to halt the inhumane treatment of slaves: "Mais entends-tu ces cris, douce blanche, beau cygne? / On châtie un esclave! . . . Oh! fais tomber d'un signe / Le fouet du commandeur, ce nègre aux yeux ardents!" (208; ellipses in original). The color binary, "douce blanche" versus "ce nègre aux yeux ardents," shifts to concentrate the locus of cruelty. Ségalas's gesture of making a black overseer the oppressor, though historically accurate, separates the Creoles from such brutality and ultimately from blame.

The fear of the oppressed, projected onto the overseer's fierce gaze ("ce nègre aux yeux ardents"), nonetheless persists. This fear prepares the split in Ségalas's thinking about the problem of slavery and its abolition:

> Dans un duel hardi, le nègre, cet atome,
> Peut contre un fouet sanglant croiser son coutelas:
> L'homme sait se plier, et se courber bien bas;
> Mais c'est comme l'acier qui bientôt vous échappe,
> Qui se ploie un instant, se redresse et vous frappe.
>
> (*La femme*, 208–9)

In a final command to her Creole sister, the speaker presages French imperialism during the Second Empire (1852–70) and the neocolonialism it would spur under the Third Republic:

> Femme, viens détacher tous ces colliers de fer,
> Et ces chaînes blessant leur âme avec leur chair.
> Épure, élève, instruis ces cœurs bruts. Va, courage!
> Plus tard la liberté finira ton ouvrage:
>
> . . . . . . . . . . . . . . . .
>
> Le nègre, libre un jour, sous tes beaux cieux brûlants,
> En brave travailleur, viendra servir les blancs.
> À l'œuvre! Sois la main qui délivre et protège.
>
> (209)

Even in promulgating abolition for humanitarian reasons, Ségalas's text inscribes a racial hierarchy. Whereas the first four lines recall the universal condition of the "homme animal" in "L'esclave," the final three lines add color to the figure. No longer a slave, yet not entirely free as a worker, the black person becomes an indentured servant to whites in the postcolonial realm Ségalas presaged at mid-century and would develop in her later prose.

"La Créole (L'esclavage)" intersects historically with *Les Créoles* (1847) by the lesser-known poet Louise de Lafaye (née Arbey). The latter's personal memories of Guadeloupe contest the myth of "la belle Créole" pivotal to Ségalas's treatment of the colonial past. The Guadeloupe-born Lafaye composed her collection while overseas.[54] However, she resided in Paris, the source of the exile expressed in her verse, which counters the perspective on Creole roots developed by Ségalas. Lafaye's nostalgic poems about her childhood, such as "Souvenirs d'enfance" and "Rêverie," dwell on Guadeloupe's natural beauty, from its native vegetation ("l'oranger," "baraguette," "goyavier") to its topography ("morne"), which supports the plantation economy ("nos champs de cannes"). A cluster of poems offers a glimpse of the political aspects of Lafaye's poetic reflections on her colonial heritage. In "Le nègre," for example, Lafaye's speaker recognizes how naïve she was as a child by expressing belated sympathy for the black slave, as if to prick her Parisian readers' conscience:

> Nègre, ne pleure plus, car voici ta maîtresse,
> Me voici de retour, plus de jours de tristesse;
>     Car je veux ton bonheur.
> Ton bonheur! j'y croyais aux jours de mon enfance,
> Et je voyais, hélas! avec indifférence,
>     Ton sort et ta couleur!
>
>                                     (*Les Créoles*, 10)

Like Ségalas, Lafaye places the Creole woman, identified by her "blanche main," in a tranquil setting: "Un hamac et des fleurs!" (17). In adding depth to the aesthetic figure stirred by the verse she's reading—"Elle pense, rêveuse"—Lafaye evokes her own thinking through poetry (17).

Lafaye's "La négresse" contradicts the image of "la belle Créole" seen in Ségalas. Instead, Lafaye portrays a Creole mistress who threatens to sell her black female slave's son, whose father she suspects to be her own husband. The black woman's plea opens the poem: "Ayez, ayez pitié de la pauvre négresse, / Oh! ne le vendez pas, chère et bonne maîtresse! / Son bras est faible encore, ses pas sont chancelants, / Mon Paul hélas! n'a pas sept ans!" (*Les Créoles*, 17). She protests that her son's father left in search of gold to buy their son's liberty, but she refuses to reveal his identity. Overcome with jealousy and suspicion, the Creole gazing upon the child's "teint, cette blancheur, à sa race étrangère" sees only "les traits de son époux" (18, 19). The black woman, given critical agency, exposes the mistress's indifference to her slaves' experience as a crime against blacks' humanity:

> Femme blanche, oh! de vous comment pouvais-je attendre
> Quelque pitié pour nous! Votre sort est si doux!
> Favorites du ciel! vos fils seront à vous,
> Et vous n'aurez jamais, dans leurs bras enchaînée;
> Baisant leurs blonds cheveux, maudit leur destinée,
> Oh! vous ne craindrez pas, vous, qu'un maître brutal,

Sur leur corps frémissant lève son fouet fatal!
Vous ne les verrez pas, oh! comble de misère!
Plaintifs et tout pleurants, arrachés à leur mère!

(21)

That Lafaye, unlike Letelier, published her volume in Paris without using a pseudonym suggests that abolitionism had gained force by that time. After abolishing slavery in all its colonies in 1848, France expanded its empire in Africa and elsewhere until the turn of the twentieth century. Travelers of both sexes logged forays into Algeria and West Africa. Ségalas, however, remained focused on the French Caribbean colonies, albeit with an increasingly conservative view of racial identity. Prose that Ségalas devoted to colonial themes from the mid-1850s onward recycled slave names from "La Créole (L'esclavage),"[55] remapping the terrain she had covered in favor of abolition to promulgate instead various phases of France's official "mission civilisatrice."

### Remapping the Colonial Empire

Three years into Napoleon III's reign, the Exposition Universelle of 1855 was held on the Champs-Élysées in Paris. The exposition reflected his desire to prove France's industrial supremacy while displaying the new empire building under way. As the French colonized North Africa, the general Louis Faidherbe, whom Napoleon had appointed governor of Senegal in 1852, directed the push into the interior of West Africa. The Palais de l'Industrie was constructed for the international exhibition in direct competition with the British venue of 1851. This is the setting and framework for Ségalas's collection of stories *Contes du nouveau Palais de Cristal* (1855), which opens by inviting readers to enter the exhibit hall: "Allons voir l'Exposition universelle!" (1).

An omniscient narrator populates the entrance with visitors from around the world, transforming Paris into "la tour de Babel" and a parade of nations or peoples of different colors (*Contes du nouveau Palais de Cristal*, 3). Recall that Ségalas evoked the tropics in her earlier poetry without specifying a site. At the exposition's entry, however, Guadeloupe is named and then transformed into the creolized female character Andrèse de Rozan: "Elle avait un petit accent traînant, nonchalant, et grasseyait comme une Parisienne qui n'a pas pris de leçons au Conservatoire. Elle passait volontiers la moitié de la journée à ne rien faire, et l'autre moitié à se reposer de n'avoir rien fait" (3–4). The beautiful yet languid Creole, whose attributes recall the opening lines of Ségalas's 1847 poem, joins a group of French visitors who are spending a week touring the exhibit halls. Authorial intrusions that describe the characters also frame or comment on the stories they tell during their visit. This narrative mode enables the author to distance herself not only from the various characters, but also from the views they express.

On the final day of the group's visit, Andrèse chances upon Adonis, a former slave "de la teinte la plus foncée," and engages him in conversation (*Contes du nouveau Palais de Cristal*, 288–89). Whereas the "bonne petite blanche," as Adonis calls the Creole, uses standard French, the black man, identified by the narrator as "le nègre," speaks patois: "Moi regarder une canne à sucre, toute pareille à celles que moi avoi planté là-bas. Adonis il ête content, il a ici une petite Améique: les belles productions du pays à li" (289). The rendering of this creolized speech, although seen by some as racist, can be read instead as a nod toward cultural authenticity.[56] This linguistic difference also raises the question of race in a post-abolition context. In Ségalas's story, a mix of narrative voices represents *both* Europeans and Creoles outside the colonial space, reproducing multiple viewpoints without resolving the tensions among them.

Andrèse steps away from Adonis to narrate the last *conte*: "L'oncle d'Amérique et le neveu de France." This story, which involves Adonis, treats abolition's immediate effects on the colonists and their former slaves together with the relationship between France and its colonies via an encounter between a Guadeloupean Creole, M. Fargès, and his Parisian nephew Rodolph Dartinville. Embedded within this tale is also the issue of racial identity, which is set forth by Andrèse in describing the Creole's daughter as being not "d'un blanc douteux," but as white as French Europeans: "Les créoles de nos Antilles sont par le fait des Françaises d'Amérique, parfaitement distinctes des noirs, qui sont d'une race africaine" (*Contes du nouveau Palais de Cristal*, 297). The sugar industry declines following slavery's abolition. Fargès faces bankruptcy and schemes with an unsuspecting Adonis to marry off his daughter, Lilia, to Rodolph, who is pretending to be a rich noble.

On the deck of a ship bound for Europe, a space laden with the memory of the Middle Passage, Fargès meets Adonis. The Creole offers to employ the black man as his "domestique," intending to pass him off to Rodolph as one of his many slaves. Adonis initially refuses. As the character invokes his rights, the narrator recalls the main figure of Haitian independence: "Moi ête un homme libre, répondit le nègre indigné, avec la pose d'un Toussaint Louverture" (*Contes du nouveau Palais de Cristal*, 303). With this allusion to the nickname "the black Napoleon" and the collective memory of Saint-Domingue, history slides into myth.[57]

A few pages later, upon seeing Adonis, who has agreed to accompany Fargès for a short period, Rodolph reacts in an irrational and vulgar way to his skin color. The black character rises to his own defense. Ségalas exploits the narrative style that enables an author to observe a character in situ, albeit from a distance, while voicing his thoughts: "Un singe! s'écria Adonis, suffoqué d'entendre comparer un homme libre à un singe" (*Contes du nouveau Palais de Cristal*, 309). Adonis rejects as vehemently the label "mulâtre," thus exposing deep racial tensions (310). Intrigued by how freely Adonis expresses his opinion, Rodolph questions Fargès about his other black charges. The Creole discloses the reality for former slaves in the colonies: "C'est vrai, ils sont très-émancipés. . . . [M]ais l'émancipation n'a fait que changer les termes: nous avions des esclaves, nous avons des domestiques et des ouvriers, voilà toute la différence" (310). There is no resolution; the story ends in Paris. Though Fargès's scheme unravels, as does Rodolph's, all ends happily for Adonis, who "quitta son maître pour vivre en homme libre et en fashionable" (328).

A shift in cultural context illuminates how the core problem of race changes in Ségalas's late colonial narrative, *Récits des Antilles: Le bois de la Soufrière*.

### Authorizing the Colonial Project

The post-abolition era witnessed the triumph of polygenism. Emblematic of this development, Arthur Gobineau's *Essai sur l'inégalité des races* (1853–55) concluded from physiology that racial differences were absolute and permanent (123–32, 151–61).[58] The Société d'anthropologie de Paris, founded in 1859, professed that blacks constituted a separate race that would not evolve either over time or through contact with whites. In the Larousse dictionary of 1866, the article "Nègre" upheld brain size and shape as evidence of black people's mental weakness: "Un fait incontestable et qui domine tous les autres, c'est qu'ils ont le cerveau plus rétréci, plus léger et moins volumineux que celui de l'espèce blanche, et comme dans toute la série animale, l'intelligence est en raison directe des dimensions du cerveau, du nombre et de la profondeur des circonvolutions, ce fait suffit pour prouver la supériorité de l'espèce blanche sur l'espèce noire" (11:904). This alleged intellectual inequality between the white and black races anticipated the rationale of the "mission civilisatrice" declared under the Third Republic: "Leur infériorité intellectuelle, loin de nous conférer le droit d'abuser de leur faiblesse, nous impose le devoir de les aider et de les protéger" (11:904).

Ségalas took on this mission in *Récits des Antilles: Le bois de la Soufrière*. She first published this narrative in 1877 as a serial story in the *Musée des Familles: Lectures du Soir*, an illustrated French literary magazine, as Barbara Cooper has documented in considering "Ségalas's changed attitude toward blacks" from the perspective of other women's pedagogical writings during the second half of the century ("Race, Gender, and Colonialism," esp. 118–20 and 127n4). Republished in a book along with some other pieces in 1884, then as a separate volume, Ségalas's novel saw eight editions between 1885 and the mid-1890s.[59] This commercial success, in line with that of *Ourika*, reflects the historical context. Ségalas's novel intersected with the 1884 declaration of France's "mission civilisatrice" by Jules Ferry, then the president of the council and the minister of public instruction and fine arts: "Il y a pour les races supérieures un droit, parce qu'il y a un devoir pour elles. Elles ont le devoir de civiliser les races inférieures" (*Discours et opinions*, 210–11). *Récits des Antilles*, like the 1884 volume, which includes a reprint of "L'oncle d'Amérique et le neveu de France," overlapped with the division of Africa among European colonial powers at the Berlin Conference (1884–85). Framed as a study of abolition's effects, Ségalas's narrative recirculates previous elements of her colonial writings, but contradicts the ideological work of her poetry.

The allusion to Offenbach's operetta *La Créole* (first performed at the Bouffes Parisiens theater on 3 November 1875) "would suggest that the action in the early part of Ségalas's novel takes place in the 1860s since ten years elapse between chapter 4 and chapter 5," Cooper has argued ("Race, Gender, and Colonialism," 127n4). The novel opens thus: "Holà! Neptune, Adonis, Apollon!" (*Récits des Antilles*, 3). A reader familiar with Ségalas's "La Créole (L'esclavage)" would recognize the slave names used here in connection with the speaker: "c'était un créole de la Guadeloupe, qui appelait ses nègres" (3). One also notices the rhetoric from her 1855 tale. In explaining blacks' role in the later post-emancipation context, however, Ségalas's omniscient narrator sets an edgy tone: "Tous les nègres sont maintenant des hommes libres: les esclaves ne sont plus que des travailleurs, qui malheureusement ne travaillent guère, et gâtent par leur inertie la pensée juste et généreuse de l'abolition de l'esclavage" (3–4). Negative perceptions of black people were expressed and yet countered in the discourse of race examined in Ségalas's verse from the 1830s and '40s, as well as in "L'oncle d'Amérique et le neveu de France." These views become more radical in *Récits des Antilles*, which draws out the hostility among whites, blacks, and other people of color after the abolition of slavery.

Recall the agency given to the black speaker ascribing beauty to his color in Ségalas's 1836 "Un nègre à une blanche." The physiognomy of Jupiter, the principal black character in *Récits des Antilles*, suggests the antithesis: "Jupiter pouvait avoir une trentaine d'années; c'était un nègre de race africaine et du noir le plus beau, ou pour mieux dire le plus laid. . . . Il n'y avait absolument de blanc dans ce sombre visage que la blancheur éclatante des dents et le blanc des yeux, au milieu duquel roulaient deux prunelles ardentes et quelque peu sauvages" (7). The civilizing role "la belle Créole" was to have played, giving black people faith and education on the eve of abolition, had apparently failed to produce the desired effects. There is no trace of this edifying discourse or the related ethos of sympathy in the narrator's view of Jupiter: "Au résumé, Jupiter était laid comme un singe, noir comme un merle, lent comme une tortue et voleur comme un pie" (7). This racial profiling extends to Jupiter's son Coco, whom the narrator depicts as an "affreux négrillon,"[60] the spitting image of his father, inside and out: "Coco n'était pas noir au dehors et blanc au dedans, son cœur était nègre aussi, noirci par tous les mauvais instincts" (7). Couched in physiological terms, this binary opposition overdetermines the theme of blind vengeance tied to fear of the oppressed, as seen in Ségalas's 1847 "La Créole (L'esclavage)."

The subtitle, *Le bois de la Soufrière*, refers to the tropical forest in Basse-Terre, Guadeloupe. This site, which Ségalas brings to life with exacting detail, signifies the natural resources of the island that were exploited for colonialists' gain: a ground ripe for revolt.[61] The volcanic terrain galvanizes the negative associations with Jupiter, the narrator barely masking irrational beliefs about black people: "Ce n'était plus le nègre apprivoisé, c'était le vrai sauvage, de race africaine, qui ne cherchait plus à cacher sa haine" (*Récits des Antilles*, 33). Charly de Tercel, the white Creole for whom Jupiter worked, mistakenly shoots Jupiter's son Coco. At two different, yet related, levels of interpretation, Jupiter's revenge against Tercel exposes the consequences of slavery *and* its abolition.

The shift in blacks' legal status, which has not been accompanied by a change in their roles or in colonial mores, exacerbates racial antipathy. Ségalas develops through the character Onélie Beaumanguier the role of "la belle Créole," who mediates between the races. Mme Beaumanguier discovers and adopts, though not legally, Charly's only daughter, Rosélis, after Jupiter kidnaps Rosélis and abandons her to die in the dense forest encircling the Soufrière. A series of chance encounters, which retrace the Atlantic slave trade route between France, Africa, and the Antilles, lead Charly to his daughter ten years later in Martinique. Her "adoptive" mother, however, disputes his paternal rights. The public trial, transposed into a battle between the races, forestalls a happy ending.

With the character Roland, visiting from Paris, Ségalas complicates her stance on race in *Récits des Antilles*. Self-styled as being "dans le progrès," Roland triangulates the view presented of the colonial world, adding a European perspective to that of African blacks and Creoles of both colors (43). Charly finds it shocking that Roland "fai[t] des visites à un mulâtre" (43). When Roland describes himself as "ému de cette touchante égalité" that now exists between the people of color and French Creoles, Charly quickly readjusts his friend's view: "Oh! l'égalité . . . existe dans nos lois, mais pas dans nos mœurs. Nous partageons avec les gens de couleur les emplois publics, mais quelles que soient leur fortune et leur position, nous ne leur ouvrons pas nos salons" (43). Here, the use of an omniscient narrator recalls Ségalas's rhetorical strategy in 1855. Ségalas borrows Roland's voice to measure "la marche du progrès dans le nouveau monde et l'effet de l'abolition de l'esclavage," registering negative attitudes toward blacks, but not closely identifying (her voice) with the harsh opinions expressed (43).

A subsequent exchange between Roland and Charly shows that the legal measure enacted on the continent has failed to dislodge the racial hierarchy in the colonies. *Récits des Antilles* builds on the cultural legacy and further textures Ségalas's colonial corpus as Charly explains the meaning of the word "créole" to Roland: "Donnez-vous donc la peine de relire l'histoire; vous verrez que les créoles de nos colonies sont les descendants des Français qui sont venus s'établir à la Guadeloupe, à la Martinique, et même à Saint-Domingue, d'où la révolte et le massacre les ont fait disparaître" (46). The memory of Saint-Domingue, distant yet haunting, is filtered only through the perspective of the French colonizers. The white Creole repeats terms used in "L'oncle d'Amérique et le neveu de France," but sharpens the use of the word "créole" in relation to whites versus blacks: "Il est vrai que les nègres nés aux colonies s'appellent nègres créoles, mais le mot *créole* seul ne désigne absolument que les blancs, qui sont, croyez-le bien, dans nos Antilles, tout aussi blancs que vos Parisiens, et sont par le fait des Français d'Amérique" (46). The narrative pivots from the past to the present as "la belle Créole," associated with racial sensitivity, mediates the negative effects of abolition.

The plot thickens against the backdrop of revenge, which pits a free black man against a white plantation owner. Convinced that Onélie has made off with his daughter, Rosélis, the night before the trial, Charly encounters an elderly black woman while seeking her mistress. Long employed by Mme Beaumanguier, "la vieille négresse" speaks "le langage des blanches," reflecting her mistress's influence, the narrator observes (*Récits des Antilles*, 71). Still loyal to her mistress, the old woman expresses nostalgia for slavery: "Aujourd'hui que les pauvres nègres ne sont plus esclaves, il faut bien que de bonnes blanches comme M^me de Beaumanguier viennent les secourir, quand ils ne peuvent plus travailler. Ah! Monsieur, où est-il, le bon temps de l'esclavage!" (72).[62] Her reminiscence excludes the cruelty toward slaves who worked as field hands, acknowledged in Ségalas's 1847 poetic narrative. This difference in attitude on the part of the domestic slave, who likely experienced better treatment while working in or around the plantation manor, accurately represents the division among colonial slaves.

In *Récits des Antilles*, as in "L'oncle d'Amérique et le neveu de France," multiple viewpoints express racial tensions. As the narrative shifts back to race and to the trial pitting whites against blacks in and outside the courtroom, Ségalas's narrator reduces the problem to color envy, which recalls the physiology of (male) genius, which excluded females: "Tout noirs qu'ils sont, les nègres sont les rouges des colonies: le blanc représente pour eux l'antique esclavage, l'autorité, la suprématie, et ils ne sont pas fâchés de se révolter à l'occasion contre ces peaux blanches qu'ils envient. Ils ont déjà la liberté, puis la fraternité des emplois publics, (excepté toutefois celle du salon): ils sont furieux de ne pouvoir joindre à cela l'égalité de la peau" (89). Can one discern behind these remarks laced with scorn what Ségalas's mother may have witnessed in Saint-Domingue?

The character Jupiter resurfaces at this juncture, inspiring cheers from the black people gathered outside the courtroom. A negative allusion to Toussaint Louverture in the same context emphasizes the slave revolt he led. The narrator glosses from this perspective the blind stance blacks took "pour le noir contre le blanc, sans raisonnement, sans conviction, uniquement parce qu'ils voyaient là une question de couleur" (*Récits des Antilles*, 89). This line of thought carries through to the novel's end. Ségalas's narrative retreats from the more balanced view in other women's writing that the French, too, especially French Creoles in the colonies, reacted irrationally to blacks. While attempting to flee, Jupiter is bitten by a poisonous snake, confesses his crime, and dies. Charly and Onélie declare their love for one another, and Rosélis is reunited with her father. This weak conclusion assimilates the two Frances in the guise of a happy ending for whites only, which leaves Ségalas open to charges of racism.[63] This issue, however, offers little insight into why Ségalas's works treating France's colonial enterprise in the nineteenth century, which nearly bookend her output, have been unevenly preserved by literary critics.

In 1890, three years before Ségalas died, François Desplantes and Paul Pouthier assessed her production and recalled *Les algériennes* as anchoring her engagement with French colonization. Yet, to explain why her œuvre had been included in the most honorable places in nineteenth-century French literature, they reiterated Eugène de Mirecourt's 1856 appraisal of Ségalas as "le poète des mères, des enfants et la famille" (*Madame Anaïs Ségalas*, 89). This is the same category that Ségalas was placed in by Louise D'Alq who in her 1893 anthology of French women writers ranked Ségalas as the most popular "poète féminin" of the century, calling her poetry "les annales du XIX$^e$ siècle mises en vers" (*Anthologie féminine*, 344).[64] In 1895, René Doumic also ignored the colonial themes probed by Ségalas, but placed her "au deuxième rang," predicting that she would fall into oblivion: "le sort commun des écrits de toutes les femmes" (*La vie et les mœurs*, 253). After the turn of the century, Edmond Pilon recalled Ségalas among the "muses plaintives du romantisme" and mentioned "La Créole (L'esclavage)" to capture the exotic flair of the poet "hantée de paysages tropicaux, de tamariniers et de déesses noires" ("Les muses plaintives du romantisme," 208).

In her anthology, Jeanine Moulin suggests Ségalas's deeper connection to French colonial history: "[L]es origines maternelles d'Anaïs Ségalas lui ont certainement mieux fait comprendre le drame des gens de couleur" (*La poésie féminine*, 292). Ségalas's heritage further textures her political affiliations in Évelyne Sullerot's history of women's press, the "douce créole" flanking the "poétesse non sans valeur qui fut de tous les clubs féministes de 1848" (*Histoire de la presse féminine*, 172). This snapshot of a more complex writer is not preserved by Luce Czyba, who reads Ségalas through the prism of twenty-first-century feminism and isolates "un conformisme conservateur" to cast her enduring legacy as a "muse chrétienne" ("Anais Ségalas," 185). Yet, as I have shown from the colonial corpus buried by the feminine works commonly listed for Ségalas, she diversified her production well beyond the Romantic "poetess" tradition that conservative critics have used to limit women's verse and thus maintain the maleness of poetic genius. In the next chapter, I reexamine the writings of the so-called late Romantic Malvina Blanchecotte, who reveals another aspect of poetic women's intellectual legacy, by positing that the labor of genius transcends class and gender.

# 5 Work, Genius, and the In-Between in Malvina Blanchecotte

A self-described "ouvrière et poète" perpetually caught between manual and mental labor, Malvina Blanchecotte (1830–1897; fig. 14) emerged on the literary scene during the early Second Empire.[1] Political stability and the resulting economic prosperity marked this regime, which spanned the years from 1852 to 1870. The gap between the rich and the poor nevertheless widened because social mobility through work or education stagnated during the same period. Despite a lifelong struggle with poverty and illness, Blanchecotte forged a serious path as a writer who delved into the creative power of thought. She won prizes from the Académie française for her poetic volume *Rêves et réalités* (1855) and her prose collection *Impressions d'une femme: Pensées, sentiments, et portraits* (1868). While Blanchecotte's poetry exhibits Romantic and Parnassian aesthetics, her prose incorporates lyricism, philosophical objectivity, and social realism. By reading Blanchecotte chiefly as a late Romantic, however, critics have silenced her intellectual legacy. Blanchecotte not only probes the meaning of genius in relation to class and gender, but also anticipates a critical turn in French poetic history by articulating the notion of the poet as worker and *voyant*.

In fashioning her poetic genealogy in the mid-1850s, Blanchecotte claimed the author of *Méditations poétiques*, Lamartine, as her model. Later, Blanchecotte revealed Charlotte Brontë as a source of inspiration for the objectivity she developed in the 1860s and '70s, extending the philosophical bent of her early verse and prose.[2] But to what tradition, if any, did Blanchecotte understand herself to belong as she exploited liminality (from the Latin *limens*, threshold) to position her voice between categories—female, worker, poet—and, in so doing, between genders and genres? What did it mean to be a poet occupying a female worker's body? As a laborer, woman, and writer, she was marginalized triply. Blanchecotte appropriated this ambiguous positioning as both a strategy of self-representation and a framework

FIG 14
Malvina Blanchecotte
as a young child
with her Scottish
deerhound. Photo:
Bibliothèque nationale
de France.

for examining inherited categories. The rival discourses of genius revealed in Blanchecotte's inaugural volume, *Rêves et réalités*, set the stage for analyzing how she cultivated work as the in-between or liminal space between material reality and the realm of creativity.

In this chapter I examine how Blanchecotte structures her poetic identity with and without markers of class and gender while reflecting on the nature of genius. I begin with letters from her mentor, Pierre de Béranger, which preserve the thought and effort Blanchecotte invested in her writing. The dialogic framing of Blanchecotte's early correspondence textures the analysis of the way that feeling overlaps with reflection across her production. In *Rêves et réalités*, she raises the question of genius, a query that I relate to her prefaces along with other paratexts of the volume, including reviews and correspondence. Blanchecotte's approach to creative writing shows how she multiplies the possibilities of authorial voice and gives fresh meaning to the *work* of originality as it evolves in her later verse and prose, treated in the second half of the chapter.

## Refiguring "Natural" Genius

Like Desbordes-Valmore, Blanchecotte fits the description of authors who, as Andrew Elfenbein argues in a related context, "seemed to have miraculously overcome their supposed lack of education to become distinguished poets. For writers who came from classes or groups that traditionally had no place in the . . . literary market, genius was a wedge into a hitherto closed system" ("Mary Wollstonecraft," 234). Blanchecotte was as candid as Desbordes-Valmore about writing against the odds and, on the surface, as reserved about her intellectualism. Yet Blanchecotte contradicted the modest posture she often adopted by actively seeking guidance to develop her craft. She also revealed through the depth of her ideas how broadly she read. This tension in Blanchecotte tempers the spontaneity commonly associated with women's discovery of verse since the Romantic era, which critics have tied specifically to an emotional blow with or *without* explicit statements from the writers themselves. Of the poets I have considered to this point, only Desbordes-Valmore and Waldor evoke pain as a catalyst for their turn to poetic writing. Grief is not the basis for creativity claimed by their contemporaries Tastu, Mercœur, Ségalas, and Colet, whose ample use of epigraphs links their development as poets to intellectual culture. Though Blanchecotte did not display her literary education as openly, the same holds true for her. In wrestling with different types of labor, menial versus transcendent, as a worker and poet, Blanchecotte gravitated toward despair but ultimately elevated thought as the greatest source of human dignity.

By 1850, three years after marrying François Blanchecotte, a bookkeeper, she had established relationships with Lamartine and Béranger, who introduced her to Louise Colet. Blanchecotte soon extended her circle by attending Colet's literary gatherings, which often focused on philosophy, and would count George Sand among her supporters.[3] From this perspective, Christine Planté notes Blanchecotte's serious preparation: "Elle lit beaucoup, apprend des langues, et travaille avec acharnement pour réaliser son ambition littéraire" (*Femmes poètes du XIXᵉ siècle*, 195). In the absence of a complete autobiography and with only a thin record of Blanchecotte's correspondence, Béranger's missives to the "jeune muse," as he addresses her in the first letter, dated 27 June 1850, allow a consideration of the early development of her poetic voice (*Correspondance*, 4:84).[4] These letters reveal that the ambitious autodidact, who learned English, German, and Latin, worked to master prosodic form, thus moderating her passion with ideation.

Béranger recognizes Blanchecotte's dual gift as cerebral and sentient, which he expresses to her this way: "votre belle et noble intelligence, avec laquelle il me semble que votre cœur rivalise avec avantage" (*Correspondance*, 4:94). That the color black permeated the world evoked in Blanchecotte's early verse was not surprising to Béranger, given the hardships she had endured as the child of common laborers.[5] Workers endured substandard living conditions, and a day's labor often stretched to fifteen hours. Financial difficulties together with poor health plagued Blanchecotte as she juggled work and writing, and motherhood was added in mid-1851.

Two poems that Blanchecotte asks Béranger to critique strike him as particularly somber in tone. An editor's note identifies one of them by title: "Après une lecture sur Napoléon."[6] In this poem (dated 29 July 1850), Blanchecotte's speaker uses the familiar form "tu" to address the fallen emperor and charge him with having created a void, the source of "le mal du siècle" explained in Musset's *La confession d'un enfant du siècle* (1836).[7] Writing to Blanchecotte on 31 July 1852, Béranger admires the lines beginning with "dont" in the following section of the poem: "Lui l'Europe, lui Tout, lui qui fut le Destin, / Lui la Toute-Puissance en un génie humain / Dont le pied comprimait la poitrine du monde, / Dont l'œil mesurait tout dans son âme profonde, / Qui commandait d'un geste aux rois de l'univers, / Le voilà sur un brick qui l'entraîne aux déserts" (*Rêves et réalités* [1855], 221). In the same letter, Béranger cautions Blanchecotte against using flowery language ("l'école des grands mots") and urges her to cultivate a lighter tone: "Vous êtes, au reste, dans l'âge où l'on s'exagère ses maux, et par malheur, votre situation excuse ici l'exagération. Pourtant je vous engage à ne pas trop user de pareilles couleurs; car l'esprit à votre âge, s'obstine souvent à vouloir tenir parole aux expressions qui lui sont échappées. Il en résulte qu'après avoir été vrai un moment on court risque d'être faux toute sa vie" (*Correspondance*, 4:145). Ultimately, Blanchecotte did not heed Béranger's advice and succeeded in capturing, through both verse and prose, the gap between visions of the ideal and the darker realities of life.

In a letter dated 15 September 1852, Béranger counsels his protégée in response to an apparent query about the sonnet form, which she would practice with aplomb: "Quant au sonnet, je ne vous en dirai rien, si ce n'est qu'il ne faut pas faire de vers au hasard. Attendez qu'un sentiment bien vif ou une idée grande ou originale vienne vous saisir pour prendre la peine de l'encadrer dans des rimes: alors vous êtes sûre de bien faire" (*Correspondance*, 4:153). Different generations of nineteenth-century poets of both genders used, or rejected, the sonnet for aesthetic reasons, as previously discussed. In the second half of the century, use of the sonnet distinguished the Parnassians and Symbolists from the Romantics.[8] Blanchecotte positioned her voice between literary schools throughout her career, however. Shifting from effusion to restraint through various poetic forms, she made the in-between a source of creative agency.

The discursive mobility developed by Blanchecotte is similarly visible in the prefaces she authored, which express both an uneasy ascription of authorship and resistance to the dominant culture. These overlapping stances could be seen as diffusing Blanchecotte's convictions, but they suggest an attempt to navigate the "field of cultural production" directly related to the authoritarian prelude to the Second Empire.[9] In 1851, Napoleon III closed the "goguettes" (bistros) that had given birth to the worker-poets' literary movement under the July Monarchy (see Thomas, *Voix d'en bas*). Censorship imposed in 1852, along with harsh measures against the enemies of the government, who were exiled in great numbers, ceded to greater liberties in the early 1860s. Workers benefited from reforms in 1864 and 1866, which granted them the right to strike and to organize, respectively. Women gained greater access to public education, having an advocate in the emperor's wife, Empress Eugénie. In 1861, Julie-Victoire Daubié became the first woman in France to receive a baccalaureate diploma. However, hostility against gifted women did not abate. Against this background, Blanchecotte's self-portrayal reproduces shifts in power relations along with her deeper sense of work energizing her relationship to creativity. Though Blanchecotte alludes to workers' difficult lives in her verse and prose, she called herself a worker *and* a poet. The conjunction allowed her to maintain a dual identity and simultaneously explore various thresholds of the liminal space between self and other, illumining the indeterminate nature of creative voice.

## The Threshold of Identity

Blanchecotte used a pseudonym, M^me M. B., for the 1855 edition of *Rêves et réalités*.[10] Such self-prescribed anonymity shields a literary woman from scorn. Directly below the author's initials in that volume are the terms "ouvrière et poète." These categories are grammatically marked as feminine and masculine, respectively. Blanchecotte exploits this ambiguity in relation to work, whereby the manual laborer flanks the creative writer. Her short preface interlocks the worker's toil with the poet's: "Les loisirs de l'étude n'ont jamais existé pour l'auteur de ces vers. Son volume a été composé entre les travaux de l'ouvrière et ceux du teneur de livres. Tel qu'il est, il se présente comme un écho des Rêves à côté des Réalités. Si l'écho est triste, c'est que les Rêves reflètent trop souvent les préoccupations de la vie. D'autres poètes ont jeté au monde un chant, une prière, une espérance; elle, la pauvre ouvrière, lui aura jeté une larme: Dieu seul recevra sans doute cette larme silencieuse" (5).[11] Likening her verse to a silent tear, Blanchecotte suggests that her contribution has little prospect of being recognized. The issue on which she insists is not gender, but a lack of time to study in order to perfect her writing. Blanchecotte refers to herself in the third person as an author and a worker, positioning her creative production across the line usually drawn between mind and matter, between brain and body. Work, however, is key to the paradoxical identity she structures by eliding mental and physical exertion and thus blurring the distance between high and low culture. Class and gender lose their sharp edges in Blanchecotte's encoding of authorship; she resists the so-called feminine tradition that had long limited the scope of women's poetry.

*Rêves et réalités* (1855) opens with the dedicatory poem "À la muse." The epigraph "I love you for ever" is addressed to the "Muse chérie," who represents the only genuine relationship the speaker has known. As a proxy for the mother as well as the motherland, the muse does not signify the force of creativity as maternity in the physiological sense but, rather, poetic self-creation: "Vous qui m'avez bercée et consolée enfant, / Qui m'avez tenu lieu de mère et de patrie, / J'irai sur votre cœur pour y rêver souvent" (7). The speaker contemplates how she overcame the pain of betrayal and desertion by writing, guided by her inner muse, whom she also calls her "ange gardien" (7). However, past sorrows linger and remind the reader of a working class blindly chained to mass production:

> À présent qu'inconnue et rivée à ma chaîne,
> Je traîne obscurément le poids de mon passé,
> Je sens votre regard rayonner sur ma peine,
> Comme un peu de soleil sur mon rêve effacé!
>
> (8)

"À la muse" prefigures the work of grief underlying Blanchecotte's writerly pursuits, which transform such loss by creating an alternate plenitude.

Dreams and realities intersect in a composite narrative of eight female figures, which constitutes the first section of *Rêves et réalités*.[12] Sainte-Beuve proposes that these figures—"Blanche," "Jobbie," "Maria," "Lucie," "Henrietta," "Madeleine," "Gabrielle," and "Conchita"—mirror Blanchecotte's secret wounds: "[P]ar toutes ces figures diverses qu'a évoquées autour d'elle l'imagination de l'ouvrière-poëte, elle s'est plu à multiplier, comme dans un miroir légèrement enchanté, des images d'elle-même, et elle n'a changé que juste ce qu'il fallait pour pouvoir dire: *Ce n'est pas moi!*" ("*Rêves et réalités*," 331; emphasis in original). In Blanchecotte, however, the poetics of pain also performs ideological work. Through this narrative, where mirror images multiply alongside alter egos, one discovers Blanchecotte's clever self-representation *among* identities. Her strategy deflects critics' aim to domesticate a gifted woman by reading her life into her writing. The worker stigmatized by her roots remains in the background while the poet engages with the issue of gender inherent to the nineteenth century's vocabulary of genius.

### The Passion of Genius

In "Blanche," which numbers more than thirty-five pages, Blanchecotte adopts the bildungsroman genre. The stanzaic narrative form exhibits a consistent rhyme scheme, pairing alexandrines (*aabb*) throughout, along with crossing octosyllabic verse (*abab*) for songs.[13] The poem also displays rich rhyme (three phonemes in common). Divided into three titled sections, called "chapters," "Blanche" represents a young woman as the embodiment of a poet. While her eyes hold mysterious depth, symbolizing vision, her forehead reflects the divine mark of giftedness:

> Elle était grande et pâle, elle était grave et belle;
> Son pas était rêveur et languissant comme elle;
> .  .  .  .  .  .  .  .  .  .  .  .  .  .  .  .  .  .  .  .  .  .  .  .

Ses yeux profonds et noirs se voilaient de mystère
Et changeaient leur douceur contre un regard austère,
Regard étrange et sombre et pourtant plein de feu,
Quand quelque mot puissant: Génie, Amour ou Dieu,
Négligemment ou non était dit devant elle.
Son sourire exprimait la pensée immortelle:
Il était fixe et long et semblait révéler
Un rêve intérieur que rien n'eût pu troubler.
On voyait sur son front le sceau des grandes âmes,
Ce blazon radieux d'élus, hommes ou femmes,
Que Dieu dès le berceau sépara d'entre tous,
Qu'il fit rois, comme, hélas! les bouffons et les fous:
(Le génie est chez nous la suprême folie!)
Pourtant elle était tendre, et sa voix amollie,
Voix qui n'a pas d'échos au grand désert humain,
Répandait sa rosée aux souffrants du chemin.

· · · · · · · · · · · · · · · · ·

Son âme était visible, on en sentait la flamme:
Malgré son diadème, enfin, elle était femme!

(Rêves et réalités [1855], 11–12)

This depiction of a woman of poetic genius exploits the history of the word "génie" and its medical inflection in mid-century France.

Blanchecotte invokes the concept "Génie," indicated by the capitalized form, which is followed by its dual meaning of an inborn talent and an exceptional individual: "(Le génie est chez nous la suprême folie!)." This parenthetical aside creates gender ambiguity, invoking "we the French" and/or "we French women" and thus gesturing toward the implied author. Blanchecotte's narrator injects as well a sardonic undertone that draws out the contemporary linkage of genius and madness. The founding of asylums early in the nineteenth century gave rise to "aliénistes," professionals who treated the mentally ill and who had begun to theorize links between psychiatric disorders and creativity by the 1830s.[14] Blanchecotte's paraphrase of the adage "Pas de génie sans quelque grain de folie" points forward to Jacques-Joseph Moreau de Tours's view in *La psychologie morbide* (1859): "Le *génie*, c'est-à-dire la plus haute expression, le *nec plus ultra* de l'activité intellectuelle, qu'une *névrose?* Pourquoi non?" (464; emphasis in original).[15] For Blanchecotte, the crux of the culture of pathology now surrounding genius was its meaning for women. Could a woman born with a gift ("On voyait sur son front . . . / Ce blazon radieux d'élus, hommes ou femmes") disentangle her creative identity from the social body she inhabited?

Read for the love plot, "Blanche" resurrects the specter of Staël's *Corinne*, but Blanchecotte considers the problem of genius otherwise. As her poetic narrator (also the implied author) asks: Why be born superior in mind, if such superiority destines one for suffering? In other words, why be born a poet with a sense of an ideal that cannot exist in reality?

> Pourquoi naître superbe entre les plus superbes,
> Et le front ceint des fleurs des plus célestes gerbes?
> Pourquoi sentir en soi l'infini déborder,
> Les vents du ciel chanter, les vents des mers gronder?
> Pourquoi naître puissant, tendre, fier, pathétique,
> Pourquoi tout contenir en son cœur sympathique?
> De souffrance et de deuil prédestination,
> C'est pour mieux accepter toute immolation!
>
> (*Rêves et réalités*, 15)

The abridged anaphora (via the repetition of "pourquoi") adds intensity. But it also defers the answer to the speaker's query about the pain inherent in superiority, meaning Blanche's exceptional vision.

The question posed about such a gifted woman's fate yields a daunting reply that targets all of humanity: "Nous naissons las déjà de notre propre poids, / Las de notre néant et pressentant nos croix" (*Rêves et réalités*, 16). From a viewpoint presaging Louise Ackermann's philosophical pessimism (discussed in chapter 7), the speaker prepares Blanche's moment of transcendence, represented as human love projected onto a mystical union with nature. Poetic vision, as suggested by Blanchecotte's portrayal of Blanche, allows one to glimpse divine harmony without being able to fuse the spiritual and physical spheres of existence. Dreams and reality (as we perceive them) coexist, albeit in separate realms of human awareness.

A docked ship provides the *locus amoenus* for a chance encounter between the lovely and talented Blanche from Paris and John Johnson, the ship's handsome commander from Liverpool. The idyllic setting of the transnational connection, which exceeds the boundaries of the subject's immediate universe, contrasts with the looming separation that will shatter the promise of happiness. In a thoroughly romantic instant, love is conceived in a glance, penetrating the tender hearts of the female protagonist and the captain who beholds her. As they redirect their gaze to the heavens while experiencing the sound of the waves, apart from the crowd gathered for the ball, Blanche and Johnson enter silently into mystical communion with nature:

> Oh! quel soupir mortel ne se trouve arrêté
> Pour se changer soudain en extase et prière
> Devant la majesté de la nature altière
> Qui semble étreindre l'homme en fascinant sa foi!
> Cet éblouissement le transfigure en roi:
> Il abdique ses sens, son esprit, son cœur même,
> Pour s'absorber plus libre en la splendeur suprême;

Tout intérêt humain disparaît et se fond
Dans l'hymne universel qui fait courber son front.
(*Rêves et réalités*, 20–21)

Humankind can only aspire to realize the unity of the natural world. The omniscient narrator comments on this projection of feeling onto nature, which fails to preserve an experience of transcendence.

Here, in "Blanche," the poetic narrator elaborates on the Romantics' confidence in a preordained harmony between humanity and nature:

O solitude, ô brise, ô flots harmonieux,
Quel puissant talisman reçûtes-vous des cieux?
Dans votre chant mystique, ô rêveuse Nature,
N'est-ce pas Dieu qui parle à toute créature?
(*Rêves et réalités*, 21)

The ensuing departure of the ship signals Blanche's awakening, as if from a dream, via an abrupt shift from the metaphysical plane of the speaker's intervention to the realm of the real: "Blanche s'interroge incertaine / Du rêve auquel son âme a cru" (22). The perfect harmony she has experienced through love was but a fleeting moment.

Passions of the mind and soul mingle in a meditation on solitude, which overlies the narrative of Blanche's emotional turmoil during Johnson's absence. The romantic thread of the narrative develops against the rendering of Blanche's superior mind. This retreat from society maps out the traditional path of the Romantic genius finding enthusiasm or inspiration (the God within) while contemplating nature:

Eloigné de la foule, on est si près de Dieu
Qu'on respire la paix dont s'empreint son ciel bleu.
Dieu parle à l'âme triste et se fait son refuge:
C'est un père attendri, ce n'est jamais un juge!
Il rafraîchit nos fronts, il nous prend par la main
Et nous fait parcourir un idéal chemin,
Sentier d'ombre ineffable et de fleurs immortelles;
Là, pour voler à lui, nos âmes ont des ailes,
Là, nous ne sentons plus le poids des passions;
Tout s'efface en nos cœurs libres d'ambitions.
(*Rêves et réalités*, 26)

The opening query about the passion of genius hovers in the background as the narrative focuses on an inconsolable Blanche pining away for Johnson: "Elle a trouvé la plaie incurable et profonde" (30). Privately, she falls into dark despair, having lost hope of ever seeing Johnson again: "Cette mort de l'espoir est la plus sombre mort" (31). Publicly, however, she continues to demonstrate her talent.

In drawing her narrative of the gifted Blanche to a close, Blanchecotte prepares an unusual denouement, where a woman of genius and a womanly woman circulate within the same discursive space; she does not bind them together nor pull them apart. In anticipation of another ball, the poet recycles the double figure of Blanche: "Allons! ceins ta double couronne / Et de génie et de beauté" (35). At the ball, Blanche chances upon Johnson and discovers that he is now betrothed to a young Italian woman. The difference between Staël's Corinne and the creative woman in Blanchecotte's poem is that, unlike Oswald, Johnson never recognizes Blanche as a woman of genius. Instead of a struggle to accept that superior intelligence and creativity neither preclude femininity nor induce masculinity, human folly guides the flight from love that Blanchecotte imagined an exceptional woman must endure with dignity.

### "Ouvrière et Poète"

Blanchecotte conceived a similar plot for "Maria." In this framed tale of an impossible romance, however, she places her female subject in a different milieu to suggest the idea that poetic creativity is blind to sex, class, and race:

> C'était une ouvrière alerte et diligente,
> D'un air royal malgré ses haillons d'indigente;
> On ne lui connaissait que des indifférents,
> Elle-même ignorait le nom de ses parents.
> Elle ne savait rien de ses jeunes années,
> Sinon que l'abandon les fit infortunées,
> Et que, croissant toujours, trop de misère enfin
> Avait changé de nom et s'appelait la faim.
> Elle chantait pourtant; Dieu l'avait fait poète.
> (*Rêves et réalités* [1855], 71–72)

Here, Blanchecotte ignores the Romantic tradition of representing genius as a divine bequest inspiring men with sublime ideas, on the one hand, and women with poetic sensibilities, on the other. She thus echoes Colet's claim in "Enthousiasme" that God has made her a poet. French grammar alone makes Blanchecotte's point clear, gendering the worker as feminine ("ouvrière") but not the poet ("Dieu l'avait fait poète"). Even more boldly than Colet, however, Blanchecotte pushes the category of "genius" beyond socioeconomic determinism. Through the figure of Maria, the poet born a worker, Blanchecotte limits the expected Romantic effusion by giving voice to existential pain.

The avian metaphor in "Maria" does not conjure up the rapture of songbirds, such as the nightingale, swallow, and dove that Desbordes-Valmore and Tastu use to symbolize poetic voice. Rather, the poet's "song" conveys intense anguish and a death wish:

> Mais son chant n'était pas un doux chant de fauvette,
> C'était le chant aigu de l'oiseau des déserts
> Qui sème ses sanglots en traversant les airs,
> Et qui laisse de lui dans chaque solitude
> Quelque lambeau de cris, quelque sombre prélude.
> O vie! ô destinée! ô lugubre combat
> De l'esprit qui s'élève et du corps qui s'abat;
> O vertige de mort! ô soif inexorable
> De sommeil, de tombeau, seul abri désirable!
> Le précipice est là dès lorsqu'il fait trop noir.
>
> (*Rêves et réalités*, 72)

Strife, exemplified by the agon between the elevated mind and the subjugated body, pervades the scene in which Blanchecotte situates Maria's solitary figure. How can the laborer reconcile the ideal envisioned in her poetic mind's eye with the reality of her despair?

The frame structure of "Maria" performs a type of doubling. A shift from narration in the third to the first person suggests the cinematic mode of the voice-over, which produces the effect of storytelling or authorial intervention by an omniscient narrator. The issue of creative identity recedes as the sentimental theme of "Maria" comes into relief via this shift. Does Blanchecotte borrow the voice of her third-person speaker to express concern over the reception she could expect as a poet who happened to be both female and a worker? Or is she playing up modesty only to question this convention and the construction of gender it supports?

> O douce Maria, n'est-ce pas violer
> Tes secrets et tes vers, que de les révéler?
> Et vous qui les lirez, avez-vous l'âme chaste?
> Avez-vous le cœur fier, l'esprit enthousiaste?
>
> (*Rêves et réalités*, 74)

To divulge Maria's verse (discovered after her death in the context of the poem) means revealing her thoughts and feelings and, at the level of Blanchecotte's meta-discourse, risking both critical scrutiny as a poet and public exposure as a woman: "Que t'importe mon nom? que t'importe ma vie / Que t'importent mes vers? que t'importent mes pleurs?" (*Rêves et réalités*, 75). Maria's response to the narrator's question echoes Blanchecotte's depiction of her verse as silent tears in the 1855 preface to *Rêves et réalités*. A four-part sequence—each part composed of quatrains and written in alexandrines with an *abab* rhyme scheme—exposes Maria's bittersweet love. In a highly sentimental text (on the surface), Maria recalls being smitten at the sight of a cavalier in a public square. Their class difference proves insurmountable, however, and she languishes for him until her premature death. The other point of "Maria" is social critique, mirroring the contestatory stance in "Blanche."

The speaker's closing remarks frame Maria's soliloquy by returning to the issue of a female worker born a poet and thus refer to Blanchecottes own crossing of social boundaries. Creative genius unsettles such limits, but may not transcend them altogether, as the poem's end implies:

> Dors ton dernier sommeil, enfant douce et candide!
> . . . . . . . . . . . . . . .
> Il était grand seigneur, et toi pauvre ouvrière;
> La curiosité le mit seul à tes pieds.
> Ne savais-tu donc pas qu'il est une barrière
> Que rien ne peut franchir, même les vœux altiers,
> Même l'essor du cœur, ni l'aile du génie . . .
> (*Rêves et réalités*, 88; ending ellipses in original)

All is possible in the realm of thought. One is free to associate disparate elements, and there is no impulse to the contrary. Within the imagination as within the heart one can transcend all barriers, Blanchecotte's speaker suggests. But according to nineteenth-century French society, class—like sex and race—denoted a barrier that one could not remove ("Ne savais-tu donc pas qu'il est une barrière / Que rien ne peut franchir"). How should one understand this retreat in "Maria" from the "claim to an imaginative life unfettered by class or gender constraints," as elaborated by Judith Rosen in a related context ("Class and Poetic Communities," 213)?[16] Through the conceptual tensions that energize Blanchecotte's trajectory, one discovers how cleverly she represented her capacity as a poet and thinker to explore opposite categories and to position her voice between them.

## Dreams and Realities

Of the remaining poems in the cluster devoted to female figures, "Lucie" and "Henrietta" treat, at first glance, the ravages of love. Yet, in a similar manner to "Blanche" and "Maria," they reflect the ideological work of the binary structure—dreams and realities—embedded in the title of Blanchecotte's collection. So, too, Blanchecotte's prefatory comparison of her verse to tears has resonance in her poetic corpus beyond the sentimental. Both are immaterial and material, emanating from the soul yet made manifest through the body—a body that Blanchecotte does not mark as maternal, nor necessarily feminine, despite the speaker's gender. In "Lucie," for example, the speaking subject refers to the mournful verses retracing Lucie's death, her "fidèle sanglot, / Larme de sang qui sur ces pages tombe" (*Rêves et réalités*, 97).[17] Similarly, to the memory of the eponymous subject of "Henrietta," the speaker closes with these lines: "J'ai déposé ces vers, qui sont aussi des pleurs" (105). Poetic expression thus navigates between the spiritual and the physical on the boundary between dreams and realities.

Near the close of the sequence, in "Madeleine," discourses of genius, love, and religion interweave. This narrative poem, exhibiting the complexity seen in "Blanche," reaches back through the myth of Mary Magdalene to develop in poetry the sublimation of passion (in the senses of both suffering and strong feeling). Framed by a prologue and an epilogue (each composed of a single stanza in octosyllabic verse with an *abab* rhyme scheme), "Madeleine" is divided into sixteen "chapters" of unequal length and different poetic structure. For example, parts 1 and 3 consist of four stanzas, each composed of seven alexandrines followed by a six-syllable line that accelerates the rhythm. Part 2 shifts to eight quatrains of alexandrines, while part 4 includes seven quatrains of alexandrines. By virtue of its asymmetrical rhythm, "Madeleine" follows the inner beat of passion, producing a prosodic mimesis of emotion. Parts 5 and 6, each a single quatrain, express short bursts of fear and doubt, respectively. Subsequent sections reveal the poem's careful design. Quatrains composed of octosyllabic lines or alexandrines further demonstrate Blanchecotte's sense of rhythm and its effects. In "Madeleine" and elsewhere, Blanchecotte's prosodic flair contradicts her self-representation as an artless muse.

From a thematic standpoint, "Madeleine" probes a woman's inner world in relation to her creative drive. Blanchecotte again deploys a framed narrative in this poem, producing a multiplicity of voices through the transfer of authority among various speakers. Here, however, instead of shifting between third- and first-person voices to distinguish the narrator from the principal character, all storytelling occurs in the first person (Je). This identifies the narrator's voice with both Madeleine and the implied author. The speaking subject recalls her passion and its (creative) sublimation:

> Plus de chants! je veux vivre attachée à ta peine;
>
> . . . . . . . . . . . . . . . . .
> Tout ce dont le cœur bat, religion, génie,
> Ce qui fait le regard perdu dans le ciel bleu,
> Tout ce qui grandit l'âme à l'idéal unie,
> Sagesse, extase, gloire, amour pur dit à Dieu!
> Ce qui donne à nos fronts une fierté soudaine,
> Tout rêve se résume au rêve de mon cœur:

Je veux être à tes pieds l'aimante Madeleine,
    La Madeleine du Sauveur!

Que le ciel resplendisse et que l'onde murmure,
Mon hymne désormais sera mon dévouement!
              (*Rêves et réalités* [1856], 102, 103)

In a familiar refrain of the female figures examined to this point, unreciprocated love produces intense grief. Does such pain precipitate a descent into fatal despair, or release the flame of poetic ascent?

The death of passion that the speaker seeks has a double meaning. The idea of suppressing desire may free the subject from the ache of unrequited love. This immolation can also be connected with sexual urges sublimated as creativity. But Blanchecotte's character does not imagine herself writing through the desiring body, or the maternal body, for that matter.[18] To render the source of creation as analogous to corporeal desire, disengaged from solely reproductive sexuality, would mean to recognize nonreproductive sexual desire in women. Madeleine's expression emerges more chastely from the depths of her soul:

Qu'ai-je donc arraché du secret de mon âme?
Taisez-vous, vains sanglots! mourez, élans de feu!
Qu'en votre sein, Dieu bon! périsse mon aveu!
J'aimerai comme un ange et non comme une femme!
              (*Rêves et réalités*, 104)

The spiritual and physical realms merge in the body of poetry. Here, the creative urge ("élan de feu")—represented as a surge of (divine) fire or (human) passion—animates the transcendence of gender through the transfiguration from woman to angel.

However, this ardor or drive to create is an autonomous force that escapes the speaker's attempt to quell its power:

Oh! laissez-moi toujours vous dévoiler mon âme,
Oh! laissez-moi toujours vous parler comme à Dieu!
À vous les chants rêveurs et les élans de flamme
    De ma pensée en feu!

À vous mon cœur ardent, vieux avant les années,
Cœur abattu, mais fier, où vous lirez des pleurs!
Il veut, lui qui rêvait les hautes destinées,
    Une tombe et des fleurs.

Pourtant il vibre encore au grand mot de génie!
Étude, art, dévoûment, patrie, et toi, vertu!

> Tu fais encor divins mes rêves d'insomnie,
>     Mon regret est vaincu!
>
> . . . . . . . . . . . . . . . . .
>
> Oh! laissez-moi toujours vous dévoiler mon âme,
> Oh! laissez-moi toujours vous parler comme à Dieu!
> À vous mes chants ailés, à vous mon cœur de femme
>     Et ma pensée en feu!
>
>             (*Rêves et réalités*, 108, 109)[19]

This section of "Madeleine" swings from self-effacement to the reclaiming of creative agency. Represented as tears and encoded as feminine ("mon cœur de femme"), personal lyricism mixes with the discourse on creative genius ("ma pensée en feu"). Such slippage between subjectivity and objectivity is expressed through the multiple voices in Blanchecotte's poetic corpus.

### Illuminating Multiplicity

No single theme provides an overarching structure for the second half of *Rêves et réalités*. In this part, entitled "Poésies diverses," what Béranger privately criticized as a lack of order highlights the impulse guiding Blanchecotte's poetry: her attempt to capture different strands of thought at a given moment.[20] The topics stretch from the personal to the universal, the real to the imaginary, and the sacred to the profane. This thematic diversity exceeds, and yet is informed by, the three principal ideas that link the cluster of female figures just examined: genius, love, and God. To pursue this triad in the volume as a whole, I consider another facet of the duality Blanchecotte shaped between the voice of the lyrical yet philosophical poet and that of the "poetess."

"Poésies diverses" opens with "À M. A. de L." Rather than carving out a space for her originality, as one might expect from the discourse of genius in the first part of *Rêves et réalités*, Blanchecotte's narrator positions herself as Lamartine's direct descendant:

> Lorsque de jeunes voix s'essayant sur la lyre,
> Font vibrer jusqu'à vous leurs chants nés de vos chants,
> Ah! donnez-leur encore un doux mot, un sourire,
> D'un accueil généreux témoignages touchants!
>
>             (131)

Self-identified as a meek child, grammatically gendered as feminine, the narrator twins her poetic efforts with artlessness:

> Mais lorsqu'une humble enfant, confidence divine,
> Sans art vous dit son âme, et son rêve et sa foi,
>   Alors, ô Lamartine,
>   Souvenez-vous de moi!
>
> (132)[21]

With the stance taken here, Blanchecotte strains the point made in the section devoted to female figures. Why would she reverse herself in the same volume, now ascribing to Lamartine the creative authority granted to women, as in "Blanche"? The dates of composition—"À M. A. de L." in June 1851 and "Blanche" on 25 September 1851—draw the texts not into a linear progression, but rather into a dialogue on the gendered hierarchy of poetic voice. Opposite modes of self-representation continually reposition the woman and the poet in relation to one another and to convention. By experimenting with different subject positions, both grammatically and thematically, Blanchecotte could escape the social space that limited her identity in real life. However, the literary public sphere posed a different obstacle. Upon what basis could a woman stake her reputation as a writer? The category of "woman poet" left little room for creativity.

Key to understanding this tension in Blanchecotte's thinking is her proximity to the subject. Whereas "Blanche" is a fictional woman of genius from whom Blanchecotte could distance herself, the speaker who pays homage to a known mentor in "À M. A. de L." could be readily identified with her. Blanchecotte's positioning of herself as inferior to her mentor, Lamartine, implies an attempt to gain the public's favor by striking the expected pose of a nineteenth-century woman as well as to please potential sponsors. Yet she simultaneously creates another entry into literary history by moving toward Parnassian formalism. A sonnet follows Blanchecotte's dedicatory poem to Lamartine in all editions of *Rêves et réalités*, showing how her increased formal control curbs the sentimental excesses of Romanticism.

The sonnet "À ma mère" (7 December 1853) is composed of two quatrains, both with the classical rhyme scheme *abab*, followed by two tercets, which also exhibit rich rhyme (*ccd, eed*). Blanchecotte harnesses the semantic power of repeated sounds, activating a phonetic network with the word "souvenirs" in the first line of the poem. The initial sibilant consonant *s* reverberates in lines 2 ("tout ce que j'ai souffert") and 3 ("un sceau de silence"), fusing the stifled memory of a traumatic past with the stillness of death:

> Ne me torturez plus, ô souvenirs d'enfance!
> J'ai besoin d'oublier tout ce que j'ai souffert;
> J'ai sur mon cœur vieilli mis un sceau de silence,
> Mon déchirant passé d'un linceul est couvert.
>
> Cependant, ô ma mère, oh! malgré moi je pense
> À ma vie isolée ainsi qu'en un désert;

Je pense aux jours passés dans votre indifférence,
Au douloureux dédain à mon amour offert.

Oh! Vous n'avez pas lu dans mon âme embrasée!
Votre enfant près de vous dut gémir épuisée:
Vous n'avez jamais su combien je vous aimais!

Maintenant que tout dort sous la tombe profonde,
Dieu vous a dit sur moi ce qu'ignorait le monde:
Votre mot de retour je ne l'aurai jamais!

*(Rêves et réalités*, 133)

A permanent end of physical being, death is irreversible. Memories long hidden from consciousness resurface, despite attempts to silence them once and for all ("Cependant, ô ma mère, oh! malgré moi je pense / À ma vie isolée ainsi qu'en un désert"). "À ma mère" recalls a miserable childhood with an apathetic mother who was incapable of sensing either her child's love or her giftedness.[22] Unlike wish fulfillment in dreams, memory rekindles the desire for a mother's affection only to rebury past loss ("Maintenant que tout dort sous la tombe profonde / . . . / Votre mot de retour je ne l'aurai jamais!"). Blanchecotte's forming of creative identity does not draw on maternity by analogy. As this poem suggests, the poet Blanchecotte did not conceive herself to inhabit her texts the way a woman inhabits her body.

Apart from a few autobiographical poems, including "À mon enfant qui va naître" (15 January 1851) and "Jalousie de mère" (14 June 1851),[23] Blanchecotte avoids the maternal themes treated by pre-Romantic and Romantic era poets such as Babois, Desbordes-Valmore, and Ségalas. Though Blanchecotte often marks the speaker in her texts as feminine, she rarely directs her poetic thinking to domestic topics. Rather, she explores problems more universal in scope, as in the sonnet "Le destin." In this meditative text, Blanchecotte's first-person speaker personifies fate as the storm of life that leaves no one unscathed:

Quand le Destin étendit sur ma tête
Le ciel de plomb, plein d'ombre et de tempête,
Qui m'enveloppe et ne s'éclaircit pas,
Et d'où la foudre éclate avec fracas;

"À tous mes maux, me dit-il, tiens-toi prête,
Car ma loi fauche et jamais ne s'arrête;
Tu m'es acquise: en vain tu te débats,
Mes nœuds de fer entraîneront tes pas.

Rêve après rêve, ivresse après ivresse,
Enthousiasme, illusion, jeunesse,
Il faut tout fuir, il faut tout arracher.

En vain ton cœur crie: Amour et Génie!
Je suis la Faim et je suis l'Ironie:
Roule où la mort t'ira bientôt chercher!"

(*Rêves et réalités*, 136)

A textual epilogue draws out poverty and hunger as the working class's lot. The bitter sense of destiny conveyed by Blanchecotte hints at personal experience: "Celui qui n'a pas vu se dresser devant lui / La misère au teint hâve . . . / Celui qui ne sait pas ce que c'est que la faim, / . . . / Rien en lui ne me touche; il n'a jamais souffert!" (137).

In "Refus," Blanchecotte's speaker also takes a defiant stance, but not one involving advocacy for workers or the contemporary women's movement. Rather, Blanchecotte expresses solidarity with poets toiling in isolation. "Refus" recalls the solitary figure of the desert bird deployed in "Maria" to represent the "ouvrière" as "poète" as well as the "désert" of the speaker's childhood in "À ma mère" in order to develop the image of a *poète maudit*. Blanchecotte situates her poetic speaker on the social margins, a commonplace of the misunderstood genius, without referring to gender:

Moi, l'oiseau du désert, épris des cieux profonds,
Au vol indépendant, à la chanson sauvage,
Quoi! timide et rampant, j'irais me mettre en cage
Et replier mon aile au niveau de leurs fronts!

Au niveau de ces fronts où la pensée hésite,
Où jamais la souffrance altière n'a sculpté
Ce pli fatal dont rit la médiocrité,
Mais qui révèle une âme où le génie habite.

(*Rêves et réalités*, 138)

Here, the reclusion of the desert bird/accursed poet does not connote inferiority. Instead, the poet-genius, the superior individual with whom the speaker (Blanchecotte) identifies, dwells within the realm of ideas that mediocre minds cannot fathom:

Il ne faut pas que l'air de vos salons joyeux
Soit un instant troublé par ma voix inquiète,
Comme ferait soudain quelque sombre tempête
Enveloppant d'éclairs vos longs rideaux soyeux.

Je retourne à mon deuil, retournez à vos fêtes!
L'oiseau meurtri soustrait sa blessure aux regards;
Il a trouvé son ciel au delà des brouillards,
Et vos félicités pour lui ne sont point faites.

(139)

This moment of self-affirmation, juxtaposed with a defensive posture that masks a sense of wounding, flows into the woeful tone of texts such as "Tristesse," "Banishment," "À la solitude," "Jamais," "L'oubli," "La morte," "La nuit," "La mort," and "N'aimez jamais." In considering these titles together with the trope in Blanchecotte's 1855 preface that equates her verse with tears, Aaron Schaffer identifies lachrymosity as "the hallmark of Mme Blanchecotte's poetry, particularly of *Rêves et réalités*" (*Genres of Parnassian Poetry*, 378). Yet, in recognizing the aesthetic quality of Blanchecotte's work, the critic places her on the Romantic edge of the Parnassian movement.

As Schaffer further observes, Blanchecotte's poetic thought developed in tandem with her prosodic discipline: "Mentally, Mme Blanchecotte may be described as having progressed from the sentimentality of Lamartine and Musset towards the intellectualism of Vigny and Leconte de Lisle; this process was paralleled by an increased concern for tightness of form and expression" (*Genres of Parnassian Poetry*, 379).[24] To take Schaffer's analysis a step further, by associating Blanchecotte's verse with "intellectualism," one desexualizes it. Blanchecotte alternately opens up and closes the space within which she explores the categories of "genius" and "worker," thus setting them apart from that of "woman." Marginality, rather than femininity, becomes a source of tension in her relationship to creativity.

The question of originality, integral to defining genius, informs the theme of origins in "Conseil," a text addressed to a young female "au front rêveur" by a speaker representing biblical authority (*Rêves et réalités*, 154). At issue is the place assigned to all living creatures: "Quand Dieu forma le ciel, et l'onde et la matière, / D'un souffle il anima son œuvre toute entière" (155). By attributing genius only to men, Blanchecotte's poem truncates the Genesis narrative that Marie Krysinska would later restore (as shown in chapter 8) in presenting Eve as the first poet:

> Or, cet accord divin de suave harmonie,
> C'est amour chez la femme, chez l'homme génie.
> Il ne doit point en nous résonner follement
> Comme une lyre neuve au premier frôlement,
> D'un souffle du midi précurseur de l'orage,
> Qui noie et l'instrument et son pieux langage.
>
> (155)

Read at face value, and in the order in which the text appears in both the 1855 and 1856 editions of *Rêves et réalités*, this discordant note in Blanchecotte's discourse of genius is perplexing.[25] But the text's date of composition, 3 March 1849, offers a plausible explanation. This early text predates the cluster in which Blanchecotte pursues the question of women's relationship to genius. Such questioning is part and parcel of identity formation, especially for a worker with a gift for abstract thought. The core conflict between manual and creative labor shapes the way that Blanchecotte works (through) the in-between to build her platform as a poet.

## Reading the Poet (Not) as the Worker

"À M. A. de L." (June 1851) and "À l'auteur: Ouvrière et poète" (27 May 1852)—the bookends of "Poésies diverses"—link Blanchecotte with Lamartine while measuring the distance between them and, by extension, between woman (worker) and poet. Recall from "À M. A. de L." that Blanchecotte traces her poetic inheritance to Lamartine without alluding to class. By aligning her voice with the aristocracy of genius represented by Lamartine, Blanchecotte surpasses the space she occupies as a female laborer. However, in "À l'auteur: Ouvrière et poète," written by Lamartine and addressed to Blanchecotte, gender and class compete with the putative recognition of the poet. In drawing attention to these markers of Blanchecotte's identity, did Lamartine have a democratized meaning of the word "auteur" in mind? Or did he understand himself and his self-proclaimed successor to be operating in different literary worlds?

On the first page of Lamartine's poem, the words "ouvrière" and "poète" are typographically displayed on the same line under "À l'auteur," thus forming a triangle that suspends the hierarchical relationship between the terms themselves. In mirroring sections of the text, however, the lexical slippage between these terms exposes differences between the creations of the male poet and those of the female worker-poet. One reads the question "What does poetry mean for an aristocratic man (like me) compared to a working-class woman (like you)?" between the lines of Lamartine's poem to Blanchecotte:

> Chanter! quand la saison qui fait monter les sèves
> Donne au lis ses parfums, à la vierge ses rêves,
> Quand du poëte ailé l'amour renfle la voix,
> Quand, accoudé sur l'herbe aux racines des frênes,
> On entend murmurer mille notes sereines
> Dans son cœur, dans les eaux, dans les airs, dans les bois,
> Chanter n'est pas chanter! c'est respirer deux fois!
>
> Mais chanter! quand l'hiver, la mère de famille
> Use ses doigts transis au froid de son aiguille,
> Quand à la vitre en vain l'oiseau vient mendier,
> Quand la cendre au foyer dispute une étincelle,
> Quand l'amour manque au cœur, le lait à la mamelle,
> Quand le travail au jour arrache son denier,
> Chanter n'est pas chanter, ô femme, c'est prier!

(Rêves et réalités, 220)

A series of binaries—harmony versus discord; leisure versus labor; idyllic, natural setting versus harsh, material reality—structures these stanzas, juxtaposing distinct sources of poetry: a second breath born of divine inspiration versus a supplication serving as a cure for personal pain. "À l'auteur" represents two types of poets (if not two canons): one inspired to re-create the harmony discerned in nature by transcending the personal to express metaphysical truths and another who finds respite from the day's labor in poetic writing. By conflating Blanchecotte's life and verse, Lamartine unwittingly widens the gap between the female worker and the poet. In his foundational appraisal of *Rêves et réalités*, Sainte-Beuve would shift the focus from class to gender, his rhetoric establishing Blanchecotte as a poet while encouraging her to adopt a more feminine persona.

By mid-century, lyrical poetry struggled to maintain its currency. Readers chose the novel, either the popular form flooding the market or more serious narratives aimed to record contemporary life through detailed observation and painstaking description, or even dissect modern society with scientific precision. But Blanchecotte's emergence proved that "la poésie n'est pas morte," Sainte-Beuve proclaims, extolling her 1855 volume as proof: "C'est ainsi qu'en ouvrant le volume que j'annonce aujourd'hui, j'ai reconnu, dès les premiers vers, un poëte et une âme, une âme douloureusement harmonieuse. On sent que ce n'est point une fiction ni une gentillesse que ce titre d'*ouvrière* se joint aux initiales de l'auteur. Une condition pénible, accablante, tient bien réellement à la gêne une intelligence qui souffre, un talent qui veut prendre l'essor" ("*Rêves et réalités*," 327–28; emphasis in original). In drawing the "poëte" closer to the "ouvrière," Sainte-Beuve touches on the existential despair expressed by Blanchecotte, "une intelligence qui souffre," which surpasses any issues related to her social status ("[u]ne condition pénible, accablante"). He makes her pain strictly personal and not fully sublimated into art, however, by mapping her biography directly onto her writing, especially the section on female figures. With one stroke, Sainte-Beuve likens Blanchecotte's cries to Sappho's. With another stroke, he imagines that, once her conditions improve, Blanchecotte will be as capable as the British Romantic Felicia Hemans of cultivating "la poésie domestique" and painting scenes of a woman's private life with sweet emotion (332). Privately, too, Sainte-Beuve blurred the lines between life and art in his correspondence with Blanchecotte from 7 December 1855 to 4 July 1868. Similar to the Dumas-Waldor and Flaubert-Colet correspondence discussed in chapter 3, this epistolary corpus is preserved mostly from Sainte-Beuve's side, yet helps to contextualize Blanchecotte's life and work. Biographical elements—including Sainte-Beuve's unrequited love for Blanchecotte—share, though not evenly, the space given to their mutual passion for the art of poetry.[26]

The editor of the 1856 edition of *Rêves et réalités* capitalized on Blanchecotte's reception, especially Sainte-Beuve's endorsement, to promote her work. Instead of an initial, the volume now bore her surname, dispelling the anonymity in the poem "À la muse" (which had also opened the 1855 edition). In a positive twist on biographical literalism, being read as a worker *and* as a poet gave Blanchecotte a creative edge along with room to maneuver among identities. Paulin Limayrac, for example, reviewing *Rêves et réalités* for *Le Constitutionnel* in May 1856, amply cited her work. She would continue to evolve, Limayrac concluded, drawing upon opposite, yet related, views of giftedness as inborn versus made: "La muse lui a souri dans son berceau. Mme Blanchecotte possède ce qui ne s'acquiert pas; il ne lui manque que ce qui s'acquiert, la correction, l'art des effets" (n.p.). Blanchecotte's prefaces to her collections of verse and prose in the 1860s and '70s suggest a delicate balancing act, if not a platform, to promote the artistic power and ideological work of poetry while appealing to critics familiar with the difficult circumstances hampering her literary aspirations. This is the provocative split in Blanchecotte's self-representation: She invited readers to associate her life and her work, but continually pushed, even dissolved, the boundaries marking off her voice and its place in literary history in relation to sex and social status.

## Thinking Poetry, Poetic Thought

The paratexts surrounding Blanchecotte's second poetic collection, *Nouvelles poésies* (1861), show how deftly she negotiated the issues of genre, gender, and class. In direct response to Sainte-Beuve's criticism of *Rêves et réalités*, she uses epigraphs to frame her prefatory comments, paratextual material uncharacteristic of her corpus. The first epigraph comes from Sainte-Beuve's untitled poem in the romance form, which begins, "Désert du cœur, en ces longues soirées / Qu'automne amène à notre hiver sans fleur"; the three-word refrain at the outset punctuates each line as well as the ending (*Nouvelles poésies*, 5). The second epigraph, citing Felicia Hemans's 1830 poem "We Return No More," begins, "'We return!—we return!—we return no more!' / So breathe sad voices our esprits o'er."[27] These choices attenuate the piercing cry Sainte-Beuve had advised her to subdue, foregrounding the aesthetics of sorrow in a transnational community of Romantics of both sexes. Nostalgia is universal, suggests Blanchecotte, preparing her defense of poetry as the sublime archive of the human condition.

It is not as a "woman poet," but rather as a poet, that Blanchecotte prefaces her *Nouvelles poésies* to advocate for poetry. The age of positivism has threatened to eclipse the unique way of knowing expressed by verse, a way of grasping ideas, from the real to the ideal, with and *without* the senses:

Des vers! A quoi bon? dira la critique.—En effet, à quoi bon? . . .

Et d'abord, le sentiment de la poésie peut-il mourir? On en a perdu le goût, soit: tant pis pour notre temps! Mais la poésie, comme la nature, comme l'art, comme le beau, comme tout ce qui fait palpiter l'esprit, épris de l'impossible, et malade du mal de l'infini, la poésie est immortelle et règne autour de nous et en nous. (6)

Through this stance on the timeless appeal of poetry, Blanchecotte counters the rise of literary naturalism, which had since the 1850s reflected the triumph of science.[28] She also seeks to authorize her new volume, but veils this objective by deferring to her critics: "Mon premier petit livre: *Rêves et réalités*, a obtenu (je le dis avec reconnaissance) un bienveillant et sympathique accueil. Avant de me recommander de nouveau à votre indulgence, ô maîtres de la littérature! laissez-moi vous remercier des encouragements que vous m'avez accordés" (7). In evoking her debut in order to garner approval from readers in 1861, Blanchecotte emphasizes her liminal position between the worker and the poet. She writes from the margins literally, but also figuratively, approaching poetry as a discourse of liminality.

As the platform for a transcendent form of work, her verse inhabits the in-between: "Ces précieux témoignages m'ont soutenue dans les épreuves de ma vie difficile et trop positive, lutte perpétuelle *entre* les laborieuses obligations à remplir et le rêve à refouler" (*Nouvelles poésies*, 7; emphasis added). With a tone that pales in comparison to that of her powerful convictions about the everlasting life of poetry, and restating Sainte-Beuve's stance on what her own emergence signifies, Blanchecotte lays bare the reality with which she still wrestles to free the poet within her: "Puissiez-vous me tenir compte encore de ces circonstances pénibles, et vous les rappeler en lisant mes vers, auxquels le travail, le loisir et l'étude ont toujours manqué!" (7). This appeal, however, has an alternative echo for her contemporary Charles Coligny: "L'enfant du peuple converse très profondément avec l'enfant du Parnasse; l'ouvrière s'adresse en pleurant à la muse" ("Les muses parisiennes," 114). His remark outlines the reflective bent that injects Blanchecotte's lyricism with universality.

The bitter remains of love, loss, and longing carry over from *Rêves et réalités* to *Nouvelles poésies*. These themes support Aaron Schaffer's appraisal of Blanchecotte as a late Romantic who "reveals herself in her poetry as a disillusioned and misanthropic victim of life and, particularly, of love" (*Genres of Parnassian Poetry*, 378). But, like other critics,[29] he also argues against the volume's sentimental grain by singling out and citing in extenso the text "Sonnet" to illustrate Blanchecotte's poetic development beyond feminine subjectivity:

> Bronze-toi, souffre à l'ombre, et, pour tous insensible,
> Souris à qui te hait, sois calme en ta fierté;
> Tais-toi, ne tente point une lutte impossible:
> Comme on aime l'éclat, aime l'obscurité.
>
> Laisse la foule en bas; demeure inaccessible;
> Demeure impénétrable et demeure indompté.
> Que ton secret, soit peine ou bonheur indicible,
> Garde l'indifférence et la sérénité.
>
> Masque-toi, revêts-toi d'une implacable armure;
> Quel que soit dans ton cœur le nom de ta blessure,
> Étouffe le cri sourd, ne le trahis jamais.

Si trop lourd est le poids en ton âme orageuse,
Va par les sentiers verts, par la vallée ombreuse:
Là tu pourras être homme et défaillir en paix.

(*Nouvelles poésies*, 132–33)

In contrast to the elegiac tone of Blanchecotte's poetry, metaphorized as tears, this sonnet advocates stoicism. The speaker urges the addressee, assumed to be female, to don "masculine" armor in order to hide her "feminine" heart and to seek escape in nature where she "can be a man" and unburden her soul. Such emotional restraint tempers Romantic effusion, as does the Parnassian aesthetic signaled by the sonnet form and thematized by the statuesque pose ("revêts-toi d'une implacable armure"). In the absence of grammatical markers, however, the gender of the speaker and of the interlocutor, who is addressed in the familiar ("tu"), is ambiguous. From this perspective, the text sheds the idea of gender-bending to suggest a broader attempt to detach the lyrical "I" from the self and to free one's writing from being read as an open book of sentiment.

Such detachment underlies the prose that Blanchecotte produced nearly concurrently; she achieves neutrality via narration in the third person ("on") not marked off by gender or class. In Jules Levallois's 1860 article, "Un poëte moraliste," there are excerpts of prose fragments Blanchecotte would publish under the title *Le long du chemin: Pensées d'une solitaire* (1864). For Levallois, in fragments focused on "l'amour dans la pauvreté . . . le poëte se trouve dans le style" ("Un poëte moraliste," 132). Youthful exuberance mingles with pithiness in strands of lyrical mysticism that express Blanchecotte's reflections on love and its discontents: "on n'a pour limites que l'infini, et l'esprit s'y plonge" (133). In this preview of *Le long du chemin*, "l'âme s'analyse," thus encapsulating Blanchecotte's trajectory as a poetic creator who demonstrates in verse and prose how words fall short of saying what we know, but allow us to imagine the unknown (133). After mentioning passages grouped as "le chapitre de la passion," Levallois selects pieces that further illustrate the contours of Blanchecotte's philosophical mind. His article closes with an excerpt from Blanchecotte's narrative about a poor working-class girl, entitled "Juliane," an unpublished story that represents "sous ses diverses faces la pensée de l'auteur" (144). The depth and intensity of expression achieved by the "poëte moraliste," Levallois concludes, stems from keen observation along with her "vigilante faculté d'analyse" (144).

One can only speculate whether Blanchecotte was uneasy about sharing the draft and thus asked Levallois not to identify her by name in citing excerpts from *Le long du chemin* (1864). The volume, though self-published and limited in circulation, garnered praise from Sainte-Beuve in a letter of 28 November 1864 ("Que de pensées fortes, pénétrantes, brûlantes"; *Correspondance générale*, 481). Gautier similarly lauded its iteration (with added material) in Blanchecotte's *Impressions d'une femme* (1868): "Elle a écrit en bonne prose des pages de moraliste qui prouvent que cette élégiaque sait observer aussi bien que sentir" ("Rapport sur le progrès de la poésie," 131). In the paratexts surrounding Blanchecotte's early prose, one recognizes the roots of her creative thinking across genres, which predates Coligny's suggestion in his 1861 review of *Nouvelles poésies* that she turn to "l'œuvre en prose, l'œuvre d'observation rigoureuse, le roman, par exemple" ("Les muses parisiennes," 115).[30] Blanchecotte continually intervened as a critical reader of her own work by incorporating elements from her previous verse or prose into new frameworks. Her return to genius in 1868 relates its poetic effect to expansive vision while privileging the work of thought as its vehicle.

## Creative Genius at Work

In prefacing *Impressions d'une femme: Pensées, sentiments, et portraits* (1868), Blanchecotte sheds her characteristic modesty.[31] She asserts that intellectual pursuits do not contradict but rather enhance a woman's contributions to society: "Avec les plus hautes intelligences de ce temps-ci, j'ose déclarer qu'il est avantageux pour tous que la femme, destinée aux plus nobles charges, soit aussi familiarisée avec les plus nobles prérogatives intellectuelles: l'observation et la culture de la pensée" (iv). Her own writerly life showcases the two practices: Close scrutiny inspires and expands reflection. The previous year she had corrected proofs of *Les quatrains de Khèyam* (1867), translated from the Persian by Jean Baptiste Nicolas, formerly the chief dragoman of the French embassy in Persia. Blanchecotte discerned from the eleventh-century mystic how, in contemplating the external world, a poet gains inner vision as well as access to the realm of the unknown.[32] This relates to the sense of poetic genius explained in *Impressions d'une femme*, a volume that subsumes, in her words, the "autopsie intérieure" performed by (her) writing, which reveals the deeper work of thought (288).

Blanchecotte associates genius with foresight or prescience. Her notion of the visionary genius calls to mind the figure of the seer-poet or *voyant*: "Les sommets sont les premiers et les derniers éclairés: le Génie voit plus tôt que les autres, et sa lumière reste après lui" (*Impressions d'une femme*, 70). She simultaneously deploys interconnected meanings of the term "genius," which transpose the inner vision of genius onto the socially recognized figure of the genius. Later in the volume, Blanchecotte distinguishes talent from genius: "L'homme de talent peut faire des élèves, l'homme de génie ne le peut pas. L'un a reçu des autres et de ses facultés patientes une méthode qu'il accepte, qu'il modifie s'il y a lieu, et qu'il transmet. L'homme de génie ne relève que de soi" (139). Blanchecotte's vocabulary calls to mind the sexing of genius, but not the attendant notions of inheritance or muscle power. She emphasizes extraordinary sight, which coheres with the disembodied nature of genius seen in *Rêves et réalités*: "Nature inattendue et spontanée, il voit plus haut, plus bas, au delà, d'un œil inspiré, surnaturel, pour ainsi dire. Ses observations sont des intuitions plutôt que des conséquences. L'homme de génie a une personnalité essentiellement sienne qui enseigne, impose, souverainement dirige, mais ne se définit pas, ne se décalque et ne se reproduit pas: il a des critiques et des vulgarisateurs; mais des disciples et des héritiers directs, des fils à son image, jamais" (139). By understanding genius as unpredictable and spontaneous, as self-generated, Blanchecotte disengages the work of originality from maleness.

Blanchecotte creates an opening for women within the category of "genius" by making autonomous creativity the primordial sign of genius. A man or woman of genius breaks with tradition—with the transmission of inherited patterns of thought or action—to illuminate the hitherto unseen. Blanchecotte's way of thinking about genius in reference to an exceptional individual is inseparable from the capacity that she refers to in another passage as "le génie du *vrai voir*" (*Impressions d'une femme*, 141; emphasis in original). The true poet and earnest thinker alike, both detached from the self, display the property of genius: "Le véritable poète, le penseur sérieux ne doivent point offrir à ce qu'on appelle l'*admiration* des autres, le tableau des petits événements qui ont marqué dans leur vie. Il ne faut parler à chacun et à tous que le langage qui les intéresse: il faut les découvrir eux-mêmes à eux-mêmes, toute personnalité d'auteur doit s'effacer. Le propre du génie est de généraliser, et sa mission est un dévouement absolu, une abdication complète" (144; emphasis in original).

In Blanchecotte, one can recognize the evolution from subjective to objective poetry that Rimbaud would advocate three years later in his *lettres du voyant* (13 and 15 May 1871; *Œuvres complètes*, 248–54).[33] In defining the poet as seer, Blanchecotte links creative voice and vision: "Le poète est un *voyant*, ouvrant pour les autres la fenêtre qu'il a en lui-même sur l'invisible et sur l'infini" (*Impressions d'une femme*, 145; emphasis in original). "La fenêtre," in Blanchecotte's definition, marks the limit between different worlds, a liminal space at once within and without, between dreams and realities. Poetry, as she depicts it, operates within this same framework: "Ainsi, sous le vent divin de la poésie, la pensée s'entr'ouvre, et soudain illumine le monde" (151). Blanchecotte mirrors the quest for the ideal alongside the reality of human passions. As she asserts in prefacing the third edition of *Rêves et réalités* (1871), poetry also has cultural responsibilities: "C'est encore et c'est toujours la langue de la poésie qui célèbre les grandes dates de l'histoire, les faits éclatants ou émouvants de la vie humaine" (x–xi).[34] In responding to historical events, just as she engages the history of ideas, Blanchecotte aligns the poet and the prose writer on the threshold of work.

## Betwixt and Between

The outbreak of the Franco-Prussian War in 1870, coupled with the siege of Paris from 9 September 1870 to 28 January 1871, delayed publication of the third edition of *Rêves et réalités* by a year. In the interim, Blanchecotte added patriotic poems and thus gave to the sentimental strand of her early verse broader historical resonance. In 1872, Alfred Marchand praised this linkage as integral to the edition's currency, recognizing the poet's universal appeal. Interestingly, he did not gender her voice: "Les émotions si variées de la lutte ont retenti dans le cœur du poëte, et il a su leur prêter une voix sonore. Il a fortifié le bras des combattants, et il a voulu relever le courage des vaincus" ("*Rêves et réalités* par Augustine-Malvina Blanchecotte," n.p.).[35] That same year Blanchecotte published *Tablettes d'une femme pendant la Commune* (1872). In the preface, Blanchecotte situates her viewpoint by referring to the ambulance in which she had crossed over enemy lines with impunity: "ma pensée revendique son privilège de neutre" (3). She thus appropriates gender idiosyncratically to position her speaking from the margins of the Paris Commune as politically neutral: "Je l'ai dit et redit avec béatitude tout le long de ma vie: Quel bonheur de n'être rien, c'est-à-dire de n'être que femme, de pouvoir, comme les enfants traités sans conséquence, penser tout et le penser tout haut, ignorer tout et porter sans contradiction sa robe d'ignorance!" (5).

In her preface to the 1996 edition of Blanchecotte's firsthand account of the Paris Commune, Christine Planté addresses the ambiguity surrounding the author's voice: "Pas assez peuple, pas assez Commune, pas assez féministe pour ceux et celles qui voudraient faire entrer l'histoire et son récit dans des catégories prédéfinies et homogènes, qui était Malvina Blanchecotte?" (*Tablettes d'une femme*, vi). Being a woman in this context was ironically emancipatory. Self-placed outside the sphere of political influence, the author distances her voice from the conflict and sides with objectivity. "[Ê]tre *femme*, pour Blanchecotte," notes Planté in describing the *Tablettes* as a testimonial about bearing witness, "c'est se trouver située, de droit et de fait, hors des enjeux et des intérêts politiques des hommes et, pour cette raison même, en position de réfléchir, de témoigner, d'agir pour la paix" (xii; emphasis in original). Just as Blanchecotte eschews taking a position on the proletarian revolt that pitted revolutionists against royalists, she avoids genre constraints: "Mes *Tablettes* n'ont aucune prétention d'aucun genre; elles représentent l'aspect d'une ville, comme la photographie reproduit ses ruines" (4). By transcribing her impressions based on daily observations through her window in the Paris of 1871 (from 11 March to 30 June) and collecting them with items such as pamphlets and posters, she creates in her words "les petites mosaïques de ces *Tablettes* intimes" (5). In her prose, as in her verse, Blanchecotte maintained her discursive mobility.

In portraying Blanchecotte as "l'image même de la Volonté unie à la Résignation," Théodore de Banville presents a feeling genius: "Car ce visage de poète, comme celui de certains prêtres, a quelque chose de l'ingénuité de l'enfance, récompense d'un ordre surnaturel et presque divin que Dieu accorde à ceux de ses serviteurs qui humblement tracent un droit sillon, sans songer un moment à se parer de leurs souffrances et à se glorifier de leur génie!" (*Camées parisiens*, 81, 82). Consonant with the humility emphasized by Banville is the Romantic gendering of divine inspiration, which Blanchecotte recycles in "Les deux voix," published in her final poetic collection, *Les militantes: Poésies* (1875). The conservative stance she takes at a time of backlash against women writers may also have been a nod to Lamartine's 1868 *Cours Familier de Littérature* (discussed in chapter 1).[36] At the end of Blanchecotte's text, the female speaker reiterates Lamartine's view that God endowed men with creativity and women with moral goodness: "Dieu m'a refusé le génie, / Mais il m'a donné la bonté" (*Les militantes*, 206). This stance does not fit Blanchecotte's overall view of genius. It parallels her self-representation, however, which reveals multiplicity as the constitutive element of her creative voice. The various subject positions explored by Blanchecotte dialogize the genius discourse in her production. Fundamentally interrogative, Blanchecotte's œuvre shows that she resisted the sociohistorical conditions of her identity, challenging women's exclusion from the category of "genius."

The tripartite composition of *Les militantes*—"Combats," "Trêves," "Paix"— harks back to the social revolution captured in *Tablettes d'une femme pendant la Commune* and links the overarching theme of strife with (self-)analysis. Blanchecotte's volume suggests the effusion of earlier collections in treating, among other topics, the wounds of lost love, only to reject such sentimentality, as in the poem "Le choix de la vie." The run-on line near the text's opening ("je me retire / Moi-même de ma vie intime") emphasizes the speaker's break with her inner life, a life she identifies with being a woman:

> J'ai choisi! je serai bonne! je me retire
> Moi-même de ma vie intime. Je déchire
> Tous les feuillets perdus, éplorés, douloureux
> De ce carnet d'amour où sont morts tant d'aveux!
> Le livre de mon cœur se ferme sur mon âme,
> Je brise avec l'espoir: je cesse d'être femme!
>
> (*Les militantes*, 200)

But in closing *Les militantes* with "À un penseur," the poet admits opposite bents of sentimentalism and intellectualism:

> Hélas! je le sais par moi-même!
> Mon long travail intérieur,
> Ma longue résistance extrême
> N'ont jamais pu changer mon cœur!
>
> (232)

Blanchecotte does not resolve the contradictions in the way she positions her voice: As a poet and prose writer she claims to be but a woman and thus in her day "nothing," but as a thinker she situates genius beyond gender.

In prefacing her last prose collection, *Le long de la vie: Nouvelles impressions d'une femme* (1875), Blanchecotte evokes her lifelong struggle as an "ouvrière et poète" to position her work. She underplays her creations as emerging from the in-between, but also presents them as the product of her own thought: "L'auteur *soussignée* ne s'est préoccupée ni de plan ni de cadre, et revendique d'avance le privilège des circonstances atténuantes. . . . Je n'ai pas besoin de dire—on le verra de reste—que je n'ai rien emprunté (à mon grand regret!) à l'étude ni aux livres. Mes maîtres ont été les vicissitudes quotidiennes: je n'ai lu qu'à travers les visages, et n'ai pensé qu'à travers ma pensée" (i, iii; emphasis in original). A self-described "esprit à l'écart en ce monde," she offers everyday impressions with the hope of reviving beleaguered souls in the modern consumer society, as suggested by the first section, "Action et courage" (iii). A "mosaïque d'observations," to use Blanchecotte's phrasing, *Le long de la vie* includes four other thematic sections: "Amour et cœur," "Lettres à Nobody," "À propos de livres," and "Études et figures" (i). Replete with poetic meditations and pithy aphorisms, these diverse clusters draw out Blanchecotte's thoughts on the meanings of genius (capacity for originality versus exceptional individual) first gleaned from *Rêves et réalités* (1855): "Les natures vraiment supérieures le sont dans toutes les conditions possibles de la vie. Ce ne sont pas les circonstances qui suscitent le génie: tout au plus le mettent-elles en lumière; et l'on a vu bien plus d'hommes inférieurs à leur situation élevée qu'on n'en a vu la dominer" (*Le long de la vie*, 37). At the outset, this key passage disengages genius from factors such as class and gender, which had been assumed to determine the conditions that give rise to genius. Blanchecotte binds the visionary faculty with the individual who possesses this innate gift: "Le don suprême d'*agir* procède du don inné de *voir*. L'homme supérieur naît avec celui-ci et le manifeste avec autorité, en quelque poste et sous quelque costume que ce soit. . . . Aucune force aveugle, inintelligente ou jalouse n'empêchera de surgir celui qui voit, celui qui discerne, celui qui veut" (37, 38; emphasis in original). It is not her gendered phrasing ("L'homme supérieur"), but rather the idea that genius knows no bounds that matches the conviction with which she imagined women of exceptional vision in *Rêves et réalités*.

Blanchecotte lifts once more her mask of modesty to lay claim to her inner life, her creative mind: "Une chose me confond, parmi les anomalies absolument incohérentes de ce monde: c'est l'espèce de pression exercée sur les natures idéales pour les accommoder au goût régnant du jour. Quoi! vous comprenez et acceptez que je préfère la couleur bleue à la couleur verte qui a toutes vos sympathies; . . . et s'il me plaît de gérer à ma guise ma vie intérieure bien vite et bien haut, vous allez opposer un: holà!" (*Le long de la vie*, 42). The prose writer recalls the poet's attempt to free her voice from her own personality or subjectivity: "Hélas! hélas! . . . je n'ai jamais su alléger le fardeau, me débarasser de moi-même" (55). But she believes all the same that within the mind reside infinite possibilities that one can work out creatively and beyond societal constraints.

In "Lettres à Nobody," the word "nobody" refers to her own imagination, and Blanchecotte reveals the world of thought she has cultivated, far beyond a material existence: "Quel champ vaste que tout l'espace de la pensée! Quels monuments j'y peux bâtir! Quelle artillerie j'y peux exercer! Quelles évolutions j'y peux réaliser!" (*Le long de la vie*, 174). It is not that Blanchecotte considers herself superior to others. Rather, as she puts it, "je me sens *autre* qu'ils ne sont" (194; emphasis in original). As a writer who has emerged from the people and as a woman who writes, she fits no category: "Je surprends quelquefois ma concierge en train de me considérer avec un regard de profonde pitié. Ces livres, ces journaux, ces lettres, ces papiers qui m'entourent, tout ce gâchis d'étrange espèce lui inspire un mépris qu'elle ne prend pas la peine de dissimuler. Le peuple . . . n'admet de travail que de travail manuel: le travail de la pensée—pour le peuple n'existe pas. . . . Et les autres? Et ceux des hautes classes? O cher travail de la pensée, labeur sublime autant qu'ingrat! Pour ceux-là, vous ne *faites rien*; pour ceux-ci, vous ne *gagnez rien*: le mépris pour vous est le même" (216; emphasis in original). In this context, Blanchecotte recalls Béranger, who had warned her that the life of the mind was one of isolation and solitude because creative production demands work (217).

Literary culture was daunting for a nineteenth-century woman, especially a worker like Blanchecotte, who read and wrote from the margins of society. Yet intelligence is precisely the realm she claims as the quintessential source of human dignity: "Il n'y a dans ce monde qu'une chose supérieure et vraiment enviable, désirable, un bien qu'il faut poursuivre et tâcher d'atteindre absolument: la possession de sa pensée, la liberté, la dignité de son intelligence" (*Le long de la vie*, 251–52). Blanchecotte does and does not gender her voice, aligning herself with originators: "Un homme de génie est tout entier en lui-même: il n'a ni prédécesseur ni successeur. Je ne puis tolérer ces stériles recherches d'école qui veulent attribuer à un esprit uniquement personnel et spontané la connaissance, l'héritage et l'assimilation du passé" (282). In the final pages of *Le long de la vie*, the worker born a poet thus reiterates the parthenogenic origins of genius. Closing her prose volume with an untitled poem, Blanchecotte carves out the intellectual path that unbinds her writing from the clichés of feminine subjectivity: "Bêche le champ, ô travailleur / Bêche le champ de la pensée" (350).

Blanchecotte worked tirelessly to cultivate her gift, as her contemporary Hippolyte Arseny noted in 1875: "Fille d'ouvriers, ouvrière elle-même, mariée très jeune à un ouvrier, elle a su, dans la condition du monde la plus laborieuse et la plus pénible, conquérir, à coups de chagrins et de malheurs, une force de volonté peu commune" ("Galerie poétique," 40). In a dedicatory poem to Lamartine dated 18 August 1878, Blanchecotte again illumines her inner force, with the critical reader joining the philosophical mind of the poet and prose writer:

> En vain m'a-t-on crié qu'il fallait de la prose:
> Je n'ai pu m'assouplir à rêver autre chose
> Que l'Idéal sans tache et, sur les sommets fins,
> La lumière immuable et la fleur des déserts!
>
> ("À Lamartine")

A posthumous tribute hints at this élan: "Mme Blanchecotte fut comme une seconde Marceline Desbordes-Valmore, la Desbordes-Valmore des pauvres. . . .

Laborieuse et résignée, Mme Blanchecotte ne fut pas cependant une mélancolique" (Claretie, *La vie à Paris*, 74). True to the social reality depicted by Lamartine and other nineteenth-century readers, the "ouvrière" labored in a realm outside that of the "poète." As a writer, however, Blanchecotte deftly crossed back and forth between spheres to express the human condition of being caught between harsh realities and absorbing dreams, forging her legacy as a creative thinker via this "travail intérieur": "Malvina Blanchecotte n'a rien gagné à être étiquetée ouvrière-poète. Sa poésie n'est pas descriptive, elle ne nous parle pas de couture, elle ne nous entretient pas de ses déboires quotidiens. Elle échappe aux petitesses du monde par le portique du rêve, en cela, et parce qu'elle l'a su exprimer bellement, elle est un vrai poète à part entière" (Somoff and Marfée, "Les muses du Parnasse," 60).

In working through the problem of pain literally as well as figuratively, Blanchecotte's contemporary Louisa Siefert also delved into memory and dreams, but in a hybrid production that splits the poetic subject between the conscious and the unconscious realms. I consider Siefert's originality and relationship to poetic genius in the next chapter.

# 6 The Poetic Edges of Dualism in Louisa Siefert

A unique blend of Romantic sensibility and Parnassian formalism characterizes the body of work that Louisa Siefert (1845–1877; fig. 15) produced while struggling physically and philosophically with the problem of pain. Siefert launched her career in December 1868 with *Rayons perdus*, which sold out within a month and saw two more editions by April 1869.[1] The best-selling volume established her reputation as a poet of contrary qualities, which Charles Asselineau formulated as "très-féminin de sentiment, & en même temps très-viril d'expression" in his preface to the second edition (vii).[2] This hybridity, unevenly appreciated by critics who puzzle over Siefert's originality, is just as striking as her intense trajectory. Despite chronic illness, including migraines, severe arthritis, and pulmonary tuberculosis, Siefert published three more poetic volumes in rapid succession: *L'année républicaine* (1869), *Les stoïques* (1870), and *Les saintes colères* (1871).[3] Her output includes plays in verse, *Comédies romanesques* (1872), and a semi-autobiographical novel, *Méline* (1876).[4] From 1871 to 1874, Siefert also wrote a literary column for the *Journal de Lyon* under the heading "Causeries poétiques."[5] This corpus of approximately thirty analytical essays, demonstrating Siefert's knowledge of French poetic history, affirms the critical role of reading in her writerly life.

As discussed in chapter 5, class factored centrally in Blanchecotte's struggle to pursue her poetic aspirations, but had nearly the opposite effect on Siefert, whose gifts were encouraged by her literate bourgeois family. Adèle-Adrienne (Belz) Siefert brought forth memoirs and some of her daughter's previously unpublished poems under the title *Souvenirs rassemblés par sa mère* (1881), recording Siefert's poetic development, works, and reception. Contemporary events and shifts in attitudes toward poetry further contextualize this record of Siefert's journey as a professional writer. Siefert's letters and other exchanges with a broad community of writers, interspersed in the volume, provide glimpses of her life and a fuller grasp

FIG 15
Louisa Siefert by
Étienne Pagny, 1880.
Museum of Fine Arts
of Lyon. Photo © MBA
Lyon (Alain Basset).

of her intellectual verve. In a posthumous tribute, the journalist Abel Peyrouton described Siefert's creative mind this way: "Le poète fut une femme, un homme, un patriote" ("Louisa Siefert et son œuvre," 41). These disparate voices suggest the deeper work of Siefert's writing, which explores how the poetic mind breaks free of the body in pain.

In this chapter I examine the aesthetic and philosophical dualism of Siefert's poetic output in relation to her working through pain. I first consider the account of Siefert's medical issues and their impact on her in her mother's introductory essay to *Souvenirs rassemblés par sa mère*. The narrative of pain that traverses Siefert's life and work is radically more complex in the creative realm. Rather than writing about her particular diseases along the lines of an autopathography, Siefert transcends the embodied experience of suffering through creative reverie and philosophical detachment. Close analysis of poems from *Rayons perdus* and *Les stoïques* in the second and third parts of the chapter, respectively, highlights the tension between material reality and the ideal, which structures the main theme of mortality versus immortality. Siefert's contemporaries tended to gender this tension, privileging the expression of feeling assumed to reflect femininity; they also praised her technical precision, contradicting the purported maleness of poetry as a higher art. Siefert's reception during her lifetime, which I treat concurrently with her production, recognized her prosodic range and diversity of topics.

Even so, Siefert has been slow to emerge from the sentimental category to which early twentieth-century critics and literary historians relegated the work of "poetesses," a category of inferior poetry upheld by some modern scholars, which says as much about our moment as her own.

## Beyond Autopathography

The habit of reading from an early age shaped both Siefert's analytical thought and her poetic creativity. Her mother recalled, "À ce goût vif et précoce pour la lecture ne tarda pas à se joindre chez Louisa une sorte d'instinct critique ou du moins une prédilection pour certains styles faisant tableau à ses yeux ou musique à ses oreilles" (*Souvenirs rassemblés*, 31–32). The young Siefert exuded mental energy, "des longues rêveries contemplatives, des réflexions au-dessus de son âge et de la concentration hâtive de son intelligence sur un point spécial d'étude ou de méditation" (32). In recounting the psychical consequences of a serious health problem Siefert faced in 1860, her mother stressed the force of mind that transposed her daughter's poetic writing into a form of struggle: "Elle a exprimé ou sous-entendu ses luttes intérieures dans un grand nombre de beaux vers où reviennent sans cesse les idées et les mots de *combat* et de *bataille*" (36–37; emphasis in original). Though Madame Siefert took this metaphor literally, she simultaneously related "cette domination souveraine sur la douleur comme sur les bouillonnements de son impétueuse nature" to the work of imagining (36).

At the age of fifteen, Siefert was suddenly incapacitated and diagnosed with "coxite ou coxalgie," as her mother described, using the medical terms for arthritis considered tubercular in origin (*Souvenirs rassemblés*, 42).[6] Excruciating pain along with the threat of joint dislocation in her right hip confined Siefert to a cast-iron bed or a lounge chair. For nearly two years, she was unable to walk. During her convalescence, guided reading and conversations with her tutor spurred her intellectual growth: "Ses entretiens et les lectures qu'il lui conseillait et facilitait suppléaient à l'instruction régulière si brusquement interrompue par la maladie, ouvraient des horizons, fournissaient des aliments à cette activité, cette curiosité d'esprit d'autant plus ardente chez Louisa que l'immobilité du corps devenait plus absolue" (45). Madame Siefert's idea that Siefert converted her immobility into psychical movement and greater acuity suggests a parallel with "splitting,"[7] the mind transcending the ailing body.

At first glance, Siefert's acute pain does not suggest an environment conducive to creativity, especially when one considers Elaine Scarry's view: "Physical pain does not simply resist language but actively destroys it, bringing about an immediate reversion to a state anterior to language, to the sounds and cries a human being makes before language is learned" (*Body in Pain*, 4). In building on this premise, however, Scarry develops the analogy between bodily trauma and its conversion into poetic power implied by Siefert's mother with the contours of a counterdiscourse. "[P]hysical pain," argues Scarry, "is exceptional in [the] whole fabric of psychic, somatic, and perceptual states for being the only one that has no object . . . in the external world" (161). The idea that pain has no content "almost prevents it from being rendered in language," whereas the imagination is "the only state that is wholly its objects" (162). This difference, however, generates a productive synergy.

The psychological effort to overcome pain engages all the senses, but cannot be expressed directly. More concretely, this effort can manifest through creative writing, which allows one to move away from the body and toward the imagined object. "Once [pain] is brought into relation with the objectifying power of the imagination," notes Scarry, "[it] will be transformed from a wholly passive and helpless occurrence into a self-modifying and, when most successful, self-eliminating one" (*Body in Pain*, 164). As Siefert's aesthetic project evolves from *Rayons perdus* to *Les stoïques*, poetry functions as a form of making that counteracts the immobilizing effects of intense pain and as a discourse that offers insight into the larger questions of life. My analysis of how Siefert voices the other in the self follows the discursive axis along which trauma and creativity mutually operate. Personal lyricism overlaps with stoic reflection as Siefert imparts with universal resonance the "projection of human pain into disembodied imagining" (Scarry, *Body in Pain*, 173). Critical reading and writing practices influenced most how Siefert developed as a poet. She thought through pain, which, like creativity, is blind to sex.

### The Poet as Reader

During her convalescence in the early 1860s, Siefert read only poetry. The list of poets given by her mother, who mentions no female poets, includes Lamartine, Hugo, Musset, Gautier, Sainte-Beuve, Victor de Laprade, and Joséphin Soulary (*Souvenirs rassemblés*, 50).[8] Immersed in the contemporary language of poetry, the teen began to compose verse that she described to her mother as given by inspiration, "comme sous la dictée" (51). The account of this episode reveals Siefert's equal concern with form. She had her mother procure a treatise on all the classical forms of French poetry, but quickly turned to studying "l'art du vers dans les maîtres de la poésie" (51). Ongoing treatment for her arthritis required Siefert and her mother to travel to thermal springs in Aix-les-Bains in Savoy at the foot of the French Alps. In 1863, a key encounter there would shape Siefert's entry into the professional arena.

That year, through a family acquaintance, Siefert met Charles Asselineau, the Parisian author and critic who was also Baudelaire's close friend and first biographer. At the time, recalled Madame Siefert, "Louisa faisait alors sa nourriture et ses délices intellectuelles d'une *Anthologie des poètes français* [*sic*]," poring over Eugène Crépet's four-volume anthology (1861–63) to which Asselineau had contributed descriptions of a number of poets, though not for any of the women poets

(*Souvenirs rassemblés*, 55). If the details of Siefert's first conversation with Asselineau had been recorded, which poets would have surfaced in their exchange? Would the aspiring poet have commented on the dearth of women, only twelve in the entire collection? How might Siefert have discussed Desbordes-Valmore, Tastu, Girardin, and Ackermann, the four women among the forty-four poets selected from the nineteenth century, especially if she had first read their verse in the anthology?

In the fourth volume of Crépet's anthology, Baudelaire introduced the works of the late Desbordes-Valmore, endorsing the way her verse embodied femaleness, "l'accent délicieux de la femme . . . rien que *l'éternel féminin*" (*Les poëtes français*, 148). Similarly, for Léon de Wailly, Tastu's writing personified womanly reserve: "une certaine mollesse gracieuse qui répand sa douce teinte sur tous les sujets, et qui au surplus convient mieux à une femme, à l'idée du moins que nous autres hommes nous aimons à nous faire de l'autre sexe" (210). The Parnassian Philoxène Boyer invoked the purported incompatibility between femininity and creativity in summing up, if not authorizing, Delphine Gay's retreat from verse. Paul Barbet-Massin, a professor and administrator at the Institution Massin, a private second-ary school in Paris, used similar rhetoric in portraying Ackermann as "le plus étonnant exemple de l'alliance des facultés les plus contradictoires: . . . ce poëte d'une imagination si gracieuse et si vive . . . est avant tout un érudit de premier ordre" (468). However, Ackermann's grief at her husband's death from tuberculo-sis in 1846, only three years into their marriage, was the basis for the sentimental-ity Barbet-Massin highlighted in *Contes et poésies* (1863). He overlooked the more reflective texts, which would surely have caught Siefert's attention as she began to experiment with fixed verse forms.

The first of Ackermann's selected texts in Crépet's anthology is a subtle theo-retical poem about not using the sonnet. Taken from the poetry section, labeled "Pensées diverses," of her 1863 volume, the untitled poem begins:

> Pour des sonnets en fasse qui les aime:
> Chacun son goût, mais ce n'est pas le mien.
> Un bon, dit-on, vaut seul un long poëme;
> Heureux qui peut en amener à bien.
>
> (*Les poëtes français*, 475)

By favoring the long poem associated with the meditations and odes of Lamartine and Hugo as well as those of Desbordes-Valmore, Tastu, and Girardin, Ackermann distanced herself from the concise and concentrated Parnassian sonnet practice taking shape at that time. Nevertheless, as shown in chapter 7, Ackermann would likewise reject unchecked lyricism, a stance consistent with the element of self-consciousness in her choice of form:

> Mon vers, hélas! a l'humeur vagabonde;
> Ne lui parlez d'entraves seulement.

Un peu de rime,—encor Dieu sait comment!—
S'il peut souffrir, c'est tout le bout du monde.

(475)

Ackermann's view of fixed verse differs from how Siefert intended to sculpt her own expression by practicing, for example, the pantoum (a series of interwoven quatrains),[9] the quintil (five-line stanzas with repeating lines), and the sonnet. Siefert's extensive sonnet practice, in particular, distinguished her among the poets who emerged from the ranks of women, even from Blanchecotte, who did not eschew the sonnet as Desbordes-Valmore had. Siefert emphasizes this aesthetic difference in her sonnet "Sur la première page de *Joseph Delorme*" (discussed in chapter 3); she explicitly refutes Asselineau, who placed her as Valmore's direct heir in prefacing *Rayons perdus*.

Soon after meeting Asselineau, Siefert corresponded with him to share her first verses and then some sonnets.[10] Her mother recalled that his mentoring (though at a distance and infrequent) was vital in tying its effect to "l'acharnement avec lequel dès lors elle travailla le mécanisme du vers, s'essayant à toutes les formes usitées dans la poésie française de tous les temps" (*Souvenirs rassemblés*, 56). To sharpen her skills, Louisa chose prosodic constraint, "s'astreignant de préférence aux plus étroites et aux plus rigoureuses, puis revenant à l'alexandrin aussi plein que possible, ou rythmant les strophes les plus variées" (56). Asselineau's letter of December 1864 supports this practice, which is reflective of Parnassian formalism: "Vous faites déjà les vers aussi bien que Madame de Girardin, et vous en avez d'aussi beaux que Madame Valmore. Leurs places vides sont à prendre; seulement le siècle est devenu plus difficile: il veut plus d'égalité, plus de souplesse, une langue plus riche. Travaillez et comptez sur l'avenir" (quoted in *Souvenirs rassemblés*, 61). The opening comparisons with Girardin and Desbordes-Valmore are favorable but ambiguous. In describing their verse as beautiful, does Asselineau mean the content, the form, or both? Had these women garnered places alongside their male counterparts, or apart from them? By urging Siefert to develop a richer poetic language, Asselineau likely meant both the formal perfection he had attributed to the sonnet's concision in *Histoire du sonnet pour servir à l'histoire de la poésie française* (1855) and its modern practice by Baudelaire.[11]

Subsequently, in a letter of 26 March 1865 addressed to Madame Siefert, Asselineau recommended that her daughter study Baudelaire: "Elle peut y apprendre l'art de concentrer en quatorze vers des horizons immenses par exemple dans le sonnet" (quoted in Scheler, "Un poète oublié," 171). For Baudelaire, who exploited the paradox between spiritual aspirations and material dimensions, the division of the sonnet into two quatrains (the octave) and two tercets (the sestet) provided him with "a form capable of embodying the dualism of experience," David Scott has argued (*Sonnet Theory and Practice*, 45). Upon close analysis of representative texts, Scott confirms: "In the majority of Baudelaire's sonnets, whereas the octave tended to be discursive, the sestet was analytical or visionary" (47). Beginning with

Siefert's preface to *Rayons perdus*, she adapted the relation of octave to sestet in developing her lyrical duality as a blend of passion and reason.

Siefert's prefatory poem reproduces, moreover, the backstory of her inaugural collection. In 1866, Siefert had sent a draft of the volume to Asselineau, which he returned to her without comment the following year. She left the manuscript untouched for some months. In the belated response her mother recorded, one can hear Siefert as a critical reader in her desire to carve out (a space for) her poetic originality: "J'y ai bien réfléchi . . . et maintenant je suis sûre d'une chose: c'est que mon œuvre est là dedans, j'entends mon œuvre originale, celle par laquelle je dois débuter ou pas du tout. Il s'agit de la dégager, de la présenter de façon à la mettre en lumière, au risque de sacrifier de bonnes pièces pour faire valoir les meilleures" (*Souvenirs rassemblés*, 79). Siefert considered in the same objective manner how to treat the issue of her gender in engaging the public as a sonnet writer.

### The "Choice" Sonnet

The 1868 edition of *Rayons perdus* opens with the poem "Préface," composed of two sonnets. This choice of form affirms her mother's account, which chronicles Siefert's intense study of French prosody well before the advice she received from Asselineau. In form, the prefatory sonnets negotiate the poet's belonging to the French literary tradition; in content, they broach her relationship to creativity. They also announce Siefert's experiments with voice; her speaker occupies different positions in the same text. Written in the third person, the first sonnet opens thus:

> *Quand, au bord du chemin, vient la biche craintive,*
> *Elle hésite un instant avant de le passer;*
> *Elle voudrait cacher sa course fugitive,*
> *Redoutant le chasseur qui la pourrait blesser.*
>
> (1; emphasis in original)

Fear of the unknown, which prevents the female subject ("elle") from advancing, as expressed in the second stanza, yields to courage. Inspired by the expanse beyond the path she must cross, "*Et, relevant la tête, elle part en courant*" (1). The poet's shift to the first person in the second sonnet produces a split subjectivity.

Siefert's speaker compares herself to a nervous doe, but also gains agency in expressing the contours of a poetic flight from pain:

> *Je suis comme la biche indécise & tremblante*
> *Devant le taillis vert au gazon savoureux;*
> *Un désir insensé prend mon cœur douloureux*
> *D'échapper à tout prix à ma vie accablante.*
>
> (*Rayons perdus* [1868], 2)[12]

For Tracy Paton, though "Siefert assumes the role of a self-effacing modest persona to appear as if she is conforming to the nineteenth-century model virtues of ideal 'femininity,'" she "simultaneously claims her status as an artist whose self-expression depends upon her explorations of identity and intimate desires from the position of an 'other' voice emerging from within her" ("Seductive Rebellions," 90–91). Siefert further illustrates this duality by suffusing her prefatory poem with private feelings, then interceding as a critical reader aware of the politics of literary reputation. In the sestet of the second sonnet of "Préface," the speaker weighs her aspirations against the bias faced by a young woman seeking entry into the literary field:

> Oh! je veux m'en aller à la gloire, là-bas! . . .
> Mais pour l'atteindre, il faut aussi franchir la route
> Où tous les préjugés font le guet l'arme au bras.
>
> Je les sais sans pitié, j'ai peur, je les redoute,
> Le trouble où je me vois accroît encor mon doute,
> Le danger est certain . . . Si je n'arrivais pas! . . .
>> (*Rayons perdus* [1868], 2; ellipses in original)

In Siefert's prefatory sonnets, the mingling of personal and impersonal voices represents an aspect of her dual style as well as the dialogical way she positions the lyrical "I" in relation to the other. The dialogue gives a palimpsestic cast to texts in *Rayons perdus* that are drawn from memory yet amplified by thought and imagination; it reveals the topography of the psyche Siefert explores as a poet's ideational realm.

### Poetic Memory

Letters Siefert wrote to her mother on 4 and 13 October 1868, while overseeing the production of her first volume in Paris, reveal that the poet chose the title *Rayons perdus*, instead of *Mirages*, which was proposed by her publisher, Alphonse Lemerre (quoted in *Souvenirs rassemblés*, 85, 86). Both titles denote optical effects; the latter refers to an illusion caused by the bending of rays of light, and the former alludes to light beams radiating from an external source such as the sun. However, Siefert's choice conveys the sense of poetic vision and its link to memory embedded in the first stanza of her poem "Anniversaire":

> Voici venir le jour où mourut mon grand-père.
> Hélas! c'est pour mon cœur encor tout éperdu
> Un de ces souvenirs sur lesquels rien n'opère,
> Et qui, toujours vivant, tantôt me désespère,
> Tantôt brille à mes yeux comme un rayon perdu.
>> (*Rayons perdus*, 83)

171

Like other texts in *Rayons perdus*, "Anniversaire" draws on personal experience, yet also raises larger issues: in this case, the workings of the mind. Subjectivity and contemplation overlap as traces of memory blend into thoughts about interiority. Sight changes to insight along a metaphorical axis drawn from the poet's "front pensif" (line 17) and "regards abaissés" (line 18) to the "lac intérieur" (line 19). The inner space deepens to link conscious and unconscious realms of the mind: "Toute âme porte en soi ce gouffre, cet abîme, / Puits sans fond, flot sans rive, espace illimité" (lines 21–22). These emblematic lines trace the turn to memory in Siefert's work, which produces the denser texture of palimpsests.[13] Poems such as "Souvenirs d'enfance" and "Marguerite" suggest screen memories of a childhood experience, which hide more difficult memories, demonstrating an aspect of how Siefert worked creatively through pain.

"Souvenirs d'enfance," which immediately follows Siefert's prefatory sonnets, telescopes the present and the past by way of the epigraph from the Renaissance poet Clément Marot: "Plus ne suis ce que j'ai été." Textual proximity produces a similar effect, whereby "plaie" correlates with "miroir" in the prism of memory:

> Il me semble parfois que ma plaie est guérie,
> Et, souriant encor, je regarde au miroir
> Revenir doucement mon enfance fleurie.
>
> Je ne sais pas comment, mais je crois la revoir
> Ce qu'elle était hier, toute rose & paisible,
> Avec son ignorance, avec son fol espoir.
>
> *(Rayons perdus, 3)*

The poet writes over past pain palimpsestically, embroidering with new thoughts the memory outlined only symbolically by a sign of injury ("ma plaie"). Suffering is not an end unto itself, but rather a means, as Siefert later states in *Méline*;[14] it heightens, if not refines, the senses. Here, in "Souvenirs d'enfance," the body represents the pain that otherwise has no object. By transposing the wound into a mirror image, the poet faintly traces the experience that can be remembered only by reimagining it.

In stanza 3, arrested by her reflection in the mirror, the speaker considers the wound traced across her forehead by a wrinkle:

> Une ride aujourd'hui court, à peine sensible,
> De l'une à l'autre tempe en fugitif sillon,
> Et rien n'effacera cette ligne invisible.
>
> . . . . . . . . . . . . .
>
> Ni l'oubli, ni la paix, ni l'amour ineffable
> Ne combleront ce pli fait en quelques instants.
> J'aurai toujours ce témoin implacable.
>
> *(Rayons perdus, 3, 4)*

The rare adjectives in "Souvenirs d'enfance" identify the poetic speaker as female ("préoccupée," line 25; "furieuse," line 29). Pain factors most in the poet's self-portrayal as an eighteen-year-old with "cette ride au front creusée avant le temps" (4). But Siefert gives considerable thought to form, as suggested by the poem's intricate rhyme scheme (*aba, bcb, cdc, ded,* and so forth). A single twelve-syllable line closes the long poem, which is composed of 235 classical alexandrines grouped in 78 tercets. Such attention to prosody, also shown by the rich rhymes sharing three phonemes, curbs the lyrical excess conventionally associated with so-called *poésie féminine.* Subsequent stanzas recall characters and places in books, ranging from stories read to the poet as a child to material she chose in broaching philosophy and religion, among other serious topics. Reason competes with free association as various elements of reading material combine into "visions sublimes" or "songes" beyond the speaker's control, which evoke the voice of the unconscious other (8).

In "Souvenirs d'enfance," the poet as reader and creative dreamer then recalls broader horizons glimpsed in the mind's eye, traveling through space and time to the New World of the Americas, to Asia, or suddenly cast back by the texts of Homer and Aeschylus to ancient Greece and Rome:

> Sans que j'en susse rien cependant, au milieu
> De ce bizarre amas de songes & d'histoires,
> La lumière pour moi, se faisait peu à peu.
>
> Les grandes vérités rayonnantes ou noires,
> Les mondes inconnus, le passé submergé,
> Remplacèrent ainsi les contes illusoires.
>
> Le menton dans la main & le regard plongé
> Dans les rangs infinis de confuses images,
> Que de jours j'ai perdus sans en avoir congé!
>
> (Rayons perdus, 10)

A rich inner world continues to emerge as the self-governing, creative impulse mines the infinite reservoir of memory:

> Soudain, comme l'oiseau lassé d'un long voyage
> Qu'emportent çà & là les vents impétueux,
> Ma pensée abordait une nouvelle plage.
>
> (14)

The poet's journey back in time through salient chapters of ancient philosophy (Plato, Epictetus) and biblical history has shaped her worldview. "Rayons éblouissants d'un seul & même prisme," extolling "le stoïcisme" or an "austère héroïsme," philosophers and prophets illuminate a similar truth for Siefert (*Rayons perdus*, 16). The philosophical dimension of her project, as it expands from *Rayons perdus* to *Les stoïques* (in progress by 1868), demonstrates how the power of mind over matter becomes the ultimate solution to the other form of pain at the heart of her verse: mental anguish. For Siefert, even memory suffused with reverie always falls short of the ideal.

## Reverie and Its Discontents

Joseph Guichard's painting *Louisa Siefert aux Ormes* (1869; fig. 16) illustrates the ambiguity surrounding the source of voice and the attendant visual field in Siefert's poem "Marguerite," as elsewhere in *Rayons perdus*. In discussing Guichard as a disciple of Jean-Auguste-Dominique Ingres and Delacroix, René Chazelle places

FIG 16
*Louisa Siefert aux Ormes* by Joseph Guichard, 1869. Museum of Fine Arts of Lyon. Photo © MBA Lyon (Alain Basset).

this painting at the uneasy intersection of neoclassicism and Romanticism, whereby "la forme se dissout dans l'embrasement des couleurs" (*Joseph Guichard*, 44). To this aesthetic frame of oppositions—controlled lines versus unrestrained colors—Chazelle adds the question of realism. Given that Guichard, also from Lyon, was a family friend and often present after dinner when Siefert read her verse aloud, he may have heard a draft of "Marguerite." The same melancholy infuses the painting and the poem, which share a dually natural and surreal landscape. The painting's title indicates a real place: Les Ormes was the Siefert family's country residence outside of Lyon. Even as a transcription of the final version of "Marguerite" published in *Rayons perdus*, Guichard's piece was likely rendered on location; as a professor of fine arts, he advocated the technique called *plein air*. This introduces an impressionist element in the painting. The play of light, however, is subtle. More resonant and suggestive of the dreamlike quality of the textual reverie rendered by Siefert are the blurred facial features of the two female subjects, which stand out against the natural landscape. What Chazelle calls "le problème des rapports entre imagination et restitution réaliste," the tension between inner and outer reality, structures the conceptual play of Siefert's dialogic imagination (*Joseph Guichard*, 50).

"Marguerite," like "Souvenirs d'enfance," highlights the role played by memory in Siefert's creative turn away from the body in pain and in the splitting of her poetic voice. From the perspective of its length and treatment of nature, the poem has a Romantic quality. A multiplicity of subject positions nonetheless complicates the source of vision. In the first nine lines of the poem, an impersonal third-person speaker ("On") portrays a natural scene to set the stage for reverie. The ensuing interplay of the real and the imagined, marked by a change in person, announces the narrator's presence ("Nous"):

> C'était un soir de juin paisible. Du midi
> Le vent soufflait chargé d'un parfum attiédi,
> Et les deux vieilles tours massives & carrées
> D'un rayon de soleil couchant étaient dorées.
> Le ciel d'un bleu d'opale avait des tons charmants,
> Les arbres & les fleurs tressaillaient par moments,
> Partout les foins coupés dormaient sur les prairies,
> On eût dit la nature en proie aux rêveries,
> Nous étions réunis tous au bout du jardin.
> (*Rayons perdus*, 25)

Because of the full stop after the word "paisible," the end of the first line flows into the second. This Romantic technique of enjambment breaks the classical rhythm of alexandrine verse. Alongside Siefert's signature ampersand (blending in non-poetic language), a mixture of rhymes (some sharing two phonemes, others three) heightens the contrastive style. The treatment of space develops the speaker's dual viewpoint as the narrator and as the lyrical "I" within and apart from the depicted scene. Reverie, which suggests the divide between mind and body together with the split subjectivity produced in language, facilitates such mobility.

Beginning with line 13, the visual field narrows as a first-person speaker recalls daydreaming while holding her cousin on her lap:

> Moi, j'étais à l'écart, tenant sur mes genoux
> Ma petite cousine aux grands yeux bleus si doux:
>
> . . . . . . . . . . . . . . . .
>
> Enlacée à mes bras, elle était immobile;
> La lumière baignait son visage tranquille;
> Elle ne dormait pas, elle semblait rêver.
> Et je la regardais se perdre & s'élever
> Dans ce cher pays bleu, splendide & solitaire,
> Où depuis si longtemps, je vis loin de la terre.
>
> *(Rayons perdus, 25–26)*

The speaker projects onto the immobile child the expansive ideation through which she transcends her earthly existence. Such psychical kinesis dominates subsequent lines as the poet dwells on the idea discussed by onlookers that the young cousin resembles her closely: "Mais je n'écoutais plus, j'entendais plus rien, / . . . / Mon cœur seul parlait haut sans craindre de témoin; / Un mot avait suffi pour l'emporter bien loin" (lines 39, 41–42). The lyrical "I," foreseeing unfulfilled desire, gives voice to pain embodied by "un long soupir" (line 44).

Nearly halfway through the poem, in the middle of line 55 (below), the full stop after the word "jeune" marks a shift in temporality from present not to past, but to a hypothetical state. The break is temporary, however, for the speaker quickly draws back from daydreaming to reality.[15] Here, as elsewhere in *Rayons perdus*, Siefert's poetic writing loosens attention without, however, surrendering the productive dialogue between conscious and unconscious mental activity. This discursive flow in "Marguerite" illumines in modern terms how the "I" is divided in and through language, a feature generally overlooked today, as it was then, by readers who view the text in light of the maternal lament:

> Marguerite est trop jeune. Oh! si c'était ma fille,
> Si j'avais une enfant, tête blonde & gentille,
> Fragile créature en qui je revivrais,
> Rose & candide avec de grands yeux indiscrets,
>
> . . . . . . . . . . . . . . . .
>
> Quel rêve, encor plus doux que celui de l'amour!
> Des larmes sourdent presque au bord de ma paupière
> Quand je pense à l'enfant qui me rendrait si fière,
> Et que je n'aurai pas, que je n'aurai jamais;

Car l'avenir, cruel en celui que j'aimais,
De cette enfant aussi veut que je désespère.[16]

. . . . . . . . . . . . .

Jamais on ne dira de moi: c'est une mère!
Et jamais un enfant ne me dira: Maman!
C'en est fini pour moi du céleste roman
Que toute jeune fille à mon âge imagine:

. . . . . . . . . . . . .

Ma vie à dix-huit ans compte tout un passé.

*(Rayons perdus*, 2729)

The sense of grief that pervades this poem, as if mourning a conscious loss, carries through much of Siefert's writing.[17] Here, in "Marguerite," the longing for maternity relates to the recurrent themes of illness, suffering, and premature death. But posterity mostly does not recall the Parnassian timbre of the motherly lament in "Marguerite" because critics insist on the poem's Romantic excess.

## Maternal Shadows

In his preface to the second edition of *Rayons perdus*, which would precede Siefert's "Préface" in all subsequent editions, Asselineau isolates part of the passage in "Marguerite" quoted above. His seven-line excerpt begins with line 70, "Quel rêve, encor plus doux que celui de l'amour!" and continues to line 75, ending with line 88: "Jamais on ne dira de moi: c'est une mère!" (iv–v). With this example Asselineau underscores Siefert's "sincérité," one of two qualities he stresses, the other being her "fermeté du langage" (v). The more general statement that most other women "jouent la poésie . . . en 'travesti,'" repeating Baudelaire, leads up to the passage from "Marguerite," which serves a twofold purpose in Asselineau's reading of Siefert (ii). To this statement Asselineau adds, "En France, constatons-le, la Poésie est un art d'hommes" (ii). For Asselineau, there are two canons of poetry, which he affirms by evoking Desbordes-Valmore. In his view, she had succeeded as a poet by remembering her place as a woman who expressed "les passions de son sexe, fille, amante, femme, mère, sans la moindre complicité avec les idées & les ambitions de l'autre sexe" (iii). Asselineau then measures the authenticity of Siefert's voice against Valmore's sincerity, framing "Marguerite" by way of the single excerpt as a gloss on "la plainte d'Antigone allant au supplice: 'Je n'aurai point connu l'amour ni l'hymen, & je n'aurai point élevé d'enfant!'" (iv). His analogy supports formulaic themes of women's writing—love, marriage, and motherhood—limiting the ideas one would expect Siefert to treat.

However, the focus of Asselineau's appraisal shifts from content to form by returning to "l'exemple de la grande Marceline dont le souvenir ne peut être évité ici à cause de l'analogie des talents signalée dès les premiers jours par les lecteurs compétents, mademoiselle Siefert procède par cris, par élans" (*Rayons perdus*, vi). Of the latter metaphors, the first assimilates Siefert's poetic expression to "cris." This recalls the "soupir naturel" Baudelaire used to depict Desbordes-Valmore's lyricism. In representing her verse as pure inspiration, he called her "un grand poète" but one who lacked artistic polish, as Rosemary Lloyd has observed ("The Demands of an Editor," 193–94). Absent from Baudelaire's description of Desbordes-Valmore is the second metaphor "élans," but not the sense of passion Asselineau transposes into energy by calling Siefert's verse "jets" or bursts that are engraved in the mind (vii).[18] Such a lasting imprint relates to the other quality accentuated by Asselineau to elevate Siefert above most other poetic women: "Mademoiselle Siefert parle une langue claire, agile, précise" (v). He cites seven other excerpts from *Rayons perdus* to underscore the blend of formal virility and feminine sentiment as Siefert's "double mérite" (vii). This contrastive style represents "une véritable originalité," Asselineau concludes, also quantifying her feat: "cinq cent exemplaires vendus en moins d'un mois" (vii).

Rimbaud was one of Siefert's keen readers. The lines that he copied out from "Marguerite" in a letter of 25 August 1870 to his professor Georges Izambard, however, do not convey a sense of the fuller body of work she had produced by then. Rimbaud, aged sixteen, writes to Izambard: "Vous aviez l'air de vouloir connaître Louisa Siefert, quand je vous ai prêté ses derniers vers; je viens de me procurer des parties de son premier volume de poésies, les *Rayons perdus*, 4e édition. J'ai là une pièce très émue et fort belle, 'Marguerite'" (*Œuvres complètes*, 239).[19] Based on this statement, Rimbaud had already introduced his professor to Siefert's most recent volume; *Les stoïques* had appeared in May of that same year.[20] A nineteenth-century reader using the critical vocabulary of the time would likely have characterized her new collection as "masculine" because of the numerous sonnets and the key theme of stoicism. But even in repeating Asselineau's comparison with Antigone—without, however, acknowledging his source—Rimbaud did not register his familiarity with Siefert's philosophical verse. As framed by the prefatory description of "Marguerite," which heightens the text's emotional charge, Rimbaud follows instead the line of pathos, thus replicating those who saw Siefert as the embodiment of femininity à la Valmore.

Eighteen lines from "Marguerite," divided into three sections in Rimbaud's letter to Izambard, begin with line 13, cited above: "Moi, j'étais à l'écart, tenant sur mes genoux / Ma petite cousine aux grands yeux bleus si doux." The first section of his excerpt includes the line describing the child: "C'est une ravissante enfant que Marguerite / Avec ses cheveux blonds, sa bouche si petite / Et son teint transparent . . ." (lines 15–17). The ellipses are Rimbaud's, truncating line 17 at the caesura. As I have mapped out elsewhere,[21] the second part of Rimbaud's selected text excludes the narrative shifts related to the speaker's creative reverie and the contours of the split subject ("Je est un autre") he would formulate less than a year later. The excerpt continues from line 55, "Marguerite est trop jeune. Oh! si c'était ma fille," to line 59, "Rose & candide avec de grands yeux indiscrets," narrowing the poem's focus to the maternal desire that bridges the distance between the speaker and child. There are no marks of omission in Rimbaud's fragment, which then moves to "Quand je pense à l'enfant qui me rendrait si fière" (line 72) and overlaps with Asselineau's selection to "De cette enfant aussi veut que je désespère" (line 75). The excerpt provided by Asselineau, which omits lines 76–87, ends with "Jamais on ne dira de moi: c'est une mère!" (line 88). Rimbaud begins the third section of his excerpt with the latter line and includes lines 89–91 (cited above), which identify the speaker as an eighteen-year-old girl. He passes over lines 92–93 to the poem's final verse declaring that her life, but a shattered dream, was now over.

Rimbaud encapsulates his selection from "Marguerite" with a single comment: "—C'est aussi beau que les plaintes d'Antigone [*anumphé*] dans Sophocle" (*Œuvres complètes*, 239). In Asselineau's rendering, Antigone was heroic in expressing her despair, her stance one of defiance coupled with stoicism. The Greek term used by Rimbaud is transliterated here: *anumphé* (unwedded). He thus focuses the comparison between Siefert and Antigone on the unfulfilled destiny central to the classical figure's lament, a destiny tied to being a wife and mother. This maternal shadow contradicts his *lettre du voyant* of 15 May 1871, predicting that women would become poets once they were liberated from a strictly domestic role. Recall that the missive identified no female contemporary. Siefert is the only woman simultaneously named and quoted by Rimbaud. Why, then, would Rimbaud isolate the excerpt from "Marguerite" in a private letter and from its fuller context? Whereas the first-person speaker in "Marguerite" injects a personal tone, a third-person speaker expresses an impersonal tone in other references to mothers, fathers, and children in *Rayons perdus*.[22] At a level of form, too, the dual edges of Siefert's project come into view. A mixture of emotion and reflection, Romantic exuberance and Parnassian reserve, carries through her sonnet practice and her long narrative poems.

Shared aspirations might have factored in Rimbaud's reaction to a sister poet "qu'il affectionne et envie," as Anne-Emmanuelle Berger proposes in sketching misprision as a basis for his thin appraisal of Siefert (*Le banquet de Rimbaud*, 18). Recall that Lemerre brought forth *Rayons perdus* and drew Siefert into the circle of Parnassian poets he was the first to publish. Asselineau accompanied Siefert to Paris to discuss the volume's production with Lemerre on 20 October 1868. In a letter to her mother later that evening, Siefert recounted that, according to Asselineau, no sooner had she left Lemerre's office that day, "tous les poètes de la maison sont arrivés," and François Coppée read aloud to them from Siefert's manuscript (*Souvenirs rassemblés*, 88). Asselineau reported to his mentee two days later that upon hearing her verse, the Parnassian leader Charles Marie René Leconte de Lisle sought him out to share very positive impressions. For Siefert, this occurrence was "d'autant plus beau qu'il passe pour l'homme le plus difficile de Paris, n'étant jamais content ni de lui ni des autres," as she wrote to her mother on 22 October (88).

The Parnassians continued to view Siefert's verse with considerable favor. They published four of her poems in the second volume of *Le Parnasse contemporain* in 1869, the periodic collection first issued in 1866 to promote their movement, and another six in the third volume in 1876.[23] However, poems Rimbaud had sent to Banville were not selected for publication in *Le Parnasse contemporain*.[24] In assessing this evidence, Berger observes, "Peut-être quelque drame de l'inconscient se joue-t-il ici. À cela s'ajoute un secret rapport de compétition" (*Le banquet de Rimbaud*, 245). The other in the self, who whispered to Siefert as she experimented with subject positions, may partly explain Rimbaud's unwitting struggle with a precursor's shadow.

## Splitting the Lyrical "I"

A group of poems in *Rayons perdus* clustered along the thematic continuum of emotions, on the one hand, and memory, on the other, exhibits Siefert's dialogical sense of voice. The epigraph taken from Alfred de Musset's dramatic poem "La coupe et les lèvres" (1831)—"Il n'est si triste amour qui n'ait son souvenir"—structures "Les remembrances," inscribing Siefert's text in a Romantic tradition.[25] In a long narrative composed of fifty-six stanzas, each consisting of three alexandrines followed by a six-syllable line, the lyrical "I" recollects a past love, then yields to the "voice" of memory in detailing moments of joy followed by heartache: "J'écoute les récits que me fait ma mémoire / Sur ce temps enchanté" (*Rayons perdus*, 60). This line calls to mind the experience of the poet as seer that Rimbaud would describe to Paul Demeny in his letter of 15 May 1871: "Car Je est un autre . . . j'assiste à l'éclosion de ma pensée: je la regarde, je l'écoute" (*Œuvres complètes*, 250).

In "Jalousie," composed of three sonnets, Siefert develops this notion of split subjectivity through a play on the dual meaning of the poem's title: envy as well as a blind through which light can pass. The first sonnet ends by equating the heartbreak of unrequited love with a thorn in the flesh: "Et tu peux donc aimer, toi, qui ne m'aimes pas? / Mais quel déchirement qu'une telle pensée, / Dans ma blessure encor, quelle épine enfoncée!" (*Rayons perdus*, 51). At once thought and felt, pain finds expression by making verse its object. A movement away from the bodily site of suffering brings imagining to the fore. This shift unfolds in the middle section of "Jalousie," where poetic writing, tied to thinking through and beyond pain, exhibits a split subject: the artist as willful creator and the creative other.

The second of the three sonnets constituting "Jalousie" displays the contrast between content and form that Asselineau gendered in Siefert. To restate Schultz's analysis of the binary thinking in traditional criticism (*Gendered Lyric*, x–xi), feminized Romantic diffusion encounters masculinized Parnassian constraint:

> Oh! ce sonnet me pèse à l'égal d'un remord!
> Que je m'occupe ou non, que je veille ou je rêve,

Ce souvenir ne peut me laisser paix ni trêve,
Car pour moi chaque vers est un serpent qui mord.

(Rayons perdus, 51)

The exclamation ("Oh!") opening the first quatrain expresses strong emotion that is immediately tempered by thought, which takes the sonnet as its object. Lines 1 and 3 blur as quickly the distinction between poetry ("ce sonnet") and memoir ("[c]e souvenir"). At a similar metadiscursive level, line 2—"Que je m'occupe ou non, que je veille ou je rêve"—evokes the unconscious as a source of poetic expression. Pain remains creativity's uncanny object, verse personified as the "serpent that bites."[26]

This image of wounding carries over to the third line of the second quatrain, which develops deep-seated emotion and the related sense of jealousy as its subject:

L'épreuve est salutaire alors qu'elle rend fort
Et d'un souffle puissant jusqu'au ciel nous enlève,
Mais tout ressentiment transperce comme un glaive,
Et ces angoisses-là sont angoisses de mort.

(Rayons perdus, 51)

The discourse of pain, now tied to mental anguish ("ces . . . angoisses de mort"), interweaves with the analysis of imagining, with the salutary effect of "l'épreuve" being the creative force that overcomes it ("d'un souffle puissant jusqu'au ciel nous enlève"). The double movement of the octave of pain and its poetic other extends to the sestet. A change in tone matches the attempt to prevail over negative emotions as the speaker rejects a fall into despair cast in the opening line against the backdrop of a Christian mythos:

Arrière donc, vipère à la langue empestée,
Amertume égoïste & vile, pour jamais
Retourne au gouffre noir qui t'avait enfantée!

Moi, je veux vivre, aimer & sentir désormais
Tout ce que peut souffrir une âme généreuse,
Qui demande au devoir le secret d'être heureuse.

(51)

In seeking quietude, the poet leans toward the philosophical practice of stoicism, which she expands in Les stoïques.

The third and final sonnet of "Jalousie" turns from suffering toward creative transcendence. Description and analysis throughout the text interweave the way that matter changes form with the transmuting of pain into poetic insight. In the first quatrain, for example, as the air once heavy with water evaporates, "Toute ligne s'efface aux horizons plus mous" (Rayons perdus, 52). In a similar manner, negative emotion ("sombre chagrin") evoked by the "I" in the second quatrain dissipates against words "de douceur & de mélancolie," closing the first tercet (52). The personal, however, becomes universal, as signaled by the change from the first-person speaker to an impersonal other. Further still, the material becomes immaterial. The final tercet maps this transformation onto the natural world through a synesthetic correspondence between vision and smell, symbolizing how creative thought transfigures pain:

> Comme aujourd'hui l'on voit la lumière affaiblie,
> Glisser avec langueur jusqu'aux prés odorants
> Et changer l'ombre humide en rayons transparents.
>
> (52)

Such doubling of poetic voice, which splits the "I" from the "other" in the self, also occurs in "Vivere memento."[27] Objectivity blends with personal lyricism as the poet creates various subject positions in contemplating the Latin imperative "Remember to live," from which the poem takes its title. At the start of "Vivere memento," composed of nineteen stanzas with the same structure and rhythm (two alexandrines followed by a six-syllable line), an omniscient speaker elicits a state of reverie and the unconscious flow of poetic vision:

> La vie est si souvent morne & décolorée,
> À l'ennui l'heure lourde est tant de fois livrée
> Que le corps s'engourdit,
> Et que l'âme, fuyant les épreuves amères,
> S'envole & vient saisir à travers les chimères
> L'idéal interdit.
>
> On trouve ainsi l'oubli des autres, de soi-même,
> On n'est plus de la terre, on plane, on rêve, on aime,
> Toute chose est à vous;
> La notion du vrai si bien est renversée
> Que, dans vos doigts, les fils, dont la vie est tissée,
> Semblent soyeux & doux.
>
> . . . . . . . . . . . . .
>
> Si jamais âme humaine a goûté ce vertige,
> Et, semblable à la fleur arrachée à sa tige
> Que soulève le vent,
> Si jamais un esprit a délaissé la terre,
> Ce fut moi, dans les jours où j'aimais à me taire
> Pour m'en aller rêvant.
>
> Que de fois je mentis à ma propre souffrance,
> Alors que s'élançait au loin mon espérance

> Fraîche et riante encor!
> Que de fois ce semblant de liberté bénie
> A brillé dans ma nuit obscure, indéfinie,
> Avec des rayons d'or!
>
> (*Rayons perdus*, 53, 54, 55)

Nearly halfway through the poem, in stanza 8, the "I" shifts from sentimental reverie to anchor a philosophical stance: "Inscrivons ces deux mots de latin pour devise: / *Vivere memento!*" (lines 53–54; emphasis in original). The latter principle works in tandem with the opposite imperative, *memento mori*, "Remember that you have to die."

In stanza 10, the poet addresses her soul, which is imprisoned in the body, by reflecting on mortality from a Platonic perspective:

> Dieu t'a donné le corps pour prison sur la terre,
> Il t'astreint à l'épreuve, à la souffrance austère,
> À la misère, au deuil.
> Le premier cri de l'être, arrivant en ce monde,
> Est un cri de douleur, dont l'angoisse profonde
> Ne finit qu'au cercueil.
>
> (*Rayons perdus*, 56)

Within the framework of a body in pain from birth until death, life is portrayed as a constant struggle ("un combat sans repos ni relâche"; line 61). To resist chronic suffering and the anguish it provokes, one cultivates moral fortitude by turning to thoughts of immortality and pursuits such as art: "Vis par l'art créateur qui des maux fait des charmes" (line 80). Stoicism overlaps with Christianity in the poet's quest for "le but idéal, héroïque, / Que mon âme comprend" (lines 92–93). However, doubts linger as she contemplates humanity's place in the universe:

> Je songe & je regarde, ô vanité bornée!
> Que sont les jours de l'homme & qu'est sa destinée
> Devant l'éternité?
> Ce qu'est l'herbe jetée au gouffre formidable,
> Ce qu'est ce monde-ci perdu dans l'insondable
> Et dans l'immensité!
>
> (58)

In asking the questions of life that escape our grasp, especially that of suffering, the poetic thinker gives universal resonance to her inner torment:

> Seigneur, qui restes seul immuable & paisible,
> Que suis-je, atome vain de ce globe invisible

Pour m'adresser à toi?
Hélas! j'ai tant souffert, console-moi, mon Père;
Viens secourir l'enfant qui ploie et désespère;
Éternel, réponds-moi!

(58)

Here, in "Vivere memento," the problem of pain—outlined from a philosophical perspective, yet punctuated with subjective lyricism—suggests the fusion of Parnassian and Romantic tendencies, whereby Siefert's form alternately matches and opposes her content.

In "Les papiers de famille," a poem composed of thirty-six quatrains in octosyllabic verse, the borders between poetry, memory, and history blur as the poet compares fallen leaves stirred by an autumn breeze with the way her verse breathes life back into her family's papers:

Dans ces lettres, tristes trophées,
Pauvre tas de papier jauni,
Vibre aussi par molles bouffées,
Le grand souffle de l'infini.

O spectres qu'aujourd'hui je touche,
Chers inconnus que j'entrevois,
La mort en vain clôt votre bouche:
Jusqu'à moi parvient votre voix!

(*Rayons perdus*, 125)

Heroic battles fought in the name of religious freedom and ideas are imagined across time and space. The past and present thus meet and nearly merge at the text's close, illustrating how Siefert explores poetry as a form of transcendence.[28]

In reflecting on the role of memory in her verse, Siefert considers her own death and resurrection in the minds of future readers:

Le souffle, qui me les apporte,
Pour jamais les remportera,
Car de mes souvenirs, moi morte,
Ici-bas qui se souviendra?

Peut-être alors un enfant triste,
Pour qui je serai le passé,
D'un œil de poëte & d'artiste
Scrutera ce feuillet froissé,

Et dira, le cœur ému comme
Le mien l'était en écrivant:

"Rien de ce qui se perd pour l'homme
"N'est perdu pour le Dieu vivant!"

(*Rayons perdus*, 132)

But Siefert's first readers, who were struck by the creativity, sincerity, and artistry of *Rayons perdus*, would not have imagined her fading into oblivion.

Reviews of the volume were unanimous: "œuvre originale, personnelle, éminemment poétique," as her mother summarized (*Souvenirs rassemblés*, 98).[29] For example, in a letter of 12 December 1868, the poet Émile Deschamps wrote to Siefert: "Vos *Rayons*, qui ne seront *perdus* pour personne, à moins que l'on ne soit insensible à toute beauté poétique, illuminent et échauffent mon âme" (quoted in *Souvenirs rassemblés*, 225). Writing on 1 March 1869, Hugo expressed similar praise: "Ce livre émouvant et charmant, signé *Louisa Siefert*, je l'ai lu d'un bout à l'autre et je le relirai. *Rayons perdus!* Non. Les rayons ne se perdent pas. Rien ne se perd de la lumière; rien ne se perd de l'âme" (226). Banville underscored that multiple readings of *Rayons perdus* had left a similar impression: "Chez vous, Mademoiselle l'artiste, le talent acquis est à la hauteur de l'inspiration poétique," adding that she richly merited "le nom glorieux de poète" (*Camées parisiens*, 227). In reviewing contemporary poets for the *Revue des Deux Mondes* in 1869, Louis Étienne ranked Siefert's volume as "le plus personnel . . . le plus remarquable peut-être et certainement le plus contraire aux habitudes du public" ("La poésie et les poètes," 732). He observed that biography and invention overlap in her œuvre—"Elle use du privilège du poète qui peut se raconter lui-même ou inventer sans nous avertir"—and thus recognized not only Siefert's use of multiple subject positions but also her ability to transform personal suffering into poetic power (733).

In *Les stoïques* (1870), Siefert further demonstrates this ability as she reflects on the stoic approach to pain, treating duality as both a philosophical problem and an aesthetic project.

## Poetic Dualism

Stoicism, an ancient Greek philosophy founded by Zeno of Citium around 300 BCE, teaches self-control. Contemplation and correct judgment lead to *apatheia* (freedom from passion). Closely related is *ataraxia*, a state of consciousness characterized by lucidity, calm, and release from suffering. Recall from "Souvenirs d'enfance" that Siefert knew the teachings of a later exponent of this philosophy: "Épictète mourant prêchant le stoïcisme" (*Rayons perdus*, 16). Siefert recognized such a practice in her maternal grandmother, whom she memorializes in the poem that opens *Les stoïques*:

> Car, si j'ai su parler de vertu simple & grande,
> C'est que tu me la fis connaître et vénérer.

*Toi donc, en qui j'ai vu l'âme de deuils brisée,*
*Dominant par la foi la nature épuisée,*
*Soumettre la mort même à l'élan de l'esprit.*

(5; emphasis in original)

Siefert turns from personal memories to the philosophy of stoicism in developing the main theme of *Les stoïques*: the manifold problem of pain. The use of different subject positions and poetic forms tempers subjective lyricism with objectivity, allowing the poet to gain agency as a thinker. Less explicitly biographical than Siefert's dedicatory text to her late grandmother, the subsequent poem, "Le départ," exploits the ambiguity of the definite article "le" in its title. The epigraph frames the notion of parting as well as a specific departure: "Ah! la patrie est belle & l'on perd à changer."[30] A further ambiguity surrounds the voice speaking the poem, which opens with a third-person speaker, "on." The inflection of the pronoun (the impersonal "they" versus the personal "we") and its gender are unmarked at the poem's start:

On s'aimait. Dans un autre on avait mis sa vie:
Aux douceurs d'être ensemble on bornait son envie;

.    .    .    .    .    .    .    .    .    .    .    .    .

Et voilà qu'on se quitte & qu'on se dit adieu;

.    .    .    .    .    .    .    .    .    .    .    .

Et que cet avenir qu'on croyait si modeste,
Avec tous les projets les plus ambitieux,
Fuit & s'évanouit comme l'aurore aux cieux.

.    .    .    .    .    .    .    .    .    .    .    .

Tout est fini. L'attente & l'absence sans terme
Remplacent maintenant l'intimité. Les ans
vont peut-être passer douloureux & pesants
Avant qu'on se retrouve & qu'on se réunisse.

(*Les stoïques*, 7, 8)

Full stops (lines 1, 14) and enjambment (lines 14–17) dislocate the classical alexandrine. This technique, which illustrates Siefert's Romantic bent, creates tension by postponing the end of a line. At the level of content, the open ending suggests how a departure of whatever nature unsettles the course of one's life. Evoked in this context is the specter of the unknown, which broadens to mean "le sort" (line 36). Death is the destiny no one escapes.

Parting, though a universal experience, also has a personal resonance. The shift to the lyrical "I" in the second and shortest section of the poem marks the poet's underlying concern about death (lines 40–46):

Frère, je n'ai jamais pu voir aucun départ
Sans qu'émue aussitôt par ces sombres pensées,

. . . . . . . . . . . . . . . . .

> Car tout départ pour moi retrace une autre perte,
> Et la Mort peut entrer par cette porte ouverte.
>
> (*Les stoïques*, 9)[31]

Here, as elsewhere in *Les stoïques*, "le doux Évangile & l'âpre stoïcisme" mutually serve as guides to navigate the difficult path of life (9).[32] In facing one's own mortality and misfortune, such as disease not under one's control, one finds peace by aligning one's desires with the will of God.[33] For the poet, deep anguish is caused by passions of the mind, particularly the desire for absolute knowledge, which is tied to a sense of the ideal. The stoic quest for serenity in light of such suffering has an aesthetic parallel in the poem "Soupir," which combines formal restraint with lyrical diffusion in transforming pain into creative work.

In "Soupir," composed of two sonnets, Siefert reflects on the vexing quest for truth from which one must seek relief. As put by Jean-Jacques Ampère in the poem's epigraph, "Sans le soupir, le monde étoufferait." A sigh restores physiological balance and mental equilibrium. Moreover, by taking in and letting out a long breath, visible to others, one moves away from the privacy of pain. Analogously, imagining remains invisible unless it takes a form others can share. The poet uses the fixed sonnet form to reflect on desire as a common source of sorrow.[34] In the first quatrain, the voice speaking the poem maintains a distance from the sentiments it apostrophizes by thinking about them:

> Rêves, anxiétés, soupirs, sanglots, murmures,
> Vœux toujours renaissants & toujours contenus,
> Instinct des cœurs naïfs, espoir de têtes mûres,
> O désirs infinis, qui ne vous a connus?
>
> (*Les stoïques*, 14)

The Romantic gesture of turning to nature for answers spins unproductively. A veiled allusion to Baudelairean *correspondances* (here, a canopy of empty brambles) illumines thwarted reciprocity:

> Les vents sont en éveil, les hautaines ramures
> Demandent le secret aux brins d'herbe ingénus,
> Et la ronce épineuse, où noircissent les mûres,
> Sur les sentiers de l'homme étend ses grands bras nus.
>
> (14)

The diversity in nature merges in universal harmony. This infinite movement, though discerned by humans, withholds its origin. Such is the paradox of humanity's quest, with the ultimate problem being whether the truth is more fully grasped in the physical world or in the mind's eye:

"Où donc la vérité?" dit l'oiseau de passage.
Le roseau chancelant répète: "Où donc le sage?"
Le bœuf à l'horizon jette un regard distrait,

Et chaque flot que roule au loin le fleuve immense
S'élève, puis retombe & soudain reparaît
Comme une question que chacun recommence.

(14–15)

The octave of the second sonnet imitates with full stops and commas the fits and starts of seeking truth. All human beings, the poet suggests, raise similar questions about the meaning of life without knowing where to find answers. The rhyme scheme (*abab*, *abab*, *ccd*, *ccd*) accentuates the vowel *i*, which stresses the anxiety that such uncertainty produces along with an underlying sense of dread. This formal pattern counters spontaneous emotion, as does the third-person speaker ("on"), who reflects on feelings at a remove:

À vingt ans, quand on a devant soi l'avenir,
Parfois le front pâlit. On va, mais on est triste;
Un pressentiment sourd qu'on ne peut définir
Accable, un trouble vague à tout effort résiste.

Les yeux brillants hier demain vont se ternir.
Les sourires perdront leurs clartés. On existe
Encor, mais on languit. On dit qu'il faut bénir,
On le veut, mais le doute au fond du cœur subsiste.

(*Les stoïques*, 15)

Can one know anything with certainty, especially if the knowledge sought is illumined by the perfect idea, evoked in Siefert's reflective poem "Voyage" as "l'idéal sacré dont l'âme est toujours veuve" (*Rayons perdus*, 146)? Here, in "Soupir," the mystery of life stirs the sentient being's desire to penetrate it while understanding that it is an impossible quest:

On se plaint, & on se heurte. Navré,
On a la lèvre en feu, le regard enfiévré.
Tout blesse, & pour souffrir on se fait plus sensible.

Chimère ou souvenir, temps futur, temps passé,
C'est comme un idéal qu'on n'a pas embrassé,
Et c'est la grande soif: celle de l'impossible!

(*Les stoïques*, 15)

Shifts in voice energize further the philosophical tug-of-war between the sensibilities of reason and passion as Siefert delves into the practice of stoicism, using form to modulate content.

## Between the Thinker and the Poet

In *Les stoïques*, Siefert often juxtaposes emotional intensity with objective scrutiny to demonstrate how a stoic philosopher reasons to overcome the sway of external impressions as well as memories and desires. The poem "Bonheur" represents this mental exercise. A line from Étienne Pivert de Senancour's pre-Romantic epistolary novel *Obermann* (1804) serves as the poem's epigraph: "Et les beaux jours sont pour moi les plus pénibles" (24). This line unfolds in Siefert's contemplative text as an ironic gloss on happiness, which is fleeting for human beings because of the agon between the senses and the mind seeking peace. The poem consists of five quintils, in which the first and fifth alexandrine verses repeat; the refrain marks prosodic restraint and, at another level of interpretation, control over emotion.[35] As expressed in the first stanza, through the senses one derives bliss from nature. Such moments of unity between humankind and the natural world represent the objective correlative of happiness, a feeling that has no object:

> Été vertigineux, négation des pleurs,
> Nuits blanches, soirs dorés, aubes resplendissantes,
> Épanouissement d'étoiles & de fleurs,
> Ivresse magnétique aux effluves puissantes:
> Été vertigineux, négation des pleurs!
>
> (24)

The speaker, hitherto omniscient, extends the joy mirrored in nature with the second stanza's refrain: "La nature aujourd'hui rit de son large rire" (lines 6, 10). But such natural pleasure originates in the sensations that incite human passions and the pain of want.

Using a first-person plural speaker to open the third stanza, Siefert the poetic thinker exposes the paradox of happiness: "Notre faiblesse est grande à porter le bonheur, / Le vent n'est pas si fort que cette douce haleine" (*Les stoïques*, 25). Human beings are so easily moved by all their senses and by external circumstances outside the realm of their control that they are unable to sustain happiness for long. Inextricably tied to the mind-body split, this weakness *is* human nature. The poet shifts to the first-person singular to reflect on her personal experience:

Cependant que la terre exaltait le Seigneur,
Mon âme a débordé comme une coupe pleine.
Notre faiblesse est grande à porter le bonheur.

(25)

From the underlying perspective of a true stoic, humans feel a continual lack and associated weariness by mistaking bodily pleasure for happiness.

The poet alternates between the first-person plural and the lyrical "I," despairing. This negative attitude belies the stoic practice of recognizing and accepting the limits of life, which brings about serenity:

Nous n'avons plus la foi de l'heure inespérée.
Sur ma lèvre tremblaient les mots du paradis,
Ceux par qui le ciel s'ouvre à l'extase sacrée.
Ces mots que je savais, je ne les ai pas dits.
Nous n'avons plus la foi de l'heure inespérée.

Le cœur énervé cède à la fatalité.
Quand vient l'amour avec le bonheur pour amorce,
Nous le regardons fuir d'un œil désenchanté,
Nous demeurons passifs, nous n'avons pas la force.
Le cœur énervé cède à la fatalité.

(*Les stoïques*, 25)

Happiness in the stoic sense of *ataraxia* can only be preserved through reason, which allows one to prevail over the limits of pleasure. Here, in "Bonheur," the speaker succumbs to passion, "la fatalité," the source of philosophical pessimism about the human condition, as expressed in a number of other poems in the volume.[36]

The final stanza of "Bonheur" was copied out by Henri-Frédéric Amiel, the Swiss philosopher and poet, in his diary on 8 November 1872; it struck him as a tension in *Les stoïques*: "Pauvre Louisa! nous faisons la stoïque et nous avons toujours au flanc le dard envenimé, *lethalis arundo*" (*Journal intime*, 532).[37] A highly sensitive and enthusiastic reader of Siefert, also familiar with *Rayons perdus*, Amiel notes the aesthetic edges of her poetic expression: "Et votre talent aussi a les deux qualités opposées, l'intimité et l'éclat, le lyrisme et la fanfare. Et vous cassez le rythme des vers en même temps que vous en soignez la rime. Et vous balancez entre Valmore et Baudelaire, entre Leconte de Lisle et Sainte-Beuve, c'est-à-dire que vos goûts aussi réunissent les extrêmes" (532). "La combe," which follows "Bonheur," exposes this tension generated by disparate aspects of the same poetic sensitivity.

The paratexts that surround "La combe" emphasize the Romantic tone in both its title and the epigraph from Sainte-Beuve's *Vies, poésies et pensées de Joseph Delo-*

*rme* (1829): "En vain elle s'est dit que la campagne est belle." A relatively long poem, composed of thirty-eight alexandrines, "La combe" presents a brooding quality:

> Non, plus pour aujourd'hui, plus de grandes pensées,
> De saintes questions à la hâte embrassées,
> D'énergiques efforts, d'élans fiers et hardis.
> Mon esprit est lassé, mes doigts sont engourdis.
> L'automne est la saison des rêves, nous y sommes,
> Elle parle; rêvons et laissons là les hommes,
> Leur bruit & leur destin.—Prenons à notre choix
> L'un des sentiers fleuris qui mènent dans les bois.
>
> (Les stoïques, 26)

The weary thinker loosens her hold on rational thought and seeks refuge in nature. For a poet exhibiting Romantic sensibilities, such a retreat into solitude normally incites creative reverie: "Il y fait bon s'asseoir au soleil & rêver. / Car l'arrière-saison est clémente aux poëtes" (27). However, the desired communion is as elusive as poetic insight:

> —Les songes! mais pourquoi toujours eux? Vainement
> Aujourd'hui je voudrais en avoir les mains pleines
> Et les jeter au vent, aux flots, aux cieux, aux plaines,
> Rouge de ma faiblesse & n'y résistant pas.
>
> .  .  .  .  .  .  .  .  .  .  .  .  .  .  .
>
> Je ne sais plus saisir le sens caché des choses,
> Et la vie assombrit les lointains les plus roses.
>
> (27, 28)

At another level of interpretation, "La combe" exposes the difficulty of seeing the true nature of reality, a principle of stoicism that informs Siefert's thinking through pain. The mixture of introspection and philosophical inquiry into the human condition throughout *Les stoïques* foregrounds Siefert's Romantic lyricism and Parnassian objectivity.[38]

"Automnales," in which pessimism is both a feeling and a thought, exemplifies Siefert's poetic duality. The poem establishes a further link with Sainte-Beuve's Romantic inheritance and concern with form via the epigraph: "Doux vents d'automne, attiédissez l'amie!"[39] Comprising four sonnets, "Automnales" also nods to the Parnassian movement in the 1860s and '70s, principally to its emphasis on metric form. In the first sonnet, the lyrical "I" projects onto nature an inner landscape strewn with memories and dashed hopes:

> Voici les vents du sud qui font tomber les fruits
> Et s'entr'ouvrir parfois les âmes plus aimées.

Ils passent sur mon front en ondes parfumées,
Hérauts des souvenirs & des espoirs détruits.

Chaque feuille qui vole aux désirs éconduits
Me ramène. J'entends bruire les ramées
Comme les mille voix confuses, animées,
Des rêves dont les cœurs de vingt ans sont séduits.

(*Les stoïques*, 29)

Yet the sestet of the first sonnet announces a more pessimistic view of developing the solace expressed in "Bonheur." The speaker questions the presumed harmony between humanity and nature as archetypal bliss and, in so doing, exposes the difference that separates them:

Que veulent-ils, ces vents qui font courber les branches,
Qui tendent le ciel bleu de fines gazes blanches,
Et gonflent le raisin de soupirs attiédis?

Que veulent-ils encore à cette âme songeuse
Qu'ils appellent, captive aux essors interdits,
Et qui brise aux murs clos son aile voyageuse?

(29–30)

The tone intensifies in the second sonnet as the speaker presses the issue further, repeating the word "pourquoi" at the start of three lines (lines 17, 19, 23): "O nature, pourquoi ces sentiers ombragés / Qu'on dirait faits exprès pour y passer ensemble?" (*Les stoïques*, 30). Why do human beings feel a sense of kinship with the natural world? Though inhabited by living creatures, nature possesses no awareness of our existence or our pain, for that matter. The opening of the third sonnet punctuates this stark reality with the full stop that breaks the second line: "Mais vents du nord ni vents du sud n'y feront rien; / Nous ne serons jamais heureux. Les solitudes / Prennent en vain leurs plus tranquilles attitudes" (31). Although nature is unconscious of the cycle of life and death and indifferent to disease and other forms of misery that plague human beings, no mortal escapes pain:

L'homme voit partout l'homme & son âme abattue,
À l'haleine du mal qui l'opprime & la tue
Ploie et cède vaincue en sa stérilité.

(31)

The distance gained through reflection by a third-person speaker changes with a shift in voice. The lyrical "I" dominating the fourth and final sonnet considers again the inspiration found in nature:

J'ai tort, n'est-il pas vrai? jours exquis, jours dorés,
De forcer mon esprit jusqu'à ce qu'il oublie
Les trésors de langueur & de mélancolie
Qu'à vos poëtes seuls en ce mois vous offrez.

(*Les stoïques*, 32)

At another level of interpretation, this questioning represents a fundamental challenge for a mind that seeks clarity of thought, but is simultaneously pulled by the senses toward the material plane and thus into the realm of pain. This struggle infuses the poet's subsequent retreat from melancholic returns to the past: "Et l'attente stoïque a remplacé l'essor / Dont la puissance m'est ravie" (73).

"Temps perdu" condenses the arc of Siefert's poetic development, which is also the subject of the untitled poem that begins, "Jadis enfant joyeuse & folle, / Toujours extrême en mes désirs" (*Les stoïques*, 79). The form, consisting of ten octosyllabic stanzas, aligns with the poem's content. Rhythmic control matches activity in the inner life. The final two stanzas evoke, through sensual exaltation, nostalgia, and suffering, a past superseded by the stoic discipline of calm acceptance:

Maintenant la vertu stoïque
Réveille en moi l'ancien espoir
Et me dit: "Il n'est d'héroïque
Que l'honneur & que le devoir!"

Mais calmant mon effervescence
Prête à partir aux grands combats:
"Sache donc tourner ta puissance
Toi-même à te vaincre tout bas."

(81)

The practice of stoic philosophy runs parallel to the aesthetic contrasts Siefert deploys, Romantic subjectivism engaging with Parnassian objectivity.

In Siefert's writing, the dialogue between the introspective poet and the lucid thinker uses creative work to rid pain of its destructive energy. In an untitled sonnet encapsulating the philosophical aspect of Siefert's project, this effort is further likened to the process of reasoning through which one dominates the passions. The epigraph taken from the third book of *Manuels d'Épictète* frames the self-conscious sonnet as a response to the stoic philosopher's teachings: "Et tu te plains?"[40] Shifts from a personal to an impersonal voice highlight how the poet works through and breaks free from pain:

C'est vrai, j'ai peu d'égards aux vains regrets d'autrui;
Pour tous, comme pour moi, je suis presque trop forte,
Et, coupable parfois au moment qu'elle exhorte,
Ma volonté superbe endure mal l'ennui.

Ah! quand on voit demain triste autant qu'aujourd'hui,
Quand on passe sa vie à dire: Que m'importe?
À repousser du pied comme une chose morte
Tout rêve qui demeure après l'espoir enfui

(Les stoïques, 92)

The relation of octave to sestet, from exposition to analysis, represents how thinking through poetry becomes a philosophy of life:

Peut-être la douleur qu'on veut garder secrète
Vous donne-t-elle aussi des mots impérieux;
Et d'un geste écartant les regards curieux,

Comme celui qui souffre en lisant Épictète,
Ravi par la vertu des Stoïques anciens,
Traite-t-on tous les maux comme on traite les siens.

(92–93)

In treating the problem of pain from the perspective of ancient stoic practice, Siefert exposed her own quest for strength of mind over matter along with an acceptance of suffering.

### Reception Matters

In the *Journal de Lyon* of 8 June 1872, the poet Joséphin Soulary rejected the idea of comparing Siefert to Desbordes-Valmore, "l'éternel idéal de la femme poète." Soulary focused on the diversity of Siefert's production and observed how unfortunate it was that *Les stoïques* appeared just before France went to war against Prussia and was thus overlooked. For him, the volume demonstrates "dans la manière du poète une indépendance fière et de superbes énergies."[41] If some critics used *Rayons perdus* to force Siefert to fit a simple definition of *poésie féminine*, he speculated whether they would now accuse her of "trop de virilité" in *Les stoïques*. He also mentioned Siefert's "Causeries poétiques," which evaluated contemporary poetic and prose production in historical and aesthetic context.

In the bibliographical record of the "Causeries poétiques" provided by Siefert's mother, the list of authors reviewed by Siefert includes Gautier, Coppée, Leconte de Lisle, Prudhomme, Léon Dierx, and Silvestre Glatigny as well as their "devanciers" Laprade, Auguste Brizeux, Louis Ménard, and Louise Ackermann (see *Souvenirs rassemblés*, 152–53). The article on Ackermann, however, is missing from the archives. One can nonetheless imagine how Ackermann's turn to science might have struck Siefert who, in a letter of 8 January 1873 to her mother, stated regarding George Sand's *Les ailes de courage* (1872) that "l'analyse scientifique . . . ne sera jamais de la poésie, quoi qu'on fasse" (*Souvenirs rassemblés*, 183). Siefert's literary criticism, which merits a study of its own, suggests the legacy she had in mind as a close reader of French prosody's evolution across the centuries.[42] In the "Causerie poétique" of 5 March 1872, which Siefert devoted to Gautier's *Tableaux du siège, Paris, 1870–1871*, she marveled at the way her fellow Parnassian's expression modeled "toutes les ressources ingénieuses de la langue et le jeu secret de ce mécanisme si bien construit et lié en toutes ses parties qui constitue le talent." In stating this, she meant the work genius demands, paraphrasing in the same context Buffon's definition: "La patience est la seconde moitié du génie."

In *Méline* (1876), Siefert raises the issue of gifted women's reception in light of societal expectations. She questions whether men can understand the difficulties intellectual and creative women still face: "Lui, qui est son seul maître après tout, dès qu'il le veut, appréciera-t-il les difficultés toujours renaissantes qu'elle trouve à reprendre un peu de liberté? . . . Non, cette marque originelle du génie de la femme, cette puissance dans le désir, ce déploiement de toutes ses facultés sur un point unique, cet élan irrésistible, impondérable qui l'amène, pour tout résultat, à un tour de force dont elle n'ose se vanter" (216). With her framed narrative about a woman born with a gift, the eponymous female protagonist intends for her doctor to realize that all women do not possess the same nature. The same could be said of their legacy as poets. Siefert's last poem, "Au revoir" (2 November 1876), highlights the limits of understanding, especially the relation of mind and body, as a source of human suffering:

> Que devant l'infini l'intelligence humaine
> Ne comprend rien, sinon qu'une loi souveraine
> Y régit toute chose en un splendide accord,
> Et que partout la vie y déborde la mort.
>
> (Souvenirs rassemblés, 361)

Siefert nonetheless hoped that her attempt to make sense of the pain associated with life by transposing its force into creative work would resound for posterity. The verse invoked in the poem's final line addresses future generations directly: "Je leur dis: 'Au revoir dans l'immortalité! . . .'" (361; ellipses in original). She died a year later.

In 1878, Claire Stephens alluded to the emergent study of tuberculosis as a catalyst for genius in praising the introspective and ailing Siefert as the young Romantic "éclairée et comme consumée par la flamme intérieure, presque diaphane, absorbée par le sentiment si pur qui l'inspire et fait briller sur son front la poétique auréole de ses *Rayons perdus*" ("Un vrai poëte," 338).[43] Two years later, Abel Peyrouton stressed Siefert's mastery of poetic form: "[C]ette fermeté de style, cette netteté, cette précision, cette virilité, tout est remarquable" ("Louisa Siefert et son œuvre," 42). In his view, Siefert was a thinker, "un esprit grave et réfléchi," whose work would withstand the test of time (42). For Emmanuel des Essarts, *Les stoïques* encapsulated Siefert's œuvre, "unissant et fondant les qualités les plus contraires"

("Poètes français contemporains," 308). Charles Fuster called Siefert a modern Sappho: "Autant le sentiment est féminin, autant la langue est mâle" ("Une Sapho moderne," 111). Ludovic Spizio related these qualities to the body in pain: "Si l'on examine la vie, la passion, les ouvrages de Louisa Siefert, on a l'étrange spectacle d'une âme virile, enfermée en un corps malade chantant des vers héroïques" ("L'âme féminine," 582). Then, as now, references to Siefert's struggle with disease suggest the transmutative force of her creativity, but also marginalize her hybrid production by drawing on categories of gender.

In 1979, Jean-Paul Somoff and Aurélien Marfée asked: "Qui peut se vanter de reconnaître si un vers est écrit par une femme ou par un homme?" ("Les muses du Parnasse," 8). They cited Siefert among the women published alongside their male contemporaries in the second volume of *Le Parnasse contemporain* (1869), refuting the idea that poetry has a sex: "De même qu'un bel alexandrin n'a pas d'âge et que frappé au coin de la beauté, il devient immortel, il n'a pas de genre; il serait aussi ridicule de gloser sur le sexe des poètes que sur celui des anges" (8). Yet they appraise Siefert's unique Romantic sensibility in these terms: "un cœur féminin virilisé par l'épreuve physique et morale" (84–85). The centenary of Rimbaud's death in 1991 encouraged closer analysis of his correspondence, specifically an 1870 letter "où Rimbaud cite favorablement et longuement Louisa Siefert," as Lucien Chovet described ("Un faux Rimbaud," 64). Graham Robb concluded about the same epistolary thread: "Rimbaud copied out a large piece of glutinously sentimental verse by Louisa Siefert about a childless young woman. One line was singled out for admiration" (*Rimbaud*, 43).[44] More productively, Lucien Scheler considered Siefert beyond the Rimbaud letter, relating her poetic history to "une vie illuminée par la beauté du verbe" ("Un poète oublié," 185). Indeed, as this reading across her production has revealed, Louisa Siefert's thinking through physical and spiritual pain illuminates language's constitutive role in our grasp of the relation of mind and body. Such a quest for knowledge also spurred Louise Ackermann's poetic engagement with modern science, which I examine in the next chapter.

# 7 Louise Ackermann's Turn to Science

A self-identified thinker who approached poetry as a way of knowing, Louise Ackermann (1813–1890; fig. 17) exposed the limits of human understanding in relation to religion and science. Ackermann burst onto the Parisian literary scene at the age of sixty-one with her 1874 collection, *Poésies: Premières poésies, Poésies philosophiques*, which saw three editions that year. The philosophical project she had developed over forty years stunned readers. In a review for the newspaper *Le Siècle*, Edmond Texier captured her volume's impact: "Pourquoi cette nature si robuste, si virile qui aborde de front tous les problèmes, qui secoue les colonnes du temple, qui abat les statues des dieux, a-t-elle livré si tard son trésor manuscrit? Quoi! tant d'audace et tant de réserve! A-t-elle voulu choisir son heure, parce qu'elle craignait, en venant trop tôt, de n'être pas comprise?" (n.p.). Ackermann later clarified why her major work had appeared so late. A cluster of philosophical poems, composed in the mid-1860s and published by various journals during that period, revealed the crisis of modern thought that had been taking shape in her mind for well over a decade.[1] None of the poems drew notice at the time, however, which discouraged her from writing for publication. Upon moving back to her native Paris early in 1871, Ackermann thus assumed the solitary and contemplative life she had led in Nice since the late 1840s. The fact that she issued a booklet of philosophical poems under the name L. Ackermann in Nice later that same year also contributed to her obscurity in the literary capital, where her *Poésies philosophiques* passed virtually unnoticed prior to 1874.

Upon learning of Ackermann's slim volume in 1873, Jules Barbey d'Aurevilly reviewed it for the newspaper *Le Constitutionnel*. He found fascinating how passionately she espoused atheism, yet made her poetry "le chaste désespoir de l'esprit *seul!*" ("Madame Ackermann," 159; emphasis in original). Having caught a glimpse of Ackermann reading her verse at a mutual acquaintance's home, he wrote that

Mᵐᵉ Ackermann, morte à Nice, le 2 août. — [Dessin de M. Paul Merwart.]

she neither looked nor sounded like "*une* poète" (162; emphasis in original).[2] Ackermann's creative mind unsexed her, but admirably so, observed Barbey d'Aurevilly, calling her "un prodige par le talent et un monstre par la pensée" (165).[3] The latter amused her, as suggested by the copy of the expanded 1874 volume she sent to him, which she signed "Un monstre reconnaissant."[4] However, his claim that Ackermann's stance reflected her own suffering provoked her to write *Ma vie* in order to rebut him and like-minded critics.[5] In tracing her pessimism to its intellectual source, Ackermann would identify science's power over religion, but emphasize their analogous failure in the search for absolute truth about the workings of the natural world and the matter of human destiny.

The philosopher Elme Caro wrote a belated review of Ackermann's 1871 *Poésies philosophiques* for the *Revue des Deux Mondes* in May 1874.[6] Critics assessing the expanded philosophical corpus in her 1874 *Poésies* would reference Caro's focus on Ackermann's original turn to contemporary science: "C'est l'écho dans une forte imagination des conceptions nouvelles que l'on nous impose sur le monde, sur l'homme et sur la vie. Là est le caractère et l'impérieuse originalité de ces poèmes" ("La poésie philosophique," 260).[7] Caro's essay, which established Ackermann as a positivist poet, brought her instant celebrity. As her contemporary Gabriel Paul Othenin de Cléron, comte d'Haussonville, later recalled, "[A]u lendemain de l'article en question, tout le monde (tout le monde, c'est-à-dire mille personnes à Paris) s'abordait en se disant: 'Avez-vous lu les vers de M^{me} Ackermann?'" ("M^{me} Ackermann," 320). Caro and those who echoed him nevertheless mistook her passion.[8] Ackermann thus interceded as the critical reader of her œuvre's span and purpose, revealing the early scientific bent crucial to grasping her despair about the human condition.

In this chapter I reconstruct the poetic development Ackermann authorizes in *Ma vie* to align her voice with objective lyricism. Ackermann's account of her intellectual journey sheds light on the complicated publication history of her output. Composed in 1874 to counter the idea that private loss had inspired her bleak view of human existence, her autobiography was published in 1882 and then prefaced subsequent editions of her poetic and prose works.[9] I consider Ackermann's production chronologically, beginning with her verse from the 1830s. First published in *Contes et poésies* (1863), then collected as *Premières poésies* with *Poésies philosophiques* in 1874, more of this early production began to circulate as part of her complete works in the 1880s. Close analysis of selected texts from the 1840s to 1871 illumines the roots of Ackermann's advanced scientific thought in *Poésies philosophiques*. Also germane to her evolving vision is the "Journal" she wrote from 1849 to 1869, some of which originally appeared as prose fragments under the title "Pensées diverses d'une solitaire" in 1881 before being posthumously published in its entirety in 1927.[10] These reflections, like Ackermann's correspondence, amplify how she studied the ascendancy of science while challenging readers' assumptions about how a poet inhabits her corpus.

## A Poet's Sensibilities

In *Ma vie*, Ackermann traces the ear she developed for poetry to works by Molière, La Fontaine, Racine, and Corneille, often read aloud by her parents. As a child, she sensed the rhythmic quality of language before understanding its meaning. While Ackermann's father encouraged both her love of reading and her writing of verse, her conservative mother attempted to "cure" her daughter's literary aspirations with catechism. In 1829, Ackermann was sent to a religious boarding school in Paris where, ironically, her poetic gift emerged.[11] She so excelled in classical prosody that her literature professor, Félix Biscarrat, had Hugo read her first alexandrines.[12] The "grand poète," recalls Ackermann, gave her advice about rhythm she never forgot (*Œuvres de Louise Ackermann*, viii). Biscarrat also facilitated her study of English and German and works by Shakespeare, Byron, Goethe, and Schiller. In relating her early development to the mix of creative and philosophical works she studied, Ackermann makes no mention of French Romantics. However, her journal and *Pensées* register criticism of Romanticism and of individual poets from that era.[13]

Ackermann stresses how widely she read, noting a translation of Plato alongside Buffon's *Époques de la nature* (1780). She writes about the latter volume:

"[C]e livre m'élargit tout à coup l'horizon" (*Œuvres de Louise Ackermann*, vi). Just when the self-described book lover encountered the naturalist's conception of the immutable laws governing the diversity in the natural world, she began to experiment with verse. Here lie the roots of Ackermann's use of poetry to engage the new science of life and its impact on humanity's relationship with creation. This is the aim Ackermann emphasizes in a passage from her 1903 *Pensées* as she reflects on the pivot in her trajectory: "J'ai autant que possible évité de parler de moi dans mes vers. Faire de la poésie subjective est une disposition maladive, un signe d'étroitesse intellectuelle. D'ailleurs, tout poète qui ne pense qu'à lui sera bientôt à bout de chants et de cris. C'est au nom de la Nature, c'est surtout au nom de l'Humanité qu'il faut élever la voix. Ces sources d'inspiration sont les seules vraiment profondes et intarissables" (49). The existential quandaries that infuse some of Ackermann's first poems anticipate her turn from subjective to objective lyricism.

Fragments of the 1830 poem "L'homme," taken from a notebook of Ackermann's early verse, portend her view of humanity's plight. The poem outlines her pessimistic thought by depicting a human's life as brief and insignificant in relation to the universe's vastness.[14] It thus truncates Blaise Pascal's paradoxical view of humans, whose grandeur consists in being conscious of their smallness.[15] It also anticipates the poem "Pascal" (1871), which is considered later in this chapter and is a fuller debate with the seventeenth-century philosopher's wager about living as if God exists. In "L'homme," Ackermann's poetic narrator makes pain the overarching experience of being human, from birth to death, adopting a thinker's impersonal stance but using the familiar "tu" to address every human being:

> Misérable grain de poussière
> Que le néant a rejeté,
> Ta vie est un jour sur la terre;
> Tu n'es rien dans l'immensité.
>
> .  .  .  .  .  .  .  .  .  .  .  .  .
>
> Ta mère en gémissant ta donna la naissance;
> Tu fus le fils de ses douleurs,
> Et tu salus l'existence
> Par des cris aigus et des pleurs,
> (*Œuvres de Louise Ackermann*, xxiii; ellipses in original)[16]

The opening stanza develops the young Ackermann's imminent rejection of faith by depicting man as the product of *creatio ex nihilo*. In contemplating humans' place in the universe, she equates life with suffering. Ackermann does not attempt to give life meaning, such as via the attainment of virtue in Siefert's rendering of stoicism. Death is not redemptive in a spiritual sense, but a release from pain, as expressed in the final stanza of the poem, with which she also ends the fragment in *Ma vie*:

Sous le poids de tes maux ton corps usé succombe
Et goûtant de la nuit le calme avant-coureur,
Ton œil se ferme enfin du sommeil de la tombe:
Réjouis-toi, vieillard, c'est ton premier bonheur.
(*Œuvres de Louise Ackermann*, xxiii)

In 1877, Ackermann added excerpts from "L'homme" to *Ma vie*. By stressing that she voiced universal despair, she also wanted to show that her pessimism was philosophical and rooted in *her* early poetic thought, not in that of Schopenhauer, whom she read in the original and to whom she was often compared.[17]

One glimpses Ackermann's solemn vision of life on earth in a telling farewell to poetry, written shortly after her father died (*Œuvres de Louise Ackermann*, xii). An ironic opening for *Premières poésies*, "Adieux à la poésie" (1835) breaks with personal verse. The poem foregrounds Ackermann's quest to penetrate the mystery of human suffering, a solitary and inescapable experience:

Mes pleurs sont à moi, nul au monde
Ne les a comptés ni reçus;
Pas un œil étranger qui sonde
Les désespoirs que j'ai conçus.

L'être qui souffre est un mystère
Parmi ses frères ici-bas;
Il faut qu'il aille solitaire
S'asseoir aux portes du trépas.

J'irai seule et brisant ma lyre,
Souffrant mes maux sans les chanter;
Car je sentirais à les dire
Plus de douleur qu'à les porter.

(3–4)[18]

Words such as "pleurs," "désespoirs," "souffre," "maux," and "douleur" extend the strand of pain from the Romantic theme of solitude. The moral accent of this theme foretells the existential angst in Ackermann's later poetry, born of the answers she sought from religion and science.

In *Ma vie*, Ackermann discusses her rejection of Catholic dogma at the boarding school in Paris where she spent three years, admitting the mystical bent that resurfaces as pantheism in her œuvre: "L'envie de croire ne me manquait pourtant pas. J'étais certainement, au fond, de nature religieuse, puisque j'eus plus tard des rechutes de mysticisme. Quant à la foi proprement dite, elle m'était devenue à tout jamais impossible" (*Œuvres de Louise Ackermann*, ix). "Élan mystique," which dates to 1832, conveys this wrestling with the realm of the divine. As a reflective poem placed directly after Ackermann's preemptive adieu to sentimental poetry, it reveals her early intellectualism and experiential sense of knowledge. Composed of thirty-two alexandrines (with four lines indicating omissions between verses 8 and 13, and three lines omitted between verses 26 and 30), the poem has a narrative quality:

> Alors j'avais quinze ans. Au sein des nuits sans voiles,
> Je m'arrêtais pour voir voyager les étoiles
> Et contemplais trembler, à l'horizon lointain,
> Des flots où leur clarté jouait jusqu'au matin.
> Un immense besoin de divine harmonie
> M'entraînait malgré moi vers la sphère infinie,
> Tant il est vrai qu'ici cet autre astre immortel,
> L'âme, gravite aussi vers un centre éternel.
>
> (5–6)

The vast universe overwhelms the observer, whose line of sight drifts from material reality to the horizon. This limit to what one can see does not quell the accompanying sense that much escapes the naked eye. Space looms as endless, but also as lack and thus longing. The poet seeks refuge from thoughts of the unknown in a preestablished harmony ordained by God. Doubt nonetheless competes for her attention.

Ackermann's nascent swerve toward scientific inquiry emerges beginning with line 13 of "Élan mystique" below. Knowledge that stems from sensory perception, however, generates uncertainty about the finite world. The poetic mind, which dwells apart from the body, also senses the infinite:

> Mais, tandis que la nuit marchait au fond des cieux,
> Des pensers me venaient, graves, silencieux,
> D'avenir large et beau, de grande destinée,
> D'amour à naître encor, de mission donnée,
> Vague image, pour moi, pareille aux flots lointains
> De la brume où nageaient mes regards incertains.
> (Œuvres de Louise Ackermann, 6)

The poet gestures toward Platonic mysticism by invoking the realm of perfect forms or ideas, for which the human soul yearns but which it cannot attain while imprisoned in the body. This impossible desire for union and illumination prompts the antithetical view:

> —Aujourd'hui tout est su; la destinée austère
> N'a plus devant mes yeux d'ombre ni de mystère,
> Et la vie, avant même un lustre révolu,
> Garde à peine un feuillet qui n'ait pas été lu.
> Humble et fragile enfant, cachant en moi ma flamme,

J'ai tout interrogé dans les choses de l'âme.
L'amour, d'abord. Jamais, le cœur endolori,
Je n'ai dit ce beau nom sans en avoir souri.

(6)

With the loss of mystery—what is known by metaphysical speculation or divine revelation—the poet's view of human destiny cedes to bitter pessimism:

Puis j'ai sondé la gloire, autre rêve enchanté,
Dans l'être d'un moment instinct d'éternité!
Mais pour moi sur la terre, où l'âme s'est ternie,
Tout s'imprégnait d'un goût d'amertume infinie.
Alors, vers le Seigneur me retournant d'effroi,
Comme un enfant en pleurs, j'osai crier: "Prends-moi!
Prends-moi, car j'ai besoin, par delà toute chose,
D'un grand et saint espoir où mon cœur se repose,
D'une idée où mon âme, à qui l'avenir ment,
S'enferme et trouve enfin un terme à son tourment."

(6–7)

The incongruous cry for salvation suggests that, in attempting to fathom the universe, the poet remains undecided about God. "Élan mystique" thus outlines Ackermann's passion for truth along with her dialectical approach to knowledge, which tests the relation of the ideal and reality.

In Ackermann's *Premières poésies*, other texts demonstrate her early questioning of humanity's true end and the existence of a benevolent God, including the introspective poem "À une artiste" (1840). Given the hostile environment that surrounds humans, evoked in the poem's second line, "Puisque le sol est froid, puisque les cieux sont lourds," the speaker asks:

Que faire de la vie? O nôtre âme immortelle,
Où jeter tes désirs et tes élans secrets?
Tu voudrais posséder, mais ici tout chancelle;
Tu veux aimer toujours, mais la tombe est si près!
(*Œuvres de Louise Ackermann*, 13)

The rhetorical use of apostrophe to address the soul assumes a mystical order, but not one identified with organized religion. Rather, in stanzas 3 and 4, the inward turn expands the realm of the artist. As a creative thinker, one detaches from the physical realm and thus gains access to the idea of beauty, which surpasses material reality:

Le meilleur est encore en quelque étude austère
De s'enfermer, ainsi qu'en un monde enchanté,

Et dans l'art bien aimé de contempler sur terre,
Sous un des ses aspects, l'éternelle beauté.

Artiste au front serein, vous l'avez su comprendre,
Vous qu'entre tous les arts le plus doux captiva,
Qui l'entourez de foi, de culte, d'amour tendre,
Lorsque la foi, le culte et l'amour, tout s'en va.

(13–14)

The enthusiasm for the ideal precipitates its opposite, illustrating Ackermann's poetic dialectics.

The poem "Renoncement" (1841) exemplifies a similar movement of thought, with pessimism being the synthesis of perfect love and its antithesis. Youthful desire, evoked in lines 3–4 of the first stanza ("Si mon cœur a rêvé, si mon cœur rêve encore / Le choix irrévocable et l'éternel amour"), is met by skepticism in the three stanzas that follow and, ultimately, by apathy in the poem's closing stanza:

Non, non! Restons plutôt dans notre indifférence.
Sacrifice . . . eh bien, soit! tu seras consommé.
Après tout, si l'amour n'est qu'erreur et souffrance,
Un cœur peut être fier de n'avoir point aimé.
(*Œuvres de Louise Ackermann*, 15–16; ellipses in original)

Even in treating the powerful feeling of love, the poet takes the gloomiest possible view.[19] Though Ackermann the thinker would resist biographical criticism, her short-lived marriage had an impact on her poetic trajectory and legacy of belatedness. Her reframing of this juncture in *Ma vie* reveals how she negotiated her relationship to creativity while keeping in mind her own poetic aspirations and the dominant view of verse produced by women: "Je puis être hardie dans mes spéculations philosophiques, mais, en revanche, j'ai toujours été extrêmement circonspecte dans ma conduite" (xiii–xiv). Ackermann distinguishes the realm of the passionate thinker from the social space she occupies as a woman: "On ne commet guère d'imprudences que du côté de ses passions; or, je n'ai jamais connu que celles de l'esprit" (xiv).

In 1838, after finally gaining her mother's permission, Ackermann studied in Berlin, which she describes as the city of her dreams: "Les questions philosophiques et littéraires y passionnaient seules les esprits. Hegel était mort, il est vrai, mais Schelling faisait mine de ressusciter" (*Œuvres de Louise Ackermann*, xiii). There, she met Paul Ackermann, an Alsatian philologist. Prior to their marriage in 1843, she had him sign a contract not to have offspring. This action resonates with her later philosophical disdain of the senses and thus of sensuality as an instinct that opposes nature to humankind, an instinct she also associated with reproduction.[20] However, Ackermann attempted to draw a strict line between her life and work to defend against their conflation. While working with her husband, she abandoned her own writing.[21] In thinking back to this decision, Ackermann reproduced her family's bias against writers along with the heightened censorship of poetic women at the time. This reflects the view of the bourgeoisie as well as the split between her creative voice and social identity: "Mon mari a toujours ignoré que j'eusse fait des vers; je ne lui ai jamais parlé de mes anciens exploits poétiques. . . . La vraie raison de mon silence, c'est que je tenais extrêmement à sa considération. Or, il ne faut pas se le dissimuler, la femme qui rime est toujours plus ou moins ridicule" (xv–xvi).[22] After her husband's untimely death in 1846, Ackermann moved to Nice and lived with one of her sisters until 1853. That year, after purchasing a small hillside estate, she began to immerse herself in study.

The poetic writing with which Ackermann broke her silence did not mirror the interest in scientific advances she simultaneously cultivated, which would become the core of her *Poésies philosophiques*. How could readers, who initially encountered the so-called late poet of science in 1874, integrate her mid-century return to writing via sentimental narratives in verse inspired by the *Mahabharata*, a major epic of ancient India?[23] Ackermann gives a terse cursor: "[J]e ne suis pas tout d'une pièce" (*Œuvres de Louise Ackermann*, xviii). In a journal entry of 3 November 1852, she writes more expansively about how her approach to poetry has evolved: "Quand j'étais jeune, ce que j'appelais inspiration n'était qu'une certaine disposition musicale; j'éprouvais le besoin de chanter. Aujourd'hui, lorsque je compose, je ne sens plus qu'une grande lucidité; je vois mieux" ("Journal," 532). As a retrospective reader of her own writing at various stages of its development, from rhythmic lyricism to objectivity, Ackermann explains her concurrent thinking about science and its linkage with poetry.

From the 1850s onward, new scientific findings inform Ackermann's poetic thought: "Les théories de l'évolution et de la transformation des forces étaient en parfait accord avec les tendances panthéistes de mon esprit" (*Œuvres de Louise Ackermann*, xix). She links poetry with science, both discourses that mutually draw on the imagination and reason to produce fresh ways of envisaging with the mind's eye: "Les côtés poétiques de cette conception des choses ne m'échappaient pas non plus. Par ses révélations, la science venait de créer un nouvel état d'âme et d'ouvrir à l'esprit des perspectives où la poésie avait évidemment beau jeu" (xix). In continuing this exposé, Ackermann separates her late work from her life: "[O]n n'y découvre . . . rien qui justifie mes plaintes et mes imprécations" (xxi). Her philosophical poetry conveys anguish and indignation, but this passion is not personal, she repeats, identifying herself as a reader of contemporary science: "Quant aux résultats récents de la science, ils ne m'ont jamais personnellement troublée; j'y étais préparée d'avance. Je puis même dire que je m'y attendais" (xxi).

Ackermann has in mind Charles Darwin's *On the Origin of Species* (1859).[24] His theory of the natural selection of living species cast human existence in the shadow of "the survival of the fittest," as rephrased in Herbert Spencer's 1864 *Principles of Biology* (444–45). She presents Darwinism in these terms: "Considéré de loin, à travers mes méditations solitaires, le genre humain m'apparaissait comme le héros d'un drame lamentable qui se joue dans un coin perdu de l'univers, en vertu de lois aveugles, devant une nature indifférente, avec le néant pour dénouement" (*Œuvres de Louise Ackermann*, xxi–xxii). Laws operating in a universe indifferent to the human race and its survival dislodge the belief in divine design, hence the poetic thinker's revolt against Christianity: "L'explication que le christianisme s'est imaginé d'en donner n'a apporté à l'humanité qu'un surcroît de ténèbres, de luttes et de tortures. En faisant intervenir le caprice divin dans l'arrangement des choses humaines, il les a compliquées, dénaturées. De là, ma haine contre lui, et surtout contre les champions et propagateurs plus ou moins convaincus, mais toujours intéressés, de ses fables et de ses doctrines" (xxi–xxii). In this context, Ackermann clarifies the passion underlying her poetic work: "Contemplateur à la fois compatissant et indigné, j'étais parfois trop émue pour garder le silence. Mais c'est au nom de l'homme collectif que j'ai élevé la voix; je crus même faire œuvre de poète en lui prêtant des accents en accord avec les horreurs de sa destinée" (xxii). Shifts in gender, from the masculine "contemplateur" to the "je" marked as feminine by "émue," distinguish the thinker from the woman considering her writerly arc. As Ackermann's view of her creative voice suggests, the poet and the woman neither inhabit the same body nor inhabit the body in the same way.

## Between the Critical Reader and the Poetic Thinker

Ackermann's *Contes* (1855) did not sell and figured little in her reception, though it is described in *Ma vie* as instrumental to her return to poetic writing at mid-century. When reissued with a selection of poems (composed between the 1830s and early 1860s) under the title *Contes et poésies* (1863), the poetry section garnered the more favorable notice.[25] In a two-part review for the newspaper *Le Temps*, published on consecutive days (7–8 June 1863), Daniel Stern (the pen name of Marie d'Agoult) distinguished the private woman from the poet, whom she depicted as "un esprit rare" (8 June). Ackermann, residing in Nice at that time, had granted Stern a rare interview in her home. In Stern's view, the stories in verse that Ackermann had drawn from diverse sources, "des littératures orientales, slaves ou germaniques," did not translate well into French (7 June). However, Ackermann had found her voice and superior vision: "Dans la seconde partie . . . l'harmonie entre la composition et l'exécution est parfaite. On sent que, dans l'intervalle, le poëte est entré en possession de lui-même et de son talent. Il ouvre une aile plus hardie, son essor monte vers des régions plus hautes" (7 June). For Stern, the poems "Les malheureux," "In memoriam," "Endymion" (dedicated to Stern), and "L'Hyménée et l'Amour," all of which express the pain of being human, captured Ackermann's emergent project on humanity's fractured relationship with nature as well as its creator. Stern also noted the striking disparity between the bold poet who pushed against established boundaries and the moderate woman who upheld strict moral standards.

The dual identity Ackermann promoted by distinguishing the creative from the social realm played an uncanny role in her relationship with Stern. As revealed in an 1859 letter to her niece Caroline Fabrègue, Ackermann had initially avoided any contact with the comtesse d'Agoult, whose morals she scorned: "[E]lle m'est antipathique sans la connaître. Je n'aime pas les femmes tarées" (quoted in Vier, *Marie d'Agoult*, 119).[26] Ackermann expressed similar reservations in a journal entry of 27 February 1860: "M^me d'Agoult est un esprit grave qui a commis des légèretés. Le contraste est discordant" ("Journal," 536). But shortly after Ackermann met the countess in Nice during the winter of 1860–61, they began a lively correspondence that lasted until d'Agoult's death in 1876.[27] Ackermann embraced the comtesse d'Agoult as her friend and supporter as well as an intellectual who shared her love of German culture. She also admired Stern the writer, who critiqued Ackermann's poems from the 1850s and early '60s before *Contes et poésies* went to press and those she composed in the mid-1860s and added to *Poésies philosophiques* (1871).[28] In the context of my analysis of Ackermann as a critical reader of her own work, their letters shed light on her aesthetic ideas. This correspondence also shows how closely Ackermann followed her critics' writings and in turn constructed her own canons of criticism.

In writing to Stern three months before Stern's article of 7–8 June 1863 appeared, Ackermann describes her *Contes* as "des jeux d'imagination": "Je n'y ai recherché que la grâce et la finesse, qualités particulières aux Français du bon temps littéraire" (quoted in Vier, *Marie d'Agoult*, 133). Her *Poésies* reflects a different aesthetic concern: "En abordant le lyrisme pur, j'ai voulu tout autre chose . . . il me fallait émouvoir et toucher par l'expression simple et profonde d'un sentiment humain. La poésie lyrique qui ne descend pas au fond des entrailles ne me paraît pas mériter ce nom" (133). Ackermann approached pure lyricism with the purpose of stirring readers' universal emotions. Her emergent poetry of science, however, like her poems drawn from ancient mythology, derived more of its effect from reasoning.[29] An earlier letter of 10 February 1862 emphasizes this leaning toward detachment. Ackermann concurs with Stern that "*désespoir scientifique*"—objective despair elicited by deep thought—characterizes the verse she produced in the 1850s and early 1860s, even her poems touching on personal loss, such as "In memoriam" (1850–52) and "Un autre cœur" (1863) (quoted in Vier, *Marie d'Agoult*, 134; emphasis in original). Ackermann notes a related thought about the creative mind in her journal on 22 June 1862: "Quelque vaste que puisse être un génie humain, il sentira toujours incomplet, plein de lacunes, entouré d'obscurité" ("Journal," 541).

As Ackermann returned to poetry, she pursued contemporary science. The poem "À la comète de 1861" stages her aesthetic project: using poetry to think about how new discoveries complicate the quest for truth.[30] Curious about the comet's sudden appearance, the erudite poet seeks to grasp its origins and its relationship to the rest of creation, including humanity. In the first of two octaves, the speaker apostrophizes the comet, appraising its sense of the world, as if to challenge the Romantic tendency of endowing nature with human aspirations and emotions:

> Bel astre voyageur, hôte qui nous arrives
> Des profondeurs du ciel et qu'on n'attendait pas,
> Où vas-tu? Quel dessein pousse vers nous tes pas?
> Toi qui vogues au large en cette mer sans rives,
> Sur ta route, aussi loin que ton regard atteint,
> N'as-tu vu comme ici que douleurs et misères?
> Dans ces mondes épars, dis, avons-nous des frères
> T'ont-ils chargé pour nous de leur salut lointain?
>
> (*Contes et poésies*, 253–54)

The great comet of 1861 was visible to the naked eye for three months and developed a spectacular tail as it approached the earth. Contemporary astronomers who measured its various positions computed a parabolic orbit of 409 years. This context unfolds in the second and final octave of Ackermann's poem from the perspective of a mortal being able to conceive, albeit not see, the comet's path. The former's finite existence, marked by a full stop in the second line below, merely intersects with the latter's infinite trajectory:

> Ah! quand tu reviendras, peut-être de la terre
> L'homme aura disparu. Du fond de ce séjour
> Si son œil ne doit pas contempler ton retour,
> Si ce globe épuisé s'est éteint solitaire,
> Dans l'espace infini poursuivant ton chemin,
> Du moins jette au passage, astre errant et rapide,
> Un regard de pitié sur le théâtre vide
> De tant de maux soufferts et du labeur humain!
>
> (*Contes et poésies*, 254)

The poet's inner dialogue with the celestial body about humanity's plight reveals a mind divided between rational power and the creative imagination. An entry from Ackermann's journal dated 14 August 1861 outlines the problem for the thinker with a pantheistic bent (equating God with nature or the laws of the universe) who is now encountering modern science: "L'ordre de l'univers ne me suggère pas l'idée d'un suprême ordonnateur, mais bien celle d'une grande loi" ("Journal," 539).

The turn from divine order toward external (yet hidden) forces operating arbitrarily in the universe yields deeper philosophical pessimism in "Les malheu-reux," which is placed near the end of the 1863 volume's poetry section. The long undated poem, composed of eighty verses not fixed in form, opens with an eerie scene: "La trompette a sonné. Des tombes entr'ouvertes / Les pâles habitants ont tout à coup frémi" (*Contes et poésies*, 281). "Why rise from the dead?" asks an omniscient first-person speaker, who recalls the earth as a harsh place where one despairs that, unpredictable in its course, life has no meaning: "Nous n'avions rencontré que désespoir et doute, / Perdus parmi les flots d'un monde indifférent" (283). The tone remains agonistic as the solace of permanent death is assessed against the faint promise of eternal life. In line 40, at the poem's midpoint, the speaking subject personifies human destiny as blind and cruel. An invisible force, which is compared to an executioner, propels humans toward the abyss:

> Au gouffre que pour nous creusait la destinée
> Une invisible main nous poussait acharnée.
> Comme un bourreau, craignant de nous voir échapper,
> À nos côtés marchait le Malheur inflexible.
> Nous portions une plaie à chaque endroit sensible,
> Et l'aveugle Hasard savait où nous frapper.
>
> (283–84)

For Gautier, who included Ackermann's *Contes et poésies* in his 1866 "Rapport sur le progrès de la poésie," she belonged neither to the Romantic school nor the Parnassian, but "à cette école des grands désespérés, Chateaubriand, Lord Byron, Shelley, Leopardi, à ces génies éternellement tristes et souffrant du mal de vivre, qui ont pris pour inspiratrice la mélancolie" (130). Harking back to the same point in Ackermann's trajectory, Louise Read considered "Les malheureux" to be the point of departure of "la vraie M$^{me}$ Ackermann," known for her philosophical power and her delving into science to clarify the purpose of human existence (*Pensées d'une solitaire* [1903], x, xii).[31]

One can see that poets wrestled with science's rise from the start of the nineteenth century, with André Chénier's "L'invention" (1787) embracing the modern muse and Lamartine's "Le désespoir" (1818) gauging science's authority over religion. In the wake of Darwin and in the shadow of a French tradition of naturalist poetry, Ackermann correlated poetic thought with scientific reasoning.[32] I now examine how her poetry (including both the poiesis and the verse) of science illustrates, at the discursive level, the production of knowledge to be both reasoned and imagined, constructivist and creative.[33] In studying the evolution of *la poésie scientifique* in France, the literary historian Casimir Fusil argues that poetry, in particular, "s'initie aux travaux des savants, à leurs vues, à leurs hypothèses; elle en déduit les conséquences morales et sentimentales, le pessimisme scientifique" (*La poésie scientifique*, 25). In the scientific strand of Ackermann's *Poésies philosophiques* our desire to know anything fully tells us that we cannot know where knowledge stops, especially given the different ways of knowing through the spirit versus the body.

Between Religion and Science

The 1871 volume, *Poésies philosophiques*, which consists of ten poems, opens with "L'amour et la mort." This long narrative poem sets the tone for Ackermann's late turn against religion toward science. In the space of thirty-four stanzas, which are divided into three unequal parts, the poet stages a dialogue about humanity's plight with various interlocutors: human beings, nature, and God. In part 1, the voice speaking the poem confronts those blinded by love with their mortality and quickly demystifies the idea of everlasting life:

> Amants, autour de vous une voix inflexible
> Crie à tout ce qui naît: aime et meurs ici-bas.
> La mort est implacable et le ciel insensible;
> Vous n'échapperez pas.
>
> (3)

Subsequent stanzas expose the sensual desire that underlies human love and similarly refute the notion that such love transcends death by emphasizing the mortal body. In part 2, stanza 11, the question asked of a personified Nature hints at her indifference:

> Toi-même, quand tes bois abritent leur délire,
> Quand tu couvres de fleurs et d'ombre leurs sentiers,
> Nature, toi leur mère, aurais-tu ce sourire
> S'ils mouraient tout entiers?
>
> (5)

Along the same lines, three stanzas later, the lyrical subject then asks God whether the spectacle of "tant d'adieux navrants et tant de funérailles" moves him to compassion (5). The speaker argues against doubt to close the second part of "L'amour et la mort" on a tenuous note of hope:

> Mais non, Dieu qu'on dit bon, tu permets qu'on espère:
> Unir pour séparer, ce n'est point ton dessein.
> Tout ce qui s'est aimé, fût-ce un jour, sur la terre
> Va s'aimer dans ton sein.
>
> (6)

In the third and longest part of the poem, the speaker mocks the promise of immortality to which human beings cling in the first two lines of stanza 17: "Éternité de l'homme, illusion! chimère! / Mensonge de l'amour et de l'orgueil humain" (*Poésies philosophiques*, 6). Nature's power to survive comes into focus against humankind's fate two stanzas later:

Vous échapperiez donc, ô rêveurs téméraires!
Seuls au pouvoir fatal qui détruit en créant?
Quittez un tel espoir; tous les limons sont frères
     En face du néant.

                                                    (6)

The Christian God having faded from view, the poet turns to pantheism by insist-
ing that Nature, though filled with living creatures, is not aware of our existence:

Heureux, vous aspirez la grande âme invisible
Qui remplit tout, les bois, les champs de ses ardeurs:
La Nature sourit, mais elle est insensible;
     Que lui font vos bonheurs?

                                                    (7)

Against this background upsurges the force that sustains Nature, which transcends
death instinctively through mindless reproduction:

Elle n'a qu'un désir, la marâtre immortelle,[34]
C'est d'enfanter toujours, sans fin, sans trêve, encor.
Mère avide, elle a pris l'éternité pour elle,
     Et vous laisse la mort.

                                                    (7)

In following the binary of nature's continuity versus humanity's limitations to
the end of the poem, the speaker links the individual human to the chain of being
while distancing God from creation. The struggle between religion and science to
reveal the nature of things in turn raises the problem of positivist thought, which
Ackermann treats from the perspective she notes in her journal on 7 July 1865: "En
face de la plupart des phénomènes de la nature, le savant constate, mais il n'expli-
que rien" ("Journal," 558).

The two-part, fifteen-line poem "Le positivisme" recalls Ackermann's resis-
tance to fixed verse forms, such as the sonnet, in representing the excess that
positivism cannot contain: the desire for definite truths. Objectivity suffuses the
short poem, written in rhyming alexandrines (apart from the hemistich that closes
the opening octave):

Il s'ouvre par delà toute science humaine
Un vide dont la Foi fut prompte à s'emparer.
De cet abîme obscur elle a fait son domaine;
En s'y précipitant elle a cru l'éclairer.
Eh bien! nous t'expulsons de tes divins royaumes,
Dominatrice ardente, et l'instant est venu:

211

Tu ne vas plus savoir où loger tes fantômes;[35]
  Nous fermons l'Inconnu!

Mais ton triomphateur expiera ta défaite.
L'homme déjà se trouble et, vainqueur éperdu,
Il se sent ruiné par sa propre conquête;
En te dépossédant nous avons tout perdu.
Nous restons sans espoir, sans recours, sans asile,
Tandis qu'obstinément le Désir qu'on exile
Revient errer autour du gouffre défendu.

  (*Poésies philosophiques*, 10)

Alternately evoked as "un vide" and "l'Inconnu," origins, like final causes, lie beyond "la science humaine." Against this gap in human understanding, which has been long appropriated as the basis for faith, positivist science established its domain. Unpublished notebooks that give Ackermann's scientific sources include this definition from the French chemist Marcellin Berthelot: "La science positive ne poursuit ni les causes premières ni la fin des choses; mais elle procède en établissant des faits et en les rattachant les uns aux autres par des relations immédiates. . . . C'est un des principes de la science positive qu'aucune réalité ne peut être établie par le raisonnement. Le monde ne saurait être deviné."[36] As Ackermann reasons in "Le positivisme," the attempt to apprehend reality via sense perceptions and the data of experience, though based on rejecting an abstract ideal, does not suppress the lack ("cet abîme obscur") that informs all systems of knowledge. Like any *scientific* inquiry, positivism cannot eradicate the desire of the unknown ("gouffre défendu"), which calls into question whether fuller understanding is possible through continued discovery.

In 1874, Caro extolled Ackermann as the first poet to engage positivism: "[L]isez cette page où, pour la première fois, le positivisme a été défini en beaux vers. Le poète triomphe des dernières conquêtes de la raison et de la science, mais quel triomphe morne et quelle peinture de l'expiation" ("La poésie philosophique," 254). Indeed, Ackermann went beyond defining positivism as a philosophical system by exposing how science is the asymptote of absolute knowledge. Auguste Laugel's *Problèmes de la nature* (1864), another of Ackermann's sources, expressed it this way: "[L]a science nous mène toujours un peu plus près de la vérité, mais plus nous approchons, plus nous demeurons convaincus que nos bras ne peuvent embrasser l'image toujours grandissante. Nous pouvons changer de point de vue: quelque chose toujours nous échappe" (178). To play on Laugel's title, the problem with nature is that nature has its reasons that reason cannot know. Ackermann's "Le nuage," a gloss on "The Cloud" (1820) by the English Romantic Percy Shelley, which she composed in 1864 and first published in 1865 with "Le positivisme," further illustrates this aporia in the pursuit of scientifically accurate knowledge about the world.[37]

In "Le nuage," Ackermann sustains a deliberate rhythm through fifteen quatrains (composed of three alexandrines followed by a single octosyllabic line) and a crossing rhyme scheme (*abab*, *cdcd*, and so forth). This aesthetic control simulates the Schopenhauerian concept of determinism as a universal law directing all observable phenomena. A Darwinian motif textures Ackermann's naturalist scheme, neatly stated by Caro: "Ce *Nuage* est tout un symbole de la doctrine de l'évolution. Son histoire, n'est-elle pas celle même des forces éternelles en circulation dans le Cosmos, qu'aucune forme ne limite, qu'aucun temps n'épuise, qu'aucun être ne contient, qu'aucun système, aucune formule ne définira jamais, qui échappent à la mort, et pour qui la naissance même n'est qu'une transformation?" ("La poésie philosophique," 255).

The epigraph to Ackermann's "Le nuage" comes from "The Cloud" by Shelley: "I change, but I cannot die." Thus personified, the cloud narrates its own story and suggests in this manner Nature's self-determination and agency:

> Levez les yeux! c'est moi qui passe sur vos têtes,
> Diaphane et léger, libre dans le ciel pur;
> L'aile ouverte, attendant le souffle des tempêtes,
>     Je plonge et nage en plein azur.
>           (*Poésies philosophiques*, 11)

In the eight stanzas that follow, the cloud details its transformation along a cyclical route. Floating as a mass of condensed water vapor by day, veiled by night, it explodes with energy, then descends as rain. Modified by movement that one perceives but cannot fully anticipate or explain, the cloud embodies how physical matter continues to evolve, as expressed in stanza 10:

> Rien ne m'arrête plus; dans mon élan rapide
> J'obéis au courant, par le désir poussé,
> Et je vole à mon but comme un grand trait liquide
>     Qu'un bras invisible a lancé.
>           (12)

Beginning with stanza 11, the cloud reverses its trajectory to show the eternal cycle in the natural world:

> Océan, ô mon père! Ouvre ton sein, j'arrive!
> Tes flots tumultueux m'ont déjà répondu.
> Ils accourent; mon onde a reculé, craintive,
>     Devant leur accueil éperdu.
>           (13)

Its time on the ground as water, which is limited to stanza 12, is fleeting. The cloud now evaporating as air represents, via metonymic adaptation, the will of Nature, which subjects all of creation, including humans, to its reproductive economy of transformation and evolution:

> Mais le soleil, baissant vers toi son œil splendide,
> M'a découvert bientôt dans tes gouffres amers.
> Son rayon tout-puissant baise mon front limpide:
>     J'ai repris le chemin des airs!

> Ainsi, jamais d'arrêt. L'immortelle matière
> Un seul instant encor n'a pu se reposer.
> La Nature ne fait, patiente ouvrière,
>     Que dissoudre et recomposer.

> Tout se métamorphose entre ses mains actives;
> Partout le mouvement incessant et divers,
> Dans le cercle éternel des formes fugitives,
>     Agitant l'immense univers.

(13)

"Le nuage" proposes that matter is the only reality. However, materialism was not Ackermann's definitive approach to the science of nature. She explains this in a letter to her nephew Jules Fabrègue: "Je déteste . . . le pur matérialisme. Le philosophe que je te recommande . . . est Spinoza. J'y mêle un peu d'Hegel et j'en compose un ragoût philosophique très sain et très fortifiant. Il a l'extrême avantage de me permettre de me passer de la nourriture vulgaire d'un Dieu personnel, sans m'enfoncer dans la matière" (quoted in Haussonville, "M^me Ackermann," 337–38). Time and again, Ackermann finds her creative inspiration in positivism and evolution. She nonetheless retains the pantheism of the Dutch philosopher Baruch Spinoza, a naturalist with a mystical side. In book 4 of the *Ethics* (1677), Spinoza argues, "Nature does not act for the sake of an end; since that eternal and infinite being whom we call God (or Nature) acts by the same necessity whereby he exists. . . . Hence the reason or cause why God (or Nature) acts and why he exists is one and the same. As therefore he exists for the sake of no end, he acts for the sake of no end" (154). Ackermann develops a similar view of the world in light of evolution.

### The Descent of Humankind

In a journal entry of 18 June 1864, Ackermann sketches out what Darwin's evolutionary scheme means for human beings: "Quel est cet idéal vers lequel la nature s'achemina à travers le temps éternel et les formes infinies? Nous ne sommes pas le terme de son évolution et de ses efforts" ("Journal," 551). A subsequent entry (1 July

1864) weighs this evidence against the biblical narrative of creation: "*À chaque creation Dieu s'applaudit de son œuvre. Il la trouva bonne.* Et cependant quelle œuvre pouvait être plus imparfaite, puisque l'éternité ne serait pas suffisante à realiser ce qui lui manque pour atteindre à l'idéal. *Ce besoin du progrès, qui est l'impulsion innée de l'univers, est en contradiction avec cette satisfaction qu'exprime le créateur*" (552–53; emphasis in original). These thoughts inform "La nature à l'homme" (November 1867), a lengthy poem of twenty-one quatrains. The poet voices the unmaking of human beings in God's image from Nature's viewpoint.[38] A prosopopoeia mimes this paradigm shift, where Nature initiates a dialogue with man (in the generic sense) about the end game of life.

The four opening quatrains of "La nature à l'homme" bring the myth of human genesis down to earth in the world created anew after Darwin:

> Dans tout l'enivrement d'un orgueil sans mesure,
> Ébloui des lueurs de ton esprit borné,
> Homme, tu m'as crié: repose-toi, Nature;
>     Ton œuvre est close: je suis né!
>
> Quoi! lorsqu'elle a l'espace et le temps devant elle,
> Quand la matière est là sous son doigt créateur,
> Elle s'arrêterait, l'ouvrière immortelle,
>     Dans l'ivresse de son labeur?
>
> Et c'est toi qui serais mes limites dernières?
> L'atome humain pourrait entraver mon essor?
> C'est à cet abrégé de toutes les misères
>     Qu'aurait tendu mon long effort?
>
> Non, tu n'es pas mon but, non, tu n'es pas ma borne
> À te franchir déjà je songe en te créant;
> Je ne viens pas du fond de l'éternité morne
>     Pour n'aboutir qu'à ton néant.
>
>                     (*Poésies philosophiques*, 23)

Evolutionary science displaces the anthropomorphism that undergirded the Romantic age, where humankind—conceived in the image of the divine Father—could project itself through a predetermined Edenic harmony into nature. "Ce n'est plus l'homme qui est le centre de la création et qui en est le but," Irène Chichmanoff later summarized the scientific turn in Ackermann ("Étude critique," 104). Here, in "Le nuage," the will or desire in the natural world, seen as perpetual change, asserts itself as the ultimate force and object of creation: "J'aspire! C'est mon cri, fatal, irrésistible" (*Poésies philosophiques*, 24).

Nature's desire for a more perfect form of evolution than that found in humanity is introduced in the eighth quatrain of "La nature à l'homme" and developed in quatrains 11–13. Unlike the discourse of progress theorized by the positivist thinker Auguste Comte in relation to the stages through which humanity would perfect its knowledge and continue to evolve, this drive is mindless:

> L'éternel mouvement n'est que l'élan des choses
> Vers l'idéal sacré qu'entrevoit mon désir;
> Dans le cours ascendant de mes métamorphoses
>     Je le poursuis sans le saisir.
>
> . . . . . . . . . . . . . . . . . . .
>
> Point d'arrêt à mes pas, point de trêve à ma tâche;
> Toujours recommencer et toujours repartir.
> Mais je n'engendre pas sans fin et sans relâche
>     Pour le plaisir d'anéantir.
>
> J'ai déjà trop longtemps fait œuvre de marâtre,
> J'ai trop enseveli, j'ai trop exterminé,
> Moi qui ne suis au fond que la mère idolâtre
>     D'un seul enfant qui n'est pas né.
>
>               (*Poésies philosophiques*, 24–25)

A return to nature's point of departure at the text's close reflects the constant motion in the universe. Birth and death are part and parcel of the life cycle of all matter and the nature of human destiny from the perspective of materialism:

> Toi-même qui te crois la couronne et le faîte
> Du monument divin qui n'est point achevé,
> Homme qui n'es au fond que l'ébauche imparfaite
>     Du chef-d'œuvre que j'ai rêvé,
>
> À ton tour, à ton heure, il faut que tu périsses.
> Ah! ton orgueil a beau s'indigner et souffrir,
> Tu ne seras jamais dans mes mains créatrices
>     Que de l'argile à repétrir.
>
>               (26)

Ackermann wrote the poem "L'homme à la nature" (February 1871) in deferred antithesis. "L'homme à la nature," which also consists of twenty-one quatrains, formally creates a mirror image of "La nature à l'homme," but in content develops the polar opposite by disputing humans' subjection to the scheme of evolution.

Though human beings cannot prevail over the forces of the physical world to which Mother Nature is paradoxically oblivious, humans are conscious of their existence. This alone renders them superior to inert matter and Nature herself. Such is the tone set in the first five quatrains of "L'homme à la nature." The poetic narrator, speaking on behalf of humanity, addresses Nature and mocks with reverse psychology her power to reproduce, which ends not in sublime creation but in death:

> Eh bien! reprends-le donc ce peu de fange obscure
> Qui pour quelques instants s'anima sous ta main;
> Dans ton dédain superbe, implacable Nature,
>     Brise à jamais le moule humain.
>
> De ces tristes débris quand tu verrais, ravie,
> D'autres créations éclore à grands essaims,
> Ton Idée éclater en des formes de vie
>     Plus dociles à tes desseins,
>
> Est-ce à dire que Lui, ton espoir, ta chimère,
> Parce qu'il fut rêvé, puisse un jour exister?
> Tu crois avoir conçu, tu voudrais être mère;
>     À l'œuvre! il s'agit d'enfanter.
>
> Change en réalité ton attente sublime.
> Mais quoi! pour les franchir, malgré tous tes élans,
> La distance est trop grande et trop profond l'abîme
>     Entre ta pensée et tes flancs.
>
> La mort est le seul fruit qu'en tes crises futures
> Il te sera donné d'atteindre et de cueillir;
> Toujours nouveaux débris, toujours des créatures
>     Que tu devras ensevelir.
>
>                (*Poésies philosophiques*, 27)

Ackermann's narrator affirms the power of the mind over matter and, by extension, elevates human creativity over Nature's analogous, yet imperfect, powers of continuity. In stanzas 6 and 8, this difference between humanity and the natural world opens up parallel spheres of the ideal and the infinite, which draws to the surface the rival bents toward pantheism and naturalism in Ackermann:

> Car sur ta route en vain l'âge à l'âge succède;
> Les tombes, les berceaux ont beau s'accumuler,
> L'Idéal qui te fuit, l'Idéal qui t'obsède,
>     À l'Infini pour reculer.
>
> . . . . . . . . . . . . . . . . . . .
>
> Il resplendit de loin, mais reste inaccessible.
> Prodigue de travaux, de luttes, de trépas,
> Ta main me sacrifie à ce fils impossible;
>     Je meurs, et Lui ne naîtra pas.
>
>                (*Poésies philosophiques*, 28)

"L'homme à la nature" interchanges in further agon the philosophies of material-
ism and idealism: the idea that matter is claimed to be the only reality versus the
notion that reality is filtered prior to experience through categories of thought,
time, and space. Ackermann had long struggled with a rational way to negotiate
the relation of nature and humankind, as suggested by her journal entry of 19 June
1864: "La nature devrait s'attendrir en faveur de l'homme, puisque c'est lui seul qui
l'aime, la comprend, la trouve belle. Tous les autres animaux n'ont pas de pensée
pour elle. . . . Nous seuls nous plongeons dans son sein avec délices et lui présentons
le miroir de notre intelligence afin qu'elle s'y réfléchisse" ("Journal," 552). It is this
thought that informs stanza 12 below. By holding up a sentient mirror to Mother
Nature, can humankind truly elevate itself above all other creatures and the bio-
logical descent of species?

> Ne suis-je point encor seul à te trouver belle?
> J'ai compté tes trésors, j'atteste ton pouvoir,
> Et mon intelligence, ô Nature éternelle!
>     T'a tendu ton premier miroir.
>
> (*Poésies philosophiques*, 29)[39]

What *is* humankind's place in an infinite universe that only the mind's eye can
conceive? Can one place any stake in the perfection of human knowledge, as pos-
itivists claim, if the answer to this fundamental question (among others) eludes
us? Herein lies the anxiety of the modern age of science expressed by Ackermann's
universal speaker, who decries the struggle to wrest from Nature the creative
potential that Darwin so admired:

> Mais, jusque sous le coup du désastre suprême,
> Moi, l'homme, je t'accuse à la face des cieux.
> Créatrice, en plein front reçois donc l'anathème
>     De cet atome audacieux.
>
> Sois maudite, ô marâtre! en tes œuvres immenses,
> Oui, maudite à ta source et dans tes éléments,
> Pour tous tes abandons, tes oublis, tes démences,
>     Aussi pour tes avortements!
>
> Que la Force en ton sein s'épuise perte à perte.
> Que la Matière, à bout de nerf et de ressort,
> Reste sans mouvement, et se refuse, inerte,
>     À te suivre dans ton essor.
>
> Qu'envahissant les cieux, l'Immobilité morne
> Sous un voile funèbre éteigne tout flambeau,

> Puisque d'un univers magnifique et sans borne
> Tu n'as su faire qu'un tombeau.
>
> *(Poésies philosophiques*, 30)

The dialectical pairing of "La nature à l'homme" and "L'homme à la nature" truncates the formulaic Hegelian logic that would seek a synthesis between opposites. For D. G. Charlton, the unresolved tension between pantheism and positivism illustrates "the opposition between [Ackermann's] aspiration towards an ideal and a knowledge of the 'Infinite' and her conviction . . . that we are all condemned to ignorance" (*Positivist Thought in France*, 182; more generally on this, see 177–89).

An undated prose fragment, related to the statements from Ackermann's journal in the summer of 1864 cited above, conveys the pessimism in "L'homme à la nature": "Je ne dirai pas à l'humanité: progresse; je lui dirai: meurs, car aucun progrès ne t'arrachera jamais aux misères de la condition terrestre" (*Pensées* [1903], 37).[40] For Ackermann, not knowing is the greatest source of suffering. By placing the force of her thinking in the gap between poiesis and knowledge, Ackermann forges an uneasy alliance of poetry and science as a way of illumining the pursuit of truth, where imagination and reality meet in "a transcendent analogue."[41] In this pursuit, she rejects the idea of God, as seen in "Prométhée" and "Pascal," the penultimate poem in her 1871 *Poésies philosophiques*. Ackermann reiterates this stance in prose from the same period: "L'élément des religions: c'est l'ignorance. La Foi disparaît devant la Science. Une humanité qui nous serait supérieure n'aurait plus besoin de croire: elle saurait" ("Pensées diverses," 621).

## Against Blind Faith

Ackermann dedicates "Prométhée" (30 November 1865) to Daniel Stern, who had critiqued drafts of the text.[42] The long narrative poem adapts to the modern scientific era the mythological person subjected to eternal suffering for having stolen fire from the gods for the benefit of humanity.[43] Prometheus's revolt against the malevolent father figure of Jupiter represents the collapse of belief in a loving God in the face of reason, as revealed midway through the poem:

> Mais ne t'abuse point; sur ce roc solitaire
> Tu ne me verras pas succomber en entier.
> Un esprit de révolte a transformé la terre,
> Et j'ai dès aujourd'hui choisi mon héritier.
> Il poursuivra mon œuvre en marchant sur ma trace,
> Né qu'il est comme moi pour tenter et souffrir.
> Aux humains affranchis je lègue mon audace,
> Héritage sacré qui ne peut plus périr.

> La raison s'affermit, le doute est prêt à naître.
> Enhardis à ce point d'interroger leur maître,
> Des mortels devant eux oseront te citer:
> Pourquoi leurs maux? Pourquoi ton caprice et ta haine?
> Oui, ton juge t'attend,—la conscience humaine;
> Elle ne peut t'absoudre et va te rejeter.
>
> (*Poésies philosophiques*, 17–18)

How can one explain the existence of suffering and evil in the world? This question, addressed to Jupiter, prepares the turn to the laws revealed by science, which Ackermann concurrently expresses in prose in terms of "[f]atalite! voilà le mot de l'univers, depuis l'atome invisible jusqu'à l'homme . . . des lois inflexibles qui enchaînent toutes les manifestations de l'Être" ("Pensées diverses d'une solitaire," 616). Against the metaphysical concept of destiny linked with faith in God, a natural force operates together with chance without distinguishing the end of humans from that of other creatures in the world:

> Délivré de la Foi comme d'un mauvais rêve,
> L'homme répudiera les tyrans immortels,
> Et n'ira plus, en proie à des terreurs sans trêve,
> Se courber lâchement au pied de tes autels.
> Las de le trouver sourd, il croira le ciel vide.
> Jetant sur toi son voile éternel et splendide,
> La Nature déjà te cache à son regard;
> Il ne découvrira dans l'univers sans borne,
> Pour tout Dieu désormais, qu'un couple aveugle et morne,
> La Force et le Hasard.
>
> (*Poésies philosophiques*, 18)

In closing, Ackermann's modern Prometheus denounces Jupiter as the author of evil, a stance developed with Christian resonance in "Pascal" as a primary reason to reject faith in God:

> Oui, tandis que du Mal, œuvre de ta colère,
> Renonçant désormais à sonder le mystère,
> L'esprit humain ailleurs portera son flambeau,
> Seul je saurai le mot de cette énigme obscure,
> Et j'aurai reconnu, pour comble de torture,
> Un Dieu dans mon bourreau.
>
> (19)[44]

As shown to this point, Ackermann steadily champions reason over belief in the quest for truth. Notes on her reading of Pascal frame her later view of his argument for God's existence. A brief comment in a journal entry of 14 May 1863 prepares the tenor of her ultimate stance: "Dans tout dévot il y a du Pascal, plus de peur que de désir" ("Journal," 544). This remains Ackermann's sense of his leap of faith, as recorded in her journal on 9 August 1865: "La peur jeta Pascal dans la religion" (559).

A longer reflection of 9 September 1866 outlines the gist of Ackermann's 1871 poem "Pascal," which she dedicated to her close advisor Ernest Havet, who had edited a second edition of Pascal's *Pensées* (1866): "Quand je lis Pascal, il me semble que je suis au bord d'un abîme; le vertige me prend; je n'ose regarder jusqu'au fond de cette passion et de ce délire. Cela passe la portée humaine" ("Journal," 570).[45] Ackermann clarifies her interest in Pascal at the outset of the same thought revised in her "Pensées diverses d'une solitaire": "Ce qui m'intéresse dans Pascal, c'est une âme aux prises et qui combat" (623). She rejects his famous wager that, in the absence of proof, humans have everything to gain and nothing to lose by believing in God's existence: "Tant de fanatisme me surpasse. . . . Nulle certitude et pourtant il faut croire, contradiction terrible où il s'est enfermé. . . . Le malheureux est emporté par la violence de sa peur et de ses désirs; il a fait le saut dans l'abîme" (623–24).[46] As she notes in a journal entry from 11 September 1866, "Oh Pascal, ton Dieu est un monstre" ("Journal," 572). This view of God as responsible for the evil pervading the world, which recalls the revolt against the gods as the authors of human suffering in "Prométhée," emerges in "Pascal," which Ackermann originally divided into four sections.[47]

In part 1, "Le sphinx," Ackermann deploys the figure of a sphinx to represent the hidden nature of things, which rational beings seek to penetrate. An adversary, the sphinx not only withholds the answer, but also tortures the seeker in the process. Part 2 evokes the mystery of Christ's passion on the cross, dispensing with the idea that such suffering is redemptive. Ackermann's speaker addresses Pascal halfway through the single stanza that comprises the section "La croix" and argues: "Tu te dis éclairé, tu n'étais qu'aveuglé" (*Poésies philosophiques*, 40). Deluded by his surrender to faith, the philosopher abdicates reason, which he had claimed to be the source of all human dignity:

> Gloire, plaisirs, travaux, ta vie et ta pensée,
> Tu jettes tout au pied d'un gibet vermoulu.
> Nous te surprenons là, spectacle qui nous navre,
> Te consumant d'amour dans les bras d'un cadavre,
> Et croyant sur son sein trouver ta guérison.
> Mais tu n'étreins, hélas! qu'une forme insensible,
> Et bien loin d'obtenir un miracle impossible,
> Dans cet embrassement tu laissas ta raison.
>
> . . . . . . . . . . . . . . . . . . . . . . . .
>
> Nous n'avons sous les yeux qu'un pauvre halluciné.

(41)          221

Part 3, "L'inconnue," refers to the unidentified woman Pascal reputedly loved, but resisted in order to devote himself to God. A shift from mortal to divine love in the final stanza of the section personifies belief as an infinite force, considered to be as merciless and treacherous as those operative in nature:

> Dans ton avidité, désastreuse, infinie,
> Tu ne lui laissas rien qu'une croix et la mort;
> Oui, tu lui ravis tout, et trésor à trésor;
> Après son chaste amour, tu lui pris son génie.
>
> (44)

In the final section, "Le dernier mot," Ackermann's poetic speaker shifts between the first-person singular and plural, refusing to succumb to faith blindly as Pascal had, and explains midway through the section:

> Car ta Foi n'était pas la Certitude encore;
> Aurais-tu tant gémi si tu n'avais douté?
> Pour avoir reculé devant ce mot: j'ignore,
> Dans quel gouffre d'erreurs t'es-tu précipité!
> Nous, nous restons au bord; aucune perspective,
> Soit Enfer, soit Néant, ne fait pâlir nos fronts;
> S'il faut accepter ta sombre alternative,
> Croire ou désespérer, nous désespérerons.
>
> (*Poésies philosophiques*, 47)

How can one embrace the infinite power of God without seeing him as apathetic to the malevolence and unpredictable disasters humans suffer?

> Comment? ne disposer de la Force infinie
> Que pour se procurer des spectacles navrants;
> Imposer le massacre, infliger l'agonie,
> Ne vouloir sous ses yeux que morts et mourants!
>
> (49)

With the idea of provoking God to destroy his creation, the poet ends with these words:

> Oh! quelle immense joie après tant de souffrance!
> À travers les débris, par-dessus les charniers,
> Pouvoir enfin jeter ce cri de délivrance:
> Plus d'hommes sous le ciel, nous sommes les derniers!
>
> (49)

"Pascal" bookends Ackermann's rejection of Christian dogma in her pursuit of the truth. The poem "Le cri," which closes the 1871 edition of her *Poésies philosophiques*, exposes the key source of the despair she voices on behalf of humanity: neither religion nor science yield definitive answers to life's major questions.

## For Posterity's Sake

As Ackermann explains in a letter of 3 October 1871 to her sister, "La place du *Cri* est à la fin du recueil que je prépare, il en est la clôture naturelle" ("Correspondance de Madame Ackermann" [1930], 432). Dated 21 March 1871, "Le cri" opens with the image of a passenger cast adrift on the open sea. The shipwreck prepares the comparison with the world of thought engaged by the poet in the fourth stanza:

> Comme ce voyageur en des mers inconnues
> J'erre et vais disparaître au sein des flots hurlants;
> Le gouffre est à mes pieds, sur ma tête les nues
> S'amoncellent, la foudre aux flancs.
> (Poésies philosophiques, 50)

The "gouffre" (dual abyss) menacing the poet recalls Pascal's perspective of man as caught between nothingness and infinity.[48] Ackermann's intellectual journey mirrors the destiny common to all, as expressed in stanza 7:

> Jouet de l'ouragan qui l'emporte et le mène
> Encombré de trésors et d'agrès submergés,
> Ce navire perdu, mais c'est la nef humaine,
> Et nous sommes les naufragés.
> (51)

The poem hurtles along the semantic axis of despair and grief, with ruin imminent: "Assise au gouvernail, la Fatalité sombre / Le dirige vers un écueil" (*Poésies philosophiques*, 51). Against this inevitable end, the poet resists fading into oblivion:

> Moi, que sans mon aveu l'aveugle Destinée
> Embarqua sur l'étrange et frêle bâtiment,
> Je ne veux pas non plus, muette et résignée,
> Subir mon engloutissement.
> (51)

This cry of resistance parallels the way Ackermann splits her identity between the woman and the poet. Tracy Paton develops this perspective of the ninth stanza (directly above) in arguing that the poet "simultaneously submits to and rebels against her disappearance into a meaningless void. It is no coincidence that this is the moment when she chooses to reveal her gender" ("Seductive Rebellions," 46).

Yet, in the final three stanzas, the thinker shifts to universal ground in expressing the angst caused by how deeply she had thought without, however, being able to determine whether the misery she sees is all there is to know:

> Afin qu'elle éclatât d'un jet plus énergique,
> J'ai, dans ma résistance à l'assaut des flots noirs,
> De tous les cœurs en moi, comme en un centre unique,
>      Rassemblé tous les désespoirs.
>
> Qu'ils vibrent donc si fort, mes accents intrépides,
> Que ces mêmes cieux sourds en tressaillent surpris;
> Les airs n'ont pas besoin, ni les vagues stupides,
>      Pour frissonner d'avoir compris.
>
> Ah! c'est un cri sacré que tout cri d'agonie;
> Il proteste, il accuse au moment d'expirer.
> Eh bien! ce cri d'angoisse et d'horreur infinie,
>      Je l'ai jeté; je puis sombrer!
>
>                    (*Poésies philosophiques*, 52)

In his 1873 review of Ackermann's *Poésies philosophiques*, Barbey d'Aurevilly reproduces "Le cri" in its entirety as representative of her voice, adding, "et c'en est un comme jamais bouche de femme n'en a poussé" ("Madame Ackermann," 168). He ends with a question that suggests the moral grounds upon which conservative critics would object to Ackermann in 1874 and onward: "L'athéisme, cette teigne du temps, aurait-il desséché sa noble tête de poète et condamné son génie à la stérilité des terres maudites?" (172).[49] Ackermann responded as a critical reader by reframing her philosophical corpus with the self-conscious poem "Mon livre" to challenge, as she did in *Ma vie*, the public's assumptions about how and why women write verse.

In Ackermann's *Poésies* of 1874, the poem "Mon livre" (7 January 1874) begins the section titled *Poésies philosophiques*. In a carefully worded, seven-stanza address, the poet speaking in the first person anticipates and questions readers' edgy response to the deep pessimism she voices:

> Je ne vous offre plus pour toutes mélodies
> Que des cris de révolte et des rimes hardies.
> Oui, mais en m'écoutant si vous alliez pâlir?
> Si, surpris des éclats de ma verve imprudente,
> Vous maudissez la voix énergique et stridente
>      Qui vous aura fait tressaillir?

Pourtant, quand je m'élève à des notes pareilles,
Je ne prétends blesser les cœurs ni les oreilles.
Même les plus craintifs n'ont point à s'alarmer;
L'accent désespéré sans doute ici domine,
Mais je n'ai pas tiré ces sons de ma poitrine
      Pour le plaisir de blasphémer.

Comment? la Liberté déchaîne ses colères;
Partout, contre l'effort des erreurs séculaires;
La Vérité combat pour s'ouvrir un chemin;
Et je ne prendrais pas parti de ce grand drame?
Quoi! ce cœur qui bat là, pour être un cœur de femme,
      En est-il moins un cœur humain?

(55–56)

Ackermann juxtaposes the melodic sentimental lyrics expected from women with her "cris de révolte." She appropriates the vocabulary used by critics to relate her poetry to the post-Romantic gush of the feminine and deftly redirects "l'accent désespéré" to its source: the ideological combat between the claims of religion and those of science. This is the aim of her book, and she hopes for posterity's sake that it survives against the odds: "En dépit du courant qui l'emporte ou l'entrave, / Qu'il se soutienne donc et surnage en épave, Sur ces flots qui vont m'engloutir!" (*Poésies*, 57).

The critic Alfred Marchand, writing for *Le Temps* (1883), grasped the intellectual roots of Ackermann's pessimism: "Ce qui a inspiré l'œuvre de Madame Ackermann c'est bien une souffrance, une passion, non du cœur, mais de l'esprit" ("Variétés: Les *Pensées* de Mme Ackermann," n.p.). Indeed, Ackermann pushed poetry to the limits of science and revealed the disjunction aligning creativity with knowledge at the threshold of the unknown.

From the perspective of this paradox, she writes her poetic testament, first published in the 1885 edition of her collected poetic works and retained for subsequent editions. Ackermann's testament, which immediately follows "Le cri," exposes the faith she has placed in science together with its limits as a way of knowing:

J'IGNORE! *un mot, le seul par lequel je réponde*
*Aux questions sans fin de mon esprit déçu;*
*Aussi quand je me plains en partant de ce monde,*
*C'est moins d'avoir souffert que de n'avoir rien su.*
  (*Œuvres de Louise Ackermann*, 183; original formatting)

In a tribute to Ackermann after her death in 1890, the historian François-Alphonse Aulard admired the unique linkage of rational and creative power she had cultivated as an intellectual who believed that "toute la poésie était dans la raison et dans les livres" ("Madame Ackermann," 623).[50] Similarly, in prefacing his selection of her texts for his 1908–9 anthology, Alphonse Séché emphasized Ackermann's fusion of science and poetry: "Son originalité tient tout entière dans son pessimisme douloureux, dans sa vision désabusée des choses et des êtres" (*Les muses françaises*, 2:323). Édouard Schuré extended her contribution to intellectual history: "[M]^me Ackermann a exprimé dans sa poésie avec une force unique un moment capital de la pensée au XIX^e siècle, je veux dire son désespoir absolu entre la perte de la foi traditionnelle et l'étouffante doctrine du positivisme" ("Un poète athée," 312). Writing in 1908, Schuré admitted that by then Ackermann had been to some extent forgotten, despite her moment of great celebrity between 1874 and 1880.[51]

With the rise in the 1880s of *vers libre* and of Symbolism (against anti-idealistic movements, such as naturalism and realism, modeled on scientific tenets), her project on the problem of knowledge fell out of favor. In her "Pensées diverses d'une solitaire" (1881), Ackermann held to a positivist model and thus rejected the search for final causes, such as the origin of genius: "Nous sommes ingrats envers les penseurs et les artistes qui nous ont précédés. Que serions-nous sans eux? Ils ont été les anneaux qui nous relient à la chaîne infinie. Comme dans un cerveau individuel une idée en amène une autre, leur œuvre a suscité la nôtre. Nous ne commençons ni n'achevons rien. Il faudrait remonter bien haut dans la pensée humaine pour trouver le point initial. Heureux, néanmoins encore, ceux à qui il est donné de continuer" (619). Ackermann's view that no thinker or artist is wholly original because all creators are influenced by, if not indebted to, predecessors was not shared by Marie Krysinska, who asserted her originality in the development of modern *vers libre*. For Krysinska, whose creative and analytical works are examined in the final chapter of this book, understanding rational evolutions was key to reclaiming the property of genius for women from the gendered narratives of religion and science.

# 8 Marie Krysinska on Eve, Evolution, and the Property of Genius

The Polish-born Marie Anastazja Wincentyna Krysinska (1857–1908; fig. 18) rarely wrote about her private life, but she produced a significant body of critical writings about her innovative practice of *vers libre* and her theory of poetic evolution.[1] Literary history thus preserves more amply her public persona and the debate generated by her claim to originality from the early 1890s on.[2] Entangled with issues of gender and xenophobia, this debate still reduces the scope of her production.[3] The transdisciplinary richness of Krysinska's writings across the musical, visual, and dramatic arts complements her approach to the aesthetics of poetry.[4] In her verse and in her analytical and imaginative prose, she challenges the narratives of religion and science that attribute creativity only to men. For Krysinska, genius is (in) the work, a force that originates from the act of making.

In the early 1870s, Krysinska left her native Poland where, as a young girl, she had studied music. Soon after arriving in Paris to study harmony and composition at the Conservatoire national de musique, she gravitated toward the iconoclastic literary clubs.[5] The only female member of the Hydropathes, Krysinska also joined the Hirsutes, Jemenfoutistes, and Zutistes.[6] By 1879, she had begun reciting her experimental verse while working as a piano-playing accompanist and singer. Her reputation as a musician with poetic flair grew at the Chat Noir, which opened in 1881. Various songs from the 1880s capture Krysinska's popularity, as suggested by this stanza from "La Marseillaise des chats noirs," signed by Vox Populi and published in an 1883 issue of the cabaret's journal, *Le Chat Noir*:

> V'là Krysinska, dans sa robe d'aurore,
> (Chante, ô mon luth, et vous, sonnez, sonnets!)
> Pour célébrer la diva qu'il adore,

FIG 18

Marie Krysinska by
Wilhelm Benque.
From *Revue
Encyclopédique* 6
(28 November 1896).
Photo courtesy John
Hay Library, Brown
University.

Tout le *Chat noir* répète en polonais:
    (REFRAIN:)
    Encore un coup d'aile dans l' bleu,
    V'là l'Idéal qui passe,
    Encore un coup d'aile dans l' bleu,
    L' bourgeois n'y voit qu' du feu![7]

In her retrospective essay "Les cénacles artistiques et littéraires" (1904), Krysinska
would emphasize "le chansonniérisme semé par le Chat Noir" and place herself
among the creative artists she identified as both "poètes et compositeurs" (488).[8]

Beginning in 1881, the year Krysinska published "Symphonie des parfums" in
*La Chronique Parisienne*, her verse regularly appeared in *Le Chat Noir* and other
literary journals, including *La Vie Moderne*, *La Libre Revue*, *La Cravache Parisi-
enne*, *La Revue Indépendante*, *Gil Blas Illustré*, *La Revue Bleue*, and *Le Figaro:
Supplément Littéraire*. Soon thereafter, she established a literary salon in her home
at rue Monge. A depiction of the room by Francis Enne, published in 1882, high-

lights her eclectic taste: "un bon piano sonore" in close proximity to "des esquisses cocasses savamment colorées" and a small bookshelf with titles by Baudelaire, Musset, Hugo, Poe, Dickens, Leconte de Lisle, Banville, and Mendès ("Chez Krysinska," n.p.).[9] In describing the volumes as "déchirés, maculés," Enne notes, "on voit que ceux qui les ont maniés les ont appris par cœur" (n.p.). While this intense absorption of reading material accentuates how seriously Krysinska approached the matter of poetic creativity, the objects Enne describes in her salon represent the interdisciplinary core of her aesthetic enterprise: music, art, and poetry. Illustrative of how Krysinska frees poetic rhythm from rhyme is her early practice of setting poems to music, including titles by Hugo, Baudelaire, Verlaine, and Charles Cros.[10] In accounts of her creations Krysinska elucidates how poetic form evolves, her *vers libre* embodying a "total work of art."[11]

A cyclical way of thinking and writing structures Krysinska's output in verse and prose. She uses a recurrent title that interweaves musicality with visuality, which invites readers to consider her three volumes of *vers libre* as a single project unified in form and content: *Rythmes pittoresques* (1890), *Joies errantes: Nouveaux rythmes pittoresques* (1894), and *Intermèdes: Nouveaux rythmes pittoresques* (1903).[12] After treating the question of form raised by one of the first poems Krysinska published, I turn to the cluster titled "Femmes" at the center of her inaugural volume. In this grouping, Krysinska anchors a revision of the myth of Eve that interweaves her three collections of poetry with a theoretical project.[13] She exploits the interpretive ambiguity surrounding the first woman and other biblical and mythical women as objects of male desire and as desiring subjects. This discourse reclaims women's quest for forbidden knowledge as a creative act and frames Krysinska's counterdiscourse as an original poet. I examine her contestatory writings in the second half of this chapter. Essays and prefaces Krysinska published from 1891 to 1903 repeat and expand the main strands of her revisionist history of modern *vers libre*, which recovers her innovative work. Krysinska's reflections deepen with each return to the dispute over her intellectual property and, ultimately, refute the sexual selection of genius.

## Working Through Poetic Form

"Symphonie en gris," the third poem published by Krysinska, appeared in *Le Chat Noir* on 4 November 1882. Long lines punctuated like prose open and close the poem, which presents through typography the prosodic fluidity that infuses Krysinska's form with discursive liminality:

> Plus d'ardentes lueurs sur le ciel alourdi, qui
>     semble tristement rêver.
> Les arbres, sans mouvement, mettent dans
> le loin une dentelle grise.

Sur le ciel qui semble tristement rêver,
plus d'ardentes lueurs.

Dans l'air gris flottent les apaisements, les résignations, et
les inquiétudes.

Du sol consterné monte une rumeur étrange, surhumaine.

Cabalistique langage entendu seulement des âmes attentives.

Les apaisements, les résignations, et les inquiétudes flot-
tent dans l'air gris.

Les silhouettes vagues ont le geste de la folie.

Les maisons sont assises disgracieusement comme de
vieilles femmes.

Les silhouettes vagues ont le geste de la folie.

C'est l'heure cruelle et stupéfiante, où la chauve-souris
déploie ses ailes grises, et s'en va rôdant comme un mal-
faiteur.

Les silhouettes vagues ont le geste de la folie.

Près de l'étang endormi le grillon fredonne d'esquises [*sic*]
romances.

Et doucement ressuscitent dans l'air gris les choses enfuies.

Près de l'étang endormi le grillon fredonne d'exquises romances.

Sous le ciel qui semble tristement rêver.

(4)

"Symphonie en gris" evokes with rhythmic, yet unpredictable, measure how the mind's eye forms what it perceives. The auditory mixes with the visual and the tactile as in synesthesia, where the senses cross. Lexical repetitions and their variations juxtapose a musical refrain with the sense of a pervasive dim light and, in turn, a murky blend of sound and color. While the vertical plane slides from "sur le ciel" to "sous le ciel" in an expansive dreamscape suffused with melancholy, "l'air gris" blurs the lines between aurality, visuality, and deep feeling. The text's musicality, generated by assonance (*u, ou, e, ê*) and alliteration (*l, s, d*), has a visual echo; end stops and dashes alternate with open-ended lines. Recurrent internal rhymes, together with repeated lines (such as "Plus d'ardentes lueurs"), create a sense of organic balance, replacing traditional metrical schemes based on syllabic symmetry with an indeterminate number of syllables. The poem ends nearly where it begins. However, the reiterated phrases gather fresh meaning as they interact with different words. For Krysinska, who conceives of poetry as visually rhythmic and rhythmically visual, such repetition produces shifts in context and thus traces the mutual shaping of poetic form and content.

Krysinska republished "Symphonie en gris" in *Rythmes pittoresques* (1890) with the same interplay of color and sound, but with a very different layout. The poem, dedicated to Rodolphe Salis, the founder and owner of the Chat

Noir cabaret where Krysinska performed, is the fifth text in the section titled "Mirages":

> Plus d'ardentes lueurs sur le ciel alourdi,
> Qui semble tristement rêver.
> Les arbres sans mouvement,
> Mettent dans le loin une dentelle grise.—
> Sur le ciel qui semble tristement rêver,
> Plus d'ardentes lueurs.—
>
> Dans l'air gris flottent les apaisements,
> Les résignations et les inquiétudes.
> Du sol consterné monte une rumeur étrange, surhumaine.
> Cabalistique langage entendu seulement
> Des âmes attentives.—
> Les apaisements, les résignations, et les inquietudes
> Flottent dans l'air gris.—
>
> Les silhouettes vagues ont le geste de la folie.
> Les maisons sont assises disgracieusement
> Comme de vieilles femmes—
> Les silhouettes vagues ont le geste de la folie.—
>
> C'est l'heure cruelle et stupéfiante,
> Où la chauve-souris déploie ses ailes grises,
> Et s'en va rôdant comme un malfaiteur.—
> Les silhouettes vagues ont le geste de la folie.—
>
> Près de l'étang endormi
> Le grillon fredonne d'exquises romances.
> Et doucement ressuscitent dans l'air gris
> Les choses enfuies.
>
> Près de l'étang endormi
> Le grillon fredonne d'exquises romances.
> Sous le ciel qui semble tristement rêver.
>
> (Rythmes pittoresques, 39–40)

Krysinska retains the original date of composition (4 November 1882) for this version of "Symphonie en gris" in which she experiments with more than just formal aspects.

Krysinska's unequivocal use of *vers libres* in the 1890 version heightens the aural-visual synergies, demonstrating how such synesthetic interaction works *between* prosodic form and creative ideation. In her article "Conflit de la rime et de la raison" (1899), she elucidates this interplay, broadly framing her poetic expression's aural, visual, and kinesthetic texture: "Aux premières tentations de traduire mes impressions sur un mode lyrique, une question pour moi s'est posée: qu'est-ce qu'une œuvre poétique" (n.p.). The questioning of poetic form mirrors Krysinska's approach to poetry as a discourse. In verse published between 1881 and 1883, she also delved into the *work* of poetry and in this way illumined the mental effort or thought displayed by a poetic work.[14] But, as Krysinska observes in 1899 and would later repeat, her experimental verse met with resistance because she is a woman: "En ce temps-là—comme disent les apôtres—une initiative émanant d'une femme était considérée comme ne venant de nulle part et tombée de droit dans le domaine public" (n.p.).

Gustave Kahn published the Symbolist manifesto by Jean Moréas and his own first *vers libre* during Krysinska's sojourn in America (1885–86) with her artist husband, Georges Bellenger.[15] For Krysinska, her exclusion from the advent of *vers libre* announced by the Symbolists in 1886 was no mistake: "Aussi mon nom fut-il scrupuleusement omis dans les manifestes faits en faveur de la nouvelle formule et les réciproques congratulations que s'adressaient les *novateurs*" ("Conflit de la rime et de la raison," n.p.; emphasis in original). Krysinska had first made this point in an essay of 1891 and would restate it in subsequent critical works, which preserve her perspective on the quarrel over both the origins and characteristics of *vers libre*.

In *Les premiers poètes du vers libre* (1922), Édouard Dujardin, a Symbolist poet, famously contests Krysinska's contribution to the history of *vers libre* by categorizing nearly all of her early production as prose poems.[16] Though Dujardin grants a leaning toward *vers libre* in "Symphonie en gris," he nevertheless reads the 1890 text as truncated lines of poetic prose and quips: "Il ne suffit pas, madame, pour faire des vers libres, de passer à la ligne à chaque membre de phrase" (21). Had Krysinska been alive and still actively responding to her critics, she would likely have related the two layouts of "Symphonie en gris" to the theoretical work of *vers libre* produced in her day. She understood the evolution of poetic form much in the way Clive Scott would assess it in 1990, although without explicitly including her contribution: "It is in the very nature of these forms [regular verse, the *verset*, prose poetry, and *vers libre*] that they should exist as the undefined interface between provenances and destinations, that they should be the unsettled sites of generical give-and-take, and formal negotiation" (*Vers Libre*, 110).[17]

Other modern scholars have since illustrated Krysinska's aesthetic sophistication. For example, in developing a revisionist dialogue between "Symphonie en gris" and Théophile Gautier's "Symphonie en blanc majeur" (1852), Gretchen Schultz has positioned Krysinska's aesthetic of *vers libre* against the neoclassical principles of Parnassian doctrine. For Schultz, the ambiguity of the color gray in Krysinska's poem represents "the variability of perception" mingling with "subjective sensations of uncertainty and anxiety" (*Gendered Lyric*, 237, 238). "Against the brightness and clarity of Gautier's white images," Schultz adds, "[Krysinska's poem] calls upon vagueness and avoids objective representation. . . . Indeed, the poem is more interested in impression and mood than representation, and relies on the indirection of metonymy rather than Gautier's expository similes" (238, 239). More recently, Seth Whidden has related the variation in the layouts of "Symphonie en gris" to a discourse on the *work* of poetry that does not change the sonorous impact of the text, but instead enhances its rhythmic structure ("Sur la *supercherie* de Marie Krysinska").

The poem's arrangement, which shifts from sixteen lines in 1882 to six stanzas set apart by blank lines in 1890, puts into relief the repetitions structuring the text. The phrase "Les silhouettes vagues," echoed three times in close proximity, suggests a visual anchor of the acoustic element. The double occurrence of "Près de l'étang endormi" extends the rhythmic effect of repetition to the poem's end, drawing out the internal recurrence of "ciel." For Whidden, this creates a suggestive harmony between the vertical and horizontal axes of the text, which makes poetic rhyme not only visual and aural, but also thematically resonant.

"Symphonie en gris" also represents the way Krysinska complicates poetic voice. "Without the mark of person, the mark of gender is frequently lacking, resulting in the absence of a clearly determinable female lyric subject," Schultz has observed (*Gendered Lyric*, 239).[18] Krysinska disputes the gendering of the lyric in conceptual ways and by examining narratives that subject females to male authority. Illustrative of such revisionism is the ambiguity that Krysinska teases out of the biblical myth of Eve, suggesting two different, yet closely related, senses of the desire to know the unknown and their consequences for women.

## The Genesis Problem

Two creation stories in the opening chapters of the book of Genesis cast the first human beings as made together in the image of God; they also separate the making of man from that of woman.[19] The "P" text, attributed to the priestly writer, founds equality between the sexes on their shared power: "Let us make man in our image, after our likeness, and let them have dominion . . . over all the earth. . . . So God created man in his own image, in the image of God he created him; male and female he created them" (Gen. 1:27).[20] According to the second creation story, known as "J" or the Yahwist source, which begins with Genesis 2:4b, woman was made of man's rib, then given to him as his companion: "Then the man said, 'This at last is bone of my bones / and flesh of my flesh; / she shall be called Woman, / because she was taken out of Man'" (Gen. 2:23). After the first couple's fall into the knowledge of good and evil, followed by their expulsion from Eden, Adam named her Eve, "the mother of all living" (Gen. 3:20). Maternity thus supplanted woman's desire for knowledge along with the authority over creation she originally shared with man.

Krysinska reconsiders the myth of the first woman before the fall, but uses the postlapsarian name "Eve" rather than "woman." This choice relates to her strategy of interweaving complicity with patriarchal culture and resistance to its power over women, thus leaving open the relation of anatomy and destiny and maintaining women's access to the realm of creation.[21] Krysinska's poem "Ève" begins by representing the mythical woman in terms of her innocent body and picturesque surroundings. A symbolic paradise, where the sacred and the profane coexist in prelapsarian harmony, teems with mystical sensuality:

> Ève au corps ingénu lasse de jeux charmants
> Avec les biches rivales et les doux léopards
> Goûte à présent le repos extatique,
> Sur la riche brocatelle des mousses.
>
> Autour d'elle, le silence de midi
> Exalte la pamoison odorante des calices,
> Et le jeune soleil baise les feuillées neuves.
>
> Tout est miraculeux dans ce Jardin de Joie:
> Les branchages s'étoilent de fruits symboliques
> Rouges comme des cœurs et blancs comme des âmes;
>
> Les Roses d'Amour encore inécloses
>                 Dorment au beau Rosier;
> Les lys premiers nés
> Balancent leurs fervents encensoirs
>                 Auprès
> Des chères coupes des Iris
> Où fermente le vin noir des mélancolies;
>
> Et le Lotus auguste rêve aux règnes futurs.
>                                     (*Rythmes pittoresques*, 65)[22]

Man's absence from the paradisial scene is ambiguous, suggesting at once woman's autonomy and responsibility.[23] While the former can be understood to accentuate her capacity for independent thought and the latter her impulse to disobey, both give her agency. Yet in this part of the poem, Krysinska's Eve dwells alone in an unmediated relation to desire. Creative play sublimates the corporeal impulses embodied by female and male beasts as various forms of vegetation submit to the sun's engendering caress. (Male) desire lurks in the (feminized) earthly garden, where "Les Roses d'Amour encore inécloses / Dorment au beau Rosier" in ecstatic repose. The calyx/chalice of the water lilies symbolizes the transcendent union of disparate worldly and spiritual domains:

> Les lys premiers nés
> Balancent leurs fervents encensoirs
>                 Auprès

Des chères coupes des Iris
Où fermente le vin noir des mélancolies.

The note of gloom intensifies as the "Jardin de Joie" reveals its internal dissonance.

As Krysinska breathes life into the majestic lotus, she implies with this image that the "J" account in Genesis, which asserts the dominion of male over female, includes the plant kingdom. The "masculine" lotus flower carries seeds that bear fruit, whereas the "feminine" water lilies possess abundant nectar but no seeds. In this way, the primeval garden embodies the difference assumed by nineteenth-century naturalists who claimed the maleness of creativity.[24] The white space that separates the line "Et le Lotus auguste rêve aux règnes futurs" from the closing stanzas of the poem also mediates a break from the harmonious fusion between Eve and her environment in the first part of the poem. The conjunction "Mais" that opens the first of the final four stanzas prepares various notes of discord:

Mais parmi les ramures,
C'est la joie criante des oiseaux;
     Bleus comme les flammes vives du Désir,
     Roses comme de chastes Caresses
     Ornés d'or clair ainsi que des Poèmes
Et vêtus d'ailes sombres comme les Trahisons.
                    (*Rythmes pittoresques*, 65)

Representative of how liberally Krysinska associates sound and color and uses *vers libre* to convey how creative thought forms, the semicolon after "oiseaux" joins the birds' cries with their plumage. This punctuation mark becomes the vehicle for linking joy with pain and blue flames of desire with chaste pink caresses as well as for transposing light gold feathers into poems and dark wings into treason. One could interpret "les Trahisons" as hinting at a future act of disobedience. However, the sequence of events in Krysinska's narrative transforms the biblical account of Eve's transgression to focus on the desire her body inspires.

The last three stanzas of "Ève" return to the subject named in the poem's first line. Krysinska recycles the opening portrayal of Eve, her body in blissful repose, but this time concentrates on the first woman's naked "flancs" or womb:

Ève repose,
Et cependant que ses beaux flancs nus,
     Ignorants de leurs prodigieuses destinées,
Dorment paisibles et par leurs grâces émerveillent
La tribu docile des antilopes,

Voici descendre des plus hautes branches
Un merveilleux Serpent à la bouche lascive
    Un merveilleux Serpent qu'attire et tente
La douceur magnétique de ces beaux flancs nus,

Et voici que pareil à un bras amoureux,
Il s'enroule autour
    De ces beaux flancs nus
Ignorants de leurs prodigieuses destinées.

           (*Rythmes pittoresques*, 65–66)

In analyzing the syntagm "Ève repose" and its link to "repos extatique" in the poem's third line, Stamos Metzidakis has observed that immobility and movement commingle at the level of discourse. "An 'ex-static' rest or repose would literally signify one that breaks out of *stasis*," Metzidakis argues, "one that *moves* in other words" ("Engendering Poetic Vision," 345; emphasis in original here and below). In standard French usage one would write "Ève *se* repose." However, as Metzidakis notes, "'[È]ve repose' does not mean 'Eve *is resting*' but 'Eve *is posing* again'" (345). For Metzidakis, this representation forms a "visual act," reinforced by "the anaphoric repetition of the emblematic letter 'E' at the start of the very next verse '*Et* cependant'" and extended by the acrostic of the name Eve "at the beginning of each opening line of the final three stanzas (E-V-E)" (345). Indeed, this creative use of typography highlights the passive figure depicted in terms of her potent womb, albeit to ironic effect. Krysinska deftly subverts the Parnassian objectification of the female body by using physical immobility to draw attention to the construct of Eve as "the mother of all living" and to generate an open ending to woman's role in creation.

The first woman, "ses beaux flancs nus / Ignorants de leurs prodigieuses destinées," as Krysinska repeats, unknowingly tempts the serpent—evil incarnate and, by analogy, the phallic tongue or, in Lacanian terms, the symbolic order—to seduce her.[25] In Krysinska's restaging of the prelapsarian encounter, the snake descends from above and coils not around the tree of knowledge of good and evil, but around Eve's "flancs" and thus makes *her* the object of desire. "Son geste est fait avant qu'elle n'allonge le bras pour cueillir le fruit interdit," Ewa Wierzbowska states in eliciting sensual undertones from the interchange of visual and olfactory stimuli in the garden evoked by Krysinska ("*Rythmes pittoresques*," 160). The sight of Eve's "beaux flancs nus," the displaced embodiment of forbidden fruit, nurtures carnality. Lust, then, symbolized by the "Serpent à la bouche lascive," brings about man's fall into animal passion and separation from pure spirituality through his yearning to know the female body (in the biblical sense of intimate penetration and possession). From this perspective, the serpentine creature represents how man's desire subordinates woman. Yet Krysinska intercepts the male gaze that delimits the female as an erotic object and, in idealized form, as mother. Her countermove invokes the power of independence of mind to transform myths.

## Eve's Shadow

In the remaining poems clustered under the title "Femmes," Krysinska engages with fictions that rob Eve's descendants of their desire and thus of subjectivity; she sketches instead models of interiority. In "Ariane," dedicated to Moréas,[26] Krysinska addresses the Greek myth of Ariadne, the daughter of Minos and sister of Phaedra. Smitten with the hero Theseus, Ariadne gives her beloved a thread that leads him out of the labyrinth after he slays the flesh-eating Minotaur hidden there. Krysinska's poem begins with the subsequent episode. Theseus has fallen in love with Phaedra and abandons Ariadne on the island of Naxos. As in "Ève," the female figure appears in a passive pose: "Ariane s'endort." The poet again focuses on the mythical woman's physical attractiveness. The accent on outward appearance shifts to the environment, depicted to mirror Ariadne's inner landscape. In the third stanza, the color of the objects surrounding the sleeping beauty stirs emotion. The melancholy of nearby roses exudes the silent figure's deep sense of pain:

> Elle dort. Les mélancoliques roses
> > Nées sous les pleurs,
> Font albatréen son beau visage.
> > > *(Rythmes pittoresques,* 67)

Cast in the image of "Ève au corps ingénu" and filtered through a quasi-male lens, Krysinska's Ariadne unknowingly incites Dionysus's lust, then falls prey to his overpowering caress:

> Le Dieu ravi
> S'émeut de délire célestement humain;
> Et sa caresse comme un aigle s'abat
> Sur le sein ingénu de la dormante belle,
> > Qui s'éveille alors.
>
> Mais la flamme des yeux noirs
> Du Dieu qui règne sur les sublimes ivresses
> A consumé dans le cœur d'Ariane
> > Les douleurs anciennes;
> Et séduite, elle se donne
> > Aux immortelles amours
> Du Dieu charmant
> > Dionisos.
> > > *(Rythmes pittoresques,* 68–69)

This female subject forsakes her own desire. But the revisionist myths of woman in "Femmes" develop the open ending in "Ève" to generate, collectively, a more

237

complex narrative. The poet deflects the phallocentric gaze that captures woman in a narcissistic mirror. Instead, she challenges man as the all-powerful, knowing subject by recasting other strong women in cultural history with inner lives and myths of their own creation.[27]

"Hélène," dedicated to Eugène Ledrain,[28] evokes the stunning Helen of Troy in captivity. Krysinska's poem renders the mythical woman from two angles, treating the surface—the physical representation of femininity—while eliciting the realm of the mind. The poem subverts the tradition of the *blason*, a short poem that celebrates an aspect of the female body, by juxtaposing the corporeal portrayal of Helen, from head to toe, with her mental state. "Hélène" opens thus:

> Aux jardins fleuris de lauriers roses
> Et parmi les vasques
> Où tombent les doux pleurs des fontaines
> Échappées au rire hiératique
> Des masques,
> Hélène, aux yeux charmants, promène
> Une indolente songerie.
>
> (*Rythmes pittoresques*, 69)

Intervening verses restrict the solitary female figure to the garden; she ambles, stopping "près des blancs gradins" to pick "les odorantes roses" and then to sit (*Rythmes pittoresques*, 69). The colors white and red, repeated throughout the poem, draw the female figure "sur ses pieds blancs" to both human production and nature, positioning her between them:

> Hélène, avec une nonchalante grâce, s'est assise
> Sur le marbre pâle d'un banc réfugié
> Dans l'ombre des lauriers roses.
>
> (70)

The hard lines of the pale marble bench, shaded by the willowy stems of the oleander, form a contrastive framework for interpreting the figure's final pose. Though objectified and thus immobilized as an object of male desire, Krysinska's female subject retreats to an inner space:

> Et, tandis que sa main enfantine mêle
> À ses beaux cheveux les odorantes roses,
> Elle rêve, l'oreille vaguement importunée
> Par le tumulte lointain du combat.
>
> (70)

As the senses of touch and smell mix, the line between the external world and the subject's interior experience blurs: "Elle rêve." This mobility in the female figure's point of reference outlines a more dynamic portrayal of a woman absorbed in thought. In a similar vein, Krysinska imagines the inner life of the Virgin Mary.

The Gospel according to Luke includes the story of Mary of Nazareth, whose humility and devotion represent in the Christian imagination a model of motherhood. The angel Gabriel, sent by God to Nazareth, greets her: "Hail, O favored one, the Lord is with you!" (Luke 1:28). The biblical narrator offers a glimpse of Mary's inner turmoil: "But she was greatly troubled at the saying, and considered in her mind what sort of greeting this must be" (Luke 1:29). Krysinska offers a prelude to this encounter in "Marie."[29] The poem's opening lines trace Mary's innermost thoughts, as suggested by the verb "rêve," which introduces her passionate reflection about God as creator of the world:

> La jeune fille nazaréenne amoureusement rêve
> Elle rêve aux exploits sans pareils
> > De l'admirable Jéhovah.
>
> —C'est lui—dit-elle dans son cœur tremblant—
> > Qui exhaussa
> Par la seule force de son Verbe
> Les murailles d'azur qui supportent son ciel.
> > > (*Rythmes pittoresques*, 71)

Interpreted from a Freudian perspective as the product of the unconscious, the creative Word of God in Mary's dream represents her wish (and Krysinska's) to manifest such verbal potency. For Freud, symbolic substitutions operate similarly in myths and in their transformations by creative writers. Freud's analysis of Shakespeare's *King Lear* from this perspective applies equally well to Krysinska's "partial return to the original [myth]" (Freud, *Standard Edition*, 12:300). The ideological work of Krysinska's poem offsets traditional Marian imagery by highlighting the biblical woman's desire as a productive force in the poetic imagination. Mary's inner life thus counterbalances the maternal destiny she assumes:

> La jeune fille nazaréenne amoureusement rêve
>
> Et le poids accablant
> D'une Humilité surhumaine
> > Fait incliner son front charmant
>
> Or, l'Ange annonciateur paraît à ce moment
> Et lui dit: "Salut, Marie,
> > Dans tes flancs tu porteras ton Dieu."
> > > (*Rythmes pittoresques*, 71)[30]

Krysinska does not resolve the tension that arises from her representations of women as "both subject of and object in poetry" (Schultz, *Gendered Lyric*, 240). Rather, in "Femmes," as in other clusters of poems about women in *Joies errantes* and *Intermèdes*, Krysinska uses various myths discursively to contest ideas about women that fail to account for their individuality and depth.[31]

Among the women who made biblical history is Mary of Magdala, whose path intersected with Jesus during his ministry, crucifixion, and resurrection. Jesus healed "Mary called Magdalene, from whom seven demons had gone out," as recorded in Luke 8:2. There is no scriptural evidence that she was a prostitute. However, in the Christian imagination, Mary Magdalene was a fallen woman who repented of her sin and followed Jesus.[32] Krysinska draws on this legacy in her poem "Magdelaine," dedicated to Arsène Houssaye, whose novels include *Les filles d'Ève* (1852). Yet Krysinska invites another interpretation of what the biblical woman mourns.[33] Krysinska's poem opens with Mary Magdalene weeping at the tomb of Jesus, as recorded in the Gospel of John:

> L'air est plus opprimant par ce soir d'orage
> Dans le creux de roche où Magdelaine pleure—
> Et des pierres émane une odeur de tristesse.
>
> > (*Rythmes pittoresques*, 72)

As in "Ariane," here too the poet avoids personal lyricism. A sense of mourning emanates from nature along an olfactory pathway, albeit from an unusual source: "des pierres émane une odeur de tristesse."[34]

This personification underscores Mary Magdalene's sorrow and its depth in her memory. Krysinska pictures the biblical woman from a double standpoint, as complicit with her own reification and as free, through self-reflection, from the external gaze that objectifies her:

> Loin sont les jours
> Où sa victorieuse beauté
> Lui était
> Comme une couronne
> Et l'éclat astral de ses yeux
> Comme une gloire—
> Un deuil cruel et cher la possède pour jamais.—
>
> Loin sont les jours
> Où la radieuse éblouissance de son corps
> Se constellait d'orfèvreries—
> Et ses beaux bras se plaisaient aux anneaux
> Amoureux de leur contour.
>
> > (*Rythmes pittoresques*, 72)

The emphasis on the female figure's outer beauty pivots to "son âme blessée," then back to the body in the throes of pleasure. The latter memory evokes the desire that divides the mythical woman against herself:

> Et pour rendre ses pensers douloureux
> > Plus navrés
> Les souvenirs maudits clament
> > Ainsi qu'un vent de rafale;—
>
> Oh! le rire de ces flûtes entendues
> > Dans les nuits damnées!
>
> Alors que couronnée de roses
> > Et la gorge nue,—
> Ivre des arômes de sa fastueuse chevelure,—
> Elle se renversait aux bras enlaçants
> > D'amants . . .
>
> > > > > (72–73; ellipses in original)

Subsequent stanzas repeat previous lines in shortened form, thus telescoping the perspective. The past and present occupy nearly the same space in the woman's inner world:

> Oh! le rire de ces flûtes!
>
> Que l'air est opprimant
> Dans le creux de roche
> Où maintenant elle pleure.
>
> Un deuil cruel et cher
> La possède pour jamais—
>
> > > > (*Rythmes pittoresques*, 73)

Neither the repetitions that structure the dual portrait of Mary Magdalene nor the olfactory pathway joining the spiritual and the human realms of existence carries through to the last stanza, which ends on an ambiguous note of color:

> Mais dans la lueur de ce soir d'orage
> Sa chevelure
> Est rose.
>
> > > > (73)

For Ewa Wierzbowska, "on pourrait dire que c'est une tête auréolée par le doigt divin" ("*Rythmes pittoresques*," 161). Yet the color pink also conveys a mix: the purity and innocence associated with white alongside the energy and passion associated with red. The different shades of meaning elicited by this final image convey the deeper revisionary work of Krysinska's compact history of ideas about women in "Femmes," which extends to her critical corpus as well.

Krysinska followed her critics closely and intervened to reclaim her rightful place among the poets of her day. In this regard, she recognized no female precursor nor any canon of so-called feminine poetry.[35] There is but a single mention of Desbordes-Valmore at the start of Krysinska's essay "Les artistes maudits" (1901), which invokes the poets discussed in Verlaine's *Poètes maudits* (1884).[36] Several paragraphs later, Krysinska references her own debut in 1881, "en vers libres publiés dans le journal le *Chat Noir*," evoking an era of rich creativity to situate the work of her contemporaries Charles de Sivry, Charles Cros, and Maurice Rollinat, all misunderstood in their day ("Les artistes maudits," 385).[37] In light of the dispute over her poetic history, a dispute that shifts between gender and originality, Krysinska identified with the "accursed poets" of both sexes.

### A Legacy at Stake

Readers who opened Krysinska's inaugural volume of poems in 1890 found this statement: "Nous désirons rappeler à ceux qui se sont intéressés aux derniers mouvements littéraires que l'auteur des *Rythmes pittoresques* est le premier qui ait eu l'initiative de ces innovations prosodiques et aussi du retour vers le symbole" (*Rythmes pittoresques*, 23).[38] Given that some of her first *vers libres* had appeared in *Le Chat Noir* and *La Vie Moderne* in 1882, add the editors, "Il y eut donc—de la part des confrères manifestants et propagateurs de symbolisme en 1885—pas mal de perfidie à ne jamais prononcer le nom de Marie Krysinska lorsqu'ils faisaient le dénombrement de leur groupe initial" (23). In prefacing the volume, J. H. Rosny addresses Krysinska as the innovator of *vers libre*: "Vous vous êtes trouvée à l'origine de ce mouvement littéraire en révolte contre la perfection routinière et qui ébranla l'idole du vers français classico-romantique" (25). Rosny describes her novel expression as having the contours of "un nouveau mode musical de la parole non chantée" (25). His attempt to describe Krysinska's verse further illumines the difficulty it posed for critics because it fit no traditional category of analysis. A mix of vocabulary relates Krysinska's *vers libre* to "prose rythmée" that retains "la saveur des images [qui] ne laissent pas un instant de doute sur le caractère nettement et bellement poétique de [son] travail," which Rosny traces to "1882–82 époque où il INNOVAIT" (25; emphasis in original).

A number of critics writing between 1890 and 1892 similarly emphasized Krysinska's unique poetic method together with her artistry, original ideas, and rich imagery.[39] They also speculated why the Symbolists had excluded her from their roster in 1886. As Vital Hocquet (writing as Narcisse Lebeau) put it, "si Mme Marie Krysinska fut si désinvoltement éliminée des articles qui battaient la grosse caisse autour des nouvelles préoccupations en art et des noms nouveaux, c'est—

uniquement—parce qu'elle est une femme . . . mais peut-être aussi parce qu'elle a eu l'indiscrétion d'être première en date dans l'affranchissement du vers" ("*Rythmes pittoresques*," 1628).

Krysinska came to her own defense the following year and positioned her contribution within a more nuanced history of modern free verse in France. Written in response to an article by Anatole France in *Le Temps*, Krysinska's essay "De la nouvelle école" (1891) redresses the critic's account of *vers libre*.[40] This poetic development, argues Krysinska, predates both the *vers libres* published in *La Vogue* in 1885 under Kahn's editorial direction and Moréas's manifesto in 1886.[41] As seen in Verlaine's *Romances sans paroles* (1874) and *Sagesse* (1881) as well as in later works, it was he, not Moréas, who rejected the classical rule of alternating masculine and feminine rhymes. In Cros's production, continues Krysinska, "le rythme du vers d'implacablement symétrique, devient souple et ondoyant" ("De la nouvelle école," 266). Suggestive of the aural principle according to which the new poetic form evolved, she mentions the effect in La Fontaine's fables of "le rythme guidé par la seule oreille d'un artiste" (266). This background situates her innovative prosody, which combines musicality and visuality and uses symbolism not to represent ideas, but to form impressions:

> Quant aux libertés définitives prises avec le mètre et la rime, effort tendant à constituer un nouveau mode prosodique, et quant à l'initiative de réaction— par le retour vers un symbolisme impressionnel—contre le réalisme et le souromantisme qui sévissaient en poésie, je me vois forcé à en réclamer pour moi-même la priorité de date; ayant dès 1881 publié dans la *Vie Moderne* et le *Chat Noir*, les premières pièces des *Rythmes pittoresques* où l'on retrouvera aussi les recherches de tels effets musicaux, des retours de phrases identiques ou *renversées*, qui eurent l'honneur d'être adoptées par les *Christophe Colombs* du Symbolisme. (266; emphasis in original)

The masculine ending of the adjective "forcé" does not agree with the pronoun subject "je." This could be merely an error by typesetters accustomed to printing male authors. Yet this grammatical "mistake," reflective of the male-dominated canon of poetry, represents the ways misinformed critics sidelined her voice. One of Krysinska's final remarks implies as much: "Que le journalisme, qui tient entre ses mains la réputation, par conséquent le gagne-pain des littérateurs, fût mieux informé et n'affublât pas les pasticheurs de l'invention apportée par tel autre" ("De la nouvelle école," 267).

Krysinska's absence from interviews that the journalist Jules Huret began publishing in March 1891 and collected under the title *Enquête sur l'évolution littéraire* further illustrates the paradox of reception that preserves, yet obscures, her role as an innovator. Despite Krysinska's stake in the debate over the emergence of free verse in France, Huret interviewed only male poets about this polemic: Mallarmé, Verlaine, Moréas, and Gustave Kahn among them. Only Verlaine mentions her contribution alongside Rimbaud's in scorning the Symbolists who claimed to have invented *vers libre*: "Où sont les *nouveautés?* Est-ce que Arthur Rimbaud,—et je ne le félicite pas—n'a pas fait tout cela avant eux? Et même Krysinska!" (quoted in Huret, *Enquête*, 69; emphasis in original). Verlaine recalls his experimental verse to which Krysinska alludes in her 1891 article on the evolution of *vers libre*. Yet his fuller comment depicts this hybrid verse form as closer to prose and utterly foreign to the French tradition: "Pour qu'il y ait vers, il faut qu'il y ait rythme. À présent, on fait des vers à mille pattes! Ça n'est plus des vers, c'est de la prose, quelquefois même ce n'est que du charabia . . . Et surtout, *ça n'est pas français*, non *ça n'est pas français!* On appelle ça des vers rythmiques! Mais nous ne sommes ni des Latins, ni des Grecs, nous autres! Nous sommes des Français, sacré nom de Dieu!" (quoted in Huret, *Enquête*, 69; emphasis and ellipses in original). However, the Greek-born Moréas derives this open form of poetry from classical French prosody as "la conséquence nécessaire des diverses transformations de l'alexandrin" (quoted in Huret, *Enquête*, 77). Kahn alludes to his foundational role as the editor of *La Vogue* in which Rimbaud's "Marine" and "Mouvement" appeared in May and June 1886, poems that critics then, as now, cite as precursors of modern *vers libres*.[42] He then invokes his own poetry and theoretical writings between 1887 and 1888, "comme créateur et esthéticien du poème libre" (quoted in Huret, *Enquête*, 396).[43]

In an article published in April 1891, "La poésie nouvelle: À propos des décadents et symbolistes," the Belgian poet Georges Rodenbach scoffs at Kahn's posturing post factum as the sole creator of *vers libre*. Using the same evidence upon which Kahn had drawn to position himself as the new poetry's founder, Rodenbach raises instead the possibility that Krysinska influenced Rimbaud: "Dans *les Illuminations*, il y avait maintes strophes libérées . . . de toutes les règles de la prosodie, sans rimes, ni césures, ni mètres officiels. Peut-être M. Arthur Rimbaud, qui avait commencé par des vers conformes, en prenant barre à Paris comme cela lui arrivait souvent, aura-t-il eu connaissance des rythmes de ce genre publiés çà et là dans des feuilles par Mᵐᵉ Marie Krysinska" (426). Rodenbach places Krysinska in the context that she would evoke to reclaim her creative property: "Dès 1879, nous l'avons entendue au cercle des Hydropathes divulguer ces premiers vers libres, parus par fragments en 1882, en 1883, dans *l'Événement*; et il est incontestable, comme l'a dit M. J.-H. Rosny dans la préface de ces proses rythmées . . . que la première 'elle constitua ce nouveau mode musical de la parole non chantée'" (426). In positioning Krysinska as an early practitioner of *vers libre*, Rodenbach relates a conversation in which she discussed reading Gérard de Nerval's translation of the German poet Heinrich Heine: "À chaque vers allemand, dans cette traduction juxtalinéaire, correspondait le sens français qui était, non pas un vers, mais de la *prose poétique*, puisqu'il traduisait sans césure ni rythme ni rime le vers allemand équivalent" (427; emphasis in original). This translation into French poetic prose of the original German verse, continues Rodenbach, "lui parut donner une apparence de strophes aux membres de phrases inégaux. . . . C'était quelque chose d'intermédiaire entre la prose et la poésie, ni tout à fait enchaîné, ni tout à fait libre, avec un rythme et une cadence quand même qui en faisait un chant" (427). In the critical corpus she produced between 1894 and 1904, Krysinska simultaneously elaborated her aesthetics and a revisionist history of modern *vers libre*.

## Misplaced Property

In the preface to *Joies errantes: Nouveaux rythmes pittoresques* (1894), Krysinska reiterates the trajectory set forth in her essay of 1891 to assert her independence from any literary school or model: "Si l'on remarque des analogies entre nos poèmes libres et ceux contenus dans les volumes et plaquettes parus en ces dernières années, nous rappellerons l'antériorité des dates de publication (1881–1882) afin que nous demeure la propriété de l'initiative bonne ou mauvaise" (v). While these dates of publication place her production in history, her definition of *vers libre* further proves her claim to prosodic innovation: "Notre proposition d'art est celle-ci: atteindre au plus de Beauté expressive possible, par le moyen lyrique, subordonnant le cadre aux exigences *imprévues* de l'image, et rechercher assidûment la *surprise de style* comme dans la libre prose avec, de plus, le souci d'un rythme particulier qui doit déterminer le caractère poétique déjà établi par le *ton* ou pour mieux dire le *diapason* ÉLEVÉ du langage" (vi; emphasis in original). Krysinska subordinates form to the symbolic power of images in a protosurrealist manner.[44] Shaped by the thought expressed, as if following the stream of consciousness, her *vers libre* translates fleeting impressions or sensations, such as those associated with "quelque capricieux coin de nature, ou quelque anxieux état de rêve" (vi). Krysinska summarizes her work's reception to date, naming among her supporters Aurélien Scholl, Ph. Gille, Henri Bauër, Anatole France, F. Champsaur, G. Montorgueil, G. Rodenbach, C. de Sainte-Croix, Ch. Maurras, G. Doncieux, and F. Féneon. She also alludes to other reviewers who were hostile "à la formule du *vers libre*," but who nevertheless recognized her effort "vers quelque beauté neuve et l'expressif inattendu" (viii).

Krysinska's preface polarized critics whose struggle over the property of genius diminished her achievement. Yet the paradox of Krysinska's reception, like that of women considered in previous chapters, suggests the impact of her work. In June 1894, for example, the Belgian writer Roland de Marès labeled Krysinska's preface "prétentieuse" and dismissed "la propriété de l'initiative" she based on her publication history: "[C]e n'est certes pas M^{me} Krysinska qui donna au mouvement actuel l'importance qu'il a acquise ces dernières années. Si elle a inventé (?) le vers libre, elle n'a pas su l'imposer; il a fallu pour cela le talent, presque le génie d'un Vielé-Griffin." For Marès, her *Joies errantes* fit the category "de la jolie littérature de femme" ("Compte rendu des *Joies errantes*," 366). The ideological work of the series "Notes féminines" and "Ombres féminines," however, counters this appraisal of Krysinska's volume, as Schultz has shown.[45]

For the journalist and poet Fernand Hauser, the founder of the literary review *Lutèce*, the appearance of *Joies errantes* confirmed instead Krysinska's exceptional status as "un des écrivains les plus complets de la génération poétique nouvelle. … [Elle] nous apporta de véritables poèmes lyriques, qui ne pouvaient être classés dans aucun des genres poétiques que nous connaissons" ("Madame Marie Krysinska," 49). Hauser highlights the aesthetic project outlined in Krysinska's preface to the volume: imagery dictating poetic form; surprising word associations; and rhythm freed from formal rhyme schemes, modeled instead upon musicality. He relates her work to that of poetic genius: "[E]lle est un des ces rares poètes qui ne dérivent de personne et qui laisse dans la littérature une trace lumineuse, telles les comètes resplendissantes" (51).[46] For Hauser, "M^me Marie Krysinska, dans la littérature, occupera une place toute particulière, car personne, à moins de la plagier, ne pourra l'imiter," and her *Rythmes pittoresques* "resteront le seul exemple d'une œuvre d'art parfaite, créée contrairement à toutes formules" (51).

In a pithy review of *Joies errantes* for *Mercure de France* published in August 1894, the novelist Rachilde (pen name of Marguerite Vallette-Eymery) straddles as well as crosses the line between exposing and upholding gender as a category of analysis in order to separate Krysinska's production from the male canon. Rachilde's review opens thus: "Depuis longtemps l'auteur nous affirme qu'il a inventé le vers libre et pour nouvelle preuve il nous offre une nouvelle série de poèmes très en dehors des règles connues. Pourquoi lui disputer cette gloire?" ("Compte rendu des *Joies errantes*," 386). Rachilde uses the word "auteur" (followed by the masculine pronoun "il") to refer to Krysinska and, at the same time, describes *vers libre* as "un charmant non sens, un bégayement délicieux et baroque convenant merveilleusement aux femmes poètes dont la paresse instinctive est souvent synonyme de génie" (386). This statement from the satiric and unconventional Rachilde, also known for her misogyny, prepares two categories of *vers libre* on the basis of gender: "Ce que Jean Moréas (de *l'école romane*) aura cru trouver en peinant terriblement sur les vieux bouquins de Ronsard et quelques dictionnaires ignorés, Marie Krysinska ne peut-elle l'avoir découvert aussi en jouant avec les frous-frous de sa jupe, les perles d'un collier, le souvenir d'un rêve?" (386). Rachilde proposes intuition rather than effort as the source of Krysinska's verse, but also suggests, to the contrary, her contemporary's thinking through prosody: "Je ne vois aucun inconvénient à ce qu'une femme pousse la versification jusqu'à sa dernière licence!" (386). Rachilde closes on another ambiguous note by praising the poet, but not the thinker, stating that she likes "[les *Joies errantes*] … mais sans explication, surtout, sans préface savante, car moins une femme s'explique et plus elle est vraiment forte" (386).

In the preface to her novel *Folle de son corps* (1895), Krysinska addresses her "lectrice éventuelle—Madame et chère inconnue," as if writing back to Rachilde, to comment on women's reception as writers. Krysinska's preface represents the hostile environment for gifted women in terms of "l'accusation de masculinité" (vi–vii).[47] In this regard, she exposes the construct of the bluestocking, universally held to characterize women writers, by teasing out of the pejorative connotation of the term "bas-bleu" the intellectual qualities and creativity that unsympathetic critics seek to veil: "Le mot *bas bleu*, cette banalité imbécile et dénuée de sens, ne fait reculer personne quand il s'agit de cataloguer une femme qui . . . pousse la coquetterie jusqu'à s'orner plus complètement. Enrichir sa mémoire de belles lectures, rompre son jugement à des opinions personnelles et sincères, s'accoutumer à voir le spectacle de la vie par les côtés esthétiques, curieux et renseignants—n'est-ce point se parer pour l'agrément des esprits délicats?" (vii). Consistent with the independence of mind she prizes, Krysinska nevertheless mocks "professionels *féministes*" (viii; emphasis in original). Her emphasis on individuality relates to the fight for notoriety, which becomes all the more acute, "si une femme se permet de révéler quelque valeur propre" (viii). Though Rachilde's review had stirred the controversy surrounding Krysinska's creations, Krysinska limits her comments to the "médiocrités mâles [qui] se conduisent alors comme si l'auteur féminin les avait attaqués et outragés grièvement et font le moulinet avec un bâton oint de bave, déguisée à peine, en éléphantine ironie" (viii). "Consciente et fière de son individualité," she would continue to engage with her critics (ix).

Krysinska would return to the question of how *vers libre* evolved to emphasize her own originality. Her analytical writings between 1901 and 1904 enrich understanding of how she engaged the narrative of evolutionary science as a space to think through poetry and its link to genius.

## On Poetic Evolution

In 1901, Krysinska presented her essay "L'évolution poétique: Devant l'Académie" as a direct response to Sully Prudhomme, the influential Parnassian poet "[qui] traite de dangereuse hérésie la tentative nouvelle, l'acheminement vers plus de liberté dans les cadres" (102).[48] Her own publication history, observes Krysinska, makes her "le premier fauteur de ce schisme" (102). In situating her *vers libre* in relation to the French poetic tradition, she reiterates from "Conflit de la rime et de la raison" (1899) the question that has shaped her aesthetic project: "Qu'est-ce qu'une œuvre poétique?" (102). Krysinska amplifies the kernel of her 1899 essay that poetry works simultaneously at phonetic and semantic levels: "*Poésie* et *rythme* ne sont point synonymes de *symétrie*. Ces dispositions asymétriques et capricieuses qui nous convenaient, nous n'avons jamais songé à les présenter comme une proposition révolutionnaire, ni même évolutionnaire. Et pourtant, l'évolution prosodique est-elle constante?" (102; emphasis in original). This query anticipates the theory of rational evolutions Krysinska would develop against Darwinism in her prefatory essay to *Intermèdes* (1903), discussed later in this chapter. For Krysinska, poetry does not follow a trajectory of progress with an ideal in mind. Rather, as the advent of *vers libre* demonstrates, new forms emerge suddenly and thus make manifest the work of creative genius.

In "L'évolution poétique," Krysinska repeats the example of La Fontaine's metric variations in the same fable, together with the "rejet" that Hugo introduced by using "enjambement," where a line of verse runs over to the next. Such prosodic experiments with rhythm raise a fundamental question about rhyme, which also concerns her *vers libre*: "[S]era-t-elle pour l'œil ou pour l'oreille?" (102).[49] Creativity re-forms tradition: "Tout cadre devenu classique depuis était à l'origine la trouvaille d'un seul poète qui l'innovait à son usage" (102). Krysinska elaborates this link by quoting her 1894 preface to *Joies errantes*: "L'artifice de l'assonance et plus tard de la rime fut, à l'origine, l'ingéniosité d'un seul—le premier qui s'en fut avisé—et non point la raison de vivre de la poésie" (102). She inserts a broader comparison with the freer forms of expression in modern visual arts and music to contextualize the asymmetrical typography that *vers libre* deploys. Krysinska's analysis of this typography, which gathers discursive folds between unexpected images, shifts to the technical aspect of sound in her own production.

A close reading of her free verse, continues Krysinska, yields regular "coupes" or metric breaks, "à la condition de garder à la lecture le rythme de la parole parlée," and thus dispenses with the rule of counting a mute *e* preceded by a consonant ("L'évolution poétique," 103). Whereas the latter prosodic syllable, upheld by Prudhomme, conforms to a word's spelling, her *vers libre* reflects a word's modern pronunciation: "vers mesurés pour la seule oreille, selon la pronunciation moderne usuelle, et assonancés pour l'oreille aussi, avec la faculté de faire rimer les pluriels avec les singuliers et toutes les finales muettes entre elles, quelle qu'en soit l'orthographe" (103). Prudhomme understood poetic evolution along a continuum and grouped artists in schools. He thus failed to recognize that "[u]ne œuvre artistique ne vaut qu'en raison de la marque personnelle que l'auteur y a pu imprimer, elle est d'essence unique," Krysinska argues (103). In "L'évolution poétique," as elsewhere in her critical writings, Krysinska interweaves reflections on originality with a revisionist history of her *vers libre*. The term "revisionist" conveys a dual perspective in the analysis proposed here: that of Krysinska's contemporaries who denied her contribution and her reevaluation of the same historical evidence.

In her 1901 analysis of poetic evolution, Krysinska revisits her absence from the official record of *vers libre* brought forth by the Symbolists and adopts the biblical figure of John the Baptist to portray herself as a poetic martyr: "Le groupe dit 'Initial' . . . (voyez les manifestes et les déclarations de principes prosodiques des années 1886, 1887, 1888, *La Vogue*, *Lutèce*, *Revue indépendante*, etc.) . . . n'a jamais prononcé notre nom, même à titre de curiosité chronologique, ne nous a même point laissé l'humble poste d'un petit saint Jean-Baptiste, annonçant en l'an 1883 (par ses essais) la glorieuse nativité, pour 1886, du fameux groupe" ("L'évolution poétique," 103). They ignored her work because of her gender: "En ce temps-là, une initiative, émanant d'une femme, était considérée autant que possible comme ne venant de nulle part et tombée de droit dans le domaine public" (103). Krysinska recycles this statement nearly verbatim from her 1899 essay, but expands its significance in relation to poetic originality across the centuries: "Tous les dispositifs prosodiques, alexandrin, coupes alternantes, sonnet, rondeau, ballade, terza rima, etc., eurent, à l'origine, chacun son novateur" (103). Infinitely diverse, poetic forms transcend evolutionary adaptation, for "tout poète original apporte sa variante plus ou moins sensible" and "comme tout autre producteur d'art, a le droit de se constituer arbitre de son œuvre en tant que moyens employés" (103).

Krysinska's critics read her as closely as she read them. Their counterdiscourse paradoxically inscribes evidence of the fuller account Krysinska gave of her poetic work and its reception. In 1902, for example, Catulle Mendès appropriated Krysinska's reference to John the Baptist in "L'évolution poétique," but feminized the figure: "Que l'aimable poétesse Marie Crysinska [*sic*] veuille bien me pardonner si je ne prends pas beaucoup plus en considération la légende qui la présente comme la sainte-Jeanne-Baptistine de l'école vers-libriste" (*Le mouvement poétique français*, 152). Mendès's use of the label "poétesse," together with the image of a cross-dressed saint he makes of Krysinska, links women's intellectual inferiority with their purported envy of male genius. That same year, Kahn similarly responded to Krysinska's criticism of the Symbolists who had omitted her from their history of *vers libre*. In *Symbolistes et décadents*, Kahn avoids naming Krysinska as he accuses her of having modeled her verse on poems he had yet to publish! Kahn claims to have chanced upon her poem "Le hibou" (published in *La Vie Moderne* in 1883) in printed matter he received while stationed for military service in Tunisia from 1880 to 1884: "Je regardais la feuille et j'y vis un poème en vers libres, ou typographié tel, poème en prose ou en vers libres, selon le gré, très directement ressemblant à mes essais. Il était signé d'une personne qui me connaissait bien, et voulait bien, moi absent, se conformer étroitement à mon esthétique; je faisais école" (29). In the prefatory essay to the poetic collection she published the following year, *Intermèdes: Nouveaux rythmes pittoresques* (1903), Krysinska retorted: "Heureux climat africain et heureux âge où l'on peut *faire école* avant d'avoir fait imprimer une seule ligne révélatrice de *son* esthétique!" (xxxiv; emphasis in original).[50] A sophisticated ars poetica, her essay "Introduction: Sur les évolutions rationnelles: Esthétique et philologie" expands on poetic evolution to theorize genius beyond gender.

## The Property of Genius

An art nouveau painting of Eve and the serpent by Bellenger serves as the cover of *Intermèdes: Nouveaux rythmes pittoresques* (1904; fig. 19).[51] Recall from *Rythmes pittoresques* how Krysinska complicated the myth of Eve the transgressor by portraying the first woman as the object of male desire. Bellenger also pictures Eve without Adam, but presents her as a desiring subject in relation to the serpent.[52] The female figure holds in place the serpent coiled around her upper torso. Eve's hair covers her ear, creating the backdrop against which the serpent's line of sight aligns with hers, the focus being the forbidden fruit of knowledge she desires. From the perspective of the subtle interplay between complicity with and resistance to

FIG 19
Cover of *Intermèdes* by Georges Bellenger.

the second creation story, Bellenger's portrayal of Eve (also known as Marie Kry-
sinska) shows the shift in meaning through which the poet gains authority over
her intellectual property. Representative of this interchange between tradition and
creativity in Krysinska's *Intermèdes* is the turn away from Eden in one of the poems
clustered under the title "Les saisons bibliques":

> Le premier couple d'amour lié
> Voit l'infini de sa tendresse

Promis par ce Jardin d'immortelle jeunesse.

Dangereux émoi de l'âme attirée
Par le charme pervers d'un bien interdit
Ève, d'une imprudente main, s'est emparée
De la branche nouvelle
Où pend le fruit
Redoutable, par qui l'Inconnu se révèle.

(137)

This gesture of reaching for the unknown, interwoven in Krysinska's poetic and analytical writings, can be interpreted as the first "creative" act.[53] An intellectual move in the opening pages of *Intermèdes* juxtaposes the narratives of religion and science to frame the underlying issue of women's relationship to creativity. Krysinska's prefatory essay addresses the limits of evolutionary science to disentangle genius from gender.

Krysinska begins "Sur les évolutions rationnelles" by explaining the concept of "evolution" in terms of Darwin's 1859 theory of natural selection, whereby the traits most useful for the survival of a species determine how it adapts to changes in the environment.[54] In this context, evolution means progress from lower to higher forms of life. To the biological paradigm, she adds social Darwinism, which had emerged by the 1870s:

> Par ce terme d'évolution, on incline à entendre: acheminement vers le mieux, et cette définition est juste en effet, sur le terrain physiologique au sens Darwinien du mot.
>
> Le vœu de perfectibilité étant un vœu manifeste de la nature, chaque espèce poursuit patiemment, à travers les âges, un idéal relatif à elle-même; elle en approche par degrés, y arrive et s'y tient jusqu'au jour où quelque révolution de milieu, quelque cataclysme déterminent sa ruine ou sa dégénérescence.
>
> Ainsi évoluent aussi les races et les nations. (*Intermèdes*, v)

Krysinska proves to be an astute reader of Darwin's *Descent of Man, and Selection in Relation to Sex* (1871). Like Galton, Darwin invokes heredity and the male-authored and male-centered annals as evidence for maintaining genius as a male property: "The chief distinction in the intellectual powers of the two sexes is shewn by man attaining to a higher eminence, in whatever he takes up, than woman can attain, whether requiring deep thought, reason, or imagination, or merely the use of the senses and hands" (*Descent of Man*, 2:327). Gender slips away, however, as Darwin buttresses this point by nuancing the gist of patience in Buffon's definition, which disengages genius from physiology: "patience, in this sense, means unflinching, undaunted perseverance" (2:328). Put another way, the intense effort central to the work of genius has no sex.

251

For Krysinska, the laws of physiology applied to nature and extrapolated to explain racial differences and societal transformations over time cannot account for the diversity among artistic productions, which stems from the autonomy of genius:

> Mais il serait fort erroné d'appliquer ces lois aux œuvres des artistes, aux productions de la Pensée et du Rêve humains, car il est du ressort de l'Art seul d'atteindre à l'Absolu, sans transitions.
>
> Le propre du Génie c'est d'être révélateur par sa manifestation soudaine, et c'est avec les exemples qu'il laisse sur son passage que sont faites la tradition, la science et la règle.
>
> Et cette tradition et cette science s'enrichissent et se complètent de la diversité des artistes créateurs qu'apparente, néanmoins, un lien mystérieux.
>
> Cette manifestation ne saurait progresser systématiquement et qu'ainsi le temps le plus récent soit le plus avancé en perfection.
>
> Toutes les fois que surgit une individualité, douée de force créatrice, un style est constitué. (*Intermèdes*, v–vi)

Krysinska assumes neither the Romantic linkage of originality with divine inspiration nor the post-Romantic turn toward an unconscious source of creativity.[55] For her, aesthetics involves a "rational" evolution: a manifestation of creative thought that unfolds outside the realm of scientific rationalizations. One cannot trace genius to its origins: "[L]e génie étant par son essence la plus tangible image de l'Absolu, n'est susceptible d'aucun progrès radical. Il est spontané et varié à l'infini" (vi). In other words, one cannot know genius apart from the work. However, "l'œuvre d'art subit des transformations," argues Krysinska, and in this sense evolves as the product of culture according to "les lois immuables d'Équilibre, d'Harmonie, et de Logique" (vi, vii). Against this background, Krysinska inscribes her own creative and intellectual legacy.

### Between the Poet and the Theoretician

In sections 2–4 of "Sur les évolutions rationnelles," Krysinska connects the evolution of philology with that of aesthetics as she maps a robust history of French poetry. This frames her return to poetic evolution in the fifth section, now referencing Sully Prudhomme's *Testament poétique* (1901). Krysinska expands her earlier response to his critique of *vers libre*, then explains "la théorie nouvelle" of her own practice in terms of a total work of art: "[A]tteindre au plus de plaisir pour l'oreille et au plus de musique possible par une eurythmie basée sur le double concours des dispositifs symétriques et des dispositifs assymétriques [*sic*]—de même que cela se voit dans tous les arts, tirant parti comme eux des effets d'opposition et de contrastes faisant à l'exemple de la musique moderne une plus large part aux *Dissonnances* [*sic*] et, comme elle, obtenant des effets de *crescendo* par une *progression* rythmique et l'effet contraire par une *régression*" (*Intermèdes*, xvii; emphasis in original). Krysinska borrows the vocabulary of music to explain the aural effect of eurythmy (rhythmic movement), which a *vers libriste* seeks to produce by creating harmony between dissonant sounds. All the arts draw on such symmetry and asymmetry, asserts Krysinska, and in this way she recalls how musicality and visuality act in concert in her *vers libre*.

At the midpoint of her reflective preface to *Intermèdes*, in section 6, Krysinska turns back to historical evidence to reinforce her place in the history of modern *vers libre*: "Nous voici engagée sur un terrain périlleux, car il s'agit de parler de nous-même en tant que—par un hasard de date: 1882—ayant précédé de cinq ans la formation de la *nouvelle école* par nos œuvres publiées dans des périodiques" (*Intermèdes*, xix; emphasis in original). The dispute over the invention of *vers libre*, which Krysinska relates to her gender, frames once again her absence from the official record:

> Ouvrons ici une parenthèse: la particularité de la nouvelle école, c'est d'être composée exclusivement de chefs qui, à des dates variées, ont tous découvert, le premier, la même nouveauté.
>
> Dans les dénombrements qu'ils ont faits de leur phalange, au cours de multiples manifestes, dont un de M. Moréas a eu les honneurs du *Figaro* en 1891, ils ont maintes fois prononcé le mot de groupe initial, et jamais notre nom n'y a été associé.
>
> Une initiative émanant d'une femme—avait sans doute décrété le groupe— peut être considérée comme ne venant de nulle part, et tombée de droit dans le domaine public. (xxi)

She analyzes her own writing as a "musicienne" who attempted "avec le moyen littéraire de traduire telle impression musicale, avec son caprice rythmique, avec son désordre parfois, usant des ressources prosodiques comme d'ornementations et de parures librement agrafées, sans symétrie obligée," leading back, in section 8, to her early verse of 1881–82 (*Intermèdes*, xxii–xxiii). As a critical reader of aesthetics, she addresses "la querelle technique en matière de poésie [qui] est permanente" (xxvii), and then, in section 9, she recalls the reception of her *Rythmes pittoresques* in greater detail than she had in her preface to *Joies errantes*.

From the standpoint of the originality that critics attributed to her first collection of poetry and recalled in assessing her poetic volume of 1894, Krysinska takes final aim at Kahn. The lengthy excerpt below, drawn from the latter part of her prefatory essay to *Intermèdes*, corroborates how actively she responded to contemporary critics about the property of *vers libre*. It also reveals Kahn's defensive posture, substantiating how seriously male detractors took her poetic creativity:

Au surplus, M. Kahn se charge lui-même de trancher la question dans son livre *Symbolistes et décadents* (page 29), où, après avoir présenté la genèse de son *invention*, comme verbalement promenée par lui le long des quais parisiens, penchée sur l'oreille confidente de témoins—morts depuis—Charles Cros, Verlaine, Laforgue, il reconnaît s'être vu "tomber sous les yeux" pendant qu'il faisait son service militaire en Algérie, le premier spécimen de vers libres, publiés dans la *Vie moderne* (1883), "il était signé *d'une personne . . .*" spécifie M. Kahn. C'était moi, "la personne" et ce poème, *Le Hibou* fut le seul, en vers libres, que la *Vie moderne* eût jamais inséré. C'est ainsi que l'on peut rétablir notre signature sous la désignation de *une personne qui me connaissait bien*, par quoi M. Kahn laisse entendre que son *invention*, alors strictement inédite, était parvenue à notre connaissance par quelque moyen occulte, sans doute, ou cambrioleur.

Si, pourtant, j'eusse été ce premier disciple, au lieu de la toute spontanée et impulsive musicienne qui essayait de transposer en poésie, sans nulle ambition de fonder une école; comment M. Kahn explique-t-il le fait de m'avoir systématiquement rejeté [*sic*] du sein de son enterprise, de ses listes, catalogues et nomenclatures d'adeptes et de sa revue propagandiste pour laquelle je lui a envoyé maints poèmes, dont il n'inséra pas un seul. (*Intermèdes*, xxxiii–xxxiv; emphasis and ellipses in original)

As Krysinska links salient chapters of the French poetic tradition with her own trajectory, she circles back to genius: "Pour que l'inépuisable champ des Possibilités en Art s'éclaire d'une éblouissante lumière, il suffit qu'un artiste original paraisse, qu'une œuvre imprévue et belle, soit" (xxxv).

Krysinska's essay forms a dense nexus. At once linear and circular, broad and deep, her line of thought moves back and forth from the center to the margins, from poetic evolution to genius, to the twinned histories of aesthetics and philology, to the French poetic tradition, to the history of *vers libre*, and then again to her reception. The poet's legacy interlocks with that of the thinker as Krysinska contests her erasure from the advent of modern *vers libre*: "Sans avoir jamais ambitionné l'emploi de chef d'école, nous déclinons avec énergie le titre de disciple et citons comme témoins de notre indépendance, des dates *imprimées* qui nous établissent *préalable* à la formation du groupe *novateur*, lequel, par omission systématique de notre nom, nous a décrétée inexistante et non advenue; 'un mythe' écrivait textuellement—je ne sais plus où—M. Viellé [*sic*] Griffin" (*Intermèdes*, xxxvi–xxxvii; emphasis in original). In reflecting on her trajectory Krysinska evokes the struggle to preserve "la vie esthétique de cette œuvre" (xxxvii). The ultimate test of any creative work emerges in the penultimate line of Krysinska's preface, which repeats the open ending of her 1901 essay on poetic evolution: "Cet acte de foi artistique qui est la production d'une œuvre vraiment belle est, de par les musées et les bibliothèques, ratifié par l'admiration des siècles; et, les enquêtes de plus tard le trouvent conforme aux Lois immuables de l'Équilibre et de l'Harmonie" (xxxviii–xxxix). All creators hope to live on in the minds of readers, but only the work of originality, defined as genius, withstands the test of time.

## Time to Rethink "Genius"

Critical response to Krysinska's preface in 1904 conveys both the polemic about her *vers libre* and the uneasy attribution of original work to a woman. For example, the Symbolist poet Pierre Quillard characterized her preface to *Intermèdes* as both "modeste" and "arrogante" ("*Intermèdes*," 178). While the latter term covers her claim that the Symbolists purloined her *vers libre*, the former refers to her invoking of La Fontaine's freer verse, which Quillard considered a precedent for her own. Quillard thus argued that her key phrase about "le propre du Génie," which he cites in its entirety, did not apply to her. To the contrary, the poet Charles Le Goffic, also a novelist and historian, stressed that, as a poet and theoretician, Krysinska had contributed to the history of French poetry:

> Il ne fait plus de doute, quand on a lu les trente-neuf pages de 'l'Introduction sur les évolutions rationnelles' dont M^me Marie Krysinska a fait précéder son nouveau recueil: *Intermèdes*, que la poésie française ne soit redevable à cette audacieuse et savante poétesse seule, de l'invention du vers libre revendiquée par M. Gustave Kahn. Voilà donc bien et dûment tranché cette fois un problème d'histoire littéraire qui ne laissait pas d'avoir sa petite importance: le vers libre est né en 1881 dans la *Chronique parisienne*, périodique aujourd'hui éteint, mais dont on peut consulter la collection à la Bibliothèque nationale. ("Compte rendu d'*Intermèdes*," 509)[56]

A review that same year in *La Revue*, signed by the editorial board, also highlighted Krysinska's erudition: "Elle nous explique, dans une préface, les lois qu'elle s'est imposées ou plutôt les libertés qu'elle s'est accordées avec une science infiniment profonde de la langue et de l'histoire littéraire" (Collaborateurs de *La Revue*, "Livres et idées," 360). In a review of *Intermèdes* for the Russian journal *Viessy*, the poet René Ghil focused on the question of originality Krysinska raises in her preface and placed her before Kahn, at the leading edge of the free verse movement. Though known as a harsh critic of *vers libre*, Ghil admired "the arabesques, almost always elegant and flexible, drawn by her verses" (51).[57] This plasticity resonates with dance, producing "une synthèse mobile" (Mallarmé, *Œuvres complètes*, 2:170).[58] Ghil then shifted from visuality to musicality to distinguish Krysinska's technique from his own verbal instrumentation.[59]

The issue of Krysinska's contribution to modern *vers libre*, however, was far from resolved for her, as suggested by the text of "Les artistes maudits" she recycles in "Les cénacles artistiques et littéraires" (1904). To reclaim her role as an innovator, the self-described "jeune poétesse déserteur de la musique et des prosodies anciennes" juxtaposes once more the history of her *vers libre* in 1882 and "dans *Le Figaro* [1886], M. Moréas annonçant aux peuples qu'il venait d'inventer le vers libre!" ("Les cénacles," 484, 485). For Krysinska, the meaning of genius posed the ultimate problem.

In *La force du désir* (1905), Krysinska borrows the voice of the character Fabien, a fin-de-siècle aesthete, to debate, one last time, the distinction between talent and genius: "Un mot dont on mésuse . . . est le mot *talent*. Il en résulte la division risible des œuvres en œuvres de *talent* et en œuvres de *génie*. Peut-on imaginer une œuvre de génie dépourvue de talent? Comment la connaîtrait-on pour telle, si elle n'était formulée avec talent, puisque le talent est la faculté de manifester dans sa forme propre un génie particulier" (177; emphasis and ellipses in original). In response to his interlocutor Hélène's comment about aesthetic judgment, Fabien adds: "à la moindre parcelle d'originalité reconnaissons le génie, par conséquent, le talent" (179). Another male character asks: "Mais à quel signe . . . reconnaître cette originalité inventive? Sera-ce à quelque réforme dans les lois qui régissent l'Art?" (179). To this, Fabien responds: "Point du tout . . . On la reconnaîtra donc, cette originalité, à l'effet de surprise agréable qu'elle apporte, surprise sans heurt, marquée d'un caractère d'opportunité comme de quelque chose qui aurait manqué si elle ne se fût jamais produite, qu'on eût été fâché de ne point connaître" (179–80; ellipses in original). This creative element of surprise echoes Krysinska's aesthetics of *vers libre* and the deeper way she wished for her originality to resonate among readers and find its place together with that of other creators: "Images, comparaisons imprévues, nouveauté du tour, inflexions inattendues qui vont émouvoir quelque coin indéfloré de nos facultés émotives. Tels sont, sommairement, les traits qui marquent les œuvres originales, au travers lesquelles nous percevons nettement une nature d'artiste, unique, et cependant apparentée malgré son indépendance à l'immortelle famille des créateurs" (180).

Imagine how Krysinska might have greeted the volume *Innovations poétiques et combats littéraires: Marie Krysinska* (2010, edited by Paliyenko, Schultz, and Whidden), following the international colloquium of 2008 in Paris on the centenary of her death. Surely she would have recognized that her œuvre has survived in all its complexity and, like the work of the other women featured in this book and still others yet to be recovered from the archives, will continue to shift from the margins to the center in shaping future accounts of French poetic history.

# Conclusion

When man assigned a gender to all things, he did not think that he was playing, but fancied that he had gained a deep insight. But at a late period, and even then only partially, he was led to admit the enormous extent of that mistake.

—FRIEDRICH NIETZSCHE,
*The Dawn of Day*

Men would not have insisted that creativity is a male prerogative unless women created—and unless men were afraid that women's creations would be taken seriously.

—CHRISTINE BATTERSBY,
*Gender and Genius*

That we have lost so many of women's creations in the context of a male-centered and male-authored literary tradition has become a commonplace of feminist criticism. That we find compelling evidence of women's contributions within the same context is the paradox left unexamined by a feminocentric approach to the past, which unwittingly maintains a separate female canon. Recovering women as creators requires a paradigm shift in the way we think about the untold history of genius because the gender binary does not allow us to account for the multiplicity of voices women have expressed as artists, writers, and thinkers across the centuries. Poetic production during the nineteenth century in France raises precisely this issue.

For well over 150 years, silence has surrounded most of the women who led this surge of creativity in France, apart from Marceline Desbordes-Valmore, whose legacy was constructed to signify the century's "poésie féminine." As shown in *Genius Envy*, the dearth of women in traditional histories of this period in French literature can be read much more productively from the perspective of the discourses that constituted their reception. Though theorists and critics had long gendered genius as masculine, the question of its source resurfaced by the start of the nineteenth century. New findings about human reproduction unsettled the assumed maleness of genius, yet left open to debate whether such creative power was blind to sex. In repeating the contradictions of medical science, however, the critical literature preserved evidence of women's contributions, which form the site of a revisionist discourse on genius and a fuller history of the French poetic past.

The deeper narrative that complicates the writing of French literary history involves the fascination generated by the upsurge of literary women in the early 1800s as well as by those who won recognition for their poetic originality across the century. By the 1840s, however, reception was mixed with scorn and even repulsion, suggesting a defensive stance on the part of critics. Most pronounced among male critics, this stance masked anxiety about women's expanding presence in the field of cultural production. The charge of "genius envy"—aimed at discrediting women's poetic work as unoriginal, if not pathologizing it as a form of psychological compensation with harmful physiological effects—anticipated phallic criticism à la Freud. Against the backdrop of this inherited narrative, however, individual women's creativity comes into greater relief, the more bold among them intervening in their own reception to contest the view that, in France, poetry was a man's art.

As I have shown, the rise of women writers during the Romantic era brought a number of poets into prominence, including those featured in this study: Desbordes-Valmore, Amable Tastu, Mélanie Waldor, Élisa Mercœur, Anaïs Ségalas, and Louise Colet. Praise from peers greeted these women, who were esteemed by poets of both genders and by critics for their original works. Sympathetic critics extolled them as "true" poets, but at times reduced a woman's poetic range by reading her life into her work, thus domesticating her writing as the expression of femininity. As a group, however, women provoked an entirely different response, with critics of the 1840s denigrating their poetry as the artless transcription of the female experience. Hostility toward the *bas-bleu poète* continued during the second part of the century, peaking in the 1870s. Some critics nevertheless remarked on the new paths women forged as poets, yet they still struggled to explain women's aesthetic and intellectual projects by using the traditional category of gender.

As seen in the chapters devoted to Malvina Blanchecotte, Louisa Siefert, Louise Ackermann, and Marie Krysinska, these later poets wrote back to their critics. They used poems and other paratextual material, including prefaces, correspondence, autobiographies, and journals, to intervene as critical readers of their own work. The complex projects these women developed and the discourses they engaged demonstrate that nineteenth-century women became more conscious of the need to distinguish their body of work from "la poésie féminine." This restrictive label did not convey an individual woman's creativity. None of these poets identified themselves as feminists, with Ackermann and Krysinska explicitly rejecting any association with the women's movement of their day. In this and other ways, they deftly avoided being made to fit a category. Poetic women's writings on topics ranging from aesthetics and human emotions, to philosophy, religion, and science, to social issues expose the sexual difference used to gender genius. The provocative interplay of feminine and masculine identifications seen in the works of women selected for this book developed more fully during the second half of the century. Women thought through their poetry in profoundly creative ways, challenging at the levels of voice, form, and content the way that maleness had been factored into originality.

Scholars today are less hobbled in their analysis of women's poetic production during nineteenth-century France than thinkers of the past who believed that genius had a sex. Thus, we can dispense with the dated notion of an inspired genius inflected with biological determinism, endorsing instead the modern view energized by scientific research. In recent decades, cognitive scientists studying various trajectories of high achievement have discerned the role of myelin, the white matter that wraps around neurons, which renders nerve conduction faster and more consistent. Myelin is universal and thus has no sex, class, or race. Increasingly seen as the key physiological factor that supports the development of exceptional creativity through deep and deliberate practice, myelin may help us understand how what is called "great talent" or "genius" develops, but it does not solve the mystery of genius's origins. There does not appear to be an all-inclusive formula for explaining greatness. Current insights in genetics support the view that "no one is genetically designed into greatness and few are biologically restricted from attaining it," David Shenk has observed (*Genius in All of Us*, 52). Rather than seeing genius as born or made, as a gift or as a process, there is ample evidence to understand its manifestation as the result of "genes interacting dynamically with environmental forces" (130). This evolution of thought, which Helvétius had in mind, invites us to read women back into French poetic history with even greater attention to their claim to the work of genius than Krysinska theorized.

To sustain the view that creative power is a divine inheritance is to believe "in sudden suggestions, so-called inspirations; as if the idea of a work of art, of poetry, the fundamental thought of a philosophy shone down from heaven like a ray of grace," Nietzsche writes (*Human, All-Too-Human*, 159). In the following fragment from *Human, All-Too-Human* (1878), he thinks beyond the genius paradigm of his time, though not beyond gender: "All great men were great workers, unwearied not only in invention but also in rejection, reviewing, transforming, and arranging" (160). Is this not precisely the critical thought foregrounded most energetically by Ackermann and Krysinska, but also displayed by Ségalas, Blanchecotte, and Siefert, and even by the Romantic era women who were less explicit in recording the stages of their creations? By examining the impact of culture on the canons of criticism, scholars can continue the work brought to light in *Genius Envy*. In women's poetic writing and in their writing about poetry and other reflections, genuinely creative work not only generates new forms and aesthetic ideas but also raises questions that reshape the way we think. "For theory, literature remains the horizon against which genius loses or acquires its worth," Ann Jefferson observes (*Genius in France*, 226).

Researchers will continue to refine our knowledge of the past with future archival findings, but works of originality will secure lasting value only if we reach for them and embrace their power to live on in the minds of their readers. Our age of digital humanities provides greater access to the literary archives across the globe without, however, re-creating the original context in which works were produced. Let us call for modern critical editions of women's complete poetic works, which will mark more concretely the way their writing circulated with men's, filling newspaper columns, almanacs, and keepsakes before being published in individual volumes, collected works, and anthologies. In this way, scholars can prepare a richer narrative for posterity. Indeed, an inclusive history of how French poetry evolved during the nineteenth century promises to shape understanding of why poetic expression in all its diversity matters.

# NOTES

## Introduction

Though the notes and bibliography refer to various printed editions of nineteenth-century sources, many of them are now available online through Gallica, the digital library of the Bibliothèque nationale de France, http://gallica.bnf.fr.

1. The marquis de Pastoret, responding to Louis XVIII (king of France from 1814 to 1824), quoted in Desbordes-Valmore, *Chefs-d'œuvre lyriques*, xxxiii.
2. Rousseau expands this footnote in *Lettre à d'Alembert sur les spectacles* (1758), arguing that, even with considerable education and effort, women cannot exhibit genius. In *Émile; ou, De l'éducation* (1762), he relates women's lack of genius to their makeup (*Œuvres*, 4:736–37).
3. In a speech of 21 February 1782 to the French Academy, Condorcet argued that, despite physical differences, the sexes share the same intellectual qualities ("Des avantages et des progrès des sciences"). His *Tableau historique des progrès de l'esprit humain* (1823) develops the argument that genius does not depend on muscles, but rather on mental acuity, which women, too, have displayed (437–39).
4. See "génie" in the *Dictionnaire de l'Académie française* (1762, 4th ed.), https://artfl-project.uchicago.edu/content/dictionnaires-dautrefois; to the meaning of "l'inclination ou disposition naturelle," synonymous with "talent," found in the first edition (1694), one finds added, "& qui appartient à l'esprit."
5. On this evolution, rooted in the eighteenth-century debate about the role of reason versus passion in creativity, see Jaffe, "The Concept of Genius"; and Jefferson, *Genius in France*, 1–15, 19–43.
6. On this development in Europe, see Mortier's *L'originalité*.
7. According to the *Oxford English Dictionary*, "It was by the Ger. writers of the 18th c. that the distinction between 'genius' and 'talent,' which had some foundation in Fr. usage, was sharpened into the strong antithesis which is now universally current, so that the one term is hardly ever defined without reference to the other. The difference between *genius*

and *talent* has been formulated very variously by different writers, but there is general agreement in regarding the former as the higher of the two, as 'creative' and 'original,' and as achieving its results by instinctive perception and spontaneous activity, rather than by processes which admit of being distinctly analyzed" (2nd ed., s.v. "genius").

8. Principal anthologies of French literature and/or poetry, both general and of the nineteenth century, as well as literary histories from the eighteenth century through the twentieth (La Porte, Petit de Julleville), nonetheless yield an inconsistent record. The number and the names of women included for a given century vary widely across the sources I consulted, precluding an accurate count. I observed an increase of women anthologized as poets beginning in the nineteenth century (Fère, Lachèvre, Lemerre, and Place and Vasseur). Yet, overall, the number of male poets greatly outweighs the female poets in anthologies and literary histories. On women's place in literary history, see Planté, "La place des femmes dans l'histoire littéraire," and chapter 2 in this book.

9. Jefferson's study *Genius in France* appeared shortly before this book went into production. In providing an incisive history of genius in France from the eighteenth century to the present, however, Jefferson focuses on its use in primarily male-authored texts, apart from her chapters on Staël's *Corinne*, 125–36, and Julia Kristeva's *Le génie féminin* (1999), 212–18.

10. Larnac cites from the 1804 *dictionnaire*, offered by Fortunée Briquet to Napoleon Bonaparte, that no cen-

tury had begun "avec un aussi grand nombre de femmes de lettres," adding that an almanac of women writers from the turn of the nineteenth century lists fifty-four poets on the leading edge of this unprecedented rise (*Histoire de la littérature féminine en France*, 166).

11. Both Hesse (*The Other Enlightenment*, 33–43) and Reid (*Des femmes en littérature*, 140–43) focus on prose in discussing the number of French women in print during and after the Revolution. In the *Bibliographie de la France* (available at http://gallica.bnf.fr), beginning with women's literary surge in the 1820s, one observes a steady rate of publication by poets, as many as twenty or more volumes in a given year. Even between 1840 and 1860, after the market for lyrical poetry fell, the numbers remained high, as suggested by the twenty-seven titles listed in 1857. The publication record was steady, though less robust, in the latter part of the century, with ten volumes on average per year.

12. In defining the "paratext" as "what enables a text to become a book and to be offered as such to its readers and, more generally, to the public," Genette adds spatial and temporal distinctions: the "peritext" (surrounding the text yet in the space of the same volume: the title, preface, epigraphs, notes, and the like) versus the "epitext" (around the text but outside the book, such as correspondence and private journals) (*Paratextes*, 1, 5).

## Chapter 1

1. The term, which originally referred to learned individuals of both sexes,

acquired a negative connotation (in English and French) in the eighteenth century in reference to literary women.

2. Latham traces Buffon's definition to a conversation in 1785 with Hérault de Séchelles ("Definition of Genius," 374).

3. Staël's statement recalls Poullain de la Barre's 1663 declaration, "l'esprit n'a point de sexe" (*Equality of the Sexes*, 84). Poullain de la Barre was "committed to the Cartesian premise that the self is the thinking subject, the mind, and that it is radically not body. From this it follows that the mind, this decorporealized self, has no sex and indeed can have no sex," Laqueur noted (*Making Sex*, 155). According to Las Cases, Napoleon recounted this incident to him (*Mémorial de Sainte-Hélène*, 141). Biographers have amplified the story. Herold maintains that Staël said this to Napoleon's butler (*Mistress to an Age*, 181), as does Cronin (*Napoleon Bonaparte*, 285), whereas P. Gautier suggests that Staël was speaking to Napoleon himself (*Napoleon Bonaparte*, 9n2). For Kete, the story is counterfeit (*Making Way for Genius*, 56).

4. Temperament was thought to derive from the four humors: phlegm (water), blood, gall or black bile (thought to be secreted by the kidneys and spleen), and choler (or yellow bile) secreted by the liver.

5. Cabanis, the first medical thinker to study intellectual activity from a biological standpoint, believed that the genitals exert the greatest influence on the brain (*Rapports du physique et du moral de l'homme*, 578).

6. On this theory in the early twentieth century, see Stockham, *Karezza*, 43, 100; and Pound, *Natural Philosophy of Love*, 205–19.

7. On Barry's discovery, see Paliyenko, "On the Physiology of Genius," 96–97.

8. A search on Gallica (http://gallica.bnf.fr) yields references to Barry from the late 1850s onward, including Virchow (1859), Giraud (1860), Robin (1873), Simpson (1874), Harris and Austen (1874), the entry on "fecundation" in *Dictionnaire encyclopédique des sciences médicales* (1877–89), Lusk (1885), and Geddes and Thomson (1892). Cf. Jacyna's perspective on Barry in "Moral Fibre."

9. See Woolf on Coleridge's statement (1 September 1832, in *Specimens of the Table Talk of S. T. Coleridge*, 1835), which depicted the great mind as "resonant and porous . . . naturally creative, incandescent and undivided" (*A Room of One's Own*, 98).

10. On medicine's authority in the nineteenth century, see Knibiehler and Fouquet, *La femme devant les médecins*, esp. 44–54, 83–87.

11. Thanks to Nathalie Charron Marcus for this reference.

12. In *De la littérature* (1800), Staël wavers on women's creative power by stating that, through their role in literary salons, women had inspired men to produce creative work, but had yet to assert their own literary influence (*Œuvres*, 1:230).

13. On Staël's defense of literary women, see the chapter in *De la littérature* that considers domestic virtue in relation to women's intellectual ambitions (*Œuvres*, 1:357).

14. In *De l'Allemagne* (1810), Staël does not sex genius (*Œuvres*, 1:81).

15. Constance de Salm wrote: "Ô femmes, c'est pour vous que j'accorde ma lyre! / . . . / Un siècle de justice à nos yeux vient de naître; / Femmes, soyez aussi ce que vous devez être"

263

(quoted in Planté, *Femmes poètes du XIX^e siècle*, 53).

16. See reference to "propriété littéraire" in *Bibliographie de la France* 41 (10 September 1811), 335–36, http://gallica.bnf.fr/ark:/12148/cb34348270x/date.r=Bibliographie+de+la+France.langFR.

17. See Porter, *Women's Vision*, 59–78; and Kete, *Making Way for Genius*, 48–72.

18. Larcher's *Le dernier mot sur les femmes*, 148, and Larcher and Martin's *Les femmes peintes par elles-mêmes*, 52, attribute to Staël this statement from Sophie Cottin's novel *Malvina* (1800): "Les femmes, n'ayant ni profondeur dans leurs aperçus, ni suite dans leurs idées, ne peuvent avoir de génie" (*Œuvres*, 2:88). In Larousse, the phrase is attributed to Sand (*Grand dictionnaire universel du dix-neuvième siècle*, s.v. "femme").

19. Freud presents this phrase as a spin on Napoleon's comment "politics is destiny" (reported by Goethe from a conversation with Bonaparte in 1808) in the *Standard Edition*, 11:189.

20. For references to physiognomy and anatomy, see Sand's *Voyage en Auvergne* (1829) in *Œuvres autobiographiques*, 826, 828, 829, 835.

21. Sandeau was Sand's lover; they wrote the novel *Rose et Blanche* (1831) together under the pseudonym J. Sand, from which Sand took her name.

22. Sand develops this theme in her first novel, *Indiana* (1832), and in her play *Gabriel* (1839).

23. On this analysis, see Terdiman, *Discourse/Counter-Discourse*, 15–18.

24. Born in Cuba and raised in Madrid, Spain, from which she fled with her family during the Napoleonic wars, the comtesse de Merlin (née Maria de las Mercedes) arrived in Paris in 1814.

A member of the literary elite, Merlin held a salon frequented by, among others, Sophie and Delphine Gay and Musset.

25. German physician Franz Joseph Gall had disseminated his pseudoneuroscience since 1819.

26. However, near the end of her career, in 1863, Sand expressed that Staël and Delphine Gay deserved entrance to the Académie française, which did not elect its first female member, Yourcenar, until 1980.

27. Two pages later, Sainte-Beuve expresses ambivalence: "Le sexe en masse ne deviendra jamais auteur, nous l'espérons bien" ("George Sand," 497).

28. A novel written in the form of a play, *Gabriel* was published in three installments in the *Revue des Deux Mondes* (1 July, 15 July, and 1 August 1839). Initially, Sand's protagonist performs the masculinity with which she was inculcated but then discovers that she was born female.

29. In the late eighteenth century, Lavater theorized that facial features reveal qualities of mind or character, postulating that expressive eyes and amply sized and nobly shaped foreheads are signs of genius (*Essays on Physiognomy*, 378–83).

30. In "To George Sand: A Desire" (1844), Browning portrays Sand as a "large-brained woman and large-hearted man" (*Poems*, 147).

31. In citing French women novelists of the Romantic era who took Staël as a model, Finch notes: "Women in the last third of the century cited Staël by name less frequently" (*Women's Writing*, 30). It is not surprising that Sand, chiefly a prose writer, was not a model for women seeking recognition as poets. Among those writing in the

second half of the century, only Ackermann mentions Sand: as an "enfant terrible" (*Pensées d'une solitaire* [1903], 28).

32. Desbordes-Valmore published her first text, the romance (or verse narrative) "Le billet," in *Le Journal Hebdomadaire* in 1807, the same year Staël published *Corinne*.

33. The *Bibliographie de la France* (http://gallica.bnf.fr) recorded the volume on 26 December 1818, but it was not available for purchase until January 1819.

34. In "À la poésie" (1818), Desbordes-Valmore identifies her heart as the source of her "chants douloureux" (*Œuvres poétiques*, 1:100).

35. *Les pleurs* was reprinted in Desbordes-Valmore, *Œuvres poétiques* (1973), 1:197–253.

36. For this poem's history, see Bertrand's commentary in Desbordes-Valmore, *Œuvres poétiques*, 1:356–57 and 2:818–20.

37. See Desbordes-Valmore's "Plus de chants" (1843; *Œuvres poétiques*, 2:503).

38. See "À. Madame A. Tastu" (*Œuvres poétiques*, 2:419–20); and Assa's article "Je n'ai pas eu le temps de consulter un livre."

39. In "Malheur à moi," Desbordes-Valmore links poetic inspiration to "l'accent qui vient des cieux" and in "À M. Alphonse de Lamartine" to the "voix d'en haut" (*Œuvres poétiques*, 1:207 and 1:225, respectively). In "À Mademoiselle Isaure Partarrieu," she refers to "mon front rêveur," the site of divinely inspired poetic reverie (2:567).

40. *Pauvres fleurs* and *Bouquets et prières* were reprinted in Desbordes-Valmore, *Œuvres poétiques* (1973), 2:373–441 and 2:443–503, respectively.

41. Sophie Gay "defended Germaine de Staël and her 1802 novel *Delphine* in the press," naming her own daughter, born in 1804, Delphine, as Morgan notes ("Sophie Gay," 228). *Delphine* is the story of a gifted woman, loved yet ultimately scorned by her male lover, in which Staël exposes "the double standards applied to men and women in all areas, but especially in those of public reputation and physical attractiveness," as Finch states in *Women's Writing*, 28.

42. On this, also see Morgan, "Death of a Poet."

43. See Mercœur's poem "Élégie" (1825), where respiratory symptoms forecast an early death (*Œuvres poétiques*, 19–20). On tuberculosis and its relationship to genius, see Munro, *Psycho-Pathology of Tuberculosis*, esp. 3–5, 17, 41–61; and Moorman, *Tuberculosis and Genius*, esp. the introduction and pages on Marie Bashkirtseff, 59–99.

44. The pre-Romantic eponymous heroïne of Staël's *Delphine* (1802) declares: "Le génie de la douleur est le plus fécond de tous" (*Œuvres*, 1:690), anticipating Musset's "La nuit de mai" (1835).

45. In the 1820s and '30s, genius had not yet been pathologized in the terms that Greenberg relates to Mercœur, quoting from the Larousse dictionary ("Le génie d'après les médecins: 'Le génie est une névrose, c'est-à-dire, une maladie nerveuse'"), which alludes to Moreau de Tours's 1859 *Psychologie morbide* ("Élisa Mercœur," 87).

46. Added to the original text by her mother, who edited Mercœur's 1843 *Œuvres poétiques*.

47. In a note on the same page, Waldor underscores that Babois's *Élégies maternelles* (first published in 1805) had appeared in a fourth edition.

48. Finch reads these lines literally ("Since you can love me"; *Women's Writing*, 29), whereas I understand from the verb *savoir* the idea of a *learned* capability.

49. Writing to Colet on 12 August 1846, Flaubert stated that whereas most women wrote to assuage their feelings because they lacked "un appétit désin-téressé du Beau," she was différent: "toi qui es née poète" (*Correspondance*, 1:296). See, by way of contrast, the artistic representation of Colet as a muse in Bergman-Carton, *Woman of Ideas in French Art*, 188–89.

50. Girardin's poetic work, however, circulated late into the century.

51. By then, Philippe Pinel's successor Jean-Étienne Dominique Esquirol had published his 1838 treatise on mental diseases. On early French psychiatry, see Goldstein, *Console and Classify*.

52. Regarding this development, see Coleman's *Biology in the Nineteenth Century*; Lesch's *Science and Medicine in France* on experimental physiology; and Jordanova's *Sexual Visions* on gender as a medical metaphor.

53. Both Adam's father and her first husband (La Messine) were doctors and likely sources.

54. See *Sex and Education: A Reply to Dr. E. H. Clarke's "Sex in Education,"* edited by Julia Ward Howe, in which his contemporaries, most of them women physicians, dispute his idea that intellectual study leads to females' physical degeneracy. For a late nineteenth-century account of the latter view, see the German neurologist Moebius's *De la débilité mentale physiologique chez la femme.*

55. The "woman question," Pyke explains, "refers to the nineteenth-century debate about whether the rights and freedoms available to men should be extended to women" ("Education and the 'Woman Question,'" 154).

56. Bonheur was the first woman artist to receive this distinction since the award's establishment by Napoleon Bonaparte in 1802. On this occasion, see Klumpke, *Rosa Bonheur*, 172–73.

57. "Éducation maternelle: À propos d'une lecture de l'Odyssée," originally published under the title "L'Odyssée" in *Cours Familier de Littérature* 4 (1857), was collected with other *entretiens* from the periodical, covering the years 1856–69, in the posthumous volume *Souvenirs et portraits* (1871). On 24 June 1848, Lamartine had lost his position in the provisional government of the Second Republic, which he had helped to establish and had led since 24 February 1848. From that point until his death in 1869, he took up writing again, yet struggled to repay his debts.

58. Lamartine's essay on Staël first appeared in *Cours Familier de Littérature* 26 (1868): 152–54.

59. Battersby expresses the double gendering of Romantic genius thus: "[I]f the male genius was 'feminine' this merely proved his cultural superiority. Creativity was displaced *male* procreativity: male sexuality made sublime" (*Gender and Genius*, 3; emphasis in original).

60. On the depopulation crisis, which was provoked not by voluntary sterility, as some medical authorities maintained, but by infant mortality, see Offen, "Depopulation, Nationalism, and Feminism in Fin-de-Siècle France," 652–53.

61. Brain science advanced rapidly after the neurological clinician Broca's 1862 discovery of the speech production center of the brain. This was followed

by Darwin's 1872 treatise on emotional responses and facial expressions and by studies of the nervous system in relation to hysteria by Charcot and Freud, among others, such as Lombroso and Pierre Janet, who developed the link between human psychology and neurology (in the lineage of Pinel, Esquirol, and Moreau de Tours).

62. See the original passage in *Un prêtre marié*, 38.

63. Darwin adapted the view of Galton, who traced a son's "intellectual superiority" to the mother, which complicates the so-called male inheritance of genius (*Hereditary Genius*, 62).

64. In 1876, Oskar Hertwig used cell theory and advances in microscopy and staining to demonstrate that fertilization occurs when the sperm penetrates the egg.

65. The English and French translations of Lombroso's *L'uomo di genio* (1889), in 1891 and 1903, respectively, differ in length, which raises the problem of partial translations and mistranslations, addressed by Rafter and Gibson in their English translation of Lombroso and Ferrero's *The Female Offender*, retitled *Criminal Woman, the Prostitute and the Normal Woman*.

66. This passage, from the French translation of Lombroso's 1889 study on the man of genius, is missing in the English translation. Nordau disputes Lombroso's association of genius with epilepsy (*Psycho-physiologie du génie et du talent*, 86, 89). On the psycho-physiology of genius, also see Winiarski, "Morituri: Essai sur le génie."

67. In their study of female criminals, whom they considered, along with degenerates, to be a biological regression to savagery, Lombroso and Ferrero tie women's lack of intellectual development and genius to their reproductive role (*Criminal Woman*, 85–87).

68. On how the nineteenth-century scientific account of male versus female reproductive physiology reproduces gender stereotypes, see Martin, "The Egg and the Sperm." Warm thanks to Sharon Johnson for this reference.

69. Writing to Flaubert in 1867, Sand questions the relevance of anatomy to gender identity: "[I]l y a ceci pour les gens forts en anatomie: *il n'y a qu'un sexe. Un homme et une femme, c'est si bien la même chose, que l'on ne comprend guère les tas de distinctions et de raisonnements subtils dont se sont nourries les sociétés sur ce chapitre-là*" (*Correspondance entre Sand et Flaubert*, 62; emphasis in original).

70. Simonton states: "[I]t is actually possible to use Darwin's idea of sexual selection to argue that both men and women might evolve the same capacity for creative genius. . . . [M]ate choice is working on both the male and the female simultaneously and equally, because these assets are of comparable value to the reproductive success of their offspring" (*Origins of Genius*, 217, 218).

## Chapter 2

1. Boutin similarly notes that the various words designating poetic women attest to "the ongoing indeterminate construction of the poetess. For many male critics, the grammatical uncertainty of the word *poète* paralleled the very untenability of women writing poetry" ("Inventing the 'Poétesse,'" 4).

2. In a related context, Vincent restates Svetlana Boym's analysis of the term

"poetess": "The word's suffix highlights an excess that is also a lack: the term poetess plays into the prescribed notion of a women's poetry that is excessively emotional and lacking in structure" (*Romantic Poetess*, xvii). In an essay in 1841, Sand uses the term while referring to worker-poet Marie Pape-Carpantier: "Une poétesse (si nous pouvons employer ce mot qui mériterait d'être dans le Dictionnaire, et qui nous paraît aussi nécessaire maintenant que celui de poète), une poétesse justement célèbre, madame Tastu, a bien voulu servir d'introductrice à sa compagne" ("Poésies, par des ouvriers," 253). That Sand overlooked the fact that the term was in the dictionary (first recorded, in 1798, in the *Dictionnaire de l'Académie française*, 5th ed.) suggests its limited usage. The entry from the sixth edition of the same dictionary (1835) states regarding "poétesse": "Il est peu usité," proposing instead "femme poète" (http://dvlf .uchicago.edu/mot/po%C3%A9tesse).

3. In "Femininity" (1933), Freud admits that "what constitutes masculinity or femininity is an unknown characteristic which anatomy cannot lay hold of," but nevertheless he asserts the effect of penis envy on women's mental life (*Standard Edition*, 22:114). A few pages later, he writes: "It seems that women have made few contributions to the discoveries and inventions in the history of civilization; there is, however, one technique which they may have invented—that of plaiting and weaving" (132). Freud relates this to shame, which he associates with "the pubic hair that conceals the [female] genitals" (132).

4. For other titles, see Lachèvre, *Bibliographie sommaire de l'Almanach des Muses*.

5. On the novel's rise, see M. Cohen, *The Sentimental Education of the Novel*.

6. Higgins, who examines how British literary magazines constructed the male Romantic genius, argues that "studying the social construction of genius makes us aware of the complex set of mechanisms—particularly the valorizing activities of critics, academics, publishers and so on—by which long-term literary reputation is secure. This, in turn, sheds light on the ways it which it has been denied to certain groups of authors (e.g., female or working-class poets)" (*Romantic Genius and the Literary Magazine*, 9).

7. In *Physiologie du poète* (1842), illustrated by Daumier, Texier likens the explosion of women writers to an infestation, the "dixième muse" propagating wildly like mushrooms, thriving uncultivated on the front pages of newspapers (118).

8. The *Revue des Deux Mondes* boasted five thousand readers by mid-century and can be compared to the *New York Review of Books*, as Gray suggests (*Rage and Fire*, 84).

9. Joly similarly argues that men of genius have few progeny (*Psychologie des grands hommes*, 53). Bach, then, who fathered twenty children (only ten of whom survived into adulthood), is an exception.

10. The label "Sappho" also associates these poets with sterile women and nonmothers.

11. Desbordes-Valmore nearly immediately rejoined with a poem, "À M. Gaschon de Molènes," which exposes the critic's blind spot. Molènes's diatribe also aggravated Colet and Ségalas; see Jackson, *Louise Colet*, 101–3.

12. The loi Falloux, passed in 1850 under the Second Republic, mandated free-

dom of education while restoring the Catholic Church's influence on the curriculum. The law's provisions included primary schools for girls in villages with more than eight hundred inhabitants.

13. Christine de Pisan, Jeanne d'Arc, Sévigné, Deshoulières, Genlis, Staël, Cottin, and Dufrénoy are among the women.

14. This poem first appeared in *Bouquets et prières* (1843).

15. "Une lettre de femme" opens Desbordes-Valmore's *Poésies inédites*: "Les femmes, je le sais, ne doivent pas écrire, / J'écris pourtant, / Afin que dans mon cœur au loin tu puisses lire / Comme en partant" (*Œuvres poétiques*, 2:506). Often cited as evidence of resistance, this poem, beginning the section titled "Amour," treats a contemporary issue. Other poems from her posthumous collection expand this diversity. See, for example, "La jeune esclave," "Le drapeau tricolore," "Sur l'inondation de Lyon," "Au poète prolétaire," "Dans la rue," "Les prisons et les prières," and "Au citoyen Raspail." Further, poems such as "Les roses de Saadi," "Un ruisseau de la Scarpe," and "Rêve intermittent d'une nuit triste" display prosodic control. On Desbordes-Valmore's hybrid production, see Planté, "Marceline Desbordes-Valmore"; Schultz, *Gendered Lyric*, 43–80; and Boutin, *Maternal Echoes*, 156–66, and "Inventing the 'Poétesse.'"

16. On Desbordes-Valmore and her male readers (Dumas, Sainte-Beuve, Baudelaire, Verlaine, and Montesquiou), see Boutin, *Maternal Echoes*, 30–48. "Since their readings of her text appear heavily invested in their own reflected maternal femininity," argues Boutin, "the object of

study, the Valmorean text, is lost to the specular logic of the reading" (48).

17. Hugo, the subject of the first chapter, dominates the volume, which is largely devoted to male poets, much as he did the poetic landscape of the nineteenth century until his death in 1885. Desbordes-Valmore and Girardin are the only women among the twenty-three poets included in Barbey d'Aurevilly's study.

18. Though I have not located the original reference in Corneille, Maury quotes the same text in *Figures littéraires*, 299.

19. In "The Paths to the Formation of Symptoms," Freud compares the formation of symptoms in the neuroses to artistic creativity (*Standard Edition*, 23:376).

20. Whereas one finds "une poète" in the 1723 *Dictionnaire historique de la langue française* without commentary, the entry on "poétesse" in the *Dictionnaire de l'Académie française* (5th ed., 1798) provides this gloss: "On dit de Sapho, de Deshoulières, qu'elles étoient Poëtes; mais on ne dit pas *La Poëte Sapho*: ce seroit le cas de dire, *La poétesse. . . .* On l'évite" (http://dvlf. uchicago.edu/mot/po%C3%A9tesse).

21. Lloyd relates Baudelaire's discussion of Desbordes-Valmore to his body of literary criticism, illuminating its ambiguities by treating "the physiological intensity of [his] reaction to art" along with the aesthetic concerns and questions about women as writers that his reading of her reveals ("The Demands of an Editor," 194). This discussion was the first iteration of the essay Baudelaire published in July 1861 in *La Revue Fantaisiste* and subsequently in the series *Réflexions sur quelques-uns de mes contemporains* (1861), reprinted in his *Œuvres complètes* (2:129–81).

22. See Schultz's chapter "Moving Statues: *Les Parnassiennes*" in her *Gendered Lyric*, 140–67.

23. Lemerre, *Anthologie*, vol. 1 (1887): Desbordes-Valmore, Tastu, Stern, Ackermann, Ségalas; vol. 2 (1887): Blanchecotte, Guyon; vol. 3 (1888): Siefert, Daudet; vol. 4 (1888): Mme Gustave Mesureur, Marie de Valandré, Alice de Chambrier, Hélène Vacaresco. Anthologies and collections of nineteenth-century French poetry, published in the early twentieth century, also integrated contributions by poets of both sexes; see works by Besson and des Essarts, Borel, Merlet, Mendès, Paraf, Pellissier, and Walch.

24. The French illuminists, traced to the philosopher Louis Claude de Saint-Martin, the playwright Antoine Fabre d'Olivet, and the economist Pierre-Samuel du Pont de Nemours, viewed the poet as a prophet-seer.

25. Rimbaud jotted down a line of poetry by Desbordes-Valmore ("Prends-y garde, ô ma vie absente!") on the back of the manuscript of "Patience." On this, see Whidden's notes in Rimbaud, *Complete Works*, 452n21, 453n22; Bivort, "Les 'vies absentes' de Rimbaud et de Marceline Desbordes-Valmore"; and Chovet, "Un faux Rimbaud." See also Schultz, *Gendered Lyric*, 219; and Boutin, *Maternal Echoes*, 43.

26. See Rimbaud's letter of 24 May 1870 to Banville in *Œuvres complètes*, 236–37.

27. Rimbaud's prophecy is the main title of Blanc's book devoted to the recovery of women's history as artists, *Elle sera poète, elle aussi: Les femmes et la création artistique* (1991), the publication of which coincided with the centenary of his death. See Schultz on Rimbaud's "feminism" (*Gendered Lyric*, 175–76).

28. On this, see Paliyenko, *Mis-reading the Creative Impulse*, 35–61.

29. See Broca's 1861 study of brain size, *Sur le volume et la forme du cerveau*, 1–16.

30. On the late nineteenth-century medical theory of female cerebral inferiority and intellectual women's resistance, see Finn, "Physiological Fictions and the Fin-de-Siècle Female Brain."

31. On these popular novelists' uneven legacy, see Constans, *Ouvrières des lettres*.

32. On the extreme hostility toward literary women in the latter part of the century, see Mesch, *The Hysteric's Revenge*.

33. Barbey d'Aurevilly refutes his contemporaries' portrayal of Staël as a masculinized *bas-bleu* by distinguishing her womanly genius (*Les bas-bleus*, 3).

34. See Baudelaire's "Conseils aux jeunes littérateurs" (1846; *Œuvres complètes*, 2:19).

35. Gilbert and Gubar use the rhetorical question "Is a pen a metaphorical penis?" to introduce their study of nineteenth-century literary culture, *The Madwoman in the Attic*, 3.

36. See Chaitin's introduction to *Cultural Wars and Literature in the French Third Republic*, 1–19.

37. Females' education did not include math, science, Latin, or Greek; see Gale, "Education, Literature and the Battle over Female Identity," 105–6, 110.

38. The women selected were Sophie Gay, Valandré, Blanchecotte, Ségalas, Girardin, Mesureur, Desbordes-Valmore, Isabelle Roche-Guyon, and Siefert.

39. He mentions Julie Fertiault, Siefert, Judith Gautier, Mme Auguste Penquer, Lucie Delarue-Mardrus, Nicolette Hennique, and Anna de Noailles.

40. This radical group, advocating a return to the monarchy, aimed to

overthrow the parlimentary Third Republic.

41. This was the pseudonym of Mme Henri de Régnier, née de Heredia.

42. Vivien was British and an open lesbian (she was the American writer Natalie Clifford Barney's love); Gérard d'Houville's father was the Cuban-born José-Maria de Heredia; Delarue-Mardrus had affairs with women her entire life; the Paris-born Noailles was of Greco-Romanian origins.

43. Chateaubriand's *Le génie du christianisme* (1802) alleges a deleterious feminine influence in post-revolutionary France to account for *le vague des passions* that tormented the male Romantic genius (272–73). This "vague des passions" was the nascent *mal du siècle* that Musset later defined in *La confession d'un enfant du siècle* (1836).

44. See Schultz's analysis of the appropriation of the female voice for masculinity in the Romantic lyric (*Gendered Lyric*, x–xi, 21–42).

45. Séché became the literary editor for Nelson Press, which published numerous anthologies.

46. By grouping Colet, Blanchecotte, Ackermann, and Siefert as late Romantics, other critics place them, together with Penquer, Isabelle Guyon, Nina de Villard, and Mélanie Bourotte, on the fringes of the Parnassian movement. Compare the accounts by Somoff and Marfée, "Les muses du Parnasse"; and Schultz, *Gendered Lyric*, 145–67.

47. Other poets included are Gabrielle d'Altenheym, Pauline de Flaugergues, Louise Bertin, Hermance Lesguillon, Waldor, Eugénie de Guérin, Antoinette Quarré, and Ondine Valmore (Chichmanoff, "Étude critique," 95).

48. Gérard published *Les muses françaises* (1943), a tribute to French women's

poetic work across the centuries, introducing the work of the poets she selected for the anthology with a prefatory poem of her own.

49. The group includes Penquer, Judith Gautier, Augusta Holmès, Simone Arnaud, Mesureur, Émilie Genevraye, Louise Michel, Bourotte, Madeline Lépine, Emmadi Rienzi, Ida Rocha, the baronne de Baxe, Mme de Montgoméry, and Vega (Mme Visme). In a final grouping of contemporary poets of foreign origin who published in French, Chichmanoff lists Marguerite Coppin (Belgium); Isabelle Kaiser, Mme de Gasparin, Mme de Pressensé, Mme Melley, and Alice de Chambrier (all from Switzerland); Hélène Vacaresco (Romania); Tola Dorian (Russia); and the baronne de Baye (Turkey).

50. Larnac provides the directory of the Société des gens de lettres from 1928 to 1929 as more evidence. He notes regarding the early twentieth century, "Jamais il n'y eut, en France, un aussi grand nombre de femmes-auteurs," which he attributes to their access to education acquired in the late nineteenth century (*Histoire de la littérature féminine en France*, 223).

51. In 1929, Woolf wrote the phrase in the heading above about the "enormous body of masculine opinion to the effect that nothing could be expected of women intellectually" (*A Room of One's Own*, 54, 55).

52. Schopenhauer's works began to appear in French translation in the early 1860s. His influence has been widespread and lasting: Auguste Burdeau's 1882 translation of *The World as Will and Representation* (*Le monde comme volonté et comme représentation*) saw its ninth edition in 1966.

53. Bertaut's explanation is not supported by statistics and is contradicted by the critical literature showing how closely many men of the time read this production.

54. He was the brother of Remy de Gourmont, an influential Symbolist poet and critic.

55. Uzanne claimed that, by 1893, women authors numbered 2,133, including 1,211 novelists and authors of children's books, 217 authors of pedagogy, 280 poets, and 237 newspaper writers (*La femme à Paris*, 164).

56. Gourmont examines more closely those he considers more artistic: Noailles, d'Houville, Marie Dauguet, Picard, and Vivien, among others. He treats Laurent Évrard as the exception and compares her artistry and intellectualism to Mallarmé's.

57. Contemporary French women's poetic writing exceeds this book's scope. On their production, see two anthologies by Bishop, *Contemporary French Women Poets* and *Women's Poetry in France*; and Shapiro, *French Women Poets*.

58. See Balzac's disparaging portrayal of the poetic woman in *Illusions perdues* (written between 1837 and 1843) in the chapter "Deux poètes," 63–66. Also see his allusion to women writers' surge in the opening pages of *La muse du département*: "Cette lèpre sentimentale a gâté beaucoup de femmes qui, sans leurs prétentions au génie, eussent été charmantes" (*Œuvres complètes de M. Honoré de Balzac*, 358).

59. Bertrand published a revised edition in 2010.

60. Larnac proposes his literary history as a corrective to those by La Porte (1769), Genlis (1811), and Jacquinet (1886).

61. Moulin's volume on the twentieth century appeared in 1963.

62. Boutin comments on the double meaning of the French term "poésie féminine," "which means explicitly poetry by women, but implicitly poetry that exalts femininity" ("Inventing the 'Poétesse,'" 6). "Poésie féminine" was established as a category of analysis during the latter part of the nineteenth century, which nuances Boutin's argument that the term gained prominence "after the publication of Jeanine Moulin's anthologies in the 1960s" (6).

63. In prefacing *Huit siècles de poésie féminine* (1975), which reproduces the record from her two-volume *La poésie féminine* and adds information on forty contemporary poets, Moulin responds to this criticism. By "poésie féminine," she means poetry by women; her selections represent the formal beauty and the life of the mind cultivated by women across the centuries. For Moulin, the word "féminitude," resonant with the term "négritude," which valorizes black culture, better captures her attempt to highlight women's particular world of ideas (7).

64. Simpson writes: "The women of France must have received very little encouragement to be poets. The situation has been changing in recent years, and today there are female poets in France who are knowledgeable, adventurous, interesting. But the poetry being written today is outside the scope of this book" (*Modern Poets of France*, xx).

65. Ezell exposes the "evolutionary narrative of women's literary history, structured on a 'great woman' or 'turning point' linear model," which cannot account for differences among women

writers (*Writing Women's Literary History*, 61).

66. Appendixes list other poetic women and their wide-ranging corpus, and others treat worker and popular poetry and the place of women in French literary history. The second edition (2010) amplifies the critical literature by including more recent Anglo-American scholarship.

67. Shapiro's 2008 bilingual anthology presents fifty-six poets to show women's range and depth across nine centuries. The section on the nineteenth century includes Babois, Desbordes-Valmore, Tastu, Girardin, Mercœur, Colet, and Ackermann, but unfortunately not Blanchecotte, Siefert, or Krysinska.

68. Lloyd similarly presents literary women as "[l]ess divisible into schools and movements than their male counterparts, more varied in their interests and less predictable in their techniques," further arguing, "it is only when their voice is fully reinstated into the period that we will begin to understand many of those ongoing conversations that give the nineteenth century its particular dynamism" ("Nineteenth Century," 145).

## Chapter 3

1. Danahy argues that modeling among women novelists was more positive than the conflict-laden Oedipal influence among male writers theorized by Harold Bloom (*Feminization of the Novel*, 199).

2. Heffernan describes how the book industry expanded after article 11 of the Déclaration des droits de l'homme et du citoyen (1789) established freedom of the press: "As early as 1823, for example, the 81 Parisian printing workshops in existence were using over 600 presses and had a combined workforce of more than 3000. Five years later, the Parisian publishing industry was producing nearly 6000 new titles a year out of a total for the whole country of 7600" ("Rogues, Rascals and Rude Books," 93).

3. Bergman-Carton notes a similar effect regarding the French journals for women, which more than doubled between 1800 and 1845 (*Woman of Ideas in French Art*, 29).

4. In a letter of 1828 to a cousin, Babois ties the discovery of her poetic voice to writing about her child's death (Montferrand, *Biographie des femmes auteurs*, 121–28). On Dufrénoy and Babois, see Planté, *Femmes poètes du XIXᵉ siècle*, 67–81 and 83–95, respectively; and Boutin and Paliyenko, "Nineteenth-Century French Women Poets," 80–81.

5. For an introduction to Ulliac-Trémadeure, see Finch, *Women's Writing*, 101–6.

6. On Desbordes-Valmore's reception through the 1950s, see Jasenas, *Marceline Desbordes-Valmore*.

7. See Boutin, *Maternal Echoes*, 10–11. On the public disapproval for Desbordes-Valmore's early indiscretions, also see Ambrière, *Le siècle des Valmore*, 1:270–73; and Jenson, *Trauma and Its Representations*, 124–29.

8. On the poetics of femininity in selected elegies, see Porter, "Poetess or Strong Poet?"

9. Alibert, a physician to Louis XVIII, then Charles X, first treated Desbordes-Valmore in 1806; see Desbordes-Valmore, *Œuvres poétiques*, 1:258.

10. This passage comes from an undated letter that was appended as a note in

Sainte-Beuve's 1833 review of Desbordes-Valmore's *Les pleurs*, published in the *Revue des Deux Mondes*. Warm thanks to Aimée Boutin for verifying that the letter was first republished in Sainte-Beuve's *Portraits contemporains*, 359–61.

11. On Deshoulières's lyrical output (madrigals, ballads, and idylls) and writing for the theater, see Shapiro, *French Women Poets*, 302–15.

12. Founded by Claude-Sixte Sautreau de Marsy in 1765, the annual published poets of both genders. On women's contributions from 1789 to 1819, see Seth, "Les muses de l'*Almanach*."

13. Ruskin coined the expression in 1856 to describe the effect of "violent feelings," which "produce in us a falseness in all our impressions of external things," together with "the habit of considering this fallacy as eminently a character of poetical description" (*Modern Painters*, 160, 161).

14. On the fictions of Sappho in nineteenth-century France, England, and Russia, which echo the topos of fatal passion associated with the Corinne myth, see Vincent, *Romantic Poetess*, 53–71.

15. Vincent suggests that Desbordes-Valmore, like Tastu, modeled herself on Dufrénoy, though there is no explicit statement on this in Desbordes-Valmore's creative or epistolary writing (*Romantic Poetess*, 58).

16. Boutin documents only one contemporary reference in her introduction to a modern edition of *Veillées* (ix).

17. In 1801, Catherine Desbordes fled to the Antilles from France with Marceline, then fourteen, to locate a rich cousin in order to reverse her family's financial problems. They docked at Saint Barthélémy, the setting of *Sarah*,

because of the slave revolt in Guadeloupe at that time. Once in Guadeloupe, they discovered that the cousin had died, leaving no inheritance. After her mother succumbed to yellow fever, Marceline made her way back to France alone.

18. See Desbordes-Valmore's poems about colonial mores (for example, "Le réveil créole") and slavery ("Chant d'une jeune esclave," "L'esclave," and "La jeune esclave") (*Œuvres poétiques*, 2:585, 1:116, 2:592, and 2:615, respectively). On the colonial themes in *Les veillées des Antilles*, see Boutin, "Colonial Memory"; Jenson, "Myth, History, and Witnessing"; Kadish, "*Sarah* and Anti-Slavery"; Paliyenko, "Returns of Marceline Desbordes-Valmore's Repressed Colonial Memory"; and Boutin's introduction to *Les veillées des Antilles*.

19. This is the title of Bertrand's study of social themes in Desbordes-Valmore.

20. Sainte-Beuve imagined that Tastu's sentimental expression would enjoy discreet glory, which he considered the most beautiful for a woman poet (*Vie, poésies et pensées de Joseph Delorme*, 161).

21. In "L'étoile de la lyre," the poet describes herself as "pensive" and laments, "Astre consolateur, ma voix faible et craintive / Ne se mêlera point à tes nobles concerts" (*Poésies complètes*, 10). In "À M. Victor Hugo," the speaker refers to her "lyre impuissante," which cannot soar like an eagle like her peer's lofty poetic expression (69).

22. For other examples of this motif in Tastu's poetry, see Finch, *Women's Writing*, 97–101.

23. On Tastu's erudition, see Boutin, "Shakespeare, Women, and French Romanticism."

24. Tastu's gift was encouraged by her parents, especially her mother, whom Sainte-Beuve described as having "une faculté poétique naturelle et remarquablement élevée" ("Poètes et romanciers," 355). In the narrative poem "Le cabinet de Robert Estienne" (1829), addressed to the Académie française, Tastu invokes the invention of the printing press and the sixteenth-century printer Estienne, the first to publish the Bible divided into standardized, numbered verses. A dialogue between the printer and his wife, also known as Joseph and Amable Tastu, suggests that the democratizing potential of print culture in the early nineteenth century was not fully realized in a society that did not value women as poets (*Poésies nouvelles*, 213–24).

25. This could also be a nod to Tastu's husband, the edition's publisher.

26. See the untitled opening poem (which alludes to the revolution of 1830, which ended the Bourbon Restoration), "La liberté," and "La France et l'industrie" (*Poésies complètes*, 1–3, 16–18, 22–26).

27. Tastu maintained a presence in keepsakes well into the 1840s, however, and reprints of her complete works appeared late into the nineteenth century.

28. See Schapira ("Amable Tastu"), who compares Tastu's decision to abandon poetry with Girardin's. Tastu placed her pedagogical writing in a tradition established by Genlis, Jeanne-Louise-Henriette Campan, Elizabeth Charlotte Pauline Guizot, Dufrénoy, Claire Élisabeth Jeanne Gravier de Vergennes de Rémusat, Albertine-Adrienne Necker-Saussure, and Desbordes-Valmore, among others. On Tastu's prose, especially *Éducation maternelle: Simples leçons d'une mère à ses enfants* (1836), her most successful book for children, which saw six editions by 1869, see Poussard-Joly, *Madame Tastu*, 107–21.

29. *Journal des Femmes* was a Christian newspaper that called for civil rights and education for women; it became a ladies' fashion journal. On its history (1832–36) and cautious feminist agenda under Fanny Richomme's leadership, see Sullerot, *Histoire de la presse féminine*, 164–84.

30. In 1837, the utopian socialist Fourier defined the principle of feminism ("doctrine visant à l'extension du rôle des femmes") but did not coin the word (http://www.cnrtl.fr). The noun first appeared in an 1871 medical thesis to describe the feminizing effects of tuberculosis on young males, "une sorte de caractère féminin que nous appellerons le FÉMINISME" (Faneau de la Cour, *Du féminisme et de l'infantilisme*, 7). The word "féministes," first used by Dumas fils in *L'homme-femme* (1872), refers to women's rights: "Les *féministes*, passez-moi ce néologisme, disent, à très bonne intention d'ailleurs: Tout le mal vient de ce qu'on ne veut pas reconnaître que la femme est l'égale de l'homme et qu'il faut lui donner la même éducation et les mêmes droits qu'à l'homme, l'homme abuse de sa force, etc., etc." (91; emphasis in original). On this lexical history, see Fraisse, *Muse de la raison*, 198–99; on the term's usage from the 1870s onward, see Offen, *European Feminisms*, 19.

31. See Chauvet, who considered Tastu's 1829 volume less inspired ("*Chroniques de France*, par Mme Amable Tastu").

32. In 1910, Souriau wondered why a woman "traitée d'égale à égal par Chateaubriand, Béranger, Victor Hugo,

275

Lamartine et Sainte-Beuve, a pu disparaître progressivement dans l'ombre, descendre dans les limbes de la littérature" ("Grandeur et décadence de Mme Tastu," 116).

33. In a letter of 7 November 1832 to her husband, Desbordes-Valmore expressed delight in having met Tastu, who agreed to market her work (*Lettres de Marceline Desbordes à Prosper Valmore*, 1:18).

34. Allusions to financial difficulties abound in Desbordes-Valmore's correspondence. On her search for a publisher for *Les pleurs*, for example, see her letter of 23 December 1833 to Jean-Baptiste Gergerès (*Lettres inédites*, 47–49).

35. According to Vincent, Tastu was "no doubt the best-known French woman poet in Britain" during the Romantic era (*Romantic Poetess*, 91).

36. These lines come from the fifteenth sonnet (chapter 26) of *La vita nuova* in which Dante Alighieri analyzes his own love poems to Beatrice in exploring poetic language and structure (76).

37. See the comment by Adélaïde Aumand, Mercœur's mother, in *Œuvres poétiques*, cxviin2. Aumand was single and abandoned her baby on the steps of the orphanage in Nantes three days after the child's birth on 24 June 1809, with a note naming her Élisa. Aumand returned to claim her child on 21 April 1811. Élisa was given the last name Mercœur after a street in Nantes, which Aumand also adopted. On this, see L. Séché, "Élisa Mercœur," 188.

38. On the support Mercœur received, see L. Séché, "Élisa Mercœur," 190–92; and Greenberg, *Uncanonical Women*, 18–19, 24–26.

39. Crapelet traced this statement to a letter of 9 October 1827 that Lamartine, then in Florence, had sent to a fellow writer (Mercœur, *Poésies*, xii). That this missive was not published in Lamartine's *Correspondance* lends weight to his later claim that it was apocryphal. Writing to the comte de Sercey on 21 February 1829, Lamartine was upset that Delphine Gay and her mother had circulated it, stating, "je n'ai lu un vers de cette demoiselle" (*Correspondance*, 3:139). It is not clear why Lamartine did not refer to Mercœur by name.

40. In a tribute shortly after Mercœur's death on 7 January 1835, Waldor wrote: "Il fallut renoncer à la poésie, faire de la prose pour la vendre et pour vivre. Elle fit de la prose avec courage, avec persévérance, mais bientôt sa santé s'altéra" ("Élisa Mercœur," 74).

41. On 15 April 1835, Desbordes-Valmore wrote to Waldor about Mercœur's death (*Correspondance intime*, 1:79–80). They initiated a financial campaign to underwrite the posthumous publication of Mercœur's poetry.

42. In opening the public session of the Académie des sciences, arts et belles-lettres de Besançon on 24 August 1826, M. Clerc, the president, so described poetry (4).

43. See Mirecourt's account, *Madame Anaïs Ségalas*, 37.

44. On this, see A. Séché, *Les muses françaises*, 2:335–36.

45. Waldor and Ségalas also worked for the *Cabinet de Lecture* (1829–46), a literary and political newspaper, exchanging in this context "des lettres rimées" (Croze, "Une héroïne romantique," 174).

46. In "À nos poëtes morts," Delphine Gay is the only woman among the poets Ségalas memorializes: "Tu partis, ô Delphine! ô muse aux blonds cheveux!" (*Nos bons parisiens*, 200).

47. Although the Desbordes-Valmore archive contains no reference to Ségalas, Waldor dedicates "La Mexicaine" to Ségalas and also cites her in the epigraph to "Le retour," the former tied to the colonial other, the latter to maternity (*Poésies du cœur*, 17, 179).

48. Married since 1822, Waldor had a daughter with her military husband, who was often absent from Paris.

49. See Beaunier's 1913 account of Waldor's incurable passion for Dumas (*Visages de femmes*, 298–305).

50. Lucot re-creates scenes from their love story in *Dumas: Père et fils*.

51. Waldor destroyed most of her letters to Dumas, according to Schopp, who edited their correspondence; on eleven letters she wrote to him, see Dumas, *Lettres*, 19, 20.

52. Mechanical reproduction, facilitated by the printing press and the development of lithography and photography in the nineteenth century, changed the impact of works of art on the public, as Benjamin discusses in "The Work of Art," 218–19, 221.

53. Despite obvious thematic overlap, Sainte-Beuve made no reference to Waldor's piece.

54. Vincent notes: "By distancing Desbordes-Valmore from all the schools and from art itself, the critic conceals the fact that her lyric persona is highly crafted and dissimulates the unsavory reality that she writes for money" (*Romantic Poetess*, 125).

55. Eugénie de Pradel pays homage to "La pléiade féminine, / De la France doux trésor," naming "La romantique *Valdor* [*sic*]" along with Delphine Gay, Salm, Desbordes-Valmore, Mercœur, Ségalas, and Tastu ("À M. le Directeur du Citateur Féminin," 41). A female critic, writing in 1835, considered Waldor's *Poésies du cœur* a superior volume of sentimental poetry and Waldor a born poet (S. D., "Reflets," 136). Chateaubriand, too, recognized "au milieu du chœur moderne des femmes poètes, en prose ou en vers: les Allart, les Waldor, les Valmore, les Ségalas, les Révoil [Colet], les Mercœur" (*Mémoires d'outre-tombe*, 2:890). Séché anthologized Waldor, as did Moulin, who admired in her verse "la souplesse des alexandrins et la sobriété des images" (*La poésie féminine*, 263–64).

56. Desbordes-Valmore does not explain why she arranged it without Waldor's consent.

57. Planté observes that "Desbordes-Valmore, même dans les moments de sa plus grande célébrité, ne semble pas constituer une autorité suffisante pour consacrer une autre poétesse" (*Femmes poètes du XIXᵉ siècle*, 41–42).

58. The pain of Dumas's betrayal was compounded by her mother's death in 1833.

59. See Musset's "blason" of Waldor, "À une muse; ou, Une valseuse dans le cénacle romantique" (1834), in *Poésies complètes*, 526.

60. Waldor interweaves epigraphs from classical and Romantic poets and novelists in her first novel, *L'écuyer Dauberon* (1832), which evokes the reign of Louis XIII. Her essay "Femmes auteurs" (*Pages de la vie intime*, 2:247–57) lists the poets Salm, Céré-Barbé (the godmother of Waldor's daughter Elisa), Babois, Desbordes-Valmore, and Tastu. Novelists include Adèle de Souza, Isabelle de Montolieu, Sophie Gay, Hilaire Belloc, and Élise Voïart. Waldor recalls Staël, Genlis, Cottin, and Dufrénoy and also names her contemporaries Girardin, Mercœur, Jenny Bastide, Hortense Allart, the

duchesse d'Abrantès, Ségalas, Marie Mennessier-Nodier, Hermance Lesguillon, and Gabrielle Soumet. Richomme has an honorable mention for founding the *Journal des Femmes* in 1832. To this cast Waldor adds Dupin, Eugénie Foa, Clémence Robert, and Aimée Harelle (*Pages de la vie intime*, 2:249–51).

61. In 1833, Sainte-Beuve used the word "talent," but defined it, like genius, in reference to "invention," "art," and "conception" ("M^me Desbordes-Valmore," 246).

62. *Contes en prose pour les enfants, Contes en vers pour les enfants*, and *Le livre des mères et des enfants* (all in 1840), *Huit femmes* (1845), and *Les anges de la famille* (1849).

63. *Les anges de la famille* (2nd ed., 1854) and *Jeunes têtes et jeunes cœurs: Contes pour les enfants* (1855).

64. See Desbordes-Valmore's letter of 20 October 1853 to her son-in-law Jacques Langlais, Ondine's husband (*Œuvres manuscrites*, 232).

65. As a loyalist, faithful to Bonaparte's memory, who welcomed the Second Empire and received financial compensation from the government, Waldor's split from Hugo was inevitable. On this, see Dumas, *Lettres*, 166–67; and Waldor's *Louis Napoléon dans le Midi* (1852) and the narrative poem *La France 1870* (1870).

66. From Chateaubriand's *Mélanges littéraires*, 83.

67. See "À Béranger," where Colet describes Béranger's genius as "une voix immense / Qui rend au peuple sa gloire et ses droits" (*Poésies complètes*, 41). Gray notes that Béranger, whose "first collection of verse . . . was marked by extreme anticlericalism and a violent hatred for the restored Bourbon monarchy," was more

famous than Lamartine and Hugo (*Rage and Fire*, 95).

68. Boismartin worked as a censor and later as the conservator at the Bibliothèque de l'Arsenal and the Bibliothèque du Sénat.

69. See Colet's 1842 letters to Paul Jacob, expressing her indignation and Ségalas's irritation about Molènes's attack in Jackson, *Louise Colet*, 102.

70. On this, see Ambrière, *Le siècle des Valmore*, 2:291–92.

71. In a letter of 14 August 1846, Flaubert begins by complimenting Colet ("Qu'ils sont beaux les vers que tu m'envoies"), then claims that she lacks "l'innéité" as well as "la persévérance au travail." He continues: "On n'arrive au style qu'avec un labeur atroce, avec une opiniâtreté fanatique et dévouée. Le mot de Buffon est un grand blasphème: le génie n'est pas une longue patience" (*Correspondance*, 1:301, 303).

72. Flaubert comments to Colet on 24 April 1852: "Tu as un côté de l'esprit . . . passionné et débordant quelquefois, auquel il faut mettre un corset et qu'il faut *durcir du dedans*" (*Correspondance*, 2:79; ellipses and emphasis in original). Flaubert and his friend Louis Bouilhet, a poet and dramatist, discussed and corrected Colet's verse at length. On this, see Flaubert's correspondence from 28 November 1852 to 23 January 1853.

73. In "Le baiser du poète" (August 1846), the reference to "muse" is not ironic: "Ce que je crois, poëte créateur, / Que votre esprit, que la muse domine, / Répand en moi son souffle inspirateur" (*Ce qui est dans le cœur des femmes*, 90).

74. Colet also distinguished herself in prose, for example, *La jeunesse de Mirabeau* (1841), *Les cœurs brisés* (1843), and *Lui* (1859). She published

three narratives in verse under the title *Le poème de la femme*: "La paysanne" (1853), "La servante" (1854), and "La religieuse" (1856), which also record her creative yet critical dialogue with Flaubert. On "La servante," see Beizer, *Ventriloquized Bodies*, 99–131.

75. A. Séché scorned Colet, "la poétesse irascible," adding: "À quatre reprises, en 1839, 1843, 1852, et 1855, l'Académie française lui décerna le prix de poésie, grâce à la protection de Victor Cousin" (*Les muses françaises*, 1:292).

76. Desbordes-Valmore's legacy did not start to take hold after 1840, as Boutin claims, but after her death ("Marceline Desbordes-Valmore," 175–76).

77. The years 1896 to 1898 saw the publication of Desbordes-Valmore's correspondence with her husband, children, and close friends. This inspired public sympathy together with "une sorte de renaissance menée avec une incroyable ferveur autour du nom de Desbordes-Valmore," as Loliée describes (*Œuvres choisies*, 2).

78. In the 1830s, a seamstress earned between 1.2 and 1.5 francs for ten to twelve hours of work (see Sullerot, *Histoire de la presse féminine*, 169). These wages were still current some thirty years later, according to the *Statistique de la France 1835–73* (http://catalog.hathitrust.org/Record/001306988).

79. Worker-poets also had the support of Chateaubriand, Hugo, and Sand. On Lamartine's relationship with women worker-poets Quarré and Reine Garde, see Jenson, *Trauma and Its Representations*, 153–56, 163–72. On French workers' poetry, see Thomas, *Voix d'en bas*.

80. Sainte-Beuve's *Œuvres choisies de Pierre de Ronsard* appeared in 1828.

On the Romantics' rejection of the sonnet, see Schultz, *Gendered Lyric*, 77–80.

81. Desbordes-Valmore wrote two sonnets: "Au livre des *Consolations*," dedicated to Sainte-Beuve and published in *Bouquets et prières* (1843), and "À la voix de Mademoiselle Mars" (1839) (*Œuvres poétiques*, 2:452, 634).

82. Baudelaire states: "Parce que la forme est contraignante, l'idée jaillit plus intense" (*Correspondance*, 1:676).

83. In her novel *Méline* (1876), Siefert cites a line concerning the agony of unrequited love: "Un vers de Louise Labé jaillit du fond de ma mémoire: 'Avec toy tout, et sans toy je n'ay rien!'" (270). On the eight French editions of Labé's works between 1815 and 1887, see Clément, "La réception de Louise Labé."

84. This is a paraphrase of Cynthia Ozick's statement about the term "woman writer" (quoted in Olsen, *Silences*, 251).

## Chapter 4

1. The 1793 decree to abolish slavery was confirmed and applied to all French colonies on 4 February 1794. Napoleon Bonaparte overturned the decision in 1802.

2. On French abolitionism from 1802 to 1848, see Jennings, *French Anti-Slavery*.

3. Midgley similarly notes "the ambivalent and complex attitudes of [British] women anti-slavery campaigners to their own social position, to their appropriate roles in the movement, and more widely to questions of women's duties and their rights" (*Women Against Slavery*, 5).

4. Pasco presents the idea that literature serves as a source, if not a repository,

279

of history by "revealing general background and individual attitudes" ("Literature as Historical Archive," 373).

5. Chateaubriand's novel *Les Natchez*, inspired by his American travels and begun in 1794, was published in 1826. Disappointed by a 1749 trip to the French colony of Martinique, in *Paul et Virginie* (1787), Bernardin de Saint-Pierre created a colonial Eden, devoid of prejudice, mirroring the purity of "la belle Créole," Virginie.

6. This phrasing comes from the American poet Eleanor Wilner: "With poetic imagination, it is precisely this distance from the ego that enables the emotional connectedness we call empathy—and because it is remote from ego-threat, as we enter imaginatively what is actually at a remove from us, we are given both vision and connection" (quoted in Lee, *Slavery and the Romantic Imagination*, 32–33).

7. On Staël's interest in slavery, developed from stories she heard in her mother's salon, including that of Ourika, see the account by her descendant the comtesse Jean de Pange (née Pauline de Broglie), "Mme de Staël et les nègres."

8. Cuvier adopted the *linea facialis* (facial angle) that the painter Petrus Camper had theorized by comparing the skulls of a European, a Mongol, a black person, and an ape. In *Leçons d'anatomie comparée* (1803), Cuvier incorporated Gall's phrenology, using the skull's structure to determine a person's character and mental capacity: "On sait en effet que l'espèce humaine présente certaines conformations héréditaires qui constituent ce qu'on appelle des *races*; et que trois d'entre elles surtout sont éminement distinctes, *la blanche* ou caucasique

... *la jaune* ou mongolique, et *la nègre* ou éthiopique" (181).

9. Barrère drew on humoral medicine and his dissections of the cadavers of African men in Cayenne to explain "la bile toujours noire comme de l'encre" coloring the Negro's blood "d'un rouge noirâtre" (*Dissertation*, 4, 5). He thus pathologized black skin: "Ne pourrait-on pas regarder en quelque façon la couleur des Nègres comme un Ictère noir naturel?" (6). On Barrère and other bioprospectors, see Schiebinger, *Plants and Empire*, 73–104.

10. Grégoire presented evidence from anatomists to dispute racial inequality (*De la littérature des nègres*, 10–87). He celebrated gifted blacks, including the military genius Abram Petrovich Hannibal (also known as Annibal), the learned Antoine-Guillaume Amo, Othello (author of *Essai contre l'esclavage des nègres*, 1788), Ottobah Cugoano (author of *Réflexions sur la traite et l'esclavage des nègres*, 1787), Ignace Sancho, and the poet Phillis Wheatley (Grégoire, *De la littérature des nègres*, 197–272).

11. Ourika's "prise de conscience" is filtered through news of "les massacres de Saint-Domingue": "maintenant j'avais honte d'appartenir à une race de barbares et d'assassins" (Duras, *Ourika*, 20).

12. The phrase comes from Kadish, "The Black Terror." During the August 1791 slave rebellion in Saint-Domingue, Toussaint Bréda remained on the plantation where he had been born, to protect his white master. Initially allied with the Spanish, he allied with the French after they abolished slavery. Renamed Toussaint "L'Ouverture" by French troops, he helped to drive the Spanish out of the north and the

British out of the south and west. After becoming the lieutenant governor of the island in 1796, he worked to rebuild Saint-Domingue. His work was cut short by Napoleon, who admired yet feared him. The French emperor had Louverture captured and deported to France in May 1802; he died in a dungeon at Fort de Joux in the Jura mountains on 7 April 1803.

13. After her father's execution in Paris in 1793, Duras fled with her mother to Martinique.

14. On Ségalas's Creole heritage, see Ratier, "Mme Anaïs Ségalas"; Mirecourt, *Madame Anaïs Ségalas*, 28; Desplantes and Pouthier, *Femmes de lettres en France*, 357; and Moulin, *La poésie féminine*, 292.

15. Roch also refers to her parents as "Créoles de Saint-Domingue" ("M^me Anaïs Ségalas," 2). Ségalas's birth certificate at the Archives numérisées de Paris shows that Ségalas (née Anne Caroline Ménard) was born on 24 September 1811 in Paris. Typographical errors by printers may explain why the biographies by Ratier and Mirecourt list the years 1814 and 1819, respectively.

16. Hervey's mention that Ségalas had recently published *Les oiseaux de passage*, "which had attracted the notice of the Academy," places the reception in 1836; he was thus mistaken about her age ("A Reception of Alfred de Vigny's," 486).

17. Charles X, then king of France, used an incident involving his consul, Pierre Deval (whom Hussein, the [Dey] Ottoman governor of Algiers, had struck with his fly whisk two years prior), as a pretext to invade Algiers on 5 July 1830. Delphine Gay de Girardin's poem "La prise d'Alger, Te Deum" recalls the incident, thank-ing God for France's victory: "On débarque—et l'Arabe a mordu la poussière: / Le dey rallie en vain ses batallions épars. / Celui qui des Français insulta la bannière / La voir flotter sur ses remparts" (*Poésies complètes*, 200–202).

18. See the reference to Clarkson in Staël's 1814 "Préface pour la traduction d'un ouvrage de Wilberforce" (291).

19. Ségalas gives as her source *Voyage dans la régence d'Alger* (the travelogue of Dr. Thomas Shaw, a British chaplain, translated into French by J. MacCarthy in 1830), 130.

20. Ségalas provides a glossary of terms (including "spahi," "aga," "zakat," "Rafazis," "chaya," and "oldaks"), which develops the context (*Les algériennes*, 129–37).

21. On 14 June 1800, the French won the battle of Marengo, which Napoleon, then the first consul of France, had waged with Austria.

22. Most had both white and black women as wives, Ségalas notes (*Les algériennes*, 131–32).

23. Sand later recalled: "J'avais en moi, comme un sentiment bien net et bien ardent, l'horreur de l'esclavage brutal et bête" (*Histoire de ma vie*, 80). On the "theme of marriage as a form of slavery by analogy," see Jenson, *Trauma and Its Representations*, 183–209.

24. The epigraph to the epilogue of the section "Poésies diverses" cites Tastu: "Que ces chants entre nous soient un secret lien; / Qu'au nom du sol natal, vos cœurs, femmes de France, / Battent à l'unison du mien" (Ségalas, *Les algériennes*, 121).

25. France established its colonial empire in the Americas (New France, the West Indies, and French Guiana) beginning in the seventeenth century.

26. A third edition appeared in 1857.

27. Spurred on by the 1833 British abolition of slavery, French citizens established the Société française pour l'abolition de l'esclavage in 1834.

28. This anecdote from Mirecourt (*Madame Anaïs Ségalas*, 59) is nuanced by Ratier ("Mme Anaïs Ségalas"), who describes Ségalas as eager to travel but limiting her explorations to Switzerland and Italy.

29. On the histories of the Antilles that Ségalas could have consulted, see the bibliography in *Récits des Antilles*, xlii–xlvii.

30. On the biblical figure Ham (one of Noah's three sons), to whom some thinkers trace the black race, see W. Cohen, *French Encounter with Africans*, 10–11, 13.

31. Virey portrays black people thus: "Au moral, cette espèce est caractérisée par un entendement borné, une civilisation imparfaite; par moins de vrai courage, d'industrie, d'habileté que l'autre espèce; elle est aussi plus portée aux plaisirs des sens qu'aux affections morales, et se rapproche d'avantage de la brute" (*Histoire naturelle*, 1:437–38).

32. The subtext is not without irony. Napoleon abolished the "parchment nobility" titles, claiming that a title was not inherited but rather earned through service to the state.

33. In arguing that "la différence des Sexes ne regarde que le Corps," Poullain de la Barre asserts with respect to the mind, "Si on le considère en lui-même, l'on trouve qu'il est égal & de même nature en tous les hommes" (*Equality of the Sexes*, 85).

34. Here, the French word "âme," meaning "soul" as well as the intellectual and moral faculties, conveys the related sense of "esprit" or mind.

35. See Lee's analysis of the relationship between creative artists (self) and their subjects (other) in *Slavery and the Romantic Imagination*, 29–43.

36. "[Personne] qui est de race blanche, d'ascendance européenne, originaire des plus anciennes colonies d'outre-mer" (*Trésor de la langue française*). English usage differs, as detailed in the *Oxford English Dictionary* (2nd ed.): "Chiefly in the Caribbean, certain parts of the Americas (esp. tropical South America, the Gulf States, and parts of Central America), and in Mauritius and Réunion: a person born in one of these countries, but of European or African descent. (Originally used to distinguish such people from those of similar descent who were born in Europe or Africa, and from indigenous peoples)."

37. In Bernardin de Saint-Pierre's *Paul et Virginie* (1787), the island of Bourbon (now called Réunion) represents a style *à la créole*. In *Bug-Jargal* (1826), Hugo distinguishes "les noirs créoles" from "les nègres congos" and suggests, in keeping with the English definition, that "créole" marks a difference not from white, but from black, more precisely from the black African (40, 51).

38. On these terms, see Kadish and Massardier-Kenney, *Translating Slavery*, 19; and Daget, "Les mots 'esclave,' 'nègre,' 'noir.'"

39. A review of the German physiologist Friedrich Tiedemann's "On the Brain of the Negro, Compared with [the] European and the Orang-Outang" (1836) appeared in French in 1837, underscoring his rival theory "que le cerveau du nègre est, dans sa totalité aussi volumineux que celui de l'Européen et des autres races humaines; le poids du cerveau, sa dimension et la capacité de la boîte osseuse démontrent ce fait" (Anon., "Du cerveau des

nègres," 172). Tiedemann also espoused intellectual equality between the sexes, considering women's brains in relation to their smaller stature proportionally larger than men's.

40. This anticipates an exchange in Ségalas's *Récits des Antilles*: "—Cependant, reprit Roland en souriant, il y a des alliances entre les deux races: si l'on a vu des rois épouser des bergères, on peut voir des blancs épouser des négresses.—Jamais, répondit Charly. On verrait encore moins, dans nos Antilles, une blanche épouser un noir" (43).

41. See the footnote by Cyrille Bissette, the journal's founder, in Letelier, "Mœurs coloniales," 86.

42. The other notable example is the response to *Ourika*, preserved in an 1825 letter sent by officers of the royal navy in Martinique to Alexander von Humboldt, a Prussian naturalist and geographer who frequented Duras's salon: "Le commerce clandestin de chair humaine va à merveille, les colons regardent chaque Français récemment arrivé comme un négrophile et le spirituel et généreux auteur d'*Ourika* est accusé à chaque instant ici d'avoir rendu intéressante dans son détestable roman une négresse qui n'avait même l'avantage d'être une négresse créole" (quoted in Pailhès, *Duchesse de Duras*, 463).

43. Letelier's husband was subsequently exiled to Saint Martin and erased from the navy registry.

44. Charles later saves Maurice through his own death.

45. Consider this exchange between Charles and his hostess: "Mme de P*** Vous, femme, vous mère, vous avez meurtri de vos mains un faible enfant, qui n'a d'autres torts que celui de fuir les douleurs atroces qui la torturent.

. . . Mais, que voulez-vous qu'on fasse? dit-elle après avoir rougi, pâli plusieurs fois; il faut bien se conformer aux habitudes du pays où l'on est forcé de vivre; sans cela on ne serait pas servi" ("Mœurs coloniales," 239).

46. "L'émancipation des esclaves," in Lamartine, *Toussaint Louverture*, 270. In speeches of 1835, 1836, 1838, 1840, and 1842 to the Chamber of Deputies, Lamartine advocated for abolition.

47. The priest consoles Ourika by saying, "[I]l n'y a pour [Dieu] ni nègres, ni blancs: tous les cœurs sont égaux devant ses yeux" (Duras, *Ourika*, 42). Waldor also references *Paul et Virginie* in *Pages de la vie intime* (2:70).

48. For the original context, see Letelier, "Mœurs coloniales," 92.

49. On the "ambiguity of racial difference within the category of the Creole," see Jenson, *Trauma and Its Representations*, 194–95.

50. Her only child, Bertile, was born on 15 December 1838.

51. In an 1848 review of *La femme*, Niboyet describes Ségalas as "une forme humanisée de la poésie," her volume exemplifying "un cours de moral à notre usage commun" (3, 4).

52. On the "clubs féminins" after the 1848 revolution, see Lucas, *Les clubs et les clubistes*.

53. There is this usage in an 1818 travelogue by J. M'Leod: "The ladies generally creolized the whole day in a delectable state of apathy. Creolizing is an easy and elegant mode of lounging in a warm climate" (*Oxford English Dictionary*, s.v. "creolize"). By 1842, "créoliser" meant "s'adapter aux mœurs et à la manière d'être creoles" (*Trésor de la langue française*).

54. Lafaye's father was part of the French military in Guadeloupe; the family moved to Paris in 1814. Poems such as

"La mer," published in *Annales Romantiques* (1835), and "La compagne du marin" in *Les Créoles* suggest that Lafaye was married to a sailor. A letter of 26 December 1846 to Gautier, with which Lafaye included a copy of the manuscript of *Les Créoles*, explains that most of the poems were composed "dans l'océan Indien, à trois milles lieues de tout contact poétique, de toute critique, de tous conseils" (Gautier, *Correspondance générale*, 125). See Antoine's references to Lafaye in *Les écrivains français*, 196, 200, 207.

55. "Tu cours dans la forêt sans nul chemin frayé, / Surprenant l'agouti qui bondit effrayé. / Tes noirs vont en avant: Apollon le superbe, / Jupiter, qui le soir revient tout chargé d'herbe, / Adonis aux cheveux crépus . . . les voici tous" (Ségalas, *La femme*, 205; ellipses in original). An agouti is a tropical rodent about the size of a rabbit.

56. Boutin similarly argues that Desbordes-Valmore "esteemed dialects to the extent that she wrote poetry in her native patois from Douai, as well as in Creole," and she also used Creole patois in her correspondence ("Colonial Memory," 67n27). In a letter of 14 May 1850 to Brizeux, Desbordes-Valmore wrote, "Une pauvre négresse disait aussi: 'Si monde, pas gagné soupir, monde là touffer!'" (*Œuvres manuscrites*, 255–56). Letelier's character, a black Guadeloupean woman, refers to her language as "parler nègre" ("Mœurs coloniales," 132).

57. Toussaint Louverture used the salutation "le premier des Noirs au premier des Blancs" in his letters to Napoleon. On this and rival transnational representations of the Haitian leader in nineteenth-century literature, see the introduction to Cashin's *Amour et liberté: Abolition de l'esclavage* (2009) and its bibliography.

58. Like Virey, Gobineau claims, "[L]es familles humaines sont marquées de différences tellement radicales, tellement essentielles, qu'on ne peut faire moins que de leur refuser l'identité d'origine. . . . [I]l n'y a pas une seule espèce; il y en a trois, quatre, davantage" (*Essai sur l'inégalité des races*, 123).

59. Serious publishers, like Delagrave, would produce a run of a thousand copies.

60. In the slavery context, the word "négrillon" meant a black boy under the age of seven.

61. An armchair traveler like Ségalas could consult tourist guides, such as Budan's *La Guadeloupe pittoresque* (1863). Cooper suggests another source: "La Soufrière, volcan de la Guadeloupe," which was published in *Le Magasin Pittoresque* (1843) ("Race, Gender, and Colonialism," 128n11).

62. In Letelier's narrative, a French Creole woman similarly comments: "[O]n les nourrit, on les habille, on les soigne depuis leur naissance, et au bout du compte, ils deviennent fous, vont marrons [runaway slaves] ou se tuent" ("Mœurs coloniales," 185–86). This, however, is a form of ironic distancing that reveals the Creoles' blindness to the inhumanity of slavery.

63. Antoine uses the terms "négrophobe" and "racisme" in reference to Ségalas's *Les oiseaux de passage* and *Récits des Antilles*, respectively (*Les écrivains français*, 279, 289).

64. D'Alq lists *Récits des Antilles* among Ségalas's works, but does not discuss it.

## Chapter 5

1. Blanchecotte, née Augustine Alphonsine Malvina Souville, was a seamstress, a trade she learned from her father.

2. On this, see Blanchecotte's dedicatory poem to Brontë (who is addressed as "la sœur de mon esprit") in the third edition of *Rêves et réalités* (1871): "Prête-moi ton génie et ta ferme sagesse / Pour que je puisse enfin, me séparant de moi, / Mettre à l'écart mon cœur dont le fardeau m'oppresse, / Et jeter ma pensée au siècle, comme toi!" (196).

3. In January 1856, Sand wrote to thank Blanchecotte for the copy of *Rêves et réalités* she had sent to her (*Correspondance*, 25:928). Sand's longer letter of 29 September 1860 praises Blanchecotte's "très grand talent" and encourages her to persevere, despite her husband's accident and confinement: "il ne faut pas qu'une si belle intelligence périsse" (25:995). In a letter of 1862 to Sainte-Beuve, Sand sought financial aid for Blanchecotte, mentioning the poet's husband, who was "aliéné" and in an asylum (16:775–76).

4. According to Boiteau, the editor of Béranger's *Correspondance*, Blanchecotte received 150 letters from Béranger, many of which were brief notes (4:83). According to Coligny, she received 200 letters from Béranger ("Les muses parisiennes," 109).

5. "Réalité" (1845), published in the first edition of *Rêves et réalités* (1855) but removed from later editions, expresses Blanchecotte's brooding: "Quand la feuille frissonne et tombe / Sous les pieds du passant rêveur / . . . / Je descends, pauvre créature, / Dans ma pensée, asile noir: / J'y cherche un rayon d'espérance / Une ombre d'un bonheur passé; / Je ne rencontre que souffrance" (165).

6. I have not identified the other text.

7. This "récit" (Béranger's term) of Napoleon's rise and fall does not appear in the 1856 and 1871 editions of *Rêves et réalités*. It may be that Blanchecotte or her editor withdrew this text, which could have been seen as an affront to Napoleon III: "Vas échouer captif comme un obscur passant, / Dans l'île où vont s'éteindre et ton rêve et ton sang" (*Rêves et réalités* [1855], 221).

8. On this, see D. Scott, *Sonnet Theory and Practice*, 9–35.

9. Bourdieu's phrasing in reference to literary works means the "social conditions of their production, circulation, and consumption" (*The Field of Cultural Production*, 11).

10. James observes that Blanchecotte used the name Malvina with her friends, a name coined by the Scottish poet James MacPherson and "made popular by his works," and highlights "Lamartine's paraphrase of the poems of Ossian" (the narrator of MacPherson's epic poems) as a possible source for Blanchecotte's "penchant for elegies" ("Malvina Blanchecotte and 'la douleur chantée,'" 148).

11. A number of poems that predate her marriage are among the eleven texts removed from the 1856 edition, including "À M. F. de R." (1846), "Edmond à Marie" (1847), "La charité" (1848), and "Sur la mort d'un enfant de 8 ans" (1849).

12. In the 1855 edition, the cluster of poems devoted to women ends with the portrait of a male poetic figure, "Léopold," not included in the 1856 edition. The removal of ten other early poems adds coherence to the section "Poésies diverses."

13. Blanchecotte's long poems feature consistent rhyme schemes and phonetic patterns. See "Elle" and "Encore elle" in *Nouvelles poésies*, 34–57 and 57–73, respectively.

14. On the establishment of asylums in France, see Goldstein, *Console and Classify*. On the linkage of madness, creativity, and dreams in nineteenth-century French psychiatric and literary discourse, see Paliyenko, "Margins of Madness and Creativity."

15. Moreau de Tours ties genius to an organic anomaly of the brain (*Psychologie morbide*, 465).

16. See Rosen's essay on how the factory worker Ellen Johnston in Victorian England "creates poetic personae that negotiate the often conflicting demands of her gender, her class, and her craft" ("Class and Poetic Communities," 207–8).

17. Composed in 1847, "Lucie" is one of Blanchecotte's earliest pieces about a friend, also a worker, who married young, had children, and then succumbed to heartbreak, poverty, and disease.

18. With the exception of "Gabrielle," which portrays familial bliss, maternity does not figure in Blanchecotte's panoply of female figures.

19. This poem was originally published under the title "À ***" (*Rêves et réalités* [1855], 114–15); in the 1856 edition, this section was added to "Madeleine" as part 7. There were other changes: section 10 became section 13; new pieces were added as sections 11 and 12; the earlier section 11 was shifted to 14; and other new pieces were added as sections 15 and 16. These revisions, however, do not alter the overall theme.

20. On 3 December 1855, a month after *Rêves et réalités* appeared, Béranger wrote to her: "Il y a beaucoup à reprendre dans votre volume; mais il est plein de poésie, malgré les inexpériences et un trop grand laisser aller. L'ordre manque; malgré tout, je vous le répète, il y a tous les éléments d'un succès mérité" (*Correspondance*, 4:295).

21. This recalls the opening lines of "À M. F. de R." (1846): "Je ne désire pas que mon nom retentisse, / Je ne désire pas que mon rêve aboutisse / À quelques sacs d'écus dans un coffre enfouis / . . . / Non! je suis faible et pauvre et je n'ai que ma lyre" (*Rêves et réalités* [1855], 182).

22. Blanchecotte describes being left alone to fend for herself while her parents worked long hours (*Le long de la vie*, 211–13).

23. As suggested by the subtitle, "Adieux à mon petit enfant âgé de quatre mois," this poem expresses a mother's sadness upon leaving her newborn ("Alphonse") with a wetnurse.

24. Schaffer adds: "[Blanchecotte] has, therefore, a more valid claim to be numbered among the Parnassians than have Mme Colet and Mme Penquer, and her poetry is unquestionably superior to theirs; essentially, however, it is with them and their Romantic masters that she belongs and like them, she is something of an interloper in the Parnassian camp" (*Genres of Parnassian Poetry*, 379). On Blanchecotte's prosody, see Planté, *Femmes poètes du XIXᵉ siècle*, 196; and Finch, *Women's Writing*, 140.

25. The second edition maintains the general order of the volume, which is divided nearly equally between the poems devoted to female figures and the section entitled "Poésies diverses."

26. This corpus of 115 letters gives details about Blanchecotte's family, health,

and whereabouts; it also reveals how closely Sainte-Beuve read her work. In June 1857, he discouraged her from pursuing the sonnet, a form he considered "si difficile et un peu vieille," telling her, "Restez plus libre et chantez-nous votre gamme à vous la note de *Sappho*" (Sainte-Beuve, *Correspondance générale*, 439; emphasis in original). Amplified with editorial notes, this correspondence helps to recover Blanchecotte's early prose production along with her circle. Among noteworthy details is mention of a letter from Desbordes-Valmore to which Blanchecotte never responded (409).

27. On this, see Paliyenko, "Illumining the Critical Reader in the Poet," 190–92.

28. Blanchecotte would continue to defend poetry, as in the preface to her biography of the eighteenth-century British poet Olivier Goldsmith: "Vous qui en toute conscience vous croyez épris du naturalisme, eh bien, au rebours de M^r Jourdain qui sans le savoir pratiquait la prose, sans le savoir, davantage vous pratiquez vous, la divine, l'impérissable, l'inéluctable poésie! . . . Poésie, poésie, poésie! C'est-à-dire cette chose sublime, essentielle, vitale qui vous met chaque jour au-dessus de vous-même, au-dessus des instincts vulgaires" (*Olivier Goldsmith*, v, vii).

29. See A. Séché, *Les muses françaises*, 2:374–75; Chichmanoff, "Étude critique," 114; and Planté, *Femmes poètes du XIX^e siècle*, 195–96.

30. James does not use this evidence to analyze Blanchecotte's development from a "poétesse dolente" to a "poète observateur" ("Malvina Blanchecotte and 'la douleur chantée,'" 157).

31. This collection, divided into three sections—"Le monde, la conscience"; "Les écrivains, les livres"; and "Les femmes, l'amour"—warrants closer study in relation to the ideological project linking Blanchecotte's verse and prose.

32. On this, see Paliyenko, "Illumining the Critical Reader in the Poet," 192–95.

33. In his personal copy of volume 2 of *Le Parnasse contemporain* (1869), in which Blanchecotte had published four "Chants élégiaques," Rimbaud apparently parodied two of her verses; see Murphy, "Détours et détournements," 85.

34. In the 1871 edition of *Rêves et réalités*, Blanchecotte criticizes the vacuous "romans pervers" popular at the time (x).

35. In "À Victor Hugo," Blanchecotte endorses patriotism as a balm for France's wounds and a matter of personal honor. In "Aux femmes," she urges women to exert moral influence.

36. "À une muse," added to the 1871 edition of *Rêves et réalités*, evokes *bas-bleu* criticism: "Eh bien! après? ô pauvre Muse! / Toi qu'on appelle *le bas bleu* / Et que tout au plus l'on excuse / D'écrire, si on t'aime un peu" (338; emphasis in original).

## Chapter 6

1. The first edition had a print run of five hundred copies, the second and third, a thousand each.

2. The page references are to the second edition of *Rayons perdus*, published in February 1869, unless otherwise indicated. The second edition included four new poems: "Le banc," "Page blanche," "Voyage," and "Solitude"; the order of the poems "L'abbaye" and "La cure" was also reversed. Subsequent editions were identical to the second;

the third edition appeared in April 1869, the fourth in 1873, and the fifth in 1878.

3. Published on the eve of the Second Empire's fall, *L'année républicaine* consists of twelve poems that follow the republican calendar, portraying the seasons. *Les saintes colères* protests Prussia's invasion of French soil.

4. During the last year of her life, Siefert translated Emilio Castelar's *L'art, la religion et la nature en Italie* with her husband, Jocelyn Pène, a journalist, whom she had married in February 1876.

5. Siefert's first article, on Banville's *Idylles prussiennes*, appeared in the 25 July 1871 issue. Although the volumes of the newspaper listed at the Bibliothèque nationale de France in Paris have been "hors d'usage" for a number of years, those recently digitized by the Bibliothèque municipale de Lyon are incomplete; most of 1871 and the second half of 1874 (July–December) are missing.

6. A bacterium that multiplies rapidly in the lungs causes tuberculosis, which can spread to other organs.

7. "Splitting" refers to "the division between the *conscious*, the *preconscious* and the *unconscious* levels," but can also denote the splitting of the ego, which "entails a simultaneous experience within the ego of two contradictory responses to reality, acceptance and denial, without the ego needing to produce a compromise between the two or repress one or the other," Sue Walrond-Skinner explains in *Dictionary of Psychotherapy*, 324.

8. The Romantic Laprade and sonneteer Soulary hailed from Lyon and were the Siefert family's friends.

9. Banville, referring to Siefert as "un poète du plus grand mérite," critiqued her pantoum "En passant en chemin de fer" (in *Rayons perdus*) in his *Petit traité de poésie française* (245). Clair Tisseur later noted Siefert's command of decasyllabic meter with a rhythmic break (5 + 5), the Romantic trimetric line with a tertiary rhythm (4 + 4 + 4), and unusual breaks in classical rhythm (*Modestes observations*, 69, 81, 106).

10. See, among early sonnets between 1865 and 1869, "Excelsior" (*Souvenirs rassemblés*, 237–38). The two-sonnet poem displays rich rhyme, beginning with "horizon"/"saison" (lines 1, 3) and "étoffée"/"trophée" (lines 6, 7). The title, the comparative of the Latin *excelsus*, meaning "higher" or "loftier," announces its theme—the quest for the ideal—and the erudition Siefert pursued in cultivating her poetry. "À mon frère E.," consisting of five sonnets, exemplifies how Siefert curbs personal lyricism with formal restraint and her acute sense of the limits of materiality ("Quelle réalité valut jamais le rêve?") (245).

11. Asselineau included Siefert in his *Livre des sonnets: Dix dizains de sonnets choisis* (1874).

12. Greenberg noted regarding the ampersand that, apart from Siefert, "no other Lemerre author or any other nineteenth-century authors used this sign," relating it to the "clash of mixing genres" in Siefert's work (*Uncanonical Women*, 37, 38).

13. A "palimpsest" refers to a manuscript that has been reused by scraping off or erasing the previous text, though not always completely; thus, traces of the original text often remain.

14. "La douleur n'est point un but, mais seulement un moyen" (*Méline*, 284).

15. See Freud, "Creative Writers and Day-Dreaming" (*Standard Edition*, 9:143–53).

16. The subsequent lines, "Pourtant elle eut porté le nom de mon grand-père, / Je l'aurais appellée Olympe comme lui," link the speaker with Siefert (*Rayons perdus*, 28).

17. In "Mourning and Melancholy" (1917), Freud states that "melancholia is in some way related to an unconscious loss of a love-object, in contradistinction to mourning, in which there is nothing unconscious about the loss" (*Standard Edition*, 15:245).

18. Baudelaire used different vocabulary to make a similar point about Desbordes-Valmore's "grandes et vigoureuses qualities qui s'imposent à la mémoire" (*Œuvres complètes*, 2:147).

19. Rimbaud was mistaken about the edition he had consulted (either the second or the third); the fourth edition appeared in 1873.

20. Completed in February 1870, *Les stoïques* was on the market by the end of May and had reached the provinces just prior to the declaration of war against the Prussians.

21. See Paliyenko, "Rereading *la femme poète*," 149–52.

22. See the sonnets "Aujourd'hui," "Hier," and "Demain," as well as "Petite sœur," "Petit enfant," "Intérieur," "Villanelle," "Berceuse," and "Enfantine."

23. The 1869 issue features a three-sonnet poem (the first two sonnets of which were published the following year under the title "Soupir"), "La combe," "Au large," and "À ce qui n'est plus." The 1876 issue has "Consolation" and "L'ennui" (not published elsewhere), the sonnet "Crépuscule" from *Rayons perdus*, "L'orage," "Adieux à Pau," and "Désir," the latter three republished in *Souvenirs rassemblés par sa mère.* According to Paton, the decision to publish Siefert was unanimous

("Seductive Rebellions," 74–75). Her inclusion, like that of other women, however, later brought ambivalent notice, discussed by Schultz in *Gendered Lyric*, 140–67.

24. See Rimbaud's 24 May 1870 letter to Banville with which he included the poems "Credo in unam" (retitled "Soleil et chair"), "Ophélie," and "Sensation" (*Œuvres complètes*, 236–37).

25. The speaker's appeal midway through the text embeds a metadiscourse highlighting the role of memory in all subjective lyricism: "Poëtes, qui pleurez, ô pléiade sacrée! / . . . / Vous tous, qui vous plaignez de votre triste histoire, / . . . / Dites-moi, dites-moi si vos regrets se fondent / Sur des bonheurs pareils à mes bonheurs anciens?" (lines 89, 93, 97–98).

26. On this image in Aeschylus's *Oresteia* and Siefert's use of it, defining a woman's relationship to poetic creativity when "the two major poetic movements in France, Romanticism and Parnassianism, were in open conflict," see O'Neill, "The Shadow of Clytemnestra," 260.

27. This is Siefert's first published poem, which appeared in the *Revue du Protestantisme Libéral* in 1867.

28. In "Promenade," poetry immortalizes memory: "Mais mes chers souvenirs, fleurs, bouquet de mon âme, / Sans que rien les entame, / En moi vivent toujours & ne sauraient mourir" (*Rayons perdus*, 99).

29. For a fuller account of this reception, see *Souvenirs rassemblés*, 96–104, 225–33.

30. The epigraph comes from Gautier's poem "La chanson de Mignon" in *La comédie de la mort* (1838).

31. "Le départ" and "Au large," which takes its epigraph, beginning "Lest de l'âme, pesant bagage," from Gautier's

poem "Tristesse en mer" in *Émaux et camées* (1852), both allude to Siefert's brother Adrien, who left for Valparaiso in January 1869. He then spent a number of years in Tahiti, from which he returned gravely ill in 1876 and died shortly thereafter.

32. The poem "La divine tragédie," dedicated to the painting on the same topic by the artist Paul Chenavard, invokes this linkage: "O stoïque chrétien! philosophe & prophète" (*Les stoïques*, 97). In the untitled poem beginning "Le ciel est sombre, il pleut, &, la tête lassée," Siefert recalls the genius of ages past; "Les mots impérieux qui traversent les temps" join ancient philosophers (Socrates, Plato, and Epictetus) with Christian martyrs (109).

33. In "Immortalité," all pass from death into eternal life: "La mort prend tout . . . / . . . / Quelqu'un ou quelque chose à tout instant s'en va. / . . . / Car ce que l'homme perd, c'est Dieu qui le recueille" (*Les stoïques*, 16–17).

34. Paton compares Siefert's two sonnets, first published untitled in *Le Parnasse contemporain*, volume 2 (1869), then retitled "Soupir" in *Les stoïques*, with Hugo's "Le firmament est plein," highlighting "[Siefert's] technique of transposing a modern sensation of fluidity into the rigid poetic form of the sonnet" ("Seductive Rebellions," 110).

35. The poem "À ce qui n'est plus," which treats the boundary between memoir and poetry ("Mes vers en sont l'écho, mais non la voix vibrante"), presents this same form, including the repeated first and fifth lines, as in Baudelaire's "Le balcon" from which Siefert takes the epigraph "Je sais l'art d'évoquer les minutes heureuses" (*Les stoïques*, 60).

36. Whereas this strand in *Les stoïques* has a universal accent, as in "Soir d'hiver"

("La terre est dure à l'homme & la mort est dans l'air"; 33) and "Au long des quais" ("La misère de l'homme & sa peine ici-bas"; 57), in the untitled poem that begins "L'orage a passé," the despair is personal ("Sur mes vers brisés la nef *Espérance*"; 64), and it is further tied to disease and death in "Et je pense à la mort" (69–71).

37. Amiel, who was also consumptive, referred in his diary to Siefert more than any other poet. In a study of the disease's impact on writers, Dormandy cites Amiel, who saw the whole of nature reflecting his own "inexorably advancing disease," quoting in English translation an entry of October 1852 from Amiel's *Journal intime*: "Sky draped in gray . . . mists trailing on the distant mountains: nature despairing, leaves falling on all sides like the lost illusions of youth under the tears of incurable grief . . . The fir tree alone in its vigour remains green and stoical in the midst of this universal phthisis" (*White Death*, 91; ellipses in original).

38. See the poem "A ce qui n'est plus": "Mon espoir est un rêve & mon rêve un secret, / Mes vers en sont l'écho, mais non la voix vibrante. / . . . / Le cœur a des retours vers les choses anciennes, / Des retours imprévus, séduisants, caressants; / Le poëte s'éveille à de si doux accents / Et s'abandonne à ces langueurs qui sont les siennes" (*Les stoïques*, 62).

39. Sainte-Beuve, "Rondeau: À une belle chasseresse" (*Poésies complètes*, 148).

40. See also Siefert's later reference to Epictetus: "Je lisais alternativement *le Manuel d'Épictète* et *L'Imitation de Jésus-Christ*. . . . j'usais mes forces dans les épreuves variées d'une exaltation moitié ascétique, moitié stoïcienne" (*Méline*, 241).

41. On *Les stoïques'* reception, see letters from Edgar Quinet, Deschamps, Blanc, and Michelet in *Souvenirs rassemblés*, 233–34.

42. See Siefert's "Causerie poétique" of 30 September 1872, which gives her sources of prosodic innovation; Crépet's anthology is among them.

43. On Shelley's analogous portrayal of John Keats's consumption "as the literal burning up of the poet's body, not by fever, but by the 'power within,'" see Bewell, *Romanticism and Colonial Disease*, 190. By the early twentieth century, this correlation was developed from the "lives and letters of many men and women of genius" (Munro, *Psycho-Pathology of Tuberculosis*, 3). Moorman, in 1940, thus prefaces his case studies of creative men and women: "In those who are endowed with exceptional mental qualities, and are at the same time suffering from tuberculosis, there often seems to be a strange psychic stimulus bent on creative accomplishment. Inescapable physical inactivity begets mental activity" (*Tuberculosis and Genius*, xi).

44. This is also Bivort's tone in depicting "les vers un peu mièvres de Louisa Siefert" ("Les 'vies absentes,'" 1272).

## Chapter 7

1. See *Ma vie* in *Œuvres de Louise Ackermann* (1893), xx. Page references are to this edition, unless otherwise indicated. The poems include "L'amour et la mort" in *Revue Germanique et Française* 29 (1864): 368–73; "Le nuage" and "Le positivisme" in *Revue Moderne* 33 (1865): 151–54; and "Prométhée" in *Revue Moderne* 36 (1866): 362–66.

2. According to Charles Buet, they met at the poet Siméon Pécontal's home (*J. Barbey d'Aurevilly*, 362).

3. Barbey d'Aurevilly continued: "[U]n monstre et un prodige, voilà le double fulminate qui a fait sauter la femme dans madame Ackermann; car, de la femme, chez elle, intellectuellement et moralement, il n'y en a plus. . . . Madame Ackermann, cette Origène femelle, est parvenue à tuer son sexe en elle et à le remplacer par quelque chose de neutre et d'horrible, mais de puissant" ("Madame Ackermann," 165). For a close analysis of his reading, see Jenson, "Gender and the Aesthetic of 'Le Mal.'"

4. See Louise Read's preface to Ackermann's *Pensées d'une solitaire* [1903], xix.

5. In a letter of 17 November 1874 to Ernest Havet, her friend and advisor, Ackermann writes regarding her autobiography: "Cette notice m'a été arrachée. Je n'ai cédé qu'à la menace d'une étude que d'Aurevilly avait annoncé vouloir faire sur moi. . . . Je me le figure, ce drôle de corps de critique . . . me disant, après m'avoir toisée du regard; 'comment, Madame, vous n'êtes pas une désespérée?' Il n'est pas d'ailleurs le seul qui m'adressait ce reproche. Une amie de Caro me racontait dernièrement, que, malgré tout ce qu'elle a pu lui dire, il persiste à croire que j'ai souffert et souffre encore excessivement" (quoted in M. Citoleux, *La poésie philosophique*, 234–35).

6. In 1873, Ackermann had sent a copy to Caro who, as a spiritualist, upheld God's existence but not a fixed idea of God.

7. To the corpus of 1871, Ackermann added two new poems, "Mon livre" and "De la lumière," as well as "À la

291

comète de 1861" and "Les malheu-
reux," previously published in *Contes
et poésies* (1863). A review of 24 May
1874 for *Le Bien Public*, signed X.Y.,
like the appraisal Francisque Sarcey
published in *Le XIXe Siècle* on 25, 27,
and 28 August 1874, references Caro.

8. Caro wrote to Ackermann about her
philosophical poems: "Ils ont une
beauté puissante et concentrée dont
j'ai été saisi, dès que je les ai connus.
Et puis il y a chez vous une telle sin-
cérité de souffrance, vous sentez si
profondément et si douloureusement
les choses humaines, que la sympathie
est entraînée avant que la raison ait
parlé. Mais je m'obstine à croire que
cette poésie du désespoir ne sera pas
votre dernier mot" (quoted in Hauss-
onville, "M^me Ackermann," 348).

9. In May 1877, Ackermann added a
two-page appendix to her autobiogra-
phy, which she had completed on 20
January 1874. Only a few handwritten
copies circulated among close con-
temporaries until it appeared in *La
Nouvelle Revue* (1882): 424–34.

10. See M. Citoleux's notes in "Journal de
M^me Ackermann." In the 1 June 1881
issue of *La Nouvelle Revue*, Acker-
mann published 77 reflections. In
1882, Lemerre published an amplified
edition of 140 fragments, retitled
*Pensées d'une solitaire*, together with
*Ma vie*, and a posthumous 1903 edi-
tion under the same title with prefa-
tory remarks by Read. For an over-
view of Ackermann's *Pensées*, treating
"1) general remarks on art (mainly
poetry) and the genius of the artist; 2)
judgments on individual writers and
on literary movements; 3) dicta
embodying Madame Ackermann's
own reactions to poetry and the
related arts," see Schaffer, "Madame
Ackermann," 26.

11. Ackermann nonetheless appreciated
her mother for having instilled in her
a similar disdain for women writers,
from whom she distanced herself as a
creative thinker (*Œuvres de Louise
Ackermann*, xiii). In a journal entry
of 30 December 1851, Ackermann
observes about a woman's relation-
ship to writing, "Nature instinctive et
spontanée, elle n'écrit bien que sous la
dictée de ses sens ou de son cœur"
("Journal," 528). A journal entry of 20
January 1863, in which Ackermann
rebuffs the emergent women's move-
ment on moral grounds, illustrates
her paradoxical hostility toward
women, including their sentimental-
ity, femininity, and feminist aspira-
tions: "Quand on ouvrirait aux
femmes les portes de la liberté, les
honnêtes et les sages ne voudraient
pas entrer" (543). See also the revised
fragment in *Pensées d'une solitaire*
(1903), 48.

12. I have not identified the verse Hugo
read.

13. "Chez les romantiques, l'expression
embrasse plus de pensées qu'elle n'en
peut étreindre. De là son caractère
vague et incomplet" (*Pensées d'une
solitaire* [1903], 44). See "Journal de
M^me Ackermann" on Lamartine, 541;
Hugo, 531 and 562; Vigny, 554; and
Musset, 562, 561, and 572.

14. A later undated prose fragment
echoes this pessimism: "On ne sort
guère de la vie sans douleurs; on n'y
était pas non plus entré sans larmes.
Une souffrance mystérieuse accom-
pagne le naître et le mourir" ("Jour-
nal," 537).

15. Pascal evokes this paradox with the
image of "un roseau pensant" and
argues: "Il ne faut pas que l'univers
entier s'arme pour l'écraser. Une
vapeur, une goutte d'eau, suffit pour le

tuer. Mais quand l'univers l'écraserait, l'homme serait encore plus noble que ce qui le tue, puisqu'il sait qu'il meurt, et l'avantage que l'univers a sur lui. L'univers n'en sait rien" (*Pensées*, 10–11).

16. For the complete text, see M. Citoleux, *La poésie philosophique*, 188–91. The text reproduced by Citoleux varies slightly from the fragment Ackermann cites: "Léger," rather than "Misérable" grain; "Par un hymne des tes pleurs," instead of "Par des cris aigus et des pleurs."

17. See *Ma vie* in *Œuvres de Louise Ackermann*, xii–xxiii. The first edition of Schopenhauer's *Die Welt als Wille und Vorstellung* (*The World as Will and Representation*) dates to 1818 and a second, expanded edition to 1844. Once his works, such as *Métaphysique de l'amour* (1861) and *Le monde comme volonté et comme représentation* (1886), appeared in French translation, Schopenhauer gained prominence in France. His notion of the "will" driving the universe intersected with Ackermann's late verse and prose on the blind forces of nature.

18. "Adieux à la poésie" opens the section "Poésies" in *Contes et poésies* (1863), then *Premières poésies* in *Poésies* from 1874 onward.

19. A journal entry of 21 December 1863 maintains this view: "Tout est pour le pire dans le plus mauvais des mondes possibles" ("Journal," 546).

20. In the prose fragment "La femme," which survives only in a secondary source, Ackermann expresses the dominant view, associating women's reproductive function with diminished intellectual capacity: "La femme . . . est un être inférieur dont la principale fonction est la reproduction de l'espèce. Malheureusement elle ne peut accomplir son œuvre toute seule, il lui faut un collaborateur. . . . Elle est un instrument aveugle entre les mains de la nature, dont elle seconde admirablement les desseins. Mais comme celle-ci a le soin d'éviter les prodigalités inutiles, elle a refusé à la femme toute sérieuse capacité intellectuelle. On ne peut concevoir ni mettre au monde de deux côtés à la fois" (quoted in Haussonville, "M^me Ackermann," 350). Ackermann did not see herself in this light, which suggests a form of ironic distancing. For related comments, see her "Journal," 530, 554, and *Pensées d'une solitaire* [1903],10, 15, 18–19, 39, 41, 54, 55. See also Jenson, "Louise Ackermann's Monstrous Nature"; and Paliyenko, "Is a Woman Poet Born or Made?"

21. Paul Ackermann's publications include *Dictionnaire des antonymes ou contremots: Ouvrage fondé sur les écrivains classiques, destiné à la jeunesse et aux écrivains français* (1842) and *Remarques sur la langue française; ou, Répertoire grammatical* (1845).

22. In 1841, Paul Ackermann published *Chants d'amour, suivis de poésies diverses* and *Du principe de la poésie et de l'éducation du poète*. In the latter work, he asserts that women lack the patience that poetic composition requires: "Leur âme est poétique, mais trop identifiée avec la nature pour pouvoir la peindre; elles goûtent vivement, mais sans produire, parce que la sensation les entraîne et les absorbe" (13).

23. Ackermann drew on the *Mahabharata* for a cluster of stories in *Contes* (1855): "Savitri," "Sakountala," and "Le coffre et le brahmane."

24. French translations of *On the Origin of Species* (1859) by Clémence Royer and *The Descent of Man* (1871) by

Jean-Jacques Moulinié appeared in 1862 and 1872, respectively.

25. The first edition appeared in Nice in 1862, the second in Paris. Sainte-Beuve mentions the volume in an 1868 essay, comparing the lament in Ackermann to Labé as well as Sappho and Musset ("Œuvres de Louise Labé," 312–17). For Haussonville, the volume, though not a market success, widened Ackermann's circle to Stern, Béranger, and Sainte-Beuve ("M^me Ackermann," 333).

26. In 1834, d'Agoult had left her husband for Franz Liszt and had several children with him.

27. According to Vier, they exchanged no letters between 9 June 1867 and 18 February 1872 (*Marie d'Agoult*, 122).

28. See M. Citoleux, "Le salon littéraire," 328–30; and Vier, *Marie d'Agoult*, 119–42.

29. The mythological strand, which warrants a separate analysis, includes "La lyre d'Orphée," "Deux vers d'Alcée," "La lampe d'Héro," "L'Hyménée et l'Amour," "Endymion," "Hébé," and "La coupe du roi Thulé."

30. A young astronomer, John Tebbutt, using a 3¼-inch marine telescope, first sighted the comet in Australia on 13 May 1861; it became visible in the northern hemisphere by late June and was seen in telescopes until March 1862.

31. A revised version of the article by Read, "Madame Louise Ackermann: Intime," was published in *La Revue Hebdomadaire* (13 January 1900): 257–70. Read was Barbey d'Aurevilly's friend and secretary.

32. For the full context of this analysis, see Paliyenko, "Illuminating the Poetic Turn to Science."

33. Considerations of space do not allow me to measure Ackermann's achievement against that of other philosophical poets, such as Népomucène Lemercier, Bouilhet, Louis-Nicolas Ménard, and Leconte de Lisle (who preceded her) or Sully Prudhomme, Jean Richepin, and Lesueur (who followed her). On Ackermann and Prudhomme, see Hunt, *Epic in Nineteenth-Century France*, 382–86.

34. Ackermann's portrayal of a personified Nature here and elsewhere can be traced to the Italian poet Giacomo Leopardi, who "portray[ed] Nature as a cruel, vicious, unforgiving 'stepmother,' insensitive to the plight of mankind and its fate" (Leopardi, *Poems and Prose*, 14). For Leopardi's influence on Ackermann, see M. Citoleux, *La poésie philosophique*, 66–72.

35. First published in 1865, the poem was republished in *Poésies philosophiques* (1871), and this line was changed, likely to eliminate the repeated "où": "Où tu ne sauras plus savoir où loger tes fantômes."

36. Quoted in M. Citoleux, *La poésie philosophique*, 102; ellipses in original. For the complete text, see Berthelot, "La science idéale et la science positive," 443. For this and Ackermann's other scientific sources, see Citoleux, *La poésie philosophique*, 100–112.

37. On Ackermann's view of Shelley, see Paliyenko, "Illumining the Critical Reader in the Poet," 201–3.

38. To this point, Ackermann notes on 30 January 1867: "Dans le système de Spinoza, Dieu existe si peu que ce n'est pas la peine de l'adorer" ("Journal," 573).

39. Ackermann outlines this thought in an undated prose fragment: "Perdu dans l'immensité de l'univers, l'homme semble disparaître, et pourtant c'est lui qui est le dépositaire

unique des images, le miroir où viennent aboutir tous les rayons et les choses. Le monde n'existe que quand il s'est reflété dans ses yeux, dans sa pensée" (*Pensées* [1903], 45).

40. The same fragment followed a reflection on universal determinism when it was first published in 1881 ("Pensées diverses d'une solitaire," 616).

41. For the original context of this turn of phrase, see Parini, *Why Poetry Matters*, 65–77.

42. See exchanges with the comtesse d'Agoult in Vier, *Marie d'Agoult*, 135–36.

43. Tracy Paton has argued that Ackermann "appropriates the masculine persona of Prometheus to signify her own contradictory lyric identity" ("Seductive Rebellions," 28; see also 48–62).

44. The poem was first published as an individual piece in *Revue Moderne* in 1865. In the version of the poem published in *Poésies philosophiques* (1871), the last stanza expands from six to fourteen lines without altering the poem's gist, but the last four lines of the text remain the same.

45. On the composition of "Pascal," see Ackermann's letter of 7 May 1871 to her nephew Jules Fabrègue, describing an earlier, unpublished draft divided into three parts ("Le sphinx," "La croix," and "L'ignorance finale") and letters of 28 July and 3 October 1871 to her sister Caroline about subsequent parts ("Dernier mot" and "Idéal") sent to Havet ("Correspondance de Madame Ackermann" [1930], 429, 430, 432).

46. Pascal articulates his wager thus: "Votre raison n'est pas plus blessée, puisqu'il faut nécessairement choisir, en choisissant l'un que l'autre. Voilà un point vidé; mais votre béatitude? Pesons le gain et la perte en prenant croix, que Dieu est. Estimons ces deux cas: si vous gagnez, vous gagnez tout; si vous perdez, vous ne perdez rien. Gagez donc qu'il est, sans hésiter" (*Pensées*, 150).

47. Ackermann added an untitled fourth section after "L'inconnue" (section 3, which was followed by section 4, "Dernier mot," in the original, 1871 version of the poem), which develops the contemporary context of scientific discovery, to the version of the poem published in *Poésies* of 1885: "La Science nous ouvre une route nouvelle, / Et du voile jeté sur la face éternelle / Sa main lève les plis. Qu'allons-nous découvrir?" (*Œuvres de Louise Ackermann*, 152). On the revised poem and the dispute surrounding it, see the correspondence between Havet's son and Haussonville in the *Revue des Deux Mondes* 108 (15 December 1891) and Greenberg's analysis in *Uncanonical Women*, 41.

48. "Car enfin qu'est-ce que l'homme dans la nature? Un néant à l'égard de l'infini, un tout à l'égard du néant, un milieu entre rien et tout" (Pascal, *Pensées*, 3).

49. See reviews by Pontmartin, "Madame Ackermann: La poésie athée," and Chauvelot, "Courrier parisien," and Fontana's overview of Ackermann's reception in relation to religion, science, and the sexing of genius, "Louise Ackermann (1813–1890)."

50. On Ackermann's intellectualism, see P. Citoleux, "Madame Ackermann"; Thérive, "À propos de Mme Ackermann"; Schaffer, *Genres of Parnassian Poetry*, 66–79; and Somoff and Marfée, "Les muses du Parnasse," 33–47, 90–93.

51. On Ackermann's international reputation, see M. Citoleux, "Madame Ackermann et les étrangers."

## Chapter 8

1. Whidden's pioneering research dispels biographical errors, confirming Krysinska's birth on 22 January 1857, her marriage to Georges Bellenger in 1885, their sojourn in America from 1885 to 1886, and her death in 1908 (see Krysinska, *Rythmes pittoresques*, 1–3). Little else is known about Krysinska, apart from the fact that she took lovers, including the artists Charles Henry and Léo Goudeau, had no children, and died destitute and alone on 22 January 1908.

2. Krysinska's detractors circulated epithets, such as "la Saint-Jean Baptistine du vers libre," "l'instigatrice du vers libre," "la verseuse de Chopin," "Marpha Bableuska," and "la vieille fée du symbolisme," which are discussed in Whidden's introduction to her *Rythmes pittoresques*, 7–10.

3. See C. Scott, *Vers Libre*, 54–74, 99; Brogniez, "Marie Krysinska et le vers libre"; Whidden, "Sur la *supercherie* de Marie Krysinska"; Izquierdo, "Les poétesses de la Belle Époque et le vers libre"; and Merello, "Pour une définition du vers libre."

4. See Krysinska's essays in this book's bibliography. For exhaustive bibliographies, including her musical scores, consult Whidden's "Marie Krysinska: A Bibliography" and his 2003 edition of Krysinska's *Rythmes pittoresques*, 161–64.

5. According to Léon de Bercy, a singer and fellow Hydropathe, Krysinska arrived in Paris in 1873 at the age of sixteen (*Montmartre et ses chansons,*

45). Krysinska abandoned formal instruction two years later.

6. For a brief history of these groups, see Whidden's introduction to Krysinska, *Rythmes pittoresques*, 2–4. The poet Ernest Raynaud, a member of the *école romane* who was opposed to the Symbolists of the late 1880s, exposes the hostility toward intellectual women in describing Krysinska and her friend the actress Denise Ahmers at a meeting of the Zutistes: "à quoi elles tâchaient de s'intéresser, par bienséance, comme les dévotes écoutent, aux offices, le latin qu'elles n'entendent point" (*La mêlée symboliste*, 24).

7. See Whidden's discussion of this and other songs as well as poems in Krysinska, *Rythmes pittoresques*, 7–8.

8. Krysinska gives a detailed history of the Chat Noir and the eclectic circle that gathered there. The female cohort consisted of a single writer of prose, Rachilde (pen name of Marguerite Vallette-Eymery); the actresses Louise France, Lucienne Dorsy, and Renée Derigny; the singers Irma Perrot (who was also an actress) and Marthe Lys; and the musicians Clémence Duquesne and Rosa Nhynn ("Les cénacles," 480, 490–91).

9. See other references to Krysinska's literary salon in *Rythmes pittoresques*, 4–5.

10. Whidden adds Jean Lorrain, Gabriel Montoya, and Xavier Privas to this list; see his introduction to Krysinska, *Poèmes choisis*, 9.

11. In the 1849 essays "Art and Revolution" and "The Artwork of the Future," the German composer Richard Wagner uses the term *Gesamtkunstwerk* (the total work of art) to express his ideal of the synthesis of all the arts through theater. Teodor de

Wyzema promoted Wagner's theory in France; see his *Beethoven et Wagner*, esp. 115–97. Krysinska refers to Wagner in her poem "Âmes sonores," treating musical genius across the centuries (*Intermèdes*, 25–28).

12. In taking "music as a model for reshaping the nature of verse," Joseph Acquisto observes, "Krysinska, a pianist and composer as well as a poet, drew loosely on musical forms such as the villanelle, minuet, and sonata to give shape to her poems, and used repeated lines of verse the way a composer might integrate a musical theme into a composition" (*French Symbolist Poetry and the Idea of Music*, 9).

13. Krysinska uses the image of Eve as the first transgressor to frame her final poetic volume, *Intermèdes* (1903). She delves into the ambiguity of the desire associated with Eve in her novels *Folle de son corps* (1896), 228, and *La force du désir* (1905), 201–2.

14. See Paton's reading of Krysinska's first published poem, "Symphonie des parfums," as a parody of "the synaesthesic analogies, tropes, and themes associated with the 'feminine'" in Baudelaire's works ("Marie Krysinska's Poetics of Parody," 149). Goulesque analyzes an associative nexus of writing, song, and dance à la Wagner in another early poem ("Le 'Hibou' qui voulait danser").

15. Best known as a lithographer, Bellenger exhibited paintings at the Salon de Paris of 1864 and in London from 1875 to 1879.

16. Krysinska published the following poems between 1881 and 1883: in 1881, "Symphonie des parfums"*; in 1882, "Chanson d'automne," "Symphonie en gris," "Ballade," and "Berceuse macabre"*; in 1883, "Le hibou," "Les bijoux

faux,"* "Les fenêtres (poème en prose),"* "Un roman dans la lune,"* and "Le démon de Rakoczi." The titles marked with an asterisk are missing from the list Dujardin establishes in *Les premiers poètes*. See Whidden, "Marie Krysinska's Prefaces and Letters," 183–86, and "Sur la *supercherie* de Marie Krysinska," 80–83.

17. The historical period used by C. Scott to mark free verse's emergence in France, 1886–1914, excludes Krysinska's early production, yet he considers her a precursor (*Vers Libre*, 74). On the forms through which Krysinska's *vers libre* evolves, see Chévrier, "La place de Marie Krysinska dans la naissance du vers libre"; and van den Bergh, "Les poèmes de Marie Krysinska dans le *Chat Noir*."

18. Schultz notes: "Krysinska exploited free verse as a vehicle with which to question alienated feminine subjectivity and to liberate women from confining models of representation" (*Gendered Lyric*, 246).

19. According to the documentary hypothesis, various editors combined independent narratives into the current form of the Bible, among them the Yahwist source (the "J" text) dated to 950 BCE and the priestly source (the "P" text) from 550 BCE.

20. In studying how nineteenth-century American feminists appropriated Darwinism to free the sexes from the narrative of Adam and Eve, Hamlin discusses how "women countered antifeminist invocations of Eve by citing the first chapter of Genesis, which describes men and women as simultaneous creations" (*From Eve to Evolution*, 31).

21. The dual figuration of Eve as desired object and as desiring subject revises

the approach I took in Paliyenko, "In the Shadow of Eve."

22. A comparison between the first version of "Ève" (published in *La Revue Indépendante* in March 1890) and the second (in *Rythmes pittoresques* in October 1890) yields four minor differences in spelling and punctuation, which alter neither form nor content; see *Rythmes pittoresques*, 40. Krysinska dedicates the poem republished in *Rythmes pittoresques* to Maurice Isabey, an architect.

23. In examining translations of Genesis 3:6b with and without the prepositional phrase "with her," from the original Hebrew word עמה, Parker develops the absence of Adam, who "is present in Gen[esis] 3:1–6 and shares responsibility for disobedience," as a way to "height[en] the blame on the woman" ("Blaming Eve Alone," 729, 730).

24. On the gendering of the arts during the French Symbolist period, see Mathews, *Passionate Discontent*, 64–85.

25. Menon similarly observes: "Adam is absent from Krysinska's consideration of Eve, who is described as beautiful and independent." In this context, she writes: "The lascivious serpent is hopelessly attracted to her and their amorous encounter is conducted 'in ignorance of their prodigious destinies'" ("Les filles d'Ève," 170). Menon's translation suggests that "their" refers to Eve and the serpent, whereas in the French text, the possessive adjective refers to Eve's "flancs."

26. Moréas broke with the Symbolists in 1891 to form the *école romane*, which rejected free verse and the poetic treatment of modern subjects, advocating for a return to classical poetry. Krysinska likely identified more with Moréas's independent spirit than with either of his aesthetics.

27. Whidden has written regarding this grouping of poems: "In response to the historical debate of the creation of free verse, Krysinska offers women who transcend history, digging up myths from antiquity and breathing new life into them" ("Marie Krysinska's Prefaces and Letters," 187).

28. A professor at the École du Louvre, a specialist in Hebraic and Assyrian inscriptions, and the curator of Oriental relics at the Louvre, Ledrain's publications include *La Bible: Traduction nouvelle d'après les textes hébreu et grec* (1886–99).

29. Krysinska dedicates the poem to Catulle Mendès, a Parnassian poet and critic who later denied her originality.

30. The layout of the two versions of "Marie," like those of "Symphonie en gris," negotiates the shaping of poetic form at the level of typography. However, the versions of "Marie," published in close proximity, throw this negotiation into greater relief; the first version appeared on 7 June 1890 in *Le Chat Noir*, the second four months later in *Rythmes pittoresques*; see *Rythmes pittoresques*, 71, 142.

31. On the series "Notes féminines" and "Ombres féminines" (in *Joies errantes*), see Schultz, *Gendered Lyric*, 240–46. See also Wierzbowska's "Figures féminines," which treats in Krysinska's three poetic collections her use of syntax, typography, and shifts in context to subvert traditional portrayals of historical and legendary women.

32. On portraits of Mary Magdalene during the July Monarchy as both sinful and contrite, exuding pleasures of the flesh versus those of the spirit, see Bergman-Carton, *Woman of Ideas in French Art*, 140–60.

33. Wierzbowska observes that "Petit oratorio sur Marie-Magdelaine" (in *Intermèdes*) "trace le portrait d'une femme à l'esprit ouvert," adding that the revisionist poem "est une voix pour la faculté intellectuelle des femmes et s'inscrit dans la réflexion de la poétesse sur l'égalité créative, intellectuelle des deux sexes" ("Figures féminines," 69, 70).

34. Wierzbowska argues that Krysinska's use of this personification "renvoie vers le panthéisme" and suggests the synesthetic way that smell interweaves Mary Magdalene's human and divine natures (*Rythmes pittoresques*," 161).

35. All of the women to whom Krysinska dedicated individual poems were French actresses: Denise Ahmers, Luce Colas, Renée Derigny, Yvette Guilbert, and Irma Perrot (who was also a singer). The transnational link created by Krysinska with nineteenth-century British women novelists and American women poets in her essays of 1901 and 1905, respectively, championing their genius, merits study.

36. The other poets are Tristan Corbière, Rimbaud, Mallarmé, and Auguste Villiers de l'Isle-Adam.

37. Krysinska comments on her contemporaries' superior intellect and original work. For example, she invokes Cros's research in chemistry, physiology, and medicine to understand the source of genius as well as his work resolving "[l]e problème de photographier des couleurs" ("Les artistes maudits," 389).

38. This comment by the editors of *Les Annales Artistiques et Littéraires* first accompanied Krysinska's poem "Sonate," published in April 1890 to announce *Rythmes pittoresques*.

39. See reviews by Champsaur, Couturat, Doncieux, Dubus, Maurras, Néronde, and Sainte-Croix.

40. The essay is Anatole France's "Examen du manifeste," *Le Temps*, 26 September 1886.

41. For a concise overview of the theories of *vers libre*, see Jones, "The First Theory of 'Vers Libre.'" Moréas's "Manifeste" was first published in *Le Figaro* on 18 September 1886, then "reproduced in Paul Adam's piece 'Le Symbolisme' (*La Vogue*, October 4–11, 1886)," as Shryock notes ("Anarchism at the Dawn of the Symbolist Movement," 293).

42. See C. Scott, *Vers Libre*, 74; and Whidden, "Marie Krysinska's Prefaces and Letters," 185.

43. Kahn references his *Palais nomades* (1887) along with critical articles and poems he published in *La Revue Indépendante* in 1888.

44. See Paliyenko, "Rereading Breton's Debt to Apollinaire," 23.

45. Schultz analyzes how these clusters "question the representation of feminine beauty in love poetry and in so doing open the possibility of non-objectifying intersubjectivity in the lyric" (*Gendered Lyric*, 243).

46. It is interesting to compare this to the way Mallarmé depicted Rimbaud bursting forth like a meteor, as if from nowhere and without any literary precedent (*Œuvres complètes*, 2:120).

47. Composed in 1890–92 and in a second edition by 1896 (from which this citation comes), Krysinska's novel represents a woman's discovery of her sexuality. See Schultz's analysis, "De la poétique féministe et la liberté sexuelle dans l'œuvre romanesque de Marie Krysinska."

48. Krysinska references Prudhomme's 1897 article "Vues générales sur le

mouvement poétique en France au dix-neuvième siècle." Prudhomme cites the article liberally in his *Testament poétique* (1901), using the rhetoric of disease, monstrosity, and perversion to reproach fin-de-siècle poets for the demise of lyrical poetry during that period.

49. In "Pour le vers libre" (1902), Krysinska recycles this question in basing poetic evolution on "*individualités originales*" (4; emphasis in original).

50. Shryock has argued that correspondence between Rachilde and Rachel Kahn supports Gustave Kahn's claim; see *Lettres à Gustave Kahn et Rachel Kahn*, 152, 154–63. For Whidden, however, "there is no evidence, in either manuscript or published form, that shows Kahn writing free-verse poems before Krysinska" ("Marie Krysinska's Prefaces and Letters," 182).

51. The copy I possess has two title pages. The painting by Bellenger serves as the front cover of the second edition, published by Messein in 1904, which includes a second title page from a 1903 edition also by Albert Messein, who purchased the Vanier holdings from his widow and in January 1903 began publishing under the name Librairie Léon Vanier, Messein Succ[r].

52. This mythical scene recurs in Krysinska's novel *La force du désir*: "Les théogonies hébraïques ont symbolisé le mensonge comme une tare originelle. Par le mensonge, le serpent entraîne la première créature hors de l'orbite de la Loi" (200–201).

53. "If Eve had not eaten the fruit of knowledge, human history could not have begun," the modern biographer Pamela Norris has noted (*Eve*, 36).

54. In his foundational book *On the Origin of Species*, Darwin did not use the term "evolution," which did not emerge until the 1870s.

55. Unlike Krysinska, the Symbolists leaned toward the view of the German philosopher Eduard von Hartmann, whose *Philosophy of the Unconscious* (translated into French in 1877) advanced the unconscious as the provenance of genius (2:300, 308). Hartmann considers the Darwinian theory of evolution to be merely descriptive of individual variations and rejects the notion of hereditary genius (1:287–91, 2:306–13).

56. In 1901, Le Goffic mocked the triumph of *vers libre*: "le ci-devant vers amorphe, le *monstrum horrendum, informe, ingens* de Mme Krysinska et de M. Gustave Kahn" ("Les conquêtes du vers français," 993; emphasis in original).

57. Warm thanks to Julie de Sherbinin for translating the review from Russian.

58. See Mallarmé's essay "Ballets" (*Œuvres complètes*, 2:170–74). For Braswell, "the rhythmic mobility of dance-forms made visual, or *pittoresque*, figures prominently in Krysinska's poetry . . . the very choice of the title *Intermèdes* is, in fact, redolent with the suggestion of dance traditions" ("Marie Krysinska," 98; ellipses in original). In her reading of "Le poème des couleurs" (in *Joies errantes*), Braswell highlights the dancer Loïe Fuller's influence on Krysinska's poetics.

59. See Ghil, *Méthode évolutive-instrumentiste d'une poésie rationnelle* (1889); and Acquisto's analysis of Ghil's theory, "Between Stéphane Mallarmé and René Ghil."

# BIBLIOGRAPHY

Académie des sciences, arts et belles-lettres de Besançon, *Séances publiques des 24 Août 1826 et 29 Janvier 1827.* Besançon: Daclin, 1827.

Ackermann, Louise. *Contes.* Paris: Garnier, 1855.

———. *Contes et poésies par L. Ackermann.* 1862. Paris: Hachette, 1863.

———. "Correspondance de Madame Ackermann pendant son séjour à Nice." *Revue d'Histoire Littéraire de la France* 36 (1929): 580–89.

———. "Correspondance de Madame Ackermann pendant son séjour à Nice." *Revue d'Histoire Littéraire de la France* 37 (1930): 80–91, 244–58, 425–33.

———. "Journal de M^me Ackermann." Edited by Marc Citoleux. *Mercure de France* (1 May 1927): 524–75.

———. "Lettres inédites de M^me Ackermann." *La Nouvelle Revue* 110, nos. 1–2 (1898): 385–403.

———. "Lettres inédites pendant ses séjours en Allemagne et en Angleterre." *Revue de Littérature Comparée* 9 (1929): 141–62, 579–89.

———. *Œuvres de L. Ackermann: Ma vie, Premières poésies, Poésies philosophiques.* 1874. Paris: L'Harmattan, 2005.

———. *Œuvres de Louise Ackermann: Ma vie, Premières poésies, Poésies philosophiques.* Paris: Lemerre, 1893.

———. "Pensées diverses d'une solitaire." *La Nouvelle Revue* 5–6 (1 June 1881): 613–29.

———. *Pensées d'une solitaire, précédées d'une autobiographie.* Paris: Lemerre, 1882.

———. *Pensées d'une solitaire, précédées de fragments inédits.* Paris: Lemerre, 1903.

———. *Poésies philosophiques.* Nice: Caisson et Mignon, 1871.

———. *Poésies: Premières poésies, Poésies philosophiques.* Paris: Lemerre, 1874.

———. "Prométhée." *Revue Moderne* 66 (1866): 362–66.

Ackermann, Paul. *Chants d'amour, suivis de poésies diverses.* Paris: Crozet, 1841.

———. *Dictionnaire des antonymes ou contremots: Ouvrage fondé sur les écrivains classiques, destiné à la jeunesse et aux écrivains français.* Paris: Treuttel and Würtz, 1842.

———. *Du principe de la poésie et de l'éducation du poète.* Paris: Brockhaus and Avenarius, 1841.

———. *Remarques sur la langue française; ou, Répertoire grammatical.* Paris: Dźorby and Magdeleine, 1845.

Acquisto, Joseph. "Between Stéphane Mallarmé and René Ghil: The Impossible Desire for Poetry." *French Forum* 29, no. 3 (Fall 2004): 27–41.

———. *French Symbolist Poetry and the Idea of Music.* London: Ashgate, 2006.

Adam, Juliette [writing as Juliette La Messine]. *Idées anti-proudhoniennes sur l'amour, la femme et le mariage.* Paris: Librarie d'Alphonse Taride, 1858.

Albistur, Maïté, and Daniel Armogathe. *Histoire du féminisme français du Moyen Âge à nos jours.* 2 vols. Paris: Des Femmes, 1977.

Alighieri, Dante. *La vita nuova.* Translated by Barbara Reynolds. Baltimore: Penguin, 1969.

Ambrière, Francis. *Le siècle des Valmore: Marceline Desbordes-Valmore et les siens.* 2 vols. Paris: Seuil, 1987.

Amiel, Henri-Frédéric. *Journal intime: Février 1872–Juin 1874.* Paris: L'Âge d'Homme, 1989.

Ancelot, Jacques. "Critique littéraire: *Poésies* de Mme Desbordes-Valmore." *Annales de la Littérature et des Arts* 2, no. 2 (1821): 197–211.

Anon. "Du cerveau des nègres comparé à celui des Européens et de l'orang-outang, par le docteur F. Tiedemann." *Revue Britannique* 9 (1837): 168–74.

Antoine, Régis. *Les écrivains français et les Antilles: Des premiers pères blancs aux surréalistes noirs.* Paris: G. P. Maisonneuve et Larose, 1978.

Arseny, Hippolyte. "Galerie poétique du XIXème siècle: M^me Blanchecotte." *Réveil Littéraire et Artistique* (20 November 1875): 40.

Assa, Sonia. "Je n'ai pas eu le temps de consulter un livre: Les lectures de Marceline Desbordes-Valmore." In "Les femmes et la lecture," edited by Catherine R. Montfort, special issue, *Women in French Studies* (2012): 85–107.

Asselineau, Charles. *Histoire du sonnet pour servir à l'histoire de la poésie française.* 2nd ed. Alençon: Poulet-Malassis and De Broise, 1856.

Audouard, Olympe. *M. Barbey d'Aurévilly: Réponse à ses réquisitoires contre les bas-bleus, conférence du 11 avril 1870.* Paris: Dentu, 1870.

Aulard, François-Alphonse. "Madame Ackermann." *Revue Politique et Littéraire: Revue Bleue* 20 (1890): 620–23.

Baale-Uittenbosch, Alexandrina-Elizabeth-Maria. *Les poétesses dolentes du romantisme.* Haarlem: De Erven F. Bohn, 1928.

Babois, Victoire. *Élégies et poésies diverses.* 3rd ed. Paris: Nepveu Libraire, 1828.

Balzac, Honoré de. *Illusions perdues.* Paris: Gallimard, 1972.

———. *Œuvres complètes de M. Honoré de Balzac: La comédie humaine.* Vol. 6. Paris: Béthune and Plon, 1843.

Banville, Théodore de. *Camées parisiens.* Paris: Pincebourde, 1873.

———. *Petit traité de poésie française.* 1872. Paris: Charpentier, 1888.

Barbey d'Aurevilly, Jules. *Les bas-bleus.* Pt. 5 of *Les œuvres et les hommes.* 1878. Geneva: Slatkine Reprints, 1968.

———. "Madame Ackermann." In *Les œuvres et les hommes: Les poètes,*

2nd ser., 157–72. 1889. Geneva: Slatkine Reprints, 1968. Reprint of "*Poésies philosophiques*, par Madame Ackermann." *Le Constitutionnel*, 28 April 1873.

———. *Les poètes*. Pt. 3, 1st ser., of *Les œuvres et les hommes*. 1862. Geneva: Slatkine Reprints, 1968.

———. *Un prêtre marié*. Vol 1. Paris: Achille Faure, 1865.

Barrère, Pierre. *Dissertation sur la cause physique de la couleur des nègres, de la qualité de leurs cheveux, et de la dégénération de l'un et de l'autre*. Paris: Simon, 1741.

Battersby, Christine. *Gender and Genius: Toward a Feminist Aesthetics*. Bloomington: Indiana University Press, 1989.

Baudelaire, Charles. *Correspondance*. Edited by Claude Pichois and Jean Ziegler. Vol. 1. Paris: Gallimard, 1973.

———. *Œuvres complètes*. Edited by Claude Pichois. 2 vols. Paris: Gallimard, 1975–76.

Beaunier, André. *Visages de femmes*. 5th ed. Paris: Plon-Nourrit, 1913.

Beauvoir, Simone de. *Le deuxième sexe*. 2 vols. Paris: Gallimard, 1949.

———. "La femme et la création." 1966. In *Les écrits de Simone de Beauvoir*, edited by Claude Francis and Fernande Gontier, 458–74. Paris: Gallimard, 1979.

Beizer, Janet. *Ventriloquized Bodies: Narratives of Hysteria in Nineteenth-Century France*. Ithaca: Cornell University Press, 1994.

Benjamin, Walter. "The Work of Art in an Age of Mechanical Reproduction." In his *Illuminations*, 217–51. New York: Schocken, 1969.

Béranger, Pierre Jean de. *Correspondance*. Edited by Paul Boiteau. 4 vols. Paris: Perrotin, 1860.

Bercy, Léon de. *Montmartre et ses chansons: Poètes et chansonniers*. Paris: H. Daragon, 1902.

Berger, Anne-Emmanuelle. *Le banquet de Rimbaud: Recherches sur l'oralité*. Seyssel: Champ Vallon, 1992.

Bergman-Carton, Janis. *The Woman of Ideas in French Art, 1830–1848*. New Haven: Yale University Press, 1995.

Bernardin de Saint-Pierre, Jacques-Henri. *Paul et Virginie*. 1787. Paris: Garnier, 1958.

Bertaut, Jules. *La littérature féminine d'aujourd'hui*. Paris: Librairie des Annales Politiques et Littéraires, 1909.

Berthelot, Marcellin. "La science idéale et la science positive." *Revue des Deux Mondes* (1 November 1863): 442–59.

Bertrand, Marc. *Une femme à l'écoute de son temps: Marceline Desbordes-Valmore*. Lyon: Cigogne, 1997.

Besson, Martial, and Emmanuel des Essarts. *Anthologie scolaire des poètes français du XIX^e siècle*. Paris: Charles Delagrave, 1891.

Bewell, Alan. *Romanticism and Colonial Disease*. Baltimore: Johns Hopkins University Press, 1999.

Bishop, Michael. *Contemporary French Women Poets*. 2 vols. Amsterdam: Rodopi, 1995.

———. *Women's Poetry in France 1965–1995: A Bilingual Anthology*. Winston-Salem: Wake Forest University Press, 1997.

Bivort, Olivier. "Les 'vies absentes' de Rimbaud et de Marceline Desbordes-Valmore." *Revue d'Histoire Littéraire de la France* 4, no. 101 (2001): 1269–73.

Blanc, Liliane. *Elle sera poète, elle aussi: Les femmes et la création artistique*. Quebec: Le Jour, 1991.

Blanchecotte, Malvina. "À Lamartine." 18 August 1878. http://beinecke.library.yale.edu.

———. *Impressions d'une femme: Pensées, sentiments, et portraits.* Paris: Didier, 1868.

———. *Lamartine: Lettre à mon temps.* Soissons: Lallart, 1867.

———. *Le long du chemin: Pensées d'une solitaire.* Paris: Chez L'Auteur, 1864.

———. *Le long de la vie: Nouvelles impressions d'une femme.* Paris: Didier, 1875.

———. *Les militantes: Poésies.* Paris: Lemerre, 1875.

———. *Nouvelles poésies.* Paris: Perrotin, 1861.

———. *Olivier Goldsmith.* Paris: Bécus et Pyot, 1882.

———. "Perlino." *Musée des Familles* 31 (3 August 1893): 489.

———. *Rêves et réalités.* Paris: Ledoyen, 1855; 2nd ed., Paris: Ledoyen, 1856; 3rd ed., Paris: Didier, 1871.

———. *Tablettes d'une femme pendant la Commune.* 1872. Paris: Du Lérot, 1996.

Bloch, Auguste. "L'intelligence est-elle en rapport avec le volume du cerveau?" *Revue d'Anthropologie* (1885): 577–619.

Boismartin, Pierre-Ange Vieillard de. "*Penserosa, poésies nouvelles,* par Mme Louise Colet." *Le Moniteur Universel* (5 January 1840): 20.

Borel, Eugène. *Album lyrique de la France moderne: Chrestomathie du XIXème siècle.* Stuttgart: Deutsche Verlags Anstalt, 1904.

Boschian-Campaner, Catherine, ed. *Le vers libre dans tous ses états: Histoire et poétique d'une forme (1886–1914).* Paris: L'Harmattan, 2009.

Bourdieu, Pierre. *The Field of Cultural Production: Essays on Art and Literature.* Edited by Randal Johnson. New York: Columbia University Press, 1993.

Bouteron, Marcel. *Les muses romantiques.* 1926. Paris: Plon, 1934.

Boutin, Aimée. "Colonial Memory, Narrative and Sentimentalism in Desbordes-Valmore's *Les veillées des Antilles.*" In "Engendering Race: Romantic-Era Women and French Colonial Memory," edited by Adrianna M. Paliyenko, special issue, *L'Esprit Créateur* 47, no. 4 (Winter 2007): 57–67.

———. Introduction to Marceline Desbordes-Valmore, *Les veillées des Antilles.* Paris: L'Harmattan, 2006.

———."Inventing the 'Poétesse': New Approaches to French Women Romantic Poets." *Transatlantic Poetess* 29–30 (February–May 2003). http://www.erudit.org/revue/ron/2003/v/n29/007725ar.html.

———. "Marceline Desbordes-Valmore and the Sorority of Poets." *Women in French Studies* (2001): 165–80.

———. *Maternal Echoes: The Poetry of Marceline Desbordes-Valmore and Alphonse de Lamartine.* Newark: University of Delaware Press, 2001.

———. "Shakespeare, Women, and French Romanticism." *Modern Language Quarterly* 65, no. 4 (December 2004): 505–29.

Boutin, Aimée, and Adrianna M. Paliyenko. "Nineteenth-Century French Women Poets: An Exceptional Legacy." In "French and Francophone Women, 16th–21st Centuries: Essays on Literature, Culture, and Society with Bibliographical and Media Resources," edited by Catherine Montfort and Marie-Christine Koop, special issue, *Women in French Studies* (October 2002): 77–109.

Braswell, Suzanne. "Marie Krysinska, Loïe Fuller, and Dynamogenic Eurhythmy." *Australian Journal of French Studies* 46, nos. 1–2 (2009): 97–110.

Broc, Hervé de. *Les femmes auteurs.* Paris: Plon, 1911.

Broca, Paul. *Sur le volume et la forme du cerveau suivant les individus et suivant les races.* Excerpt of vol. 2 of *Bulletins de la Société d'Anthropologie*, sessions of 21 March and 2 May. Paris: Hennuyer, 1861.

Brogniez, Laurence. "Marie Krysinska et le vers libre: L'outrage fait aux Muses." In *Masculin/féminin dans la poésie et les poétiques du XIX$^e$ siècle*, edited by Christine Planté, 421–36. Lyon: Presses Universitaires de Lyon, 2002.

Browning, Elizabeth Barrett. *Poems by Elizabeth Barrett Browning.* Vol. 1. London: Edward Moxon, 1844.

Brunel, Pierre. "Rimbaud et Louisa Siefert." In *Studi in onore di Mario Matucci*, edited by Silvio Loffredo, 202–10. Pisa: Pacini, 1993.

Brunetière, Ferdinand. *L'évolution de la poésie lyrique en France au dix-neuvième siècle: Leçons professées à la Sorbonne.* Paris: Hachette, 1913.

———. "L'influence des femmes dans la littérature française." In his *Questions de critique*, 23–61. Paris: Calmann Lévy, 1889.

Budan, Armand. *La Guadeloupe pittoresque.* Paris: Noblet et Baudry, 1863.

Buet, Charles. *J. Barbey d'Aurevilly: Souvenirs et impressions.* Paris: Albert Savine, 1891.

Buffon, Georges-Louis Leclerc. *Les époques de la nature.* Paris: Imprimerie Royale, 1780.

———. *Histoire naturelle, générale et particulière.* Paris: Imprimerie Royale, 1753.

Cabanis, Pierre-Jean-Georges. *Rapports du physique et du moral de l'homme.* 1802. 3rd ed. Paris: Caille et Ravier, 1815.

Caro, Elme. "La poésie philosophique dans les nouvelles écoles: Un poète positiviste." *Revue des Deux Mondes* 3 (1874): 241–63.

Cashin, A. *Amour et liberté: Abolition de l'esclavage.* Paris: L'Harmattan, 2009.

Chaitin, Gilbert, ed. *Cultural Wars and Literature in the French Third Republic.* Newcastle upon Tyne: Cambridge Scholars, 2008.

Champsaur, Félicien. "Chronique parisienne." *L'Événement* (16 October 1890): 1.

Charlton, Donald Geoffrey. *Positivist Thought in France During the Second Empire, 1852–1870.* Oxford: Clarendon, 1959.

Chateaubriand, François René de. *Le génie du christianisme.* 1802. Paris: Firmin Didot Frères, 1846.

———. *Mélanges littéraires.* Paris: Pourrat, 1833.

———. *Mémoires d'outre-tombe.* 2 vols. Paris: Gallimard, 1951.

Chauvelot, Bernard. "Courrier parisien." *L'Univers: Journal Religieux, Politique, Scientifique et Littéraire*, 30 October 1874.

Chauvet, Victor. "Chroniques de France, par Mme Amable Tastu." *Revue Encyclopédique* 42 (1829): 678–88.

———. "Poésies, par Mme Amable Tastu." *Revue Encyclopédique* 23 (1826): 648–52.

Chazelle, René. *Joseph Guichard: Peintre lyonnais (1806–1880), disciple d'Ingres et de Delacroix.* Lyon: Presses Universitaires de Lyon, 1992.

Chénier, André. *Œuvres poétiques.* Vol. 2. Paris: Librairie Garnier Frères, 1965.

Chévrier, Alain. "La place de Marie Krysinska dans la naissance du vers libre." In *Innovations poétiques et combats littéraires: Marie Krysinska*, edited by Adrianna M. Paliyenko, Gretchen Schultz, and Seth Whidden, 77–93. Lyon: Presses Universitaires de Saint-Etienne/Presses Universitaires de Lyon, 2010.

Chichmanoff, Irène. "Étude critique sur les femmes poètes en France au XIX$^e$ siècle." Doctoral thesis, University of Bern, 1910.

Chovet, Lucien. "Un faux Rimbaud non encore identifié ou Marceline Desbordes-Valmore, plagiaire par anticipation de Rimbaud." *Histoires Littéraires* 5 (2001): 61–66.

Citoleux, Marc. "Madame Ackermann et les étrangers." *Revue de Littérature Comparée* (1931): 466–72.

———. *La poésie philosophique au XIX$^e$ siècle.* 1905–6. Geneva: Slatkine Reprints, 1973.

———. "Le salon littéraire des Feuillantines: les catholiques et les neutres chez Mme Ackermann." *Mercure de France* (15 January 1932): 313–31.

Citoleux, Pierre. "Madame Ackermann." *Revue des Poètes* (20 December 1904): 265–77.

Claretie, Jules. *Élisa Mercœur.* Paris: Librairie de Mme Bachelin-Deflorenne, 1864.

———. *La vie à Paris.* Paris: Charpentier, 1898.

Clarke, Edward. *Sex in Education; or, A Fair Chance for the Girls.* Boston: James R. Osgood, 1873.

Clarkson, Thomas. *The Cries of Africa to the Inhabitants of Europe; or, A Survey of That Bloody Commerce Called the Slave Trade.* London: Harvey and Darton, 1822.

Clément, Michèle. "La réception de Louise Labé dans les éditions du XIX$^e$ siècle: La résistance au féminin, la résistance du féminin." In *Masculin/féminin dans la poésie et les poétiques du XIX$^e$ siècle*, edited by Christine Planté, 39–50. Lyon: Presses Universitaires de Lyon, 2002.

Cohen, Margaret. *The Sentimental Education of the Novel.* Princeton: Princeton University Press, 2002.

Cohen, William. *The French Encounter with Africans.* Bloomington: Indiana University Press, 1980.

Coleman, William. *Biology in the Nineteenth Century: Problems of Form, Function, and Transformation.* Cambridge: Cambridge University Press, 1978.

Colet, Louise. *Ce qui est dans le cœur des femmes: Poésies nouvelles.* Paris: Librairie Nouvelle, 1852.

———. *Poésies complètes de Madame Louise Colet.* Paris: Gosselin, 1844.

Coligny, Charles. "Les muses parisiennes: Madame Malvina Blanchecotte." *La Revue Fantaisiste* 2 (March 1861): 107–15.

Collaborateurs de *La Revue*. "Livres et idées en France et à l'étranger." *Revue* 49 (1904): 358–62.

Condorcet, Marie-Jean-Antoine-Nicolas de Caritat. "Des avantages et des progrès des sciences." 21 February

1782. www.academic-francaise.fr/immortels/index.html.

——. *Lettres d'un bourgeois de New Haven à un citoyen de Virginie, sur l'inutilité de partager le pouvoir législatif entre plusieurs corps.* In *Œuvres de Condorcet,* 9:2–93. Edited by A. Condorcet O'Connor and M. F. Arago. Paris: Firmin Didot Frères, 1847. http://gallica.bnf.fr/ark:/12148/bpt6k417228.

——. *Tableau historique des progrès de l'esprit humain: Ouvrage posthume.* Paris: Imprimerie de Constant-Chantpie, 1823.

Constans, Ellen. *Ouvrières des lettres.* Limoges: Presses Universitaires de Limoges, 2007.

Cooper, Barbara T. "Race, Gender, and Colonialism in Anaïs Ségalas's *Récits des Antilles: Le Bois de la Soufrière.*" In "Engendering Race: Romantic-Era Women and French Colonial Memory," edited by Adrianna M. Paliyenko, special issue, *L'Esprit Créateur* 47, no. 4 (Winter 2007): 118–29.

Cottin, Sophie. *Malvina, par Madame ***, auteur de Claire d'Albe.* 2 vols. Paris: Maradan, 1800.

Couturat, Jules. "Compte rendu de *Rythmes pittoresques,* par Marie Krysinska." *La Revue Indépendante* 17, no. 48 (October 1890): 120–21.

Crépet, Eugène, ed. *Les poëtes français, recueil des chefs d'oeuvres de la poésie française depuis les origines jusqu'à nos jours.* 4 vols. Paris: Gide Libraire, 1861–63.

Cronin, Vincent. *Napoleon Bonaparte: An Intimate Biography.* New York: William Morrow, 1972.

Croze, Marie-Charlotte. "Une héroïne romantique: Mélanie Waldor." *Nouvelle Revue* (1912): 167–83.

Cuvier, Georges. *Leçons d'anatomie comparée.* 1803. 2nd ed. Paris: Crochard, 1835.

——. *Tableau élémentaire de l'histoire naturelle des animaux.* Paris: Baudouin, 1798.

Czyba, Luce. "Anais Ségalas (1814–1893)." In *Femmes poètes du XIXᵉ siècle: Une anthologie,* edited by Christine Planté, 185–92. 2nd ed. Lyon: Presses Universitaires de Lyon, 2010.

Daget, Serge. "Les mots 'esclave,' 'nègre,' 'noir,' et les jugements de valeur sur la traite négrière dans la littérature abolitionniste française de 1770 à 1845." *Revue Française d'Histoire d'Outre-Mer* 60 (1973): 511–48.

D'Alq, Louise. *Anthologie féminine: Anthologie des femmes écrivains poètes et prosateurs depuis l'origine de la langue française jusqu'à nos jours.* Paris: Bureaux des Causeries Familières, 1893.

Danahy, Michael. *The Feminization of the Novel.* Gainesville: University of Florida Press, 1991.

Darwin, Charles. *The Descent of Man, and Selection in Relation to Sex.* 2 vols. London: John Murray, 1871.

——. *On the Origin of Species.* London: John Murray, 1859.

Delaville, Camille Chartier. *Mes Contemporaines.* 1st ser. Paris: P. Sévin, 1887.

Desbordes-Valmore, Marceline. "À M. Gaschon de Molènes." *Revue du Lyonnais* 16 (1842): 271–72.

——. *Les anges de la famille.* Paris: A. Desesserts, 1849.

——. *Bouquets et prières.* Paris: Dumont, 1843.

——. *Les chefs-d'œuvre lyriques de Marceline Desbordes-Valmore.* Edited by Auguste Dorchain. Paris: A. Perche, 1921.

———. *Contes en prose pour les enfants.* Lyon: L. Boitel, 1840.

———. *Contes en vers pour les enfants.* Lyon: L. Boitel, 1840.

———. *Correspondance intime.* Edited by Benjamin Rivière. 2 vols. Paris: Lemerre, 1896.

———. *Élégies, Marie, et romances.* Paris: François Louis, 1819.

———. *Huit femmes.* Edited by Marc Bertrand. Geneva: Droz, 1999.

———. *Lettres inédites (1812–1857).* Edited by Hippolyte Valmore. Paris: Louis Michaud, 1911.

———. *Lettres de Marceline Desbordes à Prosper Valmore.* 2 vols. Paris: Éditions de la Sirène, 1924.

———. *Le livre des mères et des enfants: Contes en vers et en prose.* 2 vols. Lyon: L. Boitel, 1840.

———. *Œuvres choisies de Marceline Desbordes-Valmore.* Edited by Frédéric Loliée. Paris: Delagrave, 1909.

———. *Œuvres manuscrites de Marceline Desbordes-Valmore: Albums à Pauline.* Paris: Lemerre, 1921.

———. *Œuvres poétiques.* Edited by Marc Bertrand. 2 vols. Grenoble: Presses Universitaires de Grenoble, 1973.

———. *Œuvres poétiques de Marceline Desbordes-Valmore.* Edited by Auguste Lacaussade. Paris: Lemerre, 1886.

———. *Poésies.* 1820. Edited by Charles Augustin Sainte-Beuve. Paris: Charpentier, 1842.

———. *Les veillées des Antilles.* 1820–21. Paris: L'Harmattan, 2006.

Des Essarts, Emmanuel. "À Louisa Siefert." *Lyon-Revue* 3 (1882): 357.

———. "Les morts d'hier: Louisa Siefert." *La Vie Littéraire,* 1 November 1877.

———. "Poètes français contemporains: Louisa Siefert." *Revue Politique et Littéraire: Revue Bleue* 2 (3 September 1881): 307–10.

Desplaces, Auguste. *Galerie des poètes vivants.* Paris: Charpentier, 1848.

Desplantes, François, and Paul Pouthier. *Les femmes de lettres en France.* 1890. Geneva: Slatkine Reprints, 1970.

d'Héricourt, Jenny P. *La femme affranchie: Réponse à MM. Michelet, Proudhon, É. de Girardin, A. Comte.* 2 vols. Brussels: Lacroix, 1860.

Doin, Sophie. *La famille noire, suivie de trois nouvelles blanches et noires.* 1825. Edited by Doris Kadish. Paris: L'Harmattan, 2002.

Doncieux, Georges. "*Rythmes pittoresques* par Marie Krysinska." *Revue du Siècle, Littéraire, Artistique et Scientifique* 6 (1892): 240–41.

Dormandy, Thomas. *The White Death: A History of Tuberculosis.* New York: New York University Press, 2000.

Dornis, Jean. *La sensibilité dans la poésie contemporaine.* Paris: Fayard, 1912.

Doumic, René. *La vie et les mœurs.* Paris: Perrin, 1895.

Drohojowska, Madame la Comtesse. *Les femmes illustres de la France.* Paris: P. C. Lehuby, 1850.

Dubus, Édouard. "Compte rendu des *Rythmes pittoresques,* par Marie Krysinska." *Mercure de France* 12 (December 1890): 443–44.

Dufrénoy, Adélaïde. "De Mmes Bourdic-Viot, Desroches, Verdier, Victoire Babois: De l'idylle, de l'élégie, et des poésies de Mme Desbordes-Valmore." *La Minerve Littéraire* (1820): 556–61, 617–24.

———. *Œuvres poétiques de M^{me} Dufrénoy.* Brussels: M. Hayez, 1827.

———. *Opuscules poétiques.* Paris: Arthus-Bertrand, 1806.

Dufrénoy, Adélaïde, and Amable Tastu. *Le livre des femmes: Choix de morceaux extraits des meilleurs écrivains français, sur le caractère, les mœurs et l'esprit des femmes.* 2 vols. Gand: G. de Busscher et Fils, 1823.

Dujardin, Édouard. *Les premiers poètes du vers libre.* Paris: Mercure, 1922.

Dumas fils, Alexandre. *L'homme-femme: Réponse à M. Henri d'Ideville.* 26th ed. Paris: Michel Lévy Frères, 1872.

Dumas père, Alexandre. *Lettres d'Alexandre Dumas à Mélanie Waldor.* Edited by Claude Schopp. Paris: Presses Universitaires de France, 1982.

Duras, Claire de. *Ourika: The Original French Text.* 1823. Edited by Joan Dejean. New York: Modern Language Association, 1994.

Elfenbein, Andrew. "Mary Wollstonecraft and the Sexuality of Genius." In *The Cambridge Companion to Mary Wollstonecraft*, edited by Claudia L. Johnson, 228–45. Cambridge: Cambridge University Press, 2002.

Enne, Francis. "Chez Krysinska." *Le Réveil,* 7 December 1882.

Épictète, Marc-Aurèle. *Manuels d'Épictète, suivis du tableau de Cébès.* Paris: 1798.

Étienne, Louis. "La poésie et les poètes de la nouvelle génération." *Revue des Deux Mondes* 82 (July–August 1869): 710–37.

Ezell, Margaret. *Writing Women's Literary History.* Baltimore: Johns Hopkins University Press, 1993.

Faneau de la Cour, Ferdinand Valère. *Du féminisme et de l'infantilisme chez les tuberculeux.* Paris: A. Parent, 1871.

Fère, Guyot de. *Statistique des lettres et des sciences en France, Institutions et établissements littéraires et scientifiques, Dictionnaire des hommes de lettres, des savans existant en France: Leurs ouvrages, leur domicile actuel, etc.* Paris: Chez l'Auteur, 1834.

Ferry, Jules. *Discours et opinions de Jules Ferry.* Vol. 7. Edited by Paul Robiquet. Paris: Armand Colin, 1897.

Feyrnet, Xavier [Charles Blanc]. "Rayons perdus." *Le Temps,* 10 January 1869.

Finch, Alison. *Women's Writing in Nineteenth-Century France.* Cambridge: Cambridge University Press, 2000.

Finn, Michael R. "Physiological Fictions and the Fin-de-Siècle Female Brain." *Nineteenth-Century French Studies* 39, nos. 3–4 (2011): 315–31.

Flat, Paul. *Nos femmes de lettres.* Paris: Perrin, 1909.

Flaubert, Gustave. *Correspondance.* Edited by Jean Bruneau. 4 vols. Paris: Gallimard, 1973.

Fontana, Michèle. "Louise Ackermann (1813–1890)." In *Femmes poètes du XIXᵉ siècle: Une anthologie*, edited by Christine Planté, 205–16. 2nd ed. Lyon: Presses Universitaires de Lyon, 2010.

Fouillée, Alfred. "La psychologie des sexes et ses fondements physiologiques," *Revue des Deux Mondes* 119 (15 September 1893): 397–429.

Fraisse, Geneviève. *Muse de la raison: La démocratie exclusive et la différence des sexes.* Paris: Alinéa, 1989.

France, Anatole. "Les poètes contemporains, vers inédits et notices: L. Ackermann." *Le Temps,* 19 February 1874.

Fraser, Kennedy. *Ornament and Silence: Essays on Women's Lives*. New York: Knopf, 1997.

Freud, Sigmund. *The Standard Edition of the Complete Psychological Works*. 24 vols. Edited and translated by James Strachey. London: Hogarth, 1955–74.

Fusil, Casimir Alexandre. *La poésie scientifique de 1750 à nos jours: Son élaboration, sa constitution*. Paris: Éditions Scientifica, 1917.

Fuster, Charles. "Une Sapho moderne: Louisa Siefert." In his *Essais de critique*, 99–112. 3rd ed. Paris: Giraud, 1886.

Gale, Beth W. "Education, Literature and the Battle over Female Identity in Third Republic France." In Chaitain, ed., *Cultural Wars and Literature in the French Third Republic*, 103–27.

Galton, Francis. *Hereditary Genius: An Inquiry into Its Laws and Consequences*. London: Macmillan, 1869.

Gautier, Paul. *Napoleon Bonaparte*. Paris: Plon-Nourrit, 1921.

Gautier, Théophile. *Correspondance générale*. Edited by Claudine Lacoste-Veysseyre. Vol. 5. Geneva: Droz, 1988.

———. "*Les oiseaux de passage* par Madame Anaïs Ségalas." *Le Figaro*, 8 December 1836.

———. "Rapport sur le progrès de la poésie." In *Recueil de rapports sur les progrès des lettres et des sciences en France*, edited by Sylvestre de Sacy, Paul Féval, Théophile Gautier, and Éd[ouard] Thierry, 67–141. Paris: L'Imprimerie Impériale, 1868.

Gay, Sophie. "Compte rendu de *Poésies* par Marceline Desbordes-Valmore." *Revue Encyclopédique* (October 1820): 157–59.

Genette, Gérard. *Paratextes: Thresholds of Interpretation*. Translated by Jane E. Lewin. Cambridge: Cambridge University Press, 1997.

Genlis, Stephanie-Félicité de. *De l'influence des femmes sur la littérature française*. Paris: Maradan, 1811.

Gérard, Rosemonde. *Les muses françaises: Poèmes*. Paris: Fasquelle, 1943.

Ghil, René. "*Intermèdes* de Marie Krysinska." *Viessy* 1, no. 6 (June 1904): 49–52.

———. *Méthode évolutive-instrumentiste d'une poésie rationnelle: Article-commentaire du "Traité du verbe."* Paris: Savine, 1889.

Gilbert, Sandra M., and Susan Gubar. *The Madwoman in the Attic: The Woman Writer and the Nineteenth-Century Literary Imagination*. New Haven: Yale University Press, 1979.

Girardin, Delphine [Gay] de [Charles de Launay]. *Lettres parisiennes*. 3 vols. Paris: Libraire Nouvelle, 1856.

———. *Œuvres complètes*. 6 vols. Paris: Plon, 1860–61.

———. *Poésies complètes*. Paris: Librairie Nouvelle, 1856.

Gobineau, Arthur de. *Essai sur l'inégalité des races*. 1853–55. Paris: Belfond, 1967.

Goldberg Moses, Claire. *French Feminism in the Nineteenth Century*. Albany: State University of New York Press, 1984.

Goldstein, Jan. *Console and Classify: The French Psychiatric Profession in the Nineteenth Century*. 1987. Cambridge: Cambridge University Press, 1990.

Goncourt, Edmond de, and Jules de Goncourt. *Les hommes de lettres*. Paris: E. Dentu, 1860.

———. *Journal.* Edited by A. Ricatte. 4 vols. Paris: Flammarion, 1959.

Gouges, Olympe de. "Déclaration des droits de la femme et de la citoyenne." In her *Les droits de la femme: À la reine,* 6–11. Paris: N.p., 1791.

———. *L'esclavage des noirs; ou, L'heureux naufrage.* Paris: Côté-Femmes, 1989.

———. "Réflexions sur les hommes nègres." In her *Œuvres de Madame de Gouges,* 3:92–99. 3 vols. Paris: Chez l'Auteur and Cailleau, 1788.

Goulesque, Florence. "Le 'Hibou' qui voulait danser: Marie Krysinska, une innovatrice du vers libre doublée d'une théoricienne de la poésie moderne." *Symposium* 53, no. 4 (Winter 2000): 220–33.

Gourmont, Jean de. *Muses d'aujourd'hui: Essais de physiologie poétique.* Paris: Mercure de France, 1910.

Grandeffe, Arthur de. *La pie bas-bleu.* Paris: Ledoyen, 1858.

Gray, Francine du Plessix. *Rage and Fire: A Life of Louise Colet, Pioneer Feminist, Literary Star, Flaubert's Muse.* New York: Simon and Schuster, 1994.

Greenberg, Wendy. "Élisa Mercœur: The Poetics of Genius and the Sublime." *Nineteenth-Century French Studies* 24 (Fall–Winter 1995–96): 84–96.

———. *Uncanonical Women: Feminine Voice in French Poetry (1830–1871).* Amsterdam: Rodopi, 1999.

Gregh, Fernand. *Portrait de la poésie française au XIXᵉ siècle.* Paris: Delagrave, 1936.

Grégoire, Henri de. *De la littérature des nègres; ou, Recherches sur leurs facultés intellectuelles, leurs qualités morales et de leur littérature.* Paris: Maradan, 1808.

———. *De la noblesse de la peau; ou, Du préjugé des blancs.* Paris: Baudoin, 1826.

Grenier, Édouard. "Souvenirs littéraires: Quatuor féminin." *Revue Politique et Littéraire: Revue Bleue* 52 (1893): 107–17.

Hackett, Cecil A. *Anthology of Modern French Poetry: From Baudelaire to the Present Day.* Oxford: Blackwell, 1952.

Hamlin, Kimberly A. *From Eve to Evolution: Darwin, Science, and Women's Rights in Gilded America.* Chicago: University of Chicago Press, 2014.

Hartmann, Eduard von. *Philosophy of the Unconscious.* Translated by William C. Coupland. 3 vols. 2nd ed. London: K. Paul, Trench, Trübner, 1893.

Hauser, Fernand. "Madame Marie Krysinska." *Simple Revue* (16 May 1894): 49–52.

Haussonville, [Gabriel Paul Othenin de Cléron]. "Mᵐᵉ Ackermann d'après des lettres et des papiers inédits." *Revue des Deux Mondes* 106 (1891): 310–52.

Hefferman, Michael J. "Rogues, Rascals and Rude Books: Policing the Popular Book Trade in Early-Nineteenth-Century France." *Journal of Historical Geography* 16, no. 1 (January 1990): 90–108.

Helvétius, Claude Adrien. *De l'esprit.* Paris: Durand, 1758.

———. *De l'homme: De ses facultés intellectuelles et de son éducation.* 1772. 2 vols. Londres: Société Typographique, 1773.

Herold, Christopher. *Mistress to an Age: A Life of Madame de Staël.* New York: Bobbs-Merrill, 1958.

Hervey, Charles. "A Reception of Alfred de Vigny's." *Bookmart* 6 (February 1889): 484–89.

Hesse, Carla. *The Other Enlightenment: How French Women Became Modern.* Princeton: Princeton University Press, 2001.

Higgins, David. *Romantic Genius and the Literary Magazine: Biography, Celebrity and Politics.* London: Routledge, 2004.

Hoock-Demarle, Marie-Claire. "Lire et écrire en Allemagne." In *Histoire des femmes en Occident: Le XIX<sup>e</sup> siècle*, edited by Geneviève Fraisse and Michelle Perrot, 147–67. Paris: Plon, 1991.

Howe, Julia Ward, ed. *Sex and Education: A Reply to Dr. E. H. Clarke's "Sex in Education."* 1874. New York: Arno, 1972.

Huart, Louis, and Charles Philipon. *Galerie de la presse, de la littérature et des beaux-arts.* Vol. 1. Paris: Aubert, 1841.

Hugo, Victor. *Bug-Jargal.* 1826. Paris: Hetzel, 1832.

———. *Nouvelles odes.* Paris: Ladvocat, 1824.

———. *Odes et ballades.* Paris: J. Tastu, 1826.

———. *Odes et poésies diverses.* Paris: Pélicier, 1822.

———. *Les orientales.* 5th ed. In *Œuvres de Victor Hugo.* Vol. 3. Paris: Paul Renouard, 1829.

———. "*Poésies* de Mme Desbordes-Valmore." *Le Conservateur Littéraire* 3 (February 1821): 338–45.

Hunt, Herbert J. *The Epic in Nineteenth-Century France.* Oxford: Blackwell, 1941.

Huret, Jules. *L'enquête sur l'évolution littéraire.* Paris: Charpentier, 1891.

Iung, Th[éodore]. *Lucien Bonaparte et ses mémoires, 1775–1840.* 3 vols. Paris: Charpentier, 1882.

Izquierdo, Patricia. "Les poétesses de la Belle Époque et le vers libre." In *Le vers libre dans tous ses états: Histoire et poétique d'une forme (1886–1914)*, edited by Catherine Boschian-Campaner, 109–20. Paris: L'Harmattan, 2009.

Jackson, Joseph F. *Louise Colet et ses amis littéraires.* New Haven: Yale University Press, 1937.

Jacob, Paul. "Mme Ségalas." In *Biographie des femmes auteurs*, edited by Alfred de Montferrand, 37–47. Paris: Armand-Aubrée, 1836.

Jacquinet, Paul, ed. *Les femmes de France: Poètes et prosateurs.* 1886. 2nd ed. Saint-Cloud: Vve Belin et fils, 1889.

Jacyna, L. Stephen. "Moral Fibre: The Negotiation of Microscopic Facts in Victorian Britain." *Journal of the History of Biology* 36, no. 1 (2003): 39–85.

Jaffe, Kineret S. "The Concept of Genius: Its Changing Role in Eighteenth-Century French Aesthetics." *Journal of the History of Ideas* 41, no. 4 (October–December 1980): 579–99.

James, Sara. "Malvina Blanchecotte and 'la douleur chantée': The Creation of a Female Poetic Self." In *Pleasure and Pain in Nineteenth-Century French Literature and Culture*, edited by David Evans and Kate Griffiths, 141–57. Amsterdam: Rodopi, 2008.

Janin, Jules. "Le bas-bleu." In *Les Français peints par eux-mêmes: Encyclopédie morale du dix-neuvième siècle*, 5:201–31. Paris: L. Curmer, 1841–50.

Jasenas, Éliane. *Marceline Desbordes-Valmore devant la critique.* Geneva: Droz, 1962.

Jefferson, Ann. *Genius in France: An Idea and Its Uses.* Princeton: Princeton University Press, 2015.

Jennings, Lawrence. *French Anti-Slavery: The Movement for the Abolition of Slavery in France, 1802–1848.* Cambridge: Cambridge University Press, 2000.

Jenson, Deborah. "Gender and the Aesthetic of 'Le Mal': Louise Ackermann's *Poésies philosophiques*, 1871." *Nineteenth-Century French Studies* 23, nos. 1–2 (Fall–Winter 1994–95): 175–93.

———. "Louise Ackermann's Monstrous Nature." *Symposium* 53, no. 4 (Winter 2000): 234–48.

———. "Myth, History, and Witnessing in Marceline Desbordes-Valmore's Caribbean Poetics." *L'Esprit Créateur* 47, no. 4 (Winter 2007): 81–92.

———. *Trauma and Its Representations: The Social Life of Mimesis in Post-Revolutionary France.* Baltimore: Johns Hopkins University Press, 2001.

Johnson, Barbara. "1820: The Lady in the Lake." In *A New History of French Literature*, edited by Denis Hollier, 627–32. 1989. Cambridge: Harvard University Press, 1994.

———. "Gender and Poetry: Charles Baudelaire and Marceline Desbordes-Valmore." In *Displacements: Women, Tradition, Literatures in French*, edited by Joan DeJean and Nancy K. Miller, 163–81. Baltimore: Johns Hopkins University Press, 1991.

Joly, Henri. *Psychologie des grands hommes.* Paris: Hachette, 1883.

Jones, P. Mandsell. "The First Theory of 'Vers Libre.'" *Modern Language Review* 42, no. 2 (April 1947): 207–14.

Jordanova, Ludmilla. *Sexual Visions: Images of Gender in Science and Medicine between the Eighteenth and Twentieth Centuries.* New York: Harvester Wheatsheaf, 1989.

Kadish, Doris. "The Black Terror: Women's Responses to Slave Revolts in Haiti." *French Review* 68, no. 4 (March 1995): 668–80.

———. "*Sarah* and Anti-Slavery." In "Engendering Race: Romantic-Era Women and French Colonial Memory," edited by Adrianna M. Paliyenko, special issue, *L'Esprit Créateur* 47, no. 4 (Winter 2007): 93–104.

Kadish, Doris Y., and Françoise Massardier-Kenney. *Translating Slavery: Gender and Race in French Women's Writing, 1783–1823.* Kent: Kent State University Press, 1994.

Kahn, Gustave. *Symbolistes et décadents.* Paris: Vanier, 1902.

Kete, Kathleen. *Making Way for Genius: The Aspiring Self in France from the Old Regime to the New.* New Haven: Yale University Press, 2012.

Klumpke, Anna. *Rosa Bonheur: The Artist's (Auto)biography.* Translated by Gretchen Van Slyke. Ann Arbor: University of Michigan Press, 1997.

Knibiehler, Yvonne, and Catherine Fouquet. *La femme devant les médecins.* Paris: Hachette, 1983.

Krysinska, Marie. "Les artistes maudits." *Revue* (15 August 1901): 384–97.

———. "Les cénacles artistiques et littéraires: Autour de Maurice Rollinat." *La Revue* 51 (15 August 1904): 477–91.

———. "*Chronique parisienne*: Essai sur la danse." *Revue d'Égypte et d'Orient* (February 1905): 76–84.

———. "Compte rendu d'*À se tordre*, par Alphonse Allais, et *Contes du Chat Noir*, par Rodolphe Salis." *La Revue Indépendante* 21, no. 60 (October 1891): 134.

———. "Conflit de la rime et de la raison." *La Fronde*, 11 July 1899.

———. "De la nouvelle école: À propos de l'article de M. Anatole France dans *Le Temps* sur M. Jean Moréas." *La Revue Indépendante* 18, no. 52 (February 1891): 265–67.

———. "L'évolution poétique: Devant l'Académie." *Revue Universelle* 5 (2 February 1901): 102–3.

———. "Les femmes de lettres anglaises." *Revue Universelle* 46 (16 November 1901): 1085–88. Reprinted as "Quelques femmes de lettres anglaises." *La Fronde*, 18 September 1926, 2; 19 September 1926, 2; 22 September 1926, 2.

———. *Folle de son corps*. 1895. Paris: Victor-Havard, 1896.

———. *La force du désir*. Paris: Mercure de France, 1905.

———. *Intermèdes: Nouveaux rythmes pittoresques*. Edited by Léon Vanier. 1903. Paris: Librairie Léon Vanier/Messein Succr, 1904.

———. "Introduction: Sur les évolutions rationnelles: Esthétique et philologie." In her *Intermèdes*, v–xxxix.

———. *Joies errantes: Nouveaux rythmes pittoresques*. Paris: Lemerre, 1894.

———. "La musique de Chopin." *Le Figaro: Supplément Littéraire* 27 (6 July 1895): 105.

———. *Poèmes choisis, suivis d'études critiques*. Edited by Seth Whidden. Saint-Étienne: L'Université de Saint-Étienne, 2013.

———. "Pour le vers libre." *Le XIXᵉ Siècle* (18 August 1902): 4.

———. "Psychologie du costume et de la parure." *La Plume* (1–15 March 1905): 167–78.

———. "Race Slave." *Le Figaro: Supplément Littéraire* 52 (29 December 1894): 209–10.

———. *Rythmes pittoresques*. 1890. Edited by Seth Whidden. Exeter: Exeter University Press, 2003.

———. "Symphonie des parfums." *La Chronique Parisienne* (1881): n.p.

———. "Symphonie en gris." *Le Chat Noir* 43 (4 November 1882): 4.

Labitte, Charles. "Poetæ minores." *Revue des Deux Mondes* 3 (1843): 99–138.

Lachèvre, Frédéric. *Bibliographie sommaire de l'Almanach des Muses: 1765–1833*. 2 vols. Paris: L. Giraud-Badin, 1928.

Lafaye, Louise de [née Arbey]. *Les Créoles*. Paris: J.-B. Gros, 1847.

Laforgue, Jules. *Œuvres complètes*. Vol. 1. Paris: Gallimard, 1986.

Lamartine, Alphonse de. *Correspondance de Lamartine*, vol. 3: *1827–1838*. Edited by Mme Valentine de Lamartine. 2nd ed. Paris: Hachette, 1882.

———. *Œuvres poétiques complètes*. Paris: Gallimard, 1963.

———. "Préface." In his *Méditations poétiques*, 1–26. 1820. Paris: Firmin Didot Frères, 1849.

———. *Souvenirs et portraits*. Vol. 1. Paris: Hachette, 1871.

———. *Toussaint Louverture, suivi de "L'émancipation des esclaves."* Paris: Michel Lévy Frères, 1850.

Lanson, Gustave. *Histoire de la littérature française*. Paris: Hachette, 1895.

La Porte, Joseph de. *Histoire littéraire des femmes françaises*. 5 vols. Paris: Lacombe, 1769.

Laqueur, Thomas. *Making Sex: Body and Gender from the Greeks to Freud.*

Cambridge: Harvard University Press, 1990.

Larcher, Louis-Julien. *Le dernier mot sur les femmes.* Paris: Achille Faure, 1864.

Larcher, Louis-Julien, and P.-J. Martin. *Les femmes peintes par elles-mêmes.* Paris: Hetzel, 1858.

Larnac, Jean. *Histoire de la littérature féminine en France.* Paris: Kra, 1929.

Larousse, Pierre. *Grand dictionnaire universel du dix-neuvième siècle.* 17 vols. Paris: Administration du Grand Dictionnaire Universel, 1866–78.

Las Cases, Emmanuel-Auguste-Dieudonné. *Mémorial de Sainte-Hélène.* Paris: Seuil, 1968.

Latham, Edward. "Definition of Genius." *Notes and Queries: A Medium of Intercommunication for Literary Men, General Readers. Etc.* 11 (January–June 1903): 373–74.

Latour, Antoine de. "Les femmes poètes au XIXᵉ siècle: Mme Tastu." *Revue de Paris* 17–18 (May 1835): 271–85.

Laugel, Auguste. *Les problèmes de la nature.* Paris: Germer Baillière, 1864.

Lavater, Johann Caspar. *Essays on Physiognomy: Designed to Promote the Knowledge and Love of Mankind.* London: Blake, 1842.

Lebeau, Narcisse [Vital Hocquet]. "*Rythmes pittoresques,* par Mme Marie Krysinska." *Le Chat Noir* 457 (18 October 1890): 1628.

Leconte de Lisle, Charles Marie René. *Poèmes antiques.* Paris: Ducloux, 1852.

Lee, Debbie. *Slavery and the Romantic Imagination.* Philadelphia: University of Pennsylvania Press, 2002.

Le Goffic, Charles. "Compte rendu d'*Intermèdes: Nouveaux rythmes pitto-resques,* par Mᵐᵉ Marie Krysinska." *Revue Universelle* 4, no. 118 (1904): 509.

———. "Les conquêtes du vers français." *Revue Universelle* (19 October 1901): 989–94.

Lemerre, Alphonse, ed. *Anthologie des poètes français du XIXème siècle.* 4 vols. Paris: Lemerre, 1887–88.

———. *Le Parnasse contemporain: Recueil de vers nouveaux.* 3 vols. Paris: Lemerre, 1866–76.

Leopardi, Giacomo. *Poems and Prose.* Edited by Angel Flores. Bloomington: Indiana University Press, 1966.

Lesch, John E. *Science and Medicine in France: The Emergence of Experimental Physiology, 1790–1855.* Cambridge: Cambridge University Press, 1984.

Letelier, Madame [Aline de M***]. "Mœurs coloniales." 1833. *Revue des Colonies* (1835): 86–93, 130–37, 180–87, 235–40; (1836): 272–79, 327–35.

Levallois, Jules. "Un poëte moraliste." *Revue Européenne* 10 (1860): 131–44.

Limayrac, Paulin. "Les femmes poètes: *Rêves et réalités: Poésies* par Mme A.-M. Blanchecotte." *Le Constitutionnel,* 25 May 1856.

Littré, Emile. *Dictionnaire de la langue française.* Paris: Librairie Hachette, 1863–74.

Lloyd, Rosemary. "The Demands of an Editor." In *Baudelaire's Literary Criticism,* 190–251. Cambridge: Cambridge University Press, 1981.

———. "The Nineteenth Century: Shaping Women." In *A History of Women's Writing in France,* edited by Sonya Stephens, 120–46. Cambridge: Cambridge University Press, 2000.

Lloyd, Rosemary, and Brian Nelson, eds. *Women Seeking Expression: France 1789–1914.* Melbourne: Monash Romance Studies, 2000.

Lombroso, Cesare. *L'homme de génie.* 6th ed. Translated by Colonna d'Istria. Paris: Reinwald, 1903.

———. *The Man of Genius.* Translated by Havelock Ellis. London: Walter Scott, 1891.

Lombroso, Cesare, and Guglielmo Ferrero. *Criminal Woman, the Prostitute, and the Normal Woman.* Translated by Nicole Hahn Rafter and Mary Gibson. Durham: Duke University Press, 2004.

Lourbet, Jacques. *La femme devant la science contemporaine.* Paris: F. Alcan, 1896.

Lucas, Alphonse. *Les clubs et les clubistes: Histoire complète, critique et anecdotique des clubs et des comités électoraux fondés à Paris depuis la révolution de 1848.* Paris: Dentu, 1851.

Lucot, Yves-Marie. *Dumas: Père et fils.* Woignarue: Éditions La Vague Verte, 1997.

Mallarmé, Stéphane. *Œuvres complètes.* Edited by Bertrand Marchal. 2 vols. Paris: Gallimard, 1998.

Marchand, Alfred. "*Rêves et réalités* par Augustine-Malvina Blanchecotte." *Le Temps,* 2 January 1872.

———. "Variétés: Les *Pensées* de M^me Ackermann." *Le Temps,* 5 February 1883.

Marès, Roland de. "Compte rendu des *Joies errantes,* par Marie Krysinska." *L'Ermitage* 5, no. 6 (June 1894): 366.

Marion, Henri. *Psychologie de la femme.* Paris: Colin, 1900.

Marks, Elaine. "1929: Jean Larnac Publishes a *Histoire de la littérature féminine en France.*" In *A New*

*History of French Literature,* edited by Denis Hollier, 887–91. 1989. Cambridge: Harvard University Press, 1994.

Martin, Emily. "The Egg and the Sperm: How Science Has Constructed a Romance Based on Stereotypical Male-Female Roles." *Signs* 16, no. 3 (Spring 1991): 485–501.

Mathews, Patricia. *Passionate Discontent: Creativity, Gender, and French Symbolist Art.* Chicago: Chicago University Press, 1999.

Maudsley, Henry. "Sex and Mind in Education." *Fortnightly Review* 15 (1874): 466–83.

Maurras, Charles. "Compte rendu des *Rythmes pittoresques,* par Marie Krysinska." *L'Observateur Français: Journal Politique* 4, no. 314 (10 November 1890): 1–2.

———. "Le romantisme féminin: Allégorie du sentiment désordonné." In his *L'avenir de l'intelligence,* 145–234. Paris: Flammarion, 1927.

Maury, Lucien. *Figures littéraires: Écrivains français et étrangers.* Paris: Perrin, 1911.

Meltzer, Françoise. *Hot Property: The Stakes and Claims of Literary Originality.* Chicago: University of Chicago Press, 1994.

Mendès, Catulle. *Le mouvement poétique français de 1867 à 1900: Rapport à M. le ministre de l'instruction publique et des beaux-arts.* Paris: Imprimerie Nationale, 1902.

Menon, Elizabeth. "Les filles d'Ève in Word and Image." In *Writing and Seeing: Essays on Word and Image,* edited by Rui Carvalho Homen and Maria de Fátima Lambert, 157–74. Amsterdam: Rodopi, 2006.

Mercœur, Élisa. *Œuvres poétiques: précédées de mémoires et notices sur la vie de l'auteur, écrits par sa mère*. 3 vols. Paris: Pommeret et Guenot, 1843.

———. *Poésies de M^lle Élisa Mercœur.* Edited by Georges-Adrien Crapelet. 2nd ed. Paris: Crapelet, 1829.

Merello, Ida. "Pour une définition du vers libre." In *Le vers libre dans tous ses états: Histoire et poétique d'une forme (1886–1914)*, edited by Catherine Boschian-Campaner, 123–32. Paris: L'Harmattan, 2009.

Merlet, Gustave. *Anthologie classique des poètes du XIXème siècle: Cours élémentaires et moyens.* Paris: A. Lemerre, 1890.

Mesch, Rachel. *The Hysteric's Revenge: French Women Writers at the Fin de Siècle.* Nashville: Vanderbilt University Press, 2006.

Metzidakis, Stamos. "Engendering Poetic Vision." *Rivista di Letterature Moderne e Comparate* 61, no. 3 (2008): 335–47.

Michelet, Jules. *Le peuple.* Paris: Hachette, 1846.

Midgley, Claire. *Women Against Slavery: The British Campaign 1780–1870.* London: Routledge, 1992.

Miller, Edward M. "Intelligence and Brain Myelination: A Hypothesis." *Personality and Individual Differences* 17 (1994): 803–32.

Mirecourt, Eugène de. *Les contemporains: Louise Colet.* Paris: Havard, 1857.

———. *Madame Anaïs Ségalas, précédée d'une lettre à M. Alphonse Karr.* Paris: Havard, 1856.

Moebius, P[aulus]-J[ulius]. *De la débilité mentale physiologique chez la femme.* Translated by Nicole Roche and Simone Roche. 1898. Paris: Solin, 1980.

Molènes, Paul de. "Simples essais d'histoire littéraire: Les femmes poètes." *Revue des Deux Mondes* 31 (1842): 48–76.

Montégut, Émile. "Portraits poétiques: Marceline Desbordes-Valmore." *Revue des Deux Mondes* 6 (1860): 996–1016.

Montferrand, Alfred de, ed. *Biographie des femmes auteurs contemporaines françaises.* Paris: Armand-Aubrée, 1836.

Moorman, Lewis J. *Tuberculosis and Genius.* Chicago: University of Chicago Press, 1940.

Moreau [de Tours], Jacques-Joseph. *La psychologie morbide, dans ses rapports avec la philosophie de l'histoire; ou, De l'influence des névropathies sur le dynamisme intellectuel.* Paris: Masson, 1859.

Morgan, Cheryl. "Death of a Poet: Delphine Gay's Romantic Makeover." *Symposium* 53, no. 4 (2000): 249–60.

———. "Delphine Gay de Girardin." In *Feminist Companion to French Literature*, edited by Eva Sartori and Juliette Parnell-Smith, 229–30. Westport, Conn.: Greenwood, 1999.

———. "Sophie Gay." In *Feminist Companion to French Literature*, edited by Eva Sartori and Juliette Parnell-Smith, 228–29. Westport, Conn.: Greenwood, 1999.

Mortier, Roland. *L'originalité: Une nouvelle catégorie esthétique au siècle des Lumières.* Geneva: Droz, 1982.

Moulin, Jeanine, ed. *Huit siècles de poésie féminine.* Paris: Seghers, 1975.

———. *La poésie féminine du XII^e au XIX^e siècle.* Paris: Seghers, 1966.

———. *La poésie féminine: Époque moderne.* Paris: Seghers, 1963.

Munro, Donald George Macleod. *The Psycho-Pathology of Tuberculosis.* London: Oxford University Press, 1926.

Murphy, Steve. "Détours et détournements: Rimbaud et le parodique." In "Rimbaud: Textes et contextes d'une révolution poétique," edited by Steve Murphy, special issue, *Parade sauvage* 4 (2004): 77–126.

Musset, Alfred de. *La confession d'un enfant du siècle*. 1836. In his *Œuvres complètes en prose*, edited by Maurice Allem, 63–288. Paris: Gallimard, 1951.

———. *Poésies complètes*. Edited by Maurice Allem. Paris: Gallimard, 1957.

Néronde, Chassaigne de. "Le mouvement littéraire en France." *Revue Internationale* 27 (1890): 565–80.

Niboyet, Eugénie. "*La femme: Poésies* par Anaïs Ségalas." *La Voix des Femmes* 7 (27 March 1848): 3–4.

Nietzsche, Friedrich. 1881. *The Dawn of Day*. Translated by Johanna Volz. New York: Macmillan, 1903.

———. *Human, All-Too-Human: A Book for Free Spirits*. 1878. Pt. 1. Translated by Helen Zimmern. 2nd ed. Edinburgh: T. N. Foulis, 1910.

Nordau, Max. *Psycho-physiologie du génie et du talent*. Paris: Félix Alcan, 1897.

Norris, Pamela. *Eve: A Biography*. New York: New York University Press, 1998.

Offen, Karen. "Depopulation, Nationalism, and Feminism in Fin-de-Siècle France." *American Historical Review* 89, no. 3 (June 1984): 648–76.

———. *European Feminisms 1700–1950: A Political History*. Stanford: Stanford University Press, 2000.

Olsen, Tillie. *Silences*. 1978. New York: Feminist Press, 2003.

O'Neill, Kerill. "The Shadow of Clytemnestra in Louisa Siefert's 'Jalousie': Maternity, Sexuality, and a Woman's Poetic Voice." *Classical and Modern Literature: A Quarterly* 19, no. 3 (Spring 1999): 257–77.

Pailhès, Abbé Gabriel. *La duchesse de Duras et Chateaubriand d'après des documents inédits*. Paris: Perrin, 1910.

Paliyenko, Adrianna M. "Illuminating the Poetic Turn to Science: Louise Ackermann, or the Aesthetic Stuff of Cultural Studies." In "The Cultural Currency of Nineteenth-Century French Poetry," edited by Joseph Acquisto and Adrianna M. Paliyenko, special issue, *Romance Studies* 26, no. 4 (November 2008): 308–22.

———. "Illumining the Critical Reader in the Poet: Malvina Blanchecotte and Louise Ackermann." In *Poets as Readers in Nineteenth-Century France: Critical Reflections*, edited by Joseph Acquisto, Adrianna M. Paliyenko, and Catherine Witt, 185–206. London: Institute of Modern Languages Research, 2015.

———. "In the Shadow of Eve: Marie Krysinska and the Force of Poetic Desire." In *Women Seeking Expression: France, 1789–1914*, edited by Rosemary Lloyd and Brian Nelson, 159–79. Melbourne: Monash Romance Studies, 2000.

———. "Is a Woman Poet Born or Made? Discourse of Maternity in Louisa Siefert and Louise Ackermann." *L'Esprit Créateur* 29, no. 2 (Summer 1999): 52–63.

———. "Margins of Madness and Creativity: Nineteenth-Century French Psychiatric and Literary Discourses on the Dream." In *Dreams in French Literature: The Persistent Voice*, edited by Tom

Conner, 173–98. Amsterdam: Rodopi, 1995.

———. *Mis-reading the Creative Impulse: The Poetic Subject in Rimbaud and Claudel, Restaged.* Carbondale: Southern Illinois University Press, 1997.

———. "On the Physiology of Genius: Pro/creativity in Nineteenth-Century France." In "Penser le génie à travers ses usages: The Uses of Genius," edited by Ann Jefferson and Jean-Alexandre Perras, special issue, *L'Esprit Créateur* 55, no. 2 (Summer 2015): 89–101.

———. "Rereading Breton's Debt to Apollinaire: Surrealism and Aesthetics of Creative Imaging." *Romance Quarterly* 42, no. 1 (Winter 1995): 18–27.

———. "Rereading *la femme poète*: Rimbaud and Louisa Siefert." *Nineteenth-Century French Studies* 26, nos. 1–2 (Fall–Winter 1997–98): 146–60.

———. "Returns of Marceline Desbordes-Valmore's Repressed Colonial Memory: *Sarah* and Critical Belatedness." In "Engendering Race: Romantic-Era Women and French Colonial Memory," edited by Adrianna M. Paliyenko, special issue, *L'Esprit Créateur* 47, no. 4 (Winter 2007): 68–80.

Pange, Jean de. "Mme de Staël et les nègres." *Revue de France* 5 (October 1934): 425–43.

Paraf, Pierre. *Anthologie du romantisme.* Paris: A. Michel, 1927.

Parini, Jay. *Why Poetry Matters.* New Haven: Yale University Press, 2008.

Parker, Julie Faith. "Blaming Eve Alone: Translation, Omission, and Implications of עמה in Genesis 3:6b." *Journal of Biblical Literature* 132, no. 4 (2013): 729–47.

Pascal, Blaise. *Pensées de Pascal.* Edited by Ernest Havet. 2nd ed. Paris: Ch. Delagrave, 1866.

Pasco, Allan H. "Literature as Historical Archive." *New Literary History* 35 (2004): 373–94.

Paton, Tracy. "Marie Krysinska's Poetics of Parody: Figures of the Woman Artist." *Nineteenth-Century French Studies* 33, nos. 1–2 (Autumn 2004–Winter 2005): 147–62.

———. "Seductive Rebellions: Feminine Subjectivity in the Poetry of Louise Ackermann, Louisa Siefert, and Marie Krysinska." PhD diss., University of California, Irvine, 2002.

Pellissier, Georges, ed. *Anthologie des poètes du XIXᵉ siècle.* Paris: Delagrave, 1907.

Petit de Julleville, Louis. *Histoire de la langue et de la littérature française, des origines à 1900.* 8 vols. Paris: Armand Colin, 1896–99.

Peyrouton, Abel. "Louisa Siefert et son œuvre." *Lyon-Revue* 1 (1880): 32–43.

Pilon, Edmond. "Les muses plaintives du romantisme." In his *Portraits français*, 201–21. Paris: E. Sansot, 1906.

Place, Jean-Michel, and André Vasseur. *Bibliographie des revues et journaux littéraires des XIXᵉ et XXᵉ siècles.* Paris: Éditions de la Chronique des Lettres Françaises, 1973–77.

Planté, Christine. "La place des femmes dans l'histoire littéraire: Annexe, ou point de départ d'une relecture critique?" *Revue d'Histoire Littéraire de la France* 103, no. 3 (2003): 655–68.

———. "Marceline Desbordes-Valmore: Ni poésie féminine, ni poésie féministe." *French Literature Series* 16 (1989): 78–93.

Planté, Christine, ed. *Femmes poètes du XIXᵉ siècle: Une anthologie*. 1998. 2nd ed. Lyon: Presses Universitaires de Lyon, 2010.

Pontmartin, Armand. "Madame Ackermann: La poésie athée." *Nouveaux Samedis* 11 (1875): 17–32.

Porter, Laurence. "Poetess or Strong Poet? Gender Stereotypes and the Elegies of Marceline Desbordes-Valmore." *French Forum* 18, no. 2 (1993): 185–94.

———. *Women's Vision in Western Literature: The Empathic Community*. Westport, Conn.: Praeger, 2005.

Pougin, Arthur. *La jeunesse de Marceline Desbordes-Valmore, d'après des documents nouveaux, suivie de lettres inédites de Mme Desbordes-Valmore*. Paris: Calmann-Lévy, 1898.

Poullain de la Barre, François. *The Equality of the Sexes*. Translated by A. Daniel Frankforter and Paul J. Morman. Lewiston, Maine: Edwin Mellen Press, 1989.

Pound, Ezra. *The Natural Philosophy of Love*. New York: Boni and Liveright, 1921.

Poussard-Joly, Catherine. *Madame Tastu; ou, La muse oubliée*. Palaiseau: Société Historique de Palaiseau, 1995.

Pradel, Eugénie de. "À M. le Directeur du Citateur Féminin." *Le Citateur Féminin* 1 (1835): 38–41.

Proudhon, Pierre-Joseph. *De la justice dans la révolution et dans l'église*. 3 vols. Paris: Librairie de Garnier Frères, 1858.

———. *La pornocratie; ou, Les femmes dans les temps modernes*. Paris: Lacroix, 1875.

Prudhomme, Sully. *Testament poétique*. Paris: Lemerre, 1901.

Pyke, Sandra. "Education and the 'Woman Question.'" *Canadian Psychology* 38, no. 3 (1997): 154–63.

Quillard, Pierre. "*Intermèdes*." *Mercure de France* (April 1904): 178–79.

Rachilde [Marguerite Vallette-Eymery]. "Compte rendu des *Joies errantes*, par Marie Krysinska." *Mercure de France* 56, no. 11 (August 1894): 386.

Ratier, Victor. "Mme Anaïs Ségalas." In *Galerie de la presse, de la littérature et des beaux arts*, edited by Louis Huart and Charles Philipon, n.p. Paris: Aubert, 1841.

Raynaud, Ernest. *La mêlée symboliste (1870–1890): Portraits et souvenirs*. Vol. 1. Paris: Renaissance du Livre, 1918.

Reid, Martine. *Des femmes en littérature*. Paris: Belin, 2010.

Renard, Jules. *Journal (1887–1910)*. Paris: Gallimard, 1960.

Rimbaud, Arthur. *Complete Works*. Translated by Wallace Fowlie. Revised by Seth Whidden. Chicago: University of Chicago Press, 2005.

———. *Œuvres complètes*. Paris: Gallimard, 1972.

Robb, Graham. *Rimbaud*. New York: Norton, 2000.

Roch, Francis. "Mᵐᵉ Anaïs Ségalas." *Revue Biographique des Célébrités Contemporaines* 1 (1854): 1–8.

Rodenbach, Georges. "La poésie nouvelle: À propos des décadents et des symbolistes." *Revue Politique et Littéraire: Revue Bleue* (4 April 1891): 422–30.

Rosen, Judith. "Class and Poetic Communities: The Works of Ellen Johnston, 'The Factory Girl.'" *Victorian Poetry* 39, no. 2 (Summer 2001): 207–28.

Rousseau, Jean-Jacques. *Lettre à d'Alembert sur les spectacles.* 1758. Edited by M. Fuchs. Lille: Giard, 1948.

———. *Œuvres complètes.* 4 vols. Paris, Gallimard, 1959–69.

Roussel, Pierre. *Système physique et moral de la femme; ou, Tableau philosophique de la constitution, de l'état organique, du tempérament, des moeurs, et des fonctions propres au sexe.* Paris: Vincent, 1775.

Ruskin, John. *Modern Painters,* vol. 3, containing pt. 4: *Of Many Things.* London: Smith, Elder, 1856.

S. D. "Reflets: Littérature: *Poésies du cœur.*" *Le Citateur Féminin* 2 (1835): 135–36.

Sainte-Beuve, Charles Augustin. *Correspondance générale: Lettres retrouvées (1823–1859).* Edited by Alain Bonnerot. Vol. 1. Paris: Honoré Champion, 2006.

———. "De la littérature industrielle." *Revue des Deux Mondes* 19 (1 September 1839): 673–91.

———. "George Sand: *Lélia,* 1833." In his *Portraits contemporains,* 1:495–523. Paris: M. Lévy, 1881.

———. "M^me Desbordes-Valmore." *Revue des Deux Mondes* (1 August 1833): 241–55.

———. *Madame Desbordes-Valmore: Sa vie et sa correspondance.* Paris: Michel Lévy Frères, 1870.

———. "Madame Emile de Girardin." In his *Causeries du lundi,* 3:384–406. 3rd ed. Paris: Garnier Frères, 1855.

———. "Œuvres de Louise Labé: La Belle cordière." In his *Nouveaux lundis,* 4:289–317. Paris: Calmann Lévy, 1883.

———. "Poésie: 'La vision,' par mademoiselle Delphine Gay; 'Les oiseaux du sacre,' par madame Amable Tastu." *Le Globe,* 7 July 1825.

———. *Poésies complètes.* Paris: Charpentier, 1840.

———. "Poètes et romanciers modernes de la France: Madame Tastu, *Poésies nouvelles.*" *Revue des Deux Mondes* (15 February 1835): 353–56.

———. *Portraits contemporains.* Vol. 1. Paris: Didier, 1846.

———. "*Rêves et réalités, poésies* par Madame Blanchecotte." 1855. In his *Causeries du lundi,* 15:327–32. 3rd ed. Paris: Garnier Frères, 1855.

———. *Vie, poésies et pensées de Joseph Delorme.* 1829. Paris: Michel Lévy Frères, 1863.

Sainte-Croix, Camille de. *Mœurs littéraires: Les lundis de "La Bataille" (1890–1891).* Paris: A. Savine, 1891.

Salm, Constance Pipelet de. *Œuvres complètes de Madame la Princesse Constance de Salm-Dyck.* 4 vols. Paris: Didot, 1842.

Sand, George. *Correspondance: 1812–1876.* Paris: Calmann Lévy, 1895.

———. *Correspondance de George Sand.* Edited by Georges Lubin. 24 vols. Paris: Classiques Garnier, 1964.

———. *Correspondance de George Sand.* Edited by Georges Lubin. Vol. 25. Paris: Bordas, 1991.

———. *Correspondance entre George Sand et Gustave Flaubert.* Paris: Calmann Lévy, 1904.

———. "La fille d'Albano." 1831. In her *Les sept cordes de la lyre,* 279–93. Paris: M. Lévy, 1869.

———. *Gabriel.* 1839. Edited by Kathleen Hart. New York: Modern Language Association, 2010.

———. *Histoire de ma vie.* Paris: Victor Lecou, 1855.

———. "L'homme et la femme." In her *Impressions et souvenirs*, 258–71. 3rd ed. Paris: M. Lévy, 1873.

———. *Indiana.* Paris: Calmann-Lévy, 1832.

———. *Lélia.* 1833, 1839. Paris: Garnier, 1960.

———. "Lettres à Marcie." 1837. In her *Les sept cordes de la lyre*, 165–234. Paris: M. Lévy, 1869.

———. *Le marquis de Villemer.* 1861. Paris: M. Lévy, 1864.

———. *Œuvres autobiographiques.* 2 vols. Paris: Gallimard, 1970.

———. "Poésies, par des ouvriers." *Revue Indépendante* 1 (1841): 248–67.

———. *Pourquoi les femmes à l'Académie?* Paris: Michel Lévy Frères, 1863.

———. *Préfaces de George Sand.* Edited by Anna Szabó. Debrecen: Kossuth Lajos Tudományegyetem, 1997.

———. *Questions d'art et de littérature.* Edited by Henriette Bessis and Janis Glasgow. Paris: des Femmes, 1991.

———. "Souvenirs de Madame Merlin." In *Questions d'art et de littérature*, edited by Henriette Bessis and Janis Glasgow, 83–90. Paris: Des Femmes, 1991.

Sarcey, Francisque. "Poètes contemporains." *Le XIX^e Siècle*, 25, 27, and 28 August 1874.

Scarry, Elaine. *The Body in Pain: The Making and Unmaking of the World.* New York: Oxford University Press, 1985.

Schaffer, Aaron. *The Genres of Parnassian Poetry: A Study of the Parnassian Minors.* Baltimore: Johns Hopkins University Press, 1944.

———. "Madame Ackermann as Literary Critic." *French Review* 12, no. 1 (October 1938): 25–33.

Schapira, Marie-Claude. "Amable Tastu, Delphine Gay: Le désenchantement au féminin." In *Masculin/féminin dans la poésie et les poétiques du XIX^e siècle*, edited by Christine Planté, 191–205. Lyon: Presses Universitaires de Lyon, 2002.

Scheler, Lucien. "Un poète oublié, Louisa Siefert." *Bulletin du Bibliophile* (1992): 162–85.

Schiebinger, Londa. *Plants and Empire: Colonial Bioprospecting in the Atlantic World.* Cambridge: Harvard University Press, 2004.

Schœlcher, Victor. *Des colonies françaises: Abolition immédiate de l'esclavage.* 1842. Paris: Éditions du C. T. H. S., 1998.

Schopenhauer, Arthur. *The Works of Schopenhauer.* Edited by Will Durant. New York: Simon and Schuster, 1928.

Schultz, Gretchen. "De la poétique féministe et la liberté sexuelle dans l'œuvre romanesque de Marie Krysinska." In *Innovations poétiques et combats littéraires: Marie Krysinska*, edited by Adrianna M. Paliyenko, Gretchen Schultz, and Seth Whidden, 181–200. Lyon: Presses Universitaires de Saint-Etienne/Presses Universitaires de Lyon, 2010.

———. *The Gendered Lyric: Subjectivity and Difference in Nineteenth-Century French Poetry.* West Lafayette: Purdue University Press, 1999.

Schuré, Édouard. "Un poète athée: Mme Ackermann." In his *Femmes inspiratrices et poètes annonciateurs*, 299–313. Paris: Perrin, 1908.

Scott, Clive. *Vers Libre: The Emergence of Free Verse in France, 1886–1914.* Oxford: Clarendon, 1990.

Scott, David H. T. *Sonnet Theory and Practice in Nineteenth-Century France: Sonnets on the Sonnet.* Hull: University of Hull Publications, 1977.

Séché, Alphonse. *Les muses françaises: Anthologie des femmes poètes du XIIIᵉ au XXᵉ siècles.* 2 vols. Paris: Louis Michaud, 1908–1909.

Séché, Léon. "Élisa Mercœur: À propos du centenaire de sa naissance." *Les Annales Romantiques* (1909): 188–93.

Ségalas, Anaïs. *Les algériennes: Poésies.* Paris: C. Mary, 1831.

———. *Contes du nouveau Palais de Cristal.* Paris: Janet, 1855.

———. "La Créole." *Magasin des Demoiselles: Morale, Histoire Ancienne et Moderne, Sciences, Économie Domestique, Littérature, Beaux-Arts, Voyages, Récréations, Biographie, Petit Courrier des Demoiselles* 3 (1847): 232–36.

———. *Enfantines: Poésies à ma fille.* 4th ed. Paris: Mᵐᵉ Vve Louis Janet, 1845.

———. *La femme: Poésies.* Paris: Vve L. Janet, 1847.

———. "Madame Tastu." In *Biographie des femmes auteurs contemporaines françaises*, edited by Alfred de Montferrand, 15–23. Paris: Armand-Aubrée, 1836.

———. *Nos bons parisiens.* Paris: Magnin, Blanchard, 1864.

———. *Les oiseaux de passage: Poésies.* 2nd ed. Paris: Moutardier, 1837.

———. *Poésies.* Paris: Desforges, 1844.

———. *Récits des Antilles: Le bois de la Soufrière, suivis d'un choix de poèmes.* Paris: L'Harmattan, 2004.

———. *Les romans du wagon: Le duel des femmes, Le bois de la Soufrière, Un roman de famille, Le figurant.* Paris: Dentu, 1884.

Seth, Catriona. "Les muses de l'*Almanach*: La poésie au féminin dans l'*Almanach des Muses*, 1789–1819." In *Masculin/féminin dans la poésie et les poétiques du XIXᵉ siècle*, edited by Christine Planté, 105–19. Lyon: Presses Universitaires de Lyon, 2002.

Shapiro, Norman R. *French Women Poets of Nine Centuries: The Distaff and the Pen.* Baltimore: Johns Hopkins University Press, 2008.

Shenk, David. *The Genius in All of Us: New Insights into Genetics, Talent, and IQ.* New York: Anchor, 2011.

Shryock, Richard. "Anarchism at the Dawn of the Symbolist Movement." *French Forum* 25, no. 3 (September 2000): 291–307.

———. *Lettres à Gustave Kahn et Rachel Kahn (1886–1934).* Saint-Genouph: Nizet, 1996.

Siefert, Louisa. *L'année républicaine.* Paris: Lemerre, 1869.

———. "Causeries poétiques." *Journal de Lyon.* http://collections.bm-lyon.fr/PER003189.

———. *Comédies romanesques.* Paris: Lemerre, 1872.

———. *Méline.* Paris: Lemerre, 1876.

———. *Rayons perdus.* 1868; 2nd ed. Paris: Lemerre, 1869.

———. *Les saintes colères.* Paris: Lemerre, 1871.

———. *Souvenirs rassemblés par sa mère: Poésies inédites.* Paris: Fischbacher, 1881.

———. *Les stoïques.* Paris: Lemerre, 1870.

Simonton, Dean Keith. *Origins of Genius: Darwinian Perspectives on Creativity.* New York: Oxford University Press, 1999.

Simpson, Louis. *Modern Poets of France: A Bilingual Anthology.* Brownsville, Ore.: Story Line Press, 1997.

Somoff, Jean-Paul, and Aurélien Marfée. "Les muses du Parnasse: Louise Colet, Louise Ackermann [et] Nina de Villard et cie." Special issue, *À Rebours* 9 (1979).

Sorrell, Martin, ed. and trans. *Elles: A Bilingual Anthology of Modern French Poetry by Women.* Exeter: University of Exeter Press, 1995.

Soulary, Joséphin. "M^lle Siefert: *Les stoïques.*" *Journal de Lyon*, 8 June 1872. http://collections.bm-lyon.fr/PER003189.

Soulié, Frédéric. *Physiologie du bas-bleu.* Paris: Aubert et Lavigne, 1841.

Souriau, Maurice. "Grandeur et décadence de Mme Tastu." *Revue des Cours et Conférences* (1910): 116–32.

Spencer, Herbert. *Principles of Biology.* Vol. 1. London: Williams and Norgate, 1864.

Spinoza, Benedictus de [Baruch]. *Ethics.* 1677. Edited and translated by G. H. R. Parkinson. Oxford: Oxford University Press, 2000.

Spizio, Ludovic. "L'âme féminine: Louisa Siefert." *Revue Internationale* 15 (1887): 567–84.

Staël, Germaine de. *Mirza; ou, Lettre d'un voyageur.* 1795. In her *Œuvres*, 1:147–59.

———. *Œuvres de madame de Staël-Holstein.* 2 vols. Paris: Lefèvre, 1858.

———. "Préface pour la traduction d'un ouvrage de Wilberforce sur la traite des nègres." 1814. In *Œuvres complètes de la madame la baronne de Staël-Holstein*, 2:290–91. Geneva: Slatkine Reprints, 1967.

Stanton, Domna, ed. *The Defiant Muse: French Feminist Poems from the Middle Ages to the Present. A Bilingual Anthology.* New York: Feminist Press at CUNY, 1986.

Stephens, Claire. "Un vrai poëte: Louisa Siefert." *Bibliothèque Universelle et Revue Suisse* 62 (April–June 1878): 316–38.

Stern, Daniel [Marie d'Agoult]. *Esquisses morales: Pensées, réflexions, et maximes.* 3rd ed. Paris: J. Techener, 1859.

———. "Variétés: *Contes et poésies* par M^me Ackermann." *Le Temps*, 7–8 June 1863.

Stockham, Alice Bunker. *Karezza: Ethics of Marriage.* Chicago: Progress, 1903.

Strindberg, Auguste. "De l'infériorité de la femme et comme corollaire de la justification de sa situation subordonnée selon les données dernières de la science." *Revue Blanche* (1895): 1–20.

Sullerot, Évelyne. *Histoire de la presse féminine en France, des origines à 1848.* Paris: Armand Colin, 1966.

Tastu, Amable. *La chevalerie française.* Paris: Baudoin Fils, 1821.

———. *Éducation maternelle: Simples leçons d'une mère à ses enfants.* Paris: E. Renduel, 1836.

———. *Poésies.* Paris: Ambroise Dupont, 1826.

———. *Poésies complètes.* Paris: Didier, 1858.

———. *Poésies nouvelles.* Paris: Denain et Delamare, 1835.

———, ed. *Soirées littéraires de Paris.* Paris: Crapelet, 1832.

Tellier, Jules. *Nos poètes.* Paris: Lescène et Oudin, 1889.

Terdiman, Richard. *Discourse/Counter-Discourse: The Theory and Practice of Symbolic Resistance in Nineteenth-Century France.* Ithaca: Cornell University Press, 1985.

Texier, Edmond. "Chronique." *Le Siècle*, 24 April 1874.

———. *Physiologie du poète*. Paris: J. Laisné, 1842.

Thérive, André. "À propos de Mme Ackermann." *Revue Critique des Idées et des Œuvres* 24 (January–March 1914): 142–54.

———. "Le mari de Mme Ackermann." *Revue de Paris* (1927): 140–65.

Thomas, Edmond. *Voix d'en bas: La poésie ouvrière du XIXème siècle*. Paris: La Découverte, 2002.

Tisseur, Clair. *Modestes observations sur l'art de versifier*. Lyon: Protat Frères, 1893.

*Trésor de la langue française*. http://atilf .atilf.fr.

Ulliac-Trémadeure, S[ophie]. "Madame Babois." In *Biographie des femmes auteurs contemporaines françaises*, edited by Alfred de Montferrand, 119–32. Paris: Armand-Aubrée, 1836.

Uzanne, Octave. *La femme à Paris, nos contemporaines: Notes successives sur les Parisiennes de ce temps dans leurs divers milieux, etats et conditions*. Paris: Ancienne Maison Quantin, 1894.

van den Bergh, Carla. "Les poèmes de Marie Krysinska dans le *Chat Noir*: Vers libre, prose rythmée ou versets?" In *Innovations poétiques et combats littéraires: Marie Krysinska*, edited by Adrianna M. Paliyenko, Gretchen Schultz, and Seth Whidden, 95–104. Lyon: Presses Universitaires de Saint-Etienne/ Presses Universitaires de Lyon, 2010.

Van Slyke, Gretchen. "Does Genius Have a Sex? Rosa Bonheur's Reply." *French American Review* 2 (1992): 12–23.

Verlaine, Paul. *Œuvres complètes*. Vol. 6. Paris: Villain et Bar, 1932.

———. *Les poètes maudits de Paul Verlaine*. Edited by Michel Décaudin. Paris: Société d'Edition d'Enseignement Supérieur, 1982.

Vier, Jacques. *Marie d'Agoult: Son mari, ses amis, documents inédits*. Paris: Éditions du Cèdre, 1950.

Vigny, Alfred de. *Poèmes*. Paris: Pélicier, 1822.

Vincent, Patrick. *The Romantic Poetess: European Culture, Politics and Gender 1820–1840*. Durham: University Press of New England, 2004.

Virey, Julien-Joseph. *De la femme sous ses rapports physiologique, moral et littéraire*. 1823. 2nd ed. Paris: Crochard, 1825.

———. *De la physiologie dans ses rapports avec la philosophie*. Paris: Baillière, 1844.

———. *Histoire naturelle du genre humain*. 1801. 3 vols. Paris: Crochard, 1824.

———. "Nègre." In *Dictionnaire des sciences médicales*, 35:378–432. Paris: Panckoucke, 1819.

———. "Nègre." In *Nouveau dictionnaire d'histoire naturelle*, 22:422–71. Paris: Deterville, 1818.

Vox Populi. "La Marseillaise des chats noirs." *Le Chat Noir* 2, no. 56 (3 February 1883): 16.

Walch, Gérard. *Anthologie des poètes français contemporains: Le Parnasse et les écoles postérieures au Parnasse (1866–1906)*. Paris: C. Delagrave, 1906.

Waldor, Mélanie. *L'abbaye des Fontenelles*. 2 vols. Paris: Desessart, 1839.

———. *Alphonse et Juliette*. Paris: Desessart, 1839.

———. *La coupe de corail*. Paris: L. de Potter, 1842.

———. "De l'influence que les femmes pourraient avoir sur la littérature actuelle." *Journal des Femmes* 5 (20 July 1833): 222–26.

———. *L'écuyer Dauberon; ou, L'oratoire de Bonsecours*. Paris: Moutardier, 1832.

———. "Élisa Mercœur." *Le Citateur Féminin* 1 (1835): 74–77.

———. *La France 1870*. Paris: P. Dupont, 1870.

———. *Lettres inédites de Mélanie Waldor*. Edited by Bon Gaëtan de Wismes. Nantes: C. Mellinet, 1905.

———. *Le livre des jeunes filles*. Paris: I. Pesron, 1834.

———. *Louis Napoléon dans le Midi: Impressions et souvenirs*. Paris: Le Claire, 1852.

———. *Pages de la vie intime*. 2 vols. Brussels: J. P. Meline, 1836.

———. *Poésies du cœur*. Paris: Janet, 1835.

Walrond-Skinner, Sue. *A Dictionary of Psychotherapy*. London: Routledge and Kegan Paul, 1986.

Whidden, Seth. "Marie Krysinska: A Bibliography." *Bulletin of Bibliography* 58, no. 1 (March 2001): 1–10.

———. "Marie Krysinska's Prefaces and Letters: Not d'un Voyant, but d'une Défiante." In *Women Seeking Expression: France 1789–1914*, edited by Rosemary Lloyd and Brian Nelson, 180–93. Melbourne: Monash Romance Studies, 2000.

———. "Sur la *supercherie* de Marie Krysinska: Vers une lecture sérieuse de 'Symphonie en gris.'" In *Le vers libre dans tous ses états: Histoire et poétique d'une forme*

*(1886–1914)*, edited by Catherine Boschian-Campaner, 79–88. Paris: L'Harmattan, 2009.

Wierzbowska, Ewa. "Figures féminines: Le décodage de Marie Krysinska." In *Recyclage et décalage: Esthétique de la reprise dans les littératures française et francophone*, edited by Renata Jakubczuk and Anna Maziarczyk, 65–74. Lublin: Wydawnictwo Uniwersytetu Marii Curie-Sklodowskeij, 2013.

———. "*Rythmes pittoresques*: Le jardin enchanté de Marie Krysinska." In *Odeurs de l'écriture: Expression de l'olfaction dans les littératures française et francophone*, edited by Renata Bizek-Tatara, 155–65. Lublin: Wydawnictwo Uniwersytetu Marii Curie-Sklodowskeij, 2012.

Wilwerth, Évelyne. *Visages de la littérature féminine*. Brussels: Mardaga, 1987.

Winiarski, Léon. "Morituri: Essai sur le génie." *La Revue Blanche* 14 (October–December 1897): 104–12.

Woolf, Virginia. *A Room of One's Own*. New York: Harcourt, Brace, 1929.

Wyzema, Teodor de, ed. *Beethoven et Wagner: Essais d'histoire et de critique musicales*. Paris: Perrin, 1898.

X. Y. "Variétés: Lettres posthumes au directeur du *Bien public*." *Le Bien Public*, 24 May 1874.

Y. "Poésies nouvelles." *Le Citateur Féminin* 1 (1835): 45–46.

# INDEX

*Typeset by*
COGHILL COMPOSITION COMPANY

*Printed and bound by*
SHERIDAN BOOKS

*Composed in*
MINION PRO

*Printed on*
NATURES NATURAL

*Bound in*
ARRESTOX

CPSIA information can be obtained
at www.ICGtesting.com
Printed in the USA
BVOW07*1230200417
481508BV00013B/48/P